Greasepaint Puritan

Greasepaint Puritan

Boston to *42nd Street*
in the Queer Backstage
Novels of Bradford Ropes

MAYA CANTU

University of Michigan Press
Ann Arbor

For questions or permissions, please contact um.press.perms@umich.edu

Published in the United States of America by the
University of Michigan Press
Manufactured in the United States of America
Printed on acid-free paper
First published January 2024

A CIP catalog record for this book is available from the British Library.

Library of Congress Control Number: 2023947088
LCCN record available at https://lccn.loc.gov/2023947088

ISBN 978-0-472-07657-4 (hardcover : alk. paper)
ISBN 978-0-472-05657-6 (paper : alk. paper)
ISBN 978-0-472-22143-1 (e-book)

Cover photographs (*clockwise from top*): Bradford Ropes, 1920s; Bradford Ropes
in Hollywood, 1930s; Billy Bradford (Bradford Ropes) and Marian Hamilton, 1925,
© National Portrait Gallery, London. Illustrations reproduced by permission.

In loving dedication to the memory of Cole Ansier

Contents

Digital materials related to this title can be found on
the Fulcrum platform via the following citable URL:
https://doi.org/10.3998/mpub.12180383

Illustrations

Acknowledgments

I am grateful to many colleagues, collaborators, institutions, friends, and family members for supporting my work on *Greasepaint Puritan*.

Thank you to my colleagues in the Drama Division at Bennington College for their support, understanding, and encouragement. The administration of Bennington College supported me with a fellowship that aided immensely in the writing of my manuscript. I am also grateful for the 2019 faculty grant that allowed me to develop the early stages of this project at the International Federation for Theatre Research conference in Shanghai, as part of the Music Theatre working group. Working here with Laura MacDonald, Elia Moretti, David Savran, Christine Snyder and Marcus Tan provided a vital springboard for moving my research forward into the prospect of a book.

I am very grateful for the robust support of the editorial team at the University of Michigan Press. LeAnn Fields aided the book's writing with her steadfast encouragement and editorial acumen, and Haley Winkle, Kevin Rennells, and Anne Taylor provided detailed guidance and feedback during the production process.

My research on Bradford Ropes extended from searching archives and libraries to following trails opened by Ancestry.com, and I am so grateful to have connected with members and outer circles of Ropes's family. My sincere thanks to Jeannette Marchant for her early guidance and enthusiastic interest in Ropes, extending to her own careful genealogical research. My interviews with M. G. Bullard, who also contributed wonderful photographs for this book, opened up fascinating and illuminating new dimensions into the manuscript. From these conversations, I learned about the nuances of Ropes's life in his final years in Jamaica Plain, Massachusetts, where he continued to delight young people with his storytelling and benefited from the kindness of family and friends.

My gratitude and admiration extend to the librarians, archivists, and the-ater workers who aided me with research and interviews. Conversations with Larry Carlson, director of the Wentworth Archives at the Thayer Academy in Braintree, Massachusetts, provided vital insight into Ropes's early life as he showed me around the beautiful campus, shared treasures from the archives, and allowed me, wondrously, to step foot into the former English classroom where Ropes honed his acting skills during his year as a "P.G." I appreciate the research assistance and photos provided by the Thomas Crane Public Library in Quincy, Massachusetts. Here, I started my original microfilm research on Ropes in 2018; and I am grateful to the library staff, and in particular to Therese Mosorjak, head of Technical and Local History Services, for her thor-oughness and generosity.

For assistance with archival research, my thanks, too, to Suzanne Lipkin and the staff of the Billy Rose Theatre Division at the New York Public Library for the Performing Arts and to the Morgan Library's María Isabel Molestina, who allowed me to see Ropes's personal signature for the first time, in a rare first edition of *42nd Street* inscribed to the original Dorothy Brock, Bebe Dan-iels. I am also very appreciative of the opportunity to have interviewed Jon Maas, who served as an assistant to David Merrick and as cast album produc-tion coordinator during the original 1980 Broadway production of *42nd Street*. The recollection of these memories and of the show's mythic opening night enriched my writing of this book.

In search of the elusive gravesite of Bradford Ropes, I extended my research to cemeteries. My thanks to the staff of the Forest Hills Cemetery in Jamaica Plain, as well as to the staff of the Rosedale Cemetery in Montclair, New Jer-sey. Here, I successfully located the graves of members of Ropes's immedi-ate family, including Alice Gertrude Williams Ropes, his remarkable mother, to whom he remained close throughout his life and who, against formidable social obstacles, supported his passion for theater. Just as Ropes was a difficult figure to trace in life, it sadly follows that the whereabouts of his ashes remain obscure. Ropes shares this lot with, among others, Federico García Lorca, Wolf-gang Amadeus Mozart, and Richard Rodgers, who wrote the "I'm Crazy 'bout the Charleston" number to which Billy Bradford and Marian Hamilton danced in *Cochran's Revue of 1926*.

Finally, I could not have accomplished the writing of *Greasepaint Puritan* without the unwavering love and support of my family: my father, Mario; my mother, Jean; my sister, Lynn; and my mother-in-law, Ruth. The memory of my grandparents, Florence Friend Shapiro and Bernard Shapiro, remains a beacon and a blessing in all of my scholarship. Finally, many thanks to my dear, supportive husband, the guitarist Daniel Corr, who has been an invaluable sounding board for the many conversations about stage mothers, chorus girls, and dancing Pilgrims. This book is for all of you.

Introduction

THE ENDURING MYTH OF *42ND STREET*
AND THE "FORGOTTEN MELODY"
OF BRADFORD ROPES

One of the most iconic musicals of the twentieth century, *42nd Street* rises like a skyscraper over the cultural imagination and entertainment history. Its vision of Broadway collides the gaudy underworld of Times Square with the loftiest aspirations of the American Dream. As a glamorously gritty 1933 movie musical directed by Lloyd Bacon and choreographed by Busby Berkeley, and then a nostalgic and splashy 1980 Broadway musical based on the film, *42nd Street* has consistently represented a "prime chunk of fantasy real-estate— not just a movie, but a novel, a song, a play, an act, an attitude, a dream, a racket, a rhythm, a way of life,".as film critic J. Hoberman observes.[1] Influentially, *42nd Street* proliferated the tropes, syntax, and archetypes of the backstage musical. Both the film and the show introduce Dorothy Brock (played originally by Bebe Daniels), the egotistical leading lady who threatens the unity of the ensemble in the new musical comedy *Pretty Lady*; Julian Marsh (Warner Baxter), the ailing impresario whose legacy rides on the success of the show; and Peggy Sawyer (Ruby Keeler), the youngster who, "descending on Broadway" from small-town America, rises from chorus girl to star after Brock's injury prompts a frenzied search for a new leading lady to open *Pretty Lady* out of town.

A fabled history of adaptation and reception accompanies *42nd Street*'s mythic show business narrative. Saving Warner Brothers Studios from bankruptcy, *42nd Street* also revived the movie musical, then dormant at the Hollywood box office. After a glut of insufficiently cinematic talkie musicals from

1927 through 1930, Berkeley's kaleidoscopic choreography debuted here in its maturity, establishing a new visual language for the film musical. At the same time, *42nd Street* resonated on a national scale during the depths of the Great Depression. Marketing *42nd Street* as a "New Deal in Entertainment," Warner Brothers dispatched a "42nd Street Special" train from Los Angeles, carrying the film's stars and chorus girls and timed to arrive for the inauguration of Franklin Delano Roosevelt in Washington, DC, on March 4, 1933. The musical's 1980 Broadway musical adaptation, directed and choreographed by Gower Champion, added another layer of legend to the history of *42nd Street*, "not only because of its success story, but also because of the deep sadness that descended so ironically upon it in the midst of its triumphant opening night."[2] Making headlines around the world, producer David Merrick shockingly followed the show's "twelve standing ovation curtain calls" with an announcement that Champion had died earlier in the day—and channeled the publicity into a decade-long run.[3]

Yet, if *42nd Street*'s adaptations and mythmaking iconography can be compared to "fantasy real-estate," its source 1932 backstage novel has been relatively crowded off the block. Both the film's opening credits and the stage musical's program introduce an enigmatic credit: "Based on the Novel by Bradford Ropes." Since Ropes's death in 1966, his biography has been largely unknown to historians, summarized by a few short paragraphs on Wikipedia. The out-of-print status of his books since the early 1930s has reinforced Ropes's historiographical elusiveness. Until 2021, with the appearance of reprints of *42nd Street* and *Go Into Your Dance*, Ropes's novels have proved difficult to obtain—relegated to cult antiquities sought after by bibliophiles, musical theater collectors, and those who have appreciated Ropes's contributions to gay literary history.

Yet, for all that his backstage novels have languished in the literary shadows, Ropes can be considered as one of the most distinctive writers of backstage fiction. In the trilogy of novels launched by *42nd Street* and continued with *Stage Mother* (1933) and *Go Into Your Dance* (1934), Ropes brought Broadway's characters to life with vivid colors, vernacular precision, and an acute sense of social insight. As the source of the film and stage musicals, Ropes's *42nd Street* can be read as a fountainhead of cultural myth. At the same time, the novel stands on its own terms as a trenchant and candid landscape portrait of Forty-Second Street, which Ropes depicts as a site of labor, a dream factory, an erotic marketplace, and a microcosm of gay urban life in interwar New York. Into all of his novels, Ropes incorporated elements of a life story as remarkable to recount as it has proven challenging to track down.

Surprisingly, *Greasepaint Puritan* is not the first biographical, albeit indirect and coded, engagement with the life of Ropes, a rebellious, multitalented Boston-born vaudeville performer and musical comedy dancer descended from Mayflower Pilgrims. For this, we need look no further than the screenplay of the film musical *The Gold Diggers of 1933*, which shares an iconic status with *42nd Street* and which Warner Brothers rushed into production following the smash success of the former movie. Also choreographed by Berkeley and featuring songs by Harry Warren and Al Dubin, the film teases Ropes's identity in the form of Brad Roberts (played by Dick Powell), an ostensibly down-on-his-luck songwriter in love with chorus girl Polly Parker (played by *42nd Street*'s Keeler). Polly helps secure for Brad a spot as composer-lyricist for the new Broadway musical *Forgotten Melody*, which takes the Great Depression and its "forgotten men" as context, inspiration, and subject.

It turns out that "Brad Roberts" can also beautifully croon a tune. He baffles Polly by adamantly refusing during *Forgotten Melody*'s opening night to go on for the juvenile lead, incapacitated by lumbago. When Brad—echoing Peggy's replacement of diva Dorothy in *42nd Street*—decides to go on, newspaper headlines soon reveal the reasons for his reluctance: "Robert Treat Bradford, Boston Blue Blood, Found Incognito in Broadway Musical Show." Brad has been fearful of being disowned by J. Lawrence Bradford (Warren William), the puritanical brother who controls his estate: a man who, in "Proper Bostonian" tradition, shuns publicity and considers all "people of the theater" to be "cheap and vulgar." Yet, Lawrence succumbs to the stratagems of the movie's trio of resourceful showgirls, as Brad marries Polly and pursues his passion for writing and performing popular music. Brad explains to his family:

> "I'm sorry everybody in the family's shocked, but I'd better come directly to the point too. Music is my career, you know that. . . . The kind that's sung in shows. Over the radio and on records. I don't mean the kind of music played by the Boston Symphony Orchestra. . . . I wanna write this other kind of music. This show was my opportunity."[4]

While basing the film on Avery Hopwood's 1919 play *The Gold Diggers* and its 1929 musical adaptation *The Gold Diggers of Broadway*, the screenwriters of *The Gold Diggers of 1933* draw repeated parallels to the life story of Ropes, who changed his name to Billy Bradford when he departed from his own socially prominent, "blue-blood" Massachusetts family to perform in vaudeville in 1923. The parallels are not exact. For instance, Ropes's own family were New

England Puritans who raised him in suburban Quincy rather than the Bostonian "heirs to millions" depicted in *The Gold Diggers of 1933*. Nevertheless, the screenplay suggests unmistakable connections to the life of Ropes (nicknamed "Brad" in high school), starting with the dual "incognito" journeys of Robert Treat Bradford/Brad Roberts and Bradford Ropes/Billy Bradford into Broadway show business.

Both the allusions to Ropes's biography within the screenplay of *The Gold Diggers of 1933* and his vast cultural influence with the novel *42nd Street* allegorize his placement in theatrical, cinematic, and literary canons: invisibly ubiquitous, centrally positioned, but uneasily traceable. Of the 1933 film musical, Hoberman observes that *42nd Street* "is so much a part of showbiz DNA that you've seen it even if you haven't, and, like *Casablanca*, is especially enjoyable if known by heart."[5] If *42nd Street* is a film that audiences have seen even if they haven't, then Ropes's novel, too, presents a widely known text through cultural osmosis, even if the man and his work vanished for decades.

42nd Street flows through the very bloodstream of American popular entertainment. Why, then, did Ropes's body of work, and consequently his biographical footsteps, disappear into such obscurity? While the reasons are complex and perhaps not fully knowable, some of these certainly relate to Ropes's own personal and artistic choices. Like Robert Treat Bradford in *The Gold Diggers of 1933*, Ropes understood that "Proper Bostonian" boys did not typically go into "cheap and vulgar" show business. Brad marries Polly at the end of *The Gold Diggers of 1933*, providing a happily ever after to their backstage "Cinderella romance." By contrast, Ropes lived his life and partnered as a gay man. Consistent newspaper descriptions of his "modest" public profile illuminate how Ropes may have chosen to stay out of the limelight when not performing in vaudeville as Billy Bradford.

Indeed, as Ropes climbed briefly into literary celebrity in 1932 and '33, he chose neither to exploit his fame nor to reveal too much of himself. Chronicling a screening of *42nd Street* at the Strand Theatre in Ropes's hometown, featuring a public appearance by the author, the *Quincy Patriot Ledger* observed: "Congratulated by scores who visited him at his parents' home yesterday, Mr. Ropes quietly accepted their encomiums, and displayed a marked preference for discussing events of his youth . . . and his experience on the stage as Billy Bradford."[6] The *Patriot Ledger* described Ropes's reaction to the *42nd Street* film's sensational success: he "modestly remained in the background while thousands have applauded the picturization of his novel."[7] Ropes left behind no direct descendants, and a collection of papers has not been made available.

Other reasons for Ropes's obscurity are more structural, related to issues of canonization, hierarchy, and artistic value. Adding to the critical establishment's marginalization of both backstage novels and gay-themed novels in the 1920s and '30s, the medium of the backstage novel has long slipped between the cracks of theater studies and literary criticism. This categorical elusiveness interacts with the adaptive history of *42nd Street* from book to film to stage production. Fueled by the combination of its commercial success and Berkeley's choreographic innovations, the 1933 film almost immediately eclipsed the novel while creating its own Depression-era mythology and moving its characters, themes, and historical contexts further away from Ropes's vision. Because the novel has been so overshadowed by its adaptations, and because the novel's copyright history has also been complicated and confusing, publishers may not have been eager to put *42nd Street* back into print.

Ropes's backstage trilogy deeply merits contemporary rediscovery. Identifying the core of raw candor and engrossing artifice that marks Ropes's work, *Stage Mother*'s dust cover touted a "novel that is both entertaining and true."[8] Ropes abundantly drew his style and influences from the pages of "genre" rather than "literary" fiction in his "entertaining and idiomatic" novels.[9] Here, a contemporary reader might find resonances with the Times Square gangster fables of Damon Runyon as well as the melodramatic yet shrewdly feminist middlebrow "women's fiction" of Fannie Hurst and Edna Ferber. Ropes also incorporated the rhythms of Broadway tabloids and Hollywood films, whose narrative formulas Ropes often ironizes and subverts.

Ropes converges his literary style and sensibility in his bawdy, hard-boiled, and highly quotable dialogue. In 1934's *Go Into Your Dance*, Ropes observed "show girls whose talk was embellished with the pungent aphorisms of Times Square."[10] With details as spicy as his language, Ropes creates worlds marked by caustic, self-reflexive, show business satire, threaded with roman à clef allusion. Ropes's Broadway abounds with scheming stage mothers, precocious stage children, grandiose bit players, and tart-tongued chorines.

Despite the semi-disreputable status of the backstage novel in the 1920s and early '30s, some perceptive critics took notice of Ropes as one of the masters of the genre. The *Philadelphia Public Ledger* raved of *Stage Mother*: "Mr. Ropes again explores the fascinating world of the theatre, and emerges with a crisp, consistently entertaining story. His photography of theatrical types is uncanny in its accuracy. The machinery of the theatre in all its aspects, the variegated pattern of backstage existence, emerge with the same clarity and authority which characterized *42nd Street*."[11] Almost ninety years later, in his essay "The Remarkable Out-of-Print Book That Inspired *42nd Street*," the *New Yorker*'s Richard Brody praised in similar terms Ropes's documentarian-like ability to capture the world of the theater: "In the sharpness of its incidents and the variety of its copious dialogue, it brings the era and the milieu to life in a way that no movie I've ever watched and no nonfiction account I've ever read has done; it has the ring of authenticity, the force of direct observation and conversation."[12]

Each version of *42nd Street* adapts the narrative of Peggy's Broadway ascent to the time in which it was produced: the film version to the Roosevelt New Deal and the stage adaptation to the Neoconservatism of the Reagan era. By contrast, Ropes completed his novel in 1932, toward the end of Herbert Hoover's presidency, amid the bleakest days of the Depression. Ropes wrote his *42nd Street* at a time of daunting industrial shifts. The demise of vaudeville and its eclipse by Hollywood talkies created an environment of scarcity and fierce competition for vaudevillians. This, in turn, allowed Ropes to reflect with raw honesty about the systems in which he worked. Ropes's backstage novels, largely set in the 1920s but reflecting the realities of the 1930s, illuminate the commercial mechanisms of Broadway and vaudeville theater; their labor conditions; the lives and struggles of their performers; and the liberations, repressions, and compromises of gay men working on Broadway during the Jazz Age. At the same time, Ropes also pays close attention to the exploitations of women in show business. To a lesser but still considerable extent, *42nd Street*, *Stage Mother*, and *Go Into Your Dance* explore issues of cultural appropriation and exchange between African American performers and white imitators.

The adaptors of *42nd Street*'s film and stage versions acted upon box office imperatives to sweeten the tone of the Ropes novel, which Depression-era critics received as tougher and more cynical than the film. The *Oakland Tribune* commented about these differences in 1933: "Bradford Ropes's novel from which *42nd Street* was taken was a good deal less delicate in its implications and its language than the adaptation by Rian James and James Seymour, but the translators have preserved the Broadway flavor of the piece and kept it sophisticated enough to amuse the cognoscenti and at the same time not offend the general public."[13]

If many considered Ropes's literary voice as indecorous in the 1930s and into the 1980s, his unflinching candor might well fit the tenor of contemporary times, in which the industrial shifts intensified by the COVID-19 pandemic have shone hard lights upon the fissures of theatrical traditions and structures. As informed by his outsider's perspective as a gay man, Ropes incisively questioned enduring myths about commerce, labor, power, and "the show must go on" in the 1930s. In his 2021 essay about the history of LGBTQ+ fiction, "Creating a Literary Culture," novelist Michael Nava speculates: "In literature, as in history, it is often the obscure stories, the ones that go unnoticed at the time and which are not inscribed in the Official Record that, years, decades, even centuries later, turn out to have been the true story of an age. Unsurprisingly, these are often the stories of the outcasts, the insignificant, and the despised of their era whose voices are not merely ignored but actively suppressed only to be reappraised and finally heard in a later, more evolved time."[14]

In their adaptive processes, each *42nd Street* represents the "story of an age." Yet, Ropes's centralization of the defiant voices of gay outcasts in his *42nd Street* (reflected equally in *Stage Mother* and *Go Into Your Dance*) distinguishes his novel from its later adaptations. The relationship of male characters to heroine Peggy Sawyer provides a key distinction among the three *42nd Streets*. The 1933 film tells the story of collective triumph over economic adversity, as fueled by Peggy's individualist ambition and as aided by her heterosexual suitors. The 1980 stage musical reprises these dynamics, though fueled by the era's feminist backlash. It positions Marsh as a Pygmalion figure to Peggy, whom the musical frames as a symbol of bootstrapping American Dream success. By contrast, Ropes's novel shows Peggy navigating social politics among a complex spectrum of gay male characters: most prominently, the discreet Billy Lawler (Marsh's lover in the book) and the flamboyant "fairy," Jack Winslow. Peggy's affiliation with Billy and her rejection of the unabashed Jack (cut from the film and stage versions) precipitate her fabled rise in Ropes's novel.

In six chapters, *Greasepaint Puritan* follows the writing, cultural reception, and afterlife of Ropes's *42nd Street*, within the contexts of his biography, cultural influences, and connections to his three other published novels. These are 1933's *Stage Mother*; 1934's *Go Into Your Dance*; and 1951's *Mr. Tilley Takes a Walk*, a Boston-set historical novel that Ropes cowrote with Val Burton and that the team infused with theatrical elements. Throughout *Greasepaint Puritan*, I discuss *42nd Street*, *Stage Mother*, and *Go Into Your Dance* as Ropes's "backstage trilogy," united by the author's interweaving of characters, themes, and settings throughout the three novels. Strikingly, Dorothy Brock reappears as a rival to ingénue Shirley Lorraine in *Stage Mother*. Similarly, Ropes provides a sort of prequel appearance to Julian Marsh, shown in *Go Into Your Dance* directing a mid-1920s musical comedy called *Sweet Sally*.

Greasepaint Puritan begins with a short interlude chapter that offers foundational information and synopses about the plots of the backstage trilogy.

Chapter 1 then explores how Ropes lived out a dual identity from his youth. The chapter places Ropes's family history and early biography in the context of the culture to which he frequently "peered back" in his fiction: the city of the "Boston Brahmins" and the suburb of Quincy, a town with a colorful anti-Puritan past as well as close connections to Pilgrims and Founding Fathers. Ropes grew up in a milieu characterized by Anglo-Saxon decorum and uplift. His formidable mother, born Alice Gertrude Williams, served as regent of the Wollaston chapter of the Daughters of the American Revolution and, during the Prohibition era, as the president of the Massachusetts Women's Christian Temperance Union. As the president of the Children of the American Revolution of Wollaston, Ropes grew up amid a white Anglo-Saxon Protestant culture marked by both a culture of homophobia and some degree of anti-theatrical prejudice. Yet, Ropes also grew into a precocious stagestruck teenager, a gifted dancer, and a prolific, increasingly rebellious writer with a knack for offending authorities.

Chapter 2 illustrates Ropes's transformation into the vaudevillian and musical comedy dancer Billy Bradford. Urged by his parents to seek a business career, the eighteen-year-old Ropes strayed from this path to join the female impersonator Alyn Mann in vaudeville. In 1925, Billy Bradford teamed up with the female dancer Marian Hamilton, with whom he performed in American vaudeville, in European cabarets and music halls, and on Broadway. He also entered into complex and ambivalent encounters with the Harlem Renaissance, which he later evoked consistently in his backstage novels. At the conclusion of this chapter, I explore the collisions of Puritan culture and Modernism that converged in the 1929 Boston censorship case of Eugene O'Neill's *Strange Interlude*: a battle of morals that, for Ropes, hit close to his family home.

Chapter 3 demonstrates how Ropes brought together two distinct but overlapping trends in 1920s and early 1930s popular fiction: the backstage novel and the gay-themed novels enabled by the "Pansy Craze" of 1931-34. Drawing from Rick Altman's discussion of the Hollywood backstage musical as a "white-collar form" that "rarely shows the work of production," I argue for the backstage novel as a genre that, as influenced by literary Naturalism, declines to "mask the blue-collar work of production."[15] In order to place Ropes's novels in a wider context, I look at three authors of the late 1920s and early 1930s with whom Ropes both shared theatrical backgrounds and overlapped in his narrative strategies. These include the backstage novelists J. P. McEvoy, the author of 1928's sardonic *Show Girl*, and Beth Brown, the writer of the same year's *Applause*. Among gay writers, I consider Max Ewing, who set loose his 1933 Lost Generation escapade *Going Somewhere* among New York's cabarets, nightclubs, and cruising grounds.

Chapter 4 explores Ropes's own portrayal of the intersection of gay culture with Broadway show business. In his backstage trilogy, Ropes demonstrates gay male characters thwarting social oppression through irony, parody, and discourses of "dishing the dirt." Ropes particularly focused on the figure of the Broadway chorus boy: a profession culturally linked from the early twentieth century with associations of effeminacy and homosexuality. Discussing Ropes's depictions of chorus boys Jack Winslow, Jack Thomas, and Bobby Rogers in, respectively, *42nd Street*, *Stage Mother*, and *Go Into Your Dance*, I also connect Ropes's strategies with his likely affair over the course of ten years with Roswell Jolly Black, a Seattle-born organist who concealed their relationship by listing himself as Ropes's "secretary" in Hollywood, as Ropes transitioned into a successful new career as a screenwriter.

Chapter 5 elaborates upon Ropes's portrayal of gay culture by considering the multifaceted role of the theater in the author's 1930s backstage trilogy, as well as in *Mr. Tilley Takes a Walk*. In all of these novels, Ropes probed the tensions between the "call of home" and the "lure of the theatre," between "Proper Boston" and Broadway. Strikingly, Ropes used roman à clef techniques to fictionalize a string of Jazz Age Broadway's most famous impresarios, including Gus Edwards, with whom he had performed as teenager in vaudeville. In focusing his veiled critique upon Broadway's "lords of the entertainment world," Ropes interrogates in human terms the myth of "the show must go on," while questioning the relationships among show business, the Protestant work ethic, and his own Puritan upbringing.

In chapter 6, I trace Ropes's final years, spent out of the limelight in Boston. After his death in 1966, *42nd Street* rose to the realm of cultural myth in Hollywood and on Broadway. At the same time, these adaptations eclipsed Ropes's novel and relegated its author to a footnote, as a new generation hailed Busby Berkeley as "the King of Camp."[16] Yet, in the years following the 1964 publication of Susan Sontag's "Notes on 'Camp,'" Ropes's sensibility lived on through *42nd Street*'s influence upon generations of LGBTQ+ theater artists and filmmakers. Works inspired by the film *42nd Street* included the 1966 stage musical *Dames at Sea*, originating at Off-Off-Broadway's Caffe Cino, and Ken Russell's 1971 movie musical *The Boy Friend*, based on Sandy Wilson's 1953 stage pastiche. By contrast, the 1980

Broadway adaptation of *42nd Street* veered away from the camp satire and gay themes of Ropes's novel.

Both historically and in terms of his movements among media, Ropes is a difficult figure to pin down. His shape-shifting informs the structure of this book. *Greasepaint Puritan* can be approached as an intellectual biography of Ropes, in which I have blended his personal story with theater and performance historiography; literary analysis; and a cultural landscape of Boston, Broadway, and Hollywood in the 1920s and '30s, as these cities engaged in complex dialogues about censorship, sexuality, and the limits of artistic expression. In the early 1950s, Ropes presented an autobiographical Boston lecture tour entitled "Adventures in Three Make-Believe Worlds: Footlights, Movies and Books."[17] Taking the cue from Ropes himself, *Greasepaint Puritan* engages with a blend of interdisciplinary conversations: drawing together not only the "make-believe worlds" of Broadway, Hollywood, and popular fiction but also the spheres of dance history, LGBTQ+ history, and American studies.

For all his fond reminiscence about the world of the footlights, Ropes, for many decades, has been waiting in the wings. In this, he can be compared with many gay theater artists of his generation who both sought and eluded visibility. Chronicling the life and work of such an enigmatic figure has proved both exciting and difficult, and *Greasepaint Puritan* has been a rigorous labor of love since I became enthralled with Ropes's novels while writing my dissertation in the early 2010s. Since then, I have undertaken an eclectic range of research methodologies that encompass accessing *Patriot Ledger* archives at the Thomas Crane Public Library in Quincy; tracing genealogical and biographical information; consulting collections ranging from the New York Public Library of the Performing Arts to the archives of Ropes's preparatory school alma mater; visiting sites meaningful to Ropes and his loved ones; and interviewing a relative who shared her childhood memories of Ropes.

My research process underscores the challenges of writing biographically about queer artists when complex factors of personal discretion, critical reception, and cultural canonization have contributed to archival erasure. Can we ever fully know who the author was, as he shifted between the personae of the vaudevillian Billy Bradford and the novelist Bradford Ropes? It is equally impossible to know how Ropes would have navigated questions of gender and sexuality had he lived amid 2020s American culture. Still, I believe that Ropes's bold and detailed exploration of the interior lives and relationships of gay men working on Broadway suggests that he might have wanted his story narrated with more candor than he himself could be permitted to tell it between the restricted liberations of the Jazz Age and the culture of silence during the McCarthy-era "Lavender Scare." As the influence of *42nd Street* will continue to endure, it is essential to recover the "forgotten melody" of Ropes's life and work. With *Greasepaint Puritan*, I hope to begin the process of telling Ropes's story and to bring out the elements of his backstage fiction that allow him to tell his own tale—one as "feverish and crowded with color" as one of his own novels.[18]

Interlude

THE STORIES OF ROPES'S BACKSTAGE TRILOGY

Ropes's backstage novels reveal details of his life that in turn richly illuminate his books. This intimate time step between Ropes's life and work has inspired me to closely interweave biography and literary analysis in *Greasepaint Puritan*. Yet, due to their relative obscurity and long histories out of print, *Stage Mother* and *Go Into Your Dance* tell stories that will be unfamiliar to most readers, and Ropes's *42nd Street* also varies considerably from the film and stage versions in its narrative and expanded set of characters. To help contemporary readers navigate my discussions of his backstage trilogy, I have included this interlude of plot synopses that can be perused, skimmed, or skipped according to the reader's familiarity with these novels.

42nd Street (1932)

Ropes divides his *42nd Street* into two books: those of "Rehearsal" and "Opening." By contrast with the film and stage adaptations, *Pretty Lady* itself, as embodied by impresario Julian Marsh, might be considered the central character of the novel. Ropes sets the action during the 1927-28 Broadway season: a timeline suggested both by allusions to the talkies and the identification of the Paramount Theatre (built in 1926) as "Times Square's newest landmark."[1] The novel opens with a conversation between Marsh, who directs and oversees the artistic production of his shows, and coproducers Abe Green and Si Friedman, who handle the finances. "Three good tunes and a kick in the pants for your wow blackout. Can you make a hit show out of it?" inquires Green to Marsh in the novel's first line.[2]

Pretty Lady auditions begin at the 45th Street Theatre. The Equity casting call draws both chorus girls and chorus boys to the audition, conducted by the notoriously exacting dance director Andy Lee. The call also summons stage mother Mrs. Blair, who, with the help of an agent, convinces Andy to offer her acrobatic dancer daughter Polly a specialty number in *Pretty Lady*. Peggy Sawyer, a minister's daughter who has performed in a few amateur plays in Paris, Maine, enters the audition and is taken under the wing of veteran chorines Ann Lowell and Flo Perry. All three women are selected for the ensemble. After the first day of rehearsal, they celebrate at the British Tea Room café, where Ann and Flo dispel stereotypes about chorus girls and warn Peggy about the advances of out-of-town "buyers": "So just watch your step and pal around with girl friends even when the orchids start showering."[3]

In the next sections, Ropes explores the sexual politics behind the scenes of *Pretty Lady*. At their hotel apartment, Andy Lee's wife, Amy, an ex-chorus girl, threatens to expose Andy, after having hushed up a teenage girl's accusation of sexual assault. Now involved in an affair with showgirl Lorraine Fleming, Andy strategizes his own leverage against Amy's blackmail. He considers that the revelation that Amy has been "keeping" out-of-work actor Pat Denning would sink her case in court. Ropes then introduces Terry Neill and Harry Towne, who, after discussing borrowing money from fellow chorus boy Jack Winslow and disparaging him as a "nance," are themselves mocked with antigay slurs outside the Palace Theatre.[4]

Ropes moves the action back to the producers, who resolve to "make Brock behave herself."[5] Marsh discusses with Green and Friedman how Richard Endicott, a Boston Brahmin-turned-Broadway playboy, has taken a "twenty-five percent piece of the show" as a "pay off" for his affair with leading lady Dorothy Brock: an investment now in peril since Dorothy is also having an affair with a "mysterious paramour."[6] To learn the lover's identity, Marsh visits the El Mirador nightclub run by gangster Walt McDermott, to whom Mrs. Blair reveals Pat's address in the West Forties.

Ropes continues to develop relationships among *Pretty Lady*'s cast. Billed as the "King of the Nut Comics,"[7] Danny Moran gossips with vaudevillian Maud. Danny complains of the envy sparked by his going "legitimate" in a Broadway musical comedy. He also dismisses the boredom and loneliness of his wife, Daisy, his former vaudeville partner who has not been cast in the show. Maud asks Danny about working for "Madame Marsh," who Maud has heard is "puttin' his boy friend" Billy Lawler in the show as the juvenile lead.[8] Ropes next introduces Billy. Impressed by her gentility, Billy takes a mentoring interest in Peggy, who is being both coached and courted by Terry. Back at his midtown apartment, Pat invites Geoffrey Waring, a former castmate and likely sometime lover, to attend a party in Greenwich Village. Having learned from a detective that Pat is two-timing her with Dorothy, Amy confronts him at the door of his apartment, where Pat hides Geoffrey in the bathroom. Moving on to the Village party, Pat starts an intense flirtation with Peggy. Returning to his apartment, he is beaten by McDermott's thugs outside his door. As rehearsals conclude, Ropes pulls the sexual politics of *42nd Street* back into the backstage dynamics of putting on *Pretty Lady*, as Marsh muses that "nothing must stand in the way of the show."[9]

With book 2, "Opening," *Pretty Lady* moves into out-of-town tryouts in Philadelphia. Tragedy strikes early in the run, as elderly actor Lionel Crane suffers a fatal heart attack onstage during the dress rehearsal. Marsh, Green, and Friedman conspire to avoid an inquest that would delay the opening night of the show. After a promising opening, *Pretty Lady* cast members attend a party for the show's chorus members in the hotel room shared by Harry and Terry. Here, the bawdy wisecracks of Jack Winslow and his friends both fascinate and repel the Puritan-bred Peggy. More conflicts develop at the party, where Terry issues homophobic comments to the flamboyant Jack and Peggy chastises Terry for his drinking and carousing, putting an end to the latter's courtship.

Another Philadelphia hotel party hosts *Pretty Lady*'s stars, producers, and backers. More serious conflicts develop here. An intoxicated Dorothy endangers *Pretty Lady*'s bankroll by taunting sugar daddy Endicott. Hoping that Marsh will repay her loyalty with more stage time for Polly, Mrs. Blair telephones the impresario and tips him off that Brock is still seeing Pat. Marsh calls McDermott to threaten Pat, who has written a breakup letter to Peggy informing her that he is "going back to his life of sin."[10] Though resolving to focus on her career, Peggy continues to care about Pat. Learning that he is in danger from the gangster, she runs to Pat's and Dorothy's adjoining hotel suites to warn him. After Dorothy gets belligerent, Pat ejects her from the room. Stumbling drunkenly on a carpet, Dorothy falls down the stairs and injures herself badly with a sprained back and concussion.[11]

The crisis sends Marsh and his producing partners into action. Despite objections from Abe Green, Billy prevails upon his romantically besotted lover to choose Peggy as Dorothy's replacement. Billy reflects that only Peggy, among the maligning *Pretty Lady* cast, has treated him with kindness and respect. Billy also negotiates with Marsh to more advantageously showcase his biggest dance number. Postponing *Pretty Lady*'s Philadelphia opening night, Marsh puts the show's publicity machine in motion to promote Peggy as his new star, while also replacing the show's lead comic. Ropes parallels this harsh backstage firing with a marital breakup, as Amy resolves to leave Andy and sail to Europe with Pat.

An anxious Peggy prepares to go on as the star of *Pretty Lady* in Philadelphia. Strategically, Billy takes Peggy out to the tearoom of the Ritz Lenox's Palm Court. Here, he reaffirms his support, telling Peggy that she was "bound to rise" from the chorus.[12] He advises her to drop all friends who can't help her professionally and proposes a "lavender romance" that will mutually advance their careers. Outside the Palm Court, Billy and Peggy run into Jack Winslow, whom Billy snubs and who also defiantly endures the taunting of a group of bullies. Weakly defending Jack, whom Billy dismisses as a "dirty little failure,"[13] Peggy reflects upon her gratitude to Billy. She also resolves to focus on her own performing career: "Vale Terry! Vale Pat! Long live Billy! No—that was wrong—long live Peggy Sawyer!"[14]

In the novel's conclusion, which moves from Philadelphia back to New York, Peggy triumphs a second time during her star-studded Broadway opening night. Trilling the romantic duet "In the Land Where My Dreams Come True" with her leading man, John Phillips, Peggy demonstrates that she has indeed started to master the "Forty-Second Street code" of self-interest imparted to her by Billy. In the last line of *42nd Street*, Peggy cries to *Pretty Lady*'s music director: "Wasn't it wonderful! . . . And Harry, tell Phillips not to start the second verse so soon, will you? Who the hell does he think he *is*?"[15]

Stage Mother (1933)

Ropes divides *Stage Mother* into not two but three books: "Kitty," "Chrysalis," and "Enter a Lady." "Kitty" follows the title character's transformation from vaudeville performer to stage mother. "Chrysalis" focuses on Kitty's molding of Shirley, as Kitty puts her daughter on the stage and converts all of her energy into turning Shirley into a Broadway star. The third section, "Enter a Lady," tracks Shirley's gradual rebellion against, and eventual rejection of, Kitty.

Ropes starts the novel around 1910, backstage at an Orpheum Circuit theater in Des Moines, where Kitty Lorraine is preparing to go on as the performance partner of her husband, Fred, a trick cyclist. Shortly after Kitty tells her husband she's about to go into labor, Fred dies in an onstage accident. The tragedy places Kitty at the mercy of her husband's staid Boston family, from whom "Frederick" had been a black sheep. Kitty and her infant daughter Shirley move in with the family at their Beacon Hill home, in a household consisting of Fred's mother, his father, and his "old maid" schoolteacher sister, the God-fearing Ida. Though Kitty was "raised in a wardrobe trunk,"[16] the family prohibits her from returning to the stage. She finds work behind a perfume counter in a department store, a job to which she unhappily submits for the next three years.

Kitty's situation changes dramatically after a late-night party with vaudevillian friends playing in Boston. After Kitty has a bitter exchange with Mrs. Lorraine and Ida, the two expel her from the house. In exchange for Kitty's agreement to only see Shirley in the summers, the Lorraine women offer young Shirley "the right sort of education" at a Catholic school.[17] Another five years pass, during which Kitty returns to vaudeville as the stage partner and wife of song-and-dance man Ralph Martin. However, the alcoholic, unfaithful Ralph falls into a violent love triangle and shoots the husband of his mistress. After Ralph's imprisonment, Kitty attempts to enter burlesque, only to be informed by an agent that she no longer appears youthful enough to secure bookings.

Ropes moves the action to New York City just before the United States' entrance into World War I. A fortunate encounter with Ruby Vanderbilt, an old vaudeville friend now married to theatrical agent Lew Grimes, leads to Kitty working as a secretary in Grimes's office. Now solvent, Kitty persuades Ida to let Shirley move with her to Manhattan, where Kitty enrolls her daughter in dancing lessons and secures Grimes as Shirley's agent. Befriending the dance instructor, Fritz Sterling, Kitty secures solid training for her daughter—and preferential treatment to other stage mothers. As World War I drags on, Kitty and Lew book Shirley into a succession of Elks banquets and benefits, where she performs patriotic toe-dance numbers. Soon, Kitty grows estranged from Lew, who objects to Kitty's "cold-blooded exploitation" of Shirley.[18]

Kitty next sets her sights on Mark Thorne, a celebrity producer of vaudeville youth revues. She takes Shirley to Thorne's open casting call. Here, Thorne finds Shirley's dancing "a knockout."[19] He signs her to a contract after negotiating with Kitty. As the action moves into the 1920s, Shirley, given a featured dance in Thorne's revue, performs at the glamorous big-time theaters along the Orpheum Circuit. Kitty and Thorne deal with each other warily, as Kitty informs her daughter: "Vaudeville's only a stopping place for you, darling."[20]

Using agents and producers as her own stepping stones, Kitty moves on from Thorne to the licentious and corrupt but high-profile Broadway agent

Louis Hearn. Although Hearn does not typically sign vaudevillians, Kitty lures him to the Palace Theatre, where Shirley stops the show in Thorne's revue. Kitty confronts a dilemma: she has signed an unbreakable five-year contract with Thorne. She clandestinely takes a compromising photo of Thorne in bed with one of his young cast members and successfully blackmails him. This frees Shirley to sign with Hearn, who then secures her a place in the new Broadway revue *Adam and His Eves*, starring Dorothy Brock.

During rehearsals, the death of Aunt Ida brings the Lorraine women back to Boston, for which Shirley has been nostalgic. Kitty uses the funeral to stage a publicity spectacle at the Hotel New Plymouth, commanding headlines for her daughter as a young Broadway star in mourning. Silently, Shirley fumes at her mother for having withheld letters from the dying Ida. Visiting the old Lorraine home on Beacon Hill, she meets the new owner of the property: a young Brahmin painter named Warren Foster, with whom she soon starts a passionate romance. Intercepting a letter from Warren to Shirley, alluding both to their sexual affair and to his family home on Commonwealth Avenue, Kitty resolves to break up the relationship before it can compromise Shirley's career. She successfully blackmails Mrs. Foster, whose son furiously confronts Shirley backstage, thinking the dancer had been in on her mother's scheme. Warren ends the romance with a physical slap to the face of the uncomprehending Shirley.

As a heartbroken Shirley devotes herself to rehearsals for *Adam and His Eves*, Dorothy Brock grows jealous of the young dancer. After opening night critics shower praise on Shirley, Dorothy commands Hearn to pull Shirley's ballet out of the show. The diva allows the reinstatement of the ballet only after Kitty uses her connections to plant an unflattering story about Dorothy's behavior with a Broadway columnist. As her star rises both on Broadway and in the social register, where she is pursued by Wall Street barons and Beacon Hill scions, Shirley falls in line with the hard-boiled opportunism of her mother.

Now a celebrated Broadway star at the height of the Jazz Age, Shirley finds herself pursued by Alfred P. Dexter, the much publicized and married playboy mayor of a "neighboring city" in New Jersey.[21] Both Hearn and Kitty support this lucrative liaison, even as Hearn strictly instructs Shirley to conceal it from the tabloids. Shirley befriends Jack Thomas, cast as her dancing partner in the new musical comedy *Success and Flowers*. Jack's irreverent camp wit and love of gossip threaten the clandestine nature of the affair, about which Shirley trusts Jack with "choice morsels of scandal."[22] This leads John Reilly, the ruthless political boss who keeps the mayor in power, to arrange Jack's poisoning by openly homophobic gangsters at Angelo Scarlatti's speakeasy. Reilly bribes Kitty and Shirley to depart for France before the scandal of Jack's "suicide" and press about Dexter's "orgy of wastefulness" can further intensify.[23] Stunned and disillusioned when Dexter admits his complicity in Jack's murder, Shirley sets off for the French Riviera with Kitty.

Changing her name to "Shirley Clive," the dancer plans for a new life in the Riviera and cabaret bookings in Cannes, Nice, and Monte Carlo. On the ocean liner to France, Shirley meets Geoffrey Aylesworth, an English aristocrat and businessman also bound for the Riviera. There, he falls in love with the refined Shirley while tactfully disdaining her "uncouth" vaudevillian mother. Considering Kitty as a stumbling block to Lord Aylesworth's marriage proposal, Shirley devises a strategy. She confesses to a stunned Kitty: "I've told Geoffrey you were just my stage mother. . . . I'm an orphan. . . . I've called you mother because I've always needed a chaperon."[24] Shirley adds that she plans to send Kitty a salary of one hundred dollars a week. Having severed her ties to Kitty, Shirley marries Lord Aylesworth in the London Mall, in the shadow of Buckingham Palace. "In the dark of the Mall," an unseen interloper at her daughter's wedding festivities, Kitty sobs: "Thank God I've made her happy! . . . Thank God! Thank God!"[25]

Go Into Your Dance (1934)

Unlike Ropes's previous novels, *Go Into Your Dance* is not divided into separate books but unfolds across a single forty-two chapters. Nevertheless, corresponding to *Stage Mother*, its action can be looked at as encompassing three parts. Ranging from New York's Lower East Side to Broadway to Paris and back to Broadway, it follows the rise of ambitious protagonist Ted Howard from messenger boy to professional dancer; his continued ascent from vaudeville performer to Broadway producer; and his transformation into a showman of dubious ethics whose tactics compromise both his personal relationships and the welfare of his performers.

The action starts in the early 1920s on the Lower East Side, where the stagestruck Ted Howard works as a messenger boy. Delighted when he's assigned to deliver a telegram to performers at the Star Theatre, Ted hopes he'll be able to show his dancing to idols the "Two Buddies." Making his way backstage, Ted convinces one of the Buddies, Lou Adams, to take a look at one of his routines. Impressed, Lou encourages Ted to perform at an amateur night uptown at the Regent Theatre. The plan meets the disapproval of Ted's working-class Irish American family in the Bronx. However, his sister Ellen, stagestruck herself, lends Ted her fervent conspiratorial support. Confronting a rainstorm as he steps out of the subway, Ted panics that he'll be late to the theater. However, taxi driver Abe Feinstein generously consents to drive him to the Regent without sufficient fare. As "Ted Howard, the Dancing Messenger Boy," he wins second place.

Ted enters a dancing career in vaudeville. As mentored by Lou Adams, Ted signs with Sam Weinberg. The agent books him as one of three supporting dancers in *Vanities of Terpsichore*, headlined by the tango team of Ramon and Noretta. Earning his stripes as a vaudeville trouper, Ted tires of a three-show-a-day grind and dreams of striking out on his own. Meanwhile, Ellen walks out on her disapproving family as her Ivy League sugar daddy, nicknamed "Joe Harvard," puts her up in a love-nest apartment.

Ted next finds work on Broadway. Having quit *Vanities of Terpsichore* and unable to secure a spot as a featured dancer on Broadway, Ted tries his luck as a chorus boy. With the help of chorus veteran Walt Milburn, he makes his way into the ensemble of *Sweet Sally*, a new (ostensibly pre–*Pretty Lady*) musical comedy produced by Julian Marsh with dance direction by Andy Lee. Overcoming his initial trepidation around effeminate gay men, Ted befriends Arthur and Bobby Rogers (also known as "Miss Rogers"), a pair of friends and sometime lovers who dazzle Ted with their impressions, jokes, and stories. Miss Rogers's sudden suicide at a party shocks Ted. He learns that Bobby, who jumped off the roof, had been struggling with depression under his light-hearted facade.

The tragedy precipitates a fortuitous meeting for Ted. Too devastated to carry out the task by himself, and fearful of getting "pulled in," Arthur requests Ted's help in fulfilling Miss Rogers's wish: that the dancer's ashes be scattered over New York harbor. On the Staten Island Ferry, where Arthur finally carries out the task despite adversity from crowds and high winds, Ted meets Nora Wayne: a street-smart sixteen-year-old from Staten Island who has had to quit school to help support her family, including the eight-year-old brother who accompanies her on the ferry. Nora has been taking dance lessons in Manhattan and is herself eager to enter show business. She agrees to Ted's offer to meet in the city to put together a vaudeville double act. After Ted quits the chorus of *Sweet Sally*, Weinberg books Howard and Wayne into a cross-country tour on the Orpheum Circuit, where Ted and his comedian friend Al

Davies become embroiled in a misadventure with two prostitutes: an imbroglio from which Nora disentangles the two men.

Howard and Wayne commence a "swift rise to prominence" on the Broadway revue stage.[26] At the same time, both Ted and Ellen become involved with gangsters. In vaudeville, Howard and Wayne attract the attention of Lane, New York's "most astute impresario."[27] Lane engages the team for the 1924 edition of his annual *Frivolities* revue. His ambition climbing, Ted studies Lane's method and confesses to Nora his plans to produce his own snappier Broadway revue, titled *Town Talk*. At the same time that Ellen becomes the mistress of a slot-machine mobster, Ted secures the financial backing of a Chicago beer racketeer known as "the Major." He accepts the Major's condition for playing "angel": that Ted feature his torch-singer mistress, Laura Whitney, as one the stars of *Town Talk of 1926*, also starring Nora and featuring the blues-flavored compositions of the brilliant Johnny Bartels. Still in the cast of the *Frivolities*, Ted and Nora secretly assemble the first *Town Talk*. However, Ted draws Lane's wrath when news of the new revue leaks to the theatrical columns.

Ellen's life as a gangster's moll takes its toll on *Town Talk*. Ellen's love triangle with taxi racketeer Nelson and political boss Jack Vittori places her too close to the scene of Vittori's murder. Tabloids blaze "Mystery Blonde Charged with Murder" as she refuses to talk to the police. Needing bail money, Ellen begs Ted to lend her his *Town Talk* Equity bond, covering two weeks' salary for the cast. Ted postpones rehearsals and reluctantly lends her $20,000. However, Ellen jumps her bail and goes into hiding, necessitating Equity's halting of rehearsals. Nora once again saves the day. Escaping the goons that the Major has sent on their trail, Nora suggests that she and Ted flee to her vacation home in Connecticut. Serendipitously, Ellen surrenders to the court with proof of her innocence, and tabloid publicity helps *Town Talk* rack up advance sales.

Ted and Nora encounter more obstacles with *Town Talk of 1926*. In league with the rival producing team of the Wilsons, Lane attempts to block the show from booking a Broadway theater. The show also garners mixed reviews during its out-of-town tryouts in Atlantic City, after which Nora counsels Ted to fix up "that ragged first-act finale."[28] The show then receives solid notices during its Broadway opening night. Over the next few seasons, Ted turns his *Town Talk* revues into formidable rivals of the *Frivolities*, but financial success brings increasing insecurities to Ted, who aspires to a veneer of elegance and "class." Chasing after the women in his chorus, Ted also snubs the romantic feelings of Nora, who continues to advise him on his revues.

Ted becomes more unscrupulous as a producer as he aims to outspend Lane and the Wilsons in the opulence of his shows. In Paris, where Ted hopes to find ideas for new *Town Talk* production numbers, the producer falls hard for the. blue-blooded Eunice Goddard, hailing from a recently impoverished Philadelphia Main Line family. Encouraging Ted's pursuit, Eunice breaks away from her relationship with the possessive Emmy, a fashion-industry buyer whom Eunice deceptively introduces to Ted as her chaperone and "distant cousin."[29] An aspiring tunesmith, the talented Eunice also shows him sophisticated torch songs that Ted features in *Town Talk of 1929*. Ted's ambition overcomes his better judgment as he copies a production number from the Casino de Paris. He ignores his stage manager's urgent warning: that the stage technicians need more time to fix the unsafe scenery for the "Living Trellis of Girls" number. During the dress rehearsal, the set crashes down and injures several of the chorus girls, as well as Nora, who had reluctantly agreed to appear in the number. Nora expresses her anger to Ted but continues to stand by him as he replaces the trellis number and reworks the show.

Ted continues to face both professional and personal obstacles as the Great Depression intensifies. Ted learns of declining box office sales for the new edition from his business manager. Having established herself with *Town Talk*, Eunice informs Ted that she is departing for Hollywood, to write songs for talkie film musicals. As Ted insults Eunice as an opportunist and Eunice derides Ted as a "shallow, egotistical little hoofer," the lovers bitterly part ways.[30]

The final chapter of the book shows Ted, his glory days with *Town Talk* now behind him, reflecting upon the past. The ghostlike appearance of a messenger boy in the offices of Ted Howard Theatrical Enterprises prompts the producer, and now theater owner, to gaze at an old photograph of himself in his Western Union uniform. Nora, still healing from her stage accident, interrupts his reverie with some welcome news: that her Wall Street investments harvested $25,000, which she plans to invest in his new revue. When Ted weakly protests to Nora, "I don't deserve it," she replies, "I know you don't. . . . But you always were a man to get the breaks."[31] Quipping about the likely infidelities that await her post-honeymoon, Nora picks up the phone to inform an unnamed "honey doll" she can forget about Ted's private phone number.[32] She informs the producer that she will soon be "Mrs. Ted Howard." Hollywood-like, the novel fades out with a kiss.

꙳

Only after Ropes worked steadily in Hollywood for the next sixteen years did he publish a fourth novel: 1951's *Mr. Tilley Takes a Walk*, cowritten with Val Burton. This novel, which will be discussed in some depth in the following chapter, unfolds in the city of Ropes's birth and where he spent much of his childhood and coming of age. With substantially more insight and perspective than Ted Howard at the end of *Go Into Your Dance*, Ropes focused his own backward gaze at his dual hometowns of Boston and Quincy.

CHAPTER 1

Peering Back at "Proper Boston"

In 1951's *Mr. Tilley Takes a Walk*, his and Val Burton's tart valentine of a historical novel, Ropes reflects "half-tenderly, half-derisively" upon Boston.[1] Ropes
portrays the city as a bastion of Old World tradition, waltzing placidly into the
twentieth century against an increasingly syncopated national rhythm. Much
of the novel focuses upon the insular society of the Boston Brahmins: a world
with which Ropes had considerable familiarity, due to his youthful visits to
aunts who lived for "a half century" at the exclusive residences of Louisburg
Square.[2] Near the start of the novel, Ropes evokes the inner monologue of the
title character, an Irish American mailman in love with a Beacon Hill socialite,
as he walks past the "mellowed bricks of Mount Vernon Street":

> As you strolled on your way, history peered down from every nook and
> cranny. . . . Yes, there was sedate magic in these rows of houses which were so
> tightly squeezed together that not even space for area-ways existed, as though
> they had linked arms against a common foe called Progress.[3]

Ropes connects the staid and airless row houses with a group of symphony-
subscribing society matrons known as *Les Chapeaux*. The name refers both
to "those Boston hats and the ladies who sat stiffly beneath them . . . those
amorphous creations which, never, at any given time of any given era, could
have been fashionable."[4]

   In his satiric portrait of Boston, Ropes also incorporated an allusion to the
South Side suburb where he actually grew up: the bayside neighborhood of
Wollaston, at the northern end of the town of Quincy, located nine miles south-
east of Louisburg Square. Conveying Wollaston as a site with a more louche
history than that of Boston, Ropes wryly nods to the town of his upbringing
with the characters of the Crane Sisters. Characteristically respectable citizens by day, the Cranes secretly preside over a Boston bordello at night. The

French composer Pierre Fresnay reports: "Spinsters to be sure, but mon Dieu, w'at spinsters! It is said they live in a small village a few miles to the south, a place that is called Wol-las-ton."[5] Yet, Wollaston, too, peered back at history and heritage. Raised on a block adjacent to Standish Avenue, as the only son of the state regent of Wollaston's Daughters of the American Revolution (DAR) chapter, Ropes spent his childhood in a town filled with plaques and statues honoring legendary Pilgrims, Puritans, and Founding Fathers, including Anne Hutchinson, John Hancock, and John Adams.

In 1932's *42nd Street*, Ropes captured a world of fast-paced urban modernity and industrial progress that would have jolted any one of *Les Chapeaux*, if less so the racy Crane Sisters. Ropes views Times Square through the eyes of his heroine, the Maine minister's daughter-turned-chorus girl Peggy Sawyer, who gasps, "I don't suppose there's another sight in the world like that." Ropes conjures the glittering spectacle and sensory shock of the Rialto, as he details: "On either side moved the motley of Times Square; gamblers, racketeers, sightseers and show folk. . . . The theatre signs seemed to increase in frenzy. Broadway was a world gone mad with electrical display."[6] In the title song of the 1933 Warner Brothers movie musical that Ropes's novel inspired, lyricist Al Dubin took a strong cue from Ropes, who writes of Times Square as a stream into which "pour poverty and wealth; they meet, converge in the mutual quest for pleasure, and then retire leaving Broadway to shriek in untiring raucousness."[7] Dubin, in turn, paid homage to Times Square's most iconic avenue as the "naughty, gaudy, bawdy, sporty" spot "where the underworld can meet the elite."[8]

In 1923, Ropes, bound for vaudeville's Keith Circuit, moved far beyond the world of *Les Chapeaux*. Like Peggy, Ropes found himself irresistibly compelled by the neon-lit dynamism, protean fashions, and bawdy, naughty underworld of Forty-Second Street. By contrast with Peggy, Ropes's Times Square was also a queer one, soon to be spotted with the ribald drag clubs that opened in the early 1930s. At the fashionable Club Abbey, located at Forty-Sixth Street and Eighth Avenue, Ropes might have watched burly, blond female impersonator Gene Malin caress the camp double entendres of "I'd Rather Be Spanish Than Mannish." Walking two blocks up to the Pansy Club at Forty-Eighth Street and Broadway, Ropes might also have seen "Creole Fashion Plate" Karyl Norman promenade in a succession of dazzling gowns and feathered headdresses, as the star of the floor show *Pansies on Parade*.[9]

Yet, in the pages of his backstage novels, inspired by the stages of vaudeville and Broadway, Ropes returned again and again to the old-fashioned world whose rigid social hierarchies Cleveland Amory cataloged in his 1947 book *The Proper Bostonians*. Ropes's own "Proper Boston" encompassed both Boston and Quincy, which he viewed with both fond nostalgia and caustic critique. The interrelated social landscapes of the Boston Brahmins and the New England Yankee culture essentially undergird the tensions that Ropes potently explored in his backstage novels, which are flavored as much by Boston's "codfish respectability" as by Times Square's greasepaint scandals.[10] In his novels, Ropes peered behind the scenes of Broadway show business, as informed by the contradictions of his fascinating family history.

"Where the Pilgrims Walked": Puritans, Portlanders, and Boston Brahmins

When Ropes, in 1923, transformed from the respectable Bradford Ropes into the improper vaudevillian Billy Bradford, he adopted a moniker likely intended as a cosmopolitan taunt of Mayflower Pilgrim William Bradford (1590–1657). The staunch second governor of the Plymouth Colony and the author of *Of Plymouth Plantation*, Bradford, like Ropes, was also the son of a woman named Alice. Yet the choice of "Billy Bradford" equally acknowledged the incongruity of Ropes's heritage with his hoofing. After *42nd Street*'s publication, the *Brooklyn Citizen* claimed that Ropes traced his ancestry to the same Pilgrim who inspired his stage name: "Bradford Ropes, author of the novel, is a young man who can claim descent from Governor Bradford, of early Massachusetts fame."[11] In 1921, the *Quincy Patriot Ledger* announced that Ropes "traces his ancestry back to the Mayflower on both sides of his parentage."[12]

As a teenager besotted with show business and driven by an increasingly rebellious streak, Ropes struggled to reconcile his blue-blooded ancestry with his show business calling. Both Plymouth and Salem mixed into the crucible of Ropes's upbringing, which straddled different lines of New England Puritan culture. The family of his mother, Alice Gertrude Williams Ropes, moved from Massachusetts to settle in Portland, Maine. The family of his father, Arthur Dudley Ropes, circulated between Salem; Portland; Orange, New Jersey; and Boston, where Arthur's uncle married a woman from one of the city's elite "First Families." When Ropes's parents married in 1903, they established a home not in Boston but in Quincy: a town that, as Ropes suggests with the Crane Sisters in *Mr. Tilley Takes a Walk*, exuded a less immaculate reputation than Proper Boston, despite the stalwart presence of the Wollaston Woman's Club, the Women's Christian Temperance Union, and the DAR.

If Ropes claimed William Bradford as an ancestor, he was indeed descended from Mayflower Pilgrims who occupied important places in the poetic mythology of New England. His paternal grandmother, Lydia Laurelia Bisbee, "was a direct descendant both of Captain Miles Standish and John and Priscilla Alden": the subjects of the love triangle in Henry Wadsworth Longfellow's 1858 narrative poem *The Courtship of Miles Standish*.[13] Longfellow had romanticized the colonial violence of Standish, who led a preemptive ambush at the Wessagusset Colony that killed several Massachusetts Indians near Quincy, on the ancestral land of the Massachusetts and Wampanoag tribes. In the 1933 film version of *Stage Mother*, for which Ropes coadapted the screenplay from his novel, the author alludes to the brutality of his ancestors, as Boston Brahmin Warren Foster fancifully masquerades with beautiful Shirley Lorraine that the two of them are like a modern John and Priscilla Alden. At a riverside glade, Warren calls Shirley a "Puritan maid" as she quotes Longfellow. He assures her that she belongs "Here in the woods, where the Pilgrims walked. Where John Alden courted Priscilla." When Shirley adds that Alden was "keeping a fearful eye out for Indians, I suppose," Warren responds, "Of course. He was always watching for Indians, was John. With a musket on his shoulder." Warren assists her to her feet: "Here, let me help you, Priscilla."[14] On his mother's side of the family, Ropes traced his ancestry to less mythologized Pilgrims; his great-great-great-grandfather was a direct descendant of Richard Warren, the twelfth signer of the Mayflower Compact.[15]

If Pilgrim lore laureled Ropes's upbringing, he was equally aware that both sides of his family held deep roots in Portland, Maine. In 1861, Oliver Wendell Holmes Sr. described Portland as one of the major commercial port towns of New England in the nineteenth century, if unable to match Boston in mercantile scope and activity.[16] In *Mr. Tilley Takes a Walk*, postmaster Silas Thatcher defends his own line of descent to the Irish American Tilley: "Well, I'm just as good a Yankee as any Endicott.... We folks down in Maine aren't impressed by any Bostonian family tree. No, sirree. I'll match the Snows, the Thatchers, and the Halls against all the Cabots and Lowells in their *Blue Book*."[17] Hall was, in fact, the surname of Bradford Ropes's maternal grandmother, Ellen Hall, who hailed from Portland. Both Ropes's great-grandfather Charles F. Williams I and his grandfather Charles F. Williams II (the husband of Ellen) worked as steamboat passenger agents for the Portland Steam Packet Company line between Portland and Boston. In 1898, the younger Williams's failure to send a storm warning to the ship's captain involved him in a famous maritime tragedy: the wreck of the Portland passenger steamboat, which killed all passengers and crew members on board.[18]

If Ropes's mother identified as a Maine woman, his father's family made their fortune in both Portland and Orange, New Jersey, during the nineteenth century. In the 1830s, Portland's bustling industry had attracted Ropes's paternal grandfather, David Nichols Ropes, and his brother George Ropes I, who became known as "the first manufacturers of table cutlery in this country, beginning about the year 1840."[19] Together, the siblings made a fortune as "inventors and patentees of American table knives."[20] While establishing financial success with his cutlery manufacturing, David Nichols Ropes became actively involved in philanthropy and abolitionism. The 1897 book *The Pickering Genealogy* detailed that "during his residence in Portland, ME, his home was known as one of the hiding-places for fugitive slaves, escaping by the so-called 'underground railroad.' He was one of the originators of the Republican party in Orange in 1856, and took a prominent part in the Lincoln campaign." In 1864, Ropes became mayor of Orange, of which he was one of the primary city builders. Although Ropes lost much of his fortune in the Panic of 1873, he was commemorated as a "warm friend of education" and for "his devotion to the interests of the city."[21]

In Orange, David Nichols Ropes made his home with a wife from a prominent Plymouth family. Born in 1826, Lydia Laurelia Bisbee boasted a blue-blooded pedigree not only as the descendant of the Aldens and Miles Standish but also as the daughter of Plymouth minister John Bisbee and his remarkable wife: doctor and suffragette Mercy Ruggles Bisbee (born in 1802). After the passing of her second husband, Captain Daniel Jackson (whom she married after Bisbee's death), Ruggles Bisbee embarked upon a pioneering medical career as one of the first women in the United States to receive a doctor of medicine degree. *The Pickering Genealogy* detailed that Bradford's great-grandmother "entered the New England Female Medical College of Boston, although she was then fifty-two years old, took the two years' course, received her diploma [in 1860], and practiced for twenty-three years as a homeopathic physician," specializing in obstetrics and gynecology.[22]

During this period, the Ropes family intermingled with the Boston Brahmins through the 1877 marriage of George Ropes II and Mary Minot Clark. Born in Salem, the second George Ropes grew prosperous as an ivory merchant and moved to Boston in 1872. Building upon his father's cutlery fortune, he also drew upon the colonialist models bolstering nineteenth-century Boston mercantilism. Ropes "engaged exclusively in trade with Zanzibar, Madagascar and East Africa, on his own account."[23]

With Minot Clark at his side, George Ropes II moved into 6 Louisburg Square, where he raised two daughters, Alice and Charlotte.[24] According to Amory, Louisburg Square represented an exclusive neighborhood even within the elite precinct of Beacon Hill: "If [the Proper Bostonian] lives on Beacon Hill, he will probably have a view of the Commons or perhaps a fenced-in park of his own, such as on fashionable Louisburg Square, where the twenty-two so-called proprietors or homeowners have practically no responsibility at all, own the entire square outright, and meet annually to tax themselves for the upkeep of their park and the care of their street."[25] Representing one of the elite families listed in the pages of Boston's *Blue Book*, Minot Clark supplemented her family fortune with work as a music teacher and was remembered by Ednah C. Silver, in her *Sketches of the New Church in America*, as "a lady of very superior character, and a granddaughter of the good Waltham sea captain Clark."[26]

Through his relatives residing at Louisburg Square, Ropes gleaned insight into the culture of the Boston Brahmins, the Anglo-Saxon social strata that bolstered their "First Family" fortunes on the profits of seafaring "nineteenth-century merchant princes" such as John Lowell Gardner.[27] Percival Lowell called the Brahmins, for all their material prosperity, "the most austere society the world has ever known."[28] In 1861, Oliver Wendell Holmes Sr. coined the original phrase from which "Boston Brahmin" derived in his novel of sin and eugenics, *Elsie Venner: A Romance of Destiny*. Here, Holmes's narrator both delineates and defends a "Brahmin Caste of New England," derived from the ancient and persistent Indian Hindu system of class (or *varna*) as defined by birth, in a rigid hierarchy that placed the Brahmin caste of priests and scholars at the top of the social pyramid:

> There is, however, in New England, an aristocracy, if you choose to call it so, which has a far greater character of permanence. It has grown to be a caste—not in any odious sense—but, by the repetition of the same influences, generation after generation, it has acquired a distinct organization and physiognomy, which not to recognize is mere stupidity, and not to be willing to describe would show a distrust of the good-nature and intelligence of our readers, who like to have us see all we can and tell all we see.[29]

David Strauss catalogs many of the qualities that characterized the Brahmins in his biography of Percival Lowell, who rebelled against Brahmin decorum in his adventurous life as a globe-trotting writer and astronomer. These included traditional "values of hard work, reserve, self-restraint, and understatement"; "utter loyalty to family and ancestors"; a "strong commitment to learning" that also translated into "a strong sense of social and cultural superiority"; and a heavy involvement in family affairs and interest "in a variety of philanthropic enterprises."[30]

In *Mr. Tilley Takes a Walk*, Ropes depicted the early twentieth-century WASP world of the Brahmins as not only the socially stratified domain of the "sifted few" (in the words of Wendell Holmes) but also a culture steeped in racial exclusion.[31] Ropes's depiction echoes Amory's 1947 analysis of the racial prejudice systemically common within Brahmin culture: "Not content with excluding some million Bostonians of Irish background, as well as many hundreds of thousands of Bostonians of Italian, Jewish, Polish and other backgrounds, it also cheerfully excludes another several hundred thousand or so persons whose backgrounds are undeniably as Anglo-Saxon as its First Families' own, and yet because of imperfectly established connections with a First Family, can never hope to become a Proper Bostonian."[32]

In the same novel, Ropes evokes the "never-ending feud between the Boston Irish and the old-line families."[33] Jack Beatty observes, "Surveying the city for *Harper's* in 1928, Elmer Davis found that the 'cardinal fact about Boston' remained the 'racial antithesis' between the Yankee Protestant remnant and the Irish Catholic majority."[34] At the turn of the twentieth century, Anglo-Saxon Yankees held the majority of political power in Boston, even while representing only a quarter of Boston's population. Boston's Irish American population had grown from four thousand in 1840 to more than fifty thousand by 1855, and it only continued to swell into the twentieth century.[35]

The political rise of the Irish American James Michael Curley exemplified these demographic changes. Over the course of Curley's four mayoral administrations between 1914 and 1950, Brahmin political supremacy wavered under the sway of Curley, a fervent but not incorruptible populist, as well as a magnetic political orator. Amory observed in 1947, "The Proper Bostonian maintains, for example, that he has lost all political influence. 'Look at Mayor Curley,' he says. The outsider looks and he sees Mayor Curley, but he also sees former Governor Robert P. Bradford of Mayflower ancestry, two Senators by the names of Leverett Saltonstall and Henry Cabot Lodge, and a battery of Coolidges, Codmans, Curtises, Parkmans, and Wigglesworths, all of whom have been extremely successful in the political line for men who are 'drops' in a bucket.'"[36]

While *Mr. Tilley Takes a Walk* explicitly depicted the Brahmins' efforts to halt the "common foe called Progress" in the preservation of heritage, Ropes drew extensively from the span of his ancestry and upbringing across his novels. The legacy of the Pilgrims suffuses his work, in which Ropes, tracing the image of his ancestors with a skeptical edge, critiqued American Puritanism. Ropes, with Burton, ends *Mr. Tilley*'s narrative on an ironic twist that satirizes the arbitrary nature of the "pure" family ties lionized in the pages of the *Boston Transcript* and the *Blue Book*. After years of social rejection from Cornelia Endicott's Brahmin family, the title character, who believes his County Clare ancestors to have first stepped foot on American soil in the 1870s, receives a (likely erroneous) revelation from Mayflower Society member Fanny Channing. Fanny informs George Tilley that he's the descendant of Mayflower Pilgrims John and Edward Tilley: "Also among the signers . . . was a John Tilley!"[37]

In the earlier backstage trilogy, Ropes meaningfully names characters after famous Pilgrims. Most often, Ropes connects Pilgrim heritage to patriarchal privilege and sexual hypocrisy. He names no fewer than two characters, Brahmin patriarch David Endicott in *Mr. Tilley Takes a Walk* and playboy sugar daddy Richard Endicott in *42nd Street*, after John Endicott (c. 1600-1665). The zealous governor of the Massachusetts Bay Colony, Endicott held rigidly conservative views on gender and sexuality, insisting that women dress modestly and forbidding "any man to wear [his hair] below the ears" in emulation of Pequot Indians.[38] Similarly, in his film adaptation of *Stage Mother* (in which Warren Foster's name evokes that of Ropes's Mayflower ancestor Richard Warren), Ropes critically connects Warren's appreciation of John Alden with his admiration for the Pilgrims' gender conservatism. "Little girls shouldn't have careers," Warren chastises the ambitious Shirley, before alluding to *The Courtship of Miles Standish*: "Listen, darling. John Alden is speaking for himself."[39] Ropes evoked other Pilgrims more positively. In naming *42nd Street*'s flamboyantly gay Jack Winslow after John Winslow (1597-1674), Ropes may have intended to connect Jack's rebellious spirit with one of the worldlier Pilgrims. Winslow, who eschewed religious zeal, "prospered in trade, acquiring part ownership of two ships: the *Speedwell* . . . and the intriguingly named *John's Adventure*."[40]

In numerous ways, Ropes also incorporated the Portland background shared by his parents into his novels. Whereas Ropes used his ancestral Pilgrim history toward cultural critique, he draws upon his family history in Maine more autobiographically. In 1951, Ropes spoke about his grandfather's role in the wreck of the Portland steamer boat and how the catastrophe, which killed some 200 people, inspired narrative events in *Mr. Tilley Takes a Walk*. Reporter Mabelle Fullerton wrote for the *Patriot Ledger*: "It will not surprise you to learn that back in 1898 a Wollaston man was instrumental in sending the steamer Portland to sea where she was lost with all hands, while years later, another Wollaston man, his nephew [sic], discovered the facts."[41] Fullerton noted that Ropes "was doing research for the Boston background of the novel, which deals with a postman on Beacon Hill, when he found the telegram sent by the weather bureau to his uncle, Charles Williams, then passenger agent for the Boston and Maine, who gave orders for the Portland to sail on the cruise from which she never returned."[42] The *New England Quarterly* recounted Williams's role in the events in more detail:

> At 5:30 p.m., General Manager F. Liscomb telephoned from Portland to Mr. C. F. Williams, Boston agent of the line, asking to speak with Captain Blanchard, but the captain could not be found at the time.... Mr. Liscomb instructed Mr. Williams to tell Captain Blanchard that he wanted to hold the Portland at her pier until at least nine o'clock, and if the weather was then threatening, not to start. Mr. Williams replied that he would deliver the message to Captain Blanchard. Whether or not the captain received and understood the order is not known, but it is a fact that he cast off his lines at 7:00 p.m. and steamed down the harbor.[43]

In *Mr. Tilley Takes a Walk*, Ropes inserts a fictionalized version of Charles Williams II into the action of his historical novel. The title character grieves as his father, a postmaster named John Tilley, drowns at sea as a passenger on the steamship *Portland*. In the novel, "Charley Williams" appears as a friend of the tragic John Tilley, who regards Charley as a "grand man." From his post in Boston, Charley books John passage on the steamboat to Portland. Yet, concluding that gale winds will miss the ship, he fails to respond with sufficient caution to the anxieties about weather conditions that are being raised in his office. After the "Portland Gale" sinks the ship, George Tilley (with the help of Charley Williams) attempts in vain to locate the remains of his father, whom he had watched embark upon the Portland with a sense of foreboding. Ropes writes: "All that was mortal of John Tilley had been destroyed; the sea kept forever secret the fate of the blithe, brawny Irishman from County Clare."[44] *Mr. Tilley Takes a Walk* allowed Ropes, in 1951, to empathetically, and from the perspective of the victims, imagine a tragedy that undoubtedly cast a shadow over the lives of his mother's family.

By contrast, Ropes's Maine background animated his portrayal of Peggy

Sawyer in *42nd Street*. In the later adaptations of *42nd Street*, Peggy hails from Sioux City, Iowa (in the 1933 Warner Brothers musical), and from Allentown, Pennsylvania (in the 1980 Broadway musical). Yet, in Ropes's original novel, the character descends upon Times Square from New England rather than the Midwest or the Rust Belt. "The daughter of a minister of Paris, Maine cannot look but different from the hard-boiled sisterhood of Time Square," Ropes observes.[45] Peggy reflects sarcastically upon the cultural pressures she has escaped by pursuing a performing career on Broadway: "I'll probably marry some downright Yankee farmer and retire to give birth to countless boy scouts whose moral fiber will be so tough that there will be little chance for imagination to break through."[46] Family lore about the defiant Mercy Ruggles Bisbee Jackson, in her work as a Boston "woman physician," may also have influenced Ropes in his creation of Peggy as a minister's daughter, who is both at once a stoic and genteel Yankee and a determined, ambitious woman chasing a career. Ropes himself likely shared Peggy's self-identification as a "greenhorn from New England" entering show business.[47]

Finally, Ropes drew upon the Boston Brahmin culture that encircled his family, most specifically in *Stage Mother* and *Mr. Tilley Takes a Walk*. In both novels, Ropes contrasts the stringent anti-theatricalism at the heart of Brahmin society with characters' fervent desire to go upon the stage. In *Stage Mother*, Ropes punctures Brahmin class snobbery while dramatizing the drive of the vaudevillian Kitty Lorraine for social acceptance. Here, the title character encourages her daughter, a rising Broadway star, to seek out the prestige that their profession so often prohibits. Kitty gloats when Shirley attracts a "Stage Door Johnny" from the top of the Brahmin hierarchy: "That new pair of earrings is real swell. . . . And to think a Cabot sent 'em—why I used to hear about the Cabots when I was a young punk. Only in those days, they limited their friends to God an' a coupla angels."[48] Here, Ropes invokes a famous satiric light verse: "And this is good old Boston / The home of the bean and the cod, / Where the Lowells talk to the Cabots / And the Cabots talk only to God."[49]

The stratified world of the Boston Brahmins also vitally informs the show business hierarchies of Ropes's backstage novels of the '30s. In *42nd Street*, Ropes provides detailed analysis of class distinction and status anxiety among stage performers, while portraying the industry itself as a kind of caste system. In the backstage trilogy, theatrical caste mandates distinctions between industrious chorus girls and languorous show girls, between Theatre Guild actors and vaudevillian troupers. In *42nd Street*, Ropes mordantly describes the actor Arthur Lorraine lunching at an Automat while deigning to acknowledge his less successful peers, even as Lorraine himself has fallen on hard times:

> Here (on the second floor of the Automat) the more affluent show folk dine at ease, and the observant person learns the financial status of a friend by watching to see whether he eats on the first or second floor of the automat. . . . Arthur Lorraine caught the boys' stare and returned it with a condescending nod. Caste must be observed, even in the Automat, and he had played leading roles with Robert Mantell in his time. At this moment, indeed, there might be a part for him in the new thing Al Woods was producing.[50]

Ropes's varied ancestry and family background encompassing Pilgrims, Portlanders, and Boston Brahmins provide vital context for entering the world of his backstage novels. At the same time that Ropes critiqued the anti-theatrical prejudice that pervaded all three worlds, he also drew upon his upbringing in the suburb of Quincy: an area of Boston founded by a man of "outlaw sexuality."[51] This carnivalesque figure also shared much of Ropes's Puritan-taunting spirit.

"It Belonged to a Different World": Maypoles in Merrymount

In 1907's *The Education of Henry Adams*, the eponymous historian and scion of the presidential Adams dynasty sardonically remembered Quincy as "the stoniest glacial and tidal drift known in any Puritan land."[52] Adams considered that Quincy "belonged to a different world" from the Boston of the Brahmins, though only a two hours' walk away.[53] To Adams, Quincy represented a less fashionable social address than Beacon Hill and State Street. "Quincy, the Adamses well knew, was on the wrong side of Boston's narrow-gauge social tracks," wrote Amory.[54] Boston's Brahmins, for all their repression and reserve, inhabited a bustling city of commerce, propelled by the Industrial Revolution. Though Quincy prospered upon its shoe manufacturing and granite industries, the town evoked an austere eighteenth-century world to Adams, who became a cosmopolitan of extensive global travels. Adams lamented that Quincy "smacked of colonial age" and that, as a child, he longed instead for Boston's "plush curtains."[55]

In characterizing the Crane Sisters, in *Mr. Tilley Takes a Walk*, as improbable and clandestine Boston madams, Ropes likely knew that his hometown blossomed upon more bacchanalian roots than those imagined by Adams. In Wollaston's earliest colonial history, its citizens whirled around maypoles set down by the town's English founders, Captain Richard Wollaston and Thomas Morton. In 1625, the men gave the new name of Merrymount to the land that the Massachusetts tribe called Passonagessit ("little neck of land"). The atheist Morton, who later taunted Miles Standish and John Endicott as "Captain Shrimp" and "Captain Littleworth," envisioned Merrymount in defiance of the Puritans.[56] As noted in *Improper Boston*, the name of "Mary-mount" or "Mare-mount" played upon "connotations of sodomy, buggery, and possibly, Catholicism." In Merrymount, Morton revived "the 'pagan' practice of maypole dancing in 1637, and set himself up as the 'Lord of Misrule,' a comic Renaissance master of ceremonies."[57]

Morton riled Puritan authorities with his open celebration of "the native peoples of the New World," in whom he found "dignity and worth."[58] Morton also suggested his likely bi- or homosexuality, during a time in which "sodomy, rapes and buggery" were listed among "eight offenses punishable by death" at New Plymouth Colony.[59] In *Of Plymouth Plantation*, William Bradford inveighed against Morton and his anti-Puritan motley, "They also set up a maypole, drinking and dancing about it many days together, inviting the Indian women for their consorts, and frisking together like so many fairies, or furies, rather; and worse practices."[60] In his own colonial diary, *New English Canaan*, known as "America's first banned book," Morton invited further speculation upon his sexuality.[61] He alluded to "'Ganymede and Jupiter,' a Renaissance code phrase for homosexual relations."[62] Arrested by Miles Standish's Plymouth militia, Morton was expelled from Merrymount and extradited to England in 1628. The village was left to be governed by more Proper Bostonians like Edmund Quincy, who changed the town's name to Quincy after purchasing an expanded plot of land in 1636 from the Massachusetts Indians.

Although Ropes settled upon "Billy Bradford" for his stage name, he shared far more in common with the renegade Morton than with the Plymouth Colony governor who derided men frisking together like "fairies." The Pilgrims viewed the stage, too, as what John H. Houchin calls "a chaotic and anarchic site" of religious subversion.[63] They perpetuated a tradition of anti-theatrical prejudice that extended from Plato and early church fathers like Tertullian to the condemnation of unlicensed "rogues and vagabonds" in the English Vagabonds Act of 1572. In 1750, the General Court of Massachusetts passed "An Act to Prevent Stage-Plays and Other Theatrical Entertainments." This ban was only overturned in 1792, with the help of petitioning from John Quincy Adams, among other Revolutionary and Enlightenment voices.[64]

Quincy was certainly not immune from the persistent traditions of anti-theatrical prejudice that rendered "Banned in Boston" a national punchline in the 1920s, despite the city's robust theater culture. Yet, Quincy's cultural history suggests that the town's theatrical traditions developed along different, and somewhat more permissive, lines. The town became noted as the birthplace of not only Ropes but also the flamboyantly gay Broadway and Hollywood character actor and dancer Billy De Wolfe and the actress-writer Ruth Gordon, who became a late-life legend for her film performances in *Rosemary's Baby* and *Harold and Maude*. In 1928, Quincy also made national news as a theatrical shelter for Eugene O'Neill's Pulitzer Prize-winning *Strange Interlude* after the play was banned in Boston, in a censorship case involving one of Ropes's own relatives by marriage. As Ropes grew up in Quincy in the first decades of the twentieth century, he may have perceived the historical shadow of a maypole rising from its town square, alongside the statues of venerated Puritans and Founding Fathers and the respectable clubs run by prominent townswomen. In the latter group, Ropes looked to his formidable mother, Alice.

"With Her Charities and Her Clubs": Mr. and Mrs. Arthur Dudley Ropes

When the MIT-trained civil engineer Arthur Dudley Ropes, from Orange, New Jersey, married the Portland-born Alice Gertrude Williams in Boston on October 7, 1903, the young couple forged a bond upon many commonalities. Both hailed from the stock of New England families that Ropes satirized in *42nd Street* as "good, honest-to-God Yankees."[65] Both Arthur and Alice shared family connections to Portland, Maine, as well as values as cultivated and well-traveled Christians who boasted Mayflower Society-approved pedigrees. Articles in the *Quincy Patriot Ledger* suggest that Ropes, frequently visiting his family from New York and Hollywood, remained close to his immediate family, and particularly Alice, throughout his life. While Ropes rebelled from the upstanding Christian life his parents may have intended for him, they also created space and support for Ropes's all-consuming youthful passion for theater.

As one of the four children of David Nichols Ropes and Lydia Laurelia Bisbee Ropes who lived to an adult age, Arthur Dudley belonged to a family both socially and economically prominent, as well as liberally educated and civic-minded. Bradford Ropes's father was born in Orange, New Jersey, on August 27, 1866, during David Nichols Ropes's second term as the mayor of Orange. As a young man, Arthur Dudley decided to study architecture, joining his brothers Charles Franklin and Albert Barrett as students of engineering and technical science. Whereas Charles attended the Rensselaer Polytechnic Institute and Albert studied at the Stevens Institute of Technology in Hoboken, New Jersey, Arthur Dudley decided to study architecture at MIT. As recounted in *The Pickering Genealogy*: "After graduating from the High School in 1884, Mr. Ropes entered an architect's office in New York. In 1887, he removed to Boston, and took a special course of two years in architecture at the [Massachusetts] Institute of Technology."[66]

In *Mr. Tilley Takes a Walk*, Ropes once again drew from autobiographical contexts to emphasize the importance of MIT to his father, his family, and the cultural life of Boston. In the novel, young Bill Gianelli, the son of Italian immigrants, at first plans to follow his father's dream that his son study at MIT. Instead, Bill scraps his studies of architecture to pursue a life as a Tin Pan Alley songwriter in New York. Bill finds his plan abetted by George Tilley, who helps procure a place for Bill as a boarder with the Channing sisters at Louisburg Square, despite the women's xenophobic leanings. George explains to the sisters:

> "Musician, he is, a fine one, too—and just finished at M.I.T." That was one way of explaining Bill's present position—a shrewd one, too. The Massachusetts Institute of Technology occupied a niche only slightly lower than Harvard's in the hearts of old Bostonians.[67]

Arthur Dudley Ropes's career trajectory suggests professional wanderlust, if also consistent financial stability. From 1890 to 1899, Ropes worked in the engineer corps of the Boston and Maine Railroad. After that, Ropes left the corps for a career in commerce, serving as treasurer for the Boston Envelope Company throughout the 1900s and 1910s. During this time, Arthur Dudley and Alice welcomed the birth of Bradford. The family moved to Wollaston in 1908. By 1920, Arthur Dudley had switched careers once again, now working as a commercial insurance agent. By 1924, Arthur Dudley Ropes had moved into a new profession that embraced aspects of his training as a civil engineer— and might also have influenced the neon energies of his son's backstage novels. Arthur Dudley's obituary in the *Patriot Ledger* noted: "In the early days of electrical signs, he started and for many years operated a Boston firm which produced electric signs with changeable letters."[68] Arthur Dudley Ropes's final professional role was as founding president of the Cameo Art Company in Quincy; he served in this position from 1937 through his death in 1952.

Throughout his life, Arthur Dudley expressed a devotion, passed down from his father, to the Swedenborgian New Church. At the turn of the twentieth century, this mystical strand of Christianity, based on the writings of Emanuel Swedenborg, held small but robust followings centered in Cambridge, Massachusetts, and Philadelphia. By contrast with Evangelical and Baptist strains of Protestantism, the New Church, while steeped in the conviction of Christ's divinity, emphasized a holy trinity of body, mind, and soul—and "right actions" rather than pure faith.[69] The New Church disavowed the literal existence of hell, based on Swedenborg's ideas that "heaven and hell are not rewards or punishments distributed on judgment day but the present inner experience we freely choose."[70] In the mid-nineteenth century, the more tolerant Christian cosmology of the New Church attracted Poe, Emerson, and Whitman, as well as families like that of Ropes.[71] Arthur's *Quincy Patriot Ledger* obituary mentioned that he "served as lay reader for several years at Christ church, Quincy," an Anglican Episcopal denomination.[72] Yet, the New Church held the most potent influence over Ropes's family, and Bradford, too, attended New Church services as late as the 1960s, though he was not particularly devout.[73]

Arthur's religious faith overlapped with literary interests less secular than those of his son. His *Patriot Ledger* obituary, referring to his work for the Masonic youth service organization the International Order of the Rainbow for Girls, eulogized: "Always interested in young people's organizations, Mr. Ropes wrote the national hymns now used by DeMolay and Rainbow girls. He also wrote a book of poems, *Even So Come*, and a seasonal hymn entitled 'Christmas,' both published in 1932."[74]

Born in Portland on August 30, 1870, Alice Gertrude Williams likewise conducted herself as a devoted Christian. At the same time, her range of interests suggests a degree of worldliness beyond stereotypes of the prim Proper Bostonian woman. Fascinatingly, in one 1933 issue of the *Patriot Ledger*, a news article about the motion picture sale of Ropes's novel *Stage Mother* ran adjacent to an interview with Ropes's own mother.[75] Having been elected president of the Massachusetts Woman's Christian Temperance Union (WCTU) in 1922, Alice lamented the "bottled tragedy" of alcohol consumption, illicitly unleashed by the same forces of Prohibition that inspired so much of the dynamism of *42nd Street*.[76] The fact that both Ropes and his mother commanded newspaper coverage on the front page of the *Patriot Ledger* speaks to Alice's formidable, leadership-oriented character.

The 1960 obituary of "Mrs. Arthur Ropes" published in the *Patriot Ledger* details the wide range of the charities and clubs led by Alice. The newspaper eulogized "Mrs. Alice G. (Williams) Ropes . . . [as] an active state prohibition leader throughout the 1920s and 1930s and served 16 years as president of the WCTU. Later, she was the honorary president of the organization. She was also one of the founders and first [state] president of the Wollaston Women's Club. She headed the organization from 1913 to 1915. She was also a regent of the Abigail Phillips Chapter of the DAR, and for many years gave travel lectures at the Boston Public Library."[77]

Alice, who came of age in the reform-driven American Progressive era, shared many values promoted by the national organization of the Woman's Christian Temperance Union. As Ian Tyrell describes the WCTU, which had 766,000 dues-paying international members at its peak in 1927, the organization blended support for women's suffrage with advocacy for temperance reform: "The WTCU linked the religious and the secular through concerted and far-reaching reform strategies based on applied Christianity."[78]

As Allan J. Licthman elaborates, the WCTU was one of several turn-of-the-century organizations that "espoused a liberal maternalism that shared conservative assumptions about sex differences, but sought to raise socially conscious children and apply principles of the household economy to social reform. These liberal maternalists who had led the fight for woman's suffrage were primarily middle- to upper-class white Protestants who embraced anti-pluralist Victorian values."[79] As such, the WCTU shared some commonalities with the Daughters of the American Revolution. In one 1927 interview, Alice blended her temperance activism with her DAR patriotism, asserting: "The WCTU is waging a war against organized liquor traffic and dominant enemy of America, greater than ever was George III of England."[80] Alice considered that the repeal of the Eighteenth Amendment would lead to "more drunkenness, more crime, and more poverty."[81]

Alice likely did not belong to the Lucy Stone League, whose members advocated for women keeping their maiden names after marriage, and throughout her public life attracted newspaper publicity under her married name of "Mrs. Arthur Dudley Ropes." Nevertheless, the strong-willed and ambitious women that Bradford Ropes created in his backstage novels, from Peggy in *42nd Street* to Kitty Lorraine in *Stage Mother* and Nora Wayne in *Go Into Your Dance*, can only have been influenced by his mother's willingness to take up public

WOLLASTON WOMAN IS ELECTED STATE PRESIDENT OF W. C. T. U.

Mrs. Alice G. Ropes, Long Active in the Temperance Movement, Honored at Annual Convention Held at Hyannis

Mrs. Alice G. Ropes of Wollaston, who has been active in W. C. T. U. movements through the State, having served the past year as state vice-president, was elected to the office of president of the Mass. W. C. T. U. yesterday at the annual convention held in Hyannis.

Mrs. Ropes succeeds Mrs. Ella Aldrich Gleason of Winchester, who has been chosen honorary president for life. Miss Laura A. Jones of Wellesley, was elected vice president at large; Mrs. Ada B. Frisbee, of Boston re-elected corresponding secretary; Mrs. Jeanette H. Mann of Brookline, and Mrs. Lillia W. Magwood, assistant recording secretary and recording secretary; Mrs. Helen H. Worrell of Dorchester, treasurer.

"Whither Bound" was the subject of a talk by Mrs. Mary E. Marsh, state superintendent of peace and arbitration of Rhode Island. Mrs. Marsh's talk was inspiring and impressive. Mrs. Deborah Knox Livingston, national lecturer, also addressed the convention, talking on "South Africa and Its Social Problems."

The convention closed last evening with a "good citizenship" banquet, at which Mrs. Gleason was toastmistress. The speakers of the evening were ex-Rep. Thomas C. Thacher of Yarmouth, Rep. Edward C. Hinckley of Hyannis, Principal William A. Baldwin of the State normal school at Hyannis, James H. Kimball of Hingham, Selectman Harry B. Albro of Falmouth, W. P. Kelley of South Boston, Mrs. Alice G. Ropes of Wollaston, Mrs. Deborah Knox Livingston, and Mrs. Everett A. Bond, president of the Hyannis Woman's club.

The 1922 convention was the largest ever held by the Union, with over 550 delegates present. Convention meetings were held in the Federated church at Hyannis.

After the election of officers yesterday Mrs. Ella Gleason was presented with a brooch, in the style of the white ribbon bow which represents the temperance workers. The brooch was made of seed pearls, with an amethist in the center. Mrs. Gleason has served as president of the State Union for a number of years, and her retirement from the office was accompanied by much solemnity.

On Tuesday evening three of the delegates from Wollaston presented a playlet, "My Place, Your Place, Any Place" written by Amanda Landes especially for W. C. T. U. presentation. The part of Mrs. Elizabeth Morton, temperance leader, and true blue

MRS. ALICE G. ROPES,
State President of the W. C. T. U.

American, was taken by Mrs. William H. Warren. Mrs. Cad Wallader Rittenhouse-Jones, a leader of fashion, was impersonated by Mrs. Alice Gertrude Ropes. Mrs. Amy Phipps played the part of Mrs. Cooney, a Dutch immigrant, and the part of officer of a federal enforcement squad was taken by Mr. Kelley, of Yarmouthport, husband of the W. C. T. U. president in that town.

Wednesday evening was featured by a pageant in which the principal characters were Alcohol, Pleasure, Vanity, Wealth, and Christianity. The pageant was presented in the Baptist church.

On the whole the delegates from Wollaston and Quincy feel that the days spent at the convention were well worth while, and they have returned home with renewed spirit to carry on the work.

The Quincy delegates were Mrs. Clarence Sanborn, president of the Quincy W. C. T. U. and Mrs. Otho Hayward. Wollaston was represented by Mrs. William H. Warren, president Mrs. Jessie F. Dodge, Mrs. Paul Eldridge, Mrs. Amy Phipps and Mrs. Nettie Shay.

space and, standing at a podium, to raise her voice for the issues in which she believed. In this sense, Alice might also be considered something of a stage mother, if substantively different from the vaudevillian Kitty.

In many ways, Alice conformed to the archetype of the industrious and abstinent Proper Bostonian woman chronicled by Cleveland Amory. Amory satirically characterized the type: "Psychologists have long been interested in this problem of the phenomenal activity of the Boston Amazon. . . . Many have come to the conclusion that energy, pent up by the Puritan inhibitions of Boston life, will, like truth, out in the end."[82] In *Mr. Tilley Takes a Walk*, Ropes cheekily evoked the type, as well. "She's been working so strenuously with her charities and her clubs," remarks the rebellious young debutante Sarah Elizabeth Endicott of her mother, Cornelia.[83]

In his book, Cleveland Amory discussed the Proper Bostonian woman's "zeal for reform," expressing itself in a passion for cultural uplift, attendance at symphony, philanthropy, and, particularly, lectures.[84] Somewhat derisively, Amory called the Boston woman the "locomotive" of the Lyceum, the civil association with which Boston's culture of popular education was most strongly associated.[85] Amory observed that since the entrance of "the Boston woman of the nineteenth century" into the Lyceum, "she has made the city a recognized Garden of Eden on the American lectures circuit, and the intense seriousness with which she attends any and all offerings has become proverbial."[86] As Mrs. Arthur Dudley Ropes, Alice regularly delivered educational lectures in the World War I era and into the 1920s. She dedicated her services to the Boston Public Library's Ruskin Club: a popular education society named after the British art historian and aesthete John Ruskin.

The subjects of Alice's Ruskin Club lectures suggest Bradford's mother less as a zealous reformer than a well-traveled Christian woman with a robust interest in art and culture. Records of the Boston Public Library list Mrs. Arthur Dudley Ropes, from 1916 to 1927, presenting a series of lantern-illustrated travel lectures. A March 1920 issue of the *Newton Graphic* reported: "Mrs. Arthur Dudley Ropes, a former President of the Wollaston Woman's Club, gave an illustrated lecture on her delightful trip through Scotland. She started from Edinburgh, the capitol [sic], and then through the picturesque scenery of the Scottish Lakes to Glasgow, and finally to the haunts and homes of two great poets, Robert Burns and Sir Walter Scott."[87] While Alice repeated this lecture in 1923, as "Bonnie Scotland, the Land of the Broom and Heather," she also presented other Ruskin Club lectures: "Yellowstone Park and Yosemite Valley" (1916), "Rome and Northern Italy" (1917), "The Beauties of Switzerland" (1922), "The Wonderland of America" (1922), and "From London to Land's End" (1927).[88]

In *Mr. Tilley Takes a Walk*, Ropes paid fond but satiric tribute to the cultural edification of the Ruskin Club and Alice's love of travel lectures. As the book skips generations, from the 1900s to the 1920s, both mother and daughter Endicotts—Cornelia and Sarah Elizabeth—successively use the Boston Public Library and Ruskin Club lectures as a decoy to conduct socially taboo romances with, respectively, George Tilley and the Italian American, MIT-deserting songwriter Bill Gianelli. At the library, George uses his experience to help Bill clandestinely meet Sarah Elizabeth near Edwin Austin Abbey's murals of the Holy Grail: "The murals are in the delivery room at the Library. . . . Only a matter of a few yards from the hall where the Ruskin Club meets." In another scene, Bill refers to Sarah Elizabeth "trotting off with some old-maid cousin to lectures at the Ruskin Club."[89]

Yet, for all of Alice Williams's cultivated polish, she also belonged to the zealously patriotic and anti-pluralist WASP culture of the Daughters of the American Revolution. In a later chapter of *Mr. Tilley Takes a Walk*, the title character realizes that young Sarah Elizabeth is picking up the prejudices of her Boston Brahmin family; he adapts the pen-pal alter ego of "Billy Beau," sending her light verses to instill tolerance and egalitarianism. One of these reads: *"Helga Svenson's talk is strange because she comes from Sweden / But so was the talk of Adam and Eve who lived in the Garden of Eden / And the Viking, Leif, from Helga's Land, discovered the U.S.A. / Before the folks of the D.A.R. thought of steering their boats this way."*[90] While pointing to the DAR's racially exclusive definition of Anglo-Saxon heritage, Ropes also alludes to his mother's DAR leadership in *Mr. Tilley*, through the Brahmin character of Abby Frothingham: She "rapped sharply with her gavel, the one presented to her by the Daughters of the American Revolution when she retired as State Regent."[91]

In his critique of DAR values in *Mr. Tilley*, through his portrayal of the forbidden romance between Sarah Elizabeth Endicott and Bill Gianelli, Ropes appears to have drawn upon another autobiographical context. This was the transgressive multicultural marriage between his cousin Sarah Elizabeth Pottinger, a San Francisco socialite and grandniece of Arthur Dudley Ropes, to the Ecuadorian American Emile Bigue.[92] The two wed in a closed ceremony in 1933, following the cancellation of a planned "large formal wedding."[93] The addition of Bigue to Ropes's extended family may have later influenced the writer's positive, sometimes stereotype-subverting depiction of Latin Americans in his films, including 1941's *Angels with Broken Wings*.

Proud of her American colonial heritage, Alice pledged lifelong dedication to the DAR. A 1922 edition of the *Daughters of the American Revolution Magazine* chronicles the work of Mrs. Arthur D. Ropes as state regent of the "Abigail Phillips Quincy Chapter of Wollaston, Daughters of the American Revolution." On April 28, 1922, Alice presided over a ceremonial "marking of the grave of Abigail Phillips Quincy, in the old Hancock Cemetery of Quincy, Mass" and spoke about one of the prominent, Revolutionary-era female members of her town's storied Adams and Quincy dynasties. The magazine reported:

> She gave a historical sketch of the life of Abigail Phillips Quincy (for whom our chapter is named) and spoke of the service her husband Josiah Quincy Jr. gave to the colonies. Mr. Quincy died on his way home from England, where he had gone on diplomatic business for the colonies, in April, 1775, within sight of the land he loved so well.[94]

The same article describes the flag-waving role of Alice's seven-year-old son at the ceremony: "Bradford Ropes, president of the Hannah Watts Weston Society, Children of the American Revolution of Wollaston, which has the largest charter membership in the state of Massachusetts, assisted in the unveiling."[95] Similarly, in a 1953 lecture for the women's union of a Congregational church, "Mr. Ropes, relat[ed] his life story, start[ing] with his public appearance before an audience at the age of six when he appeared at a meeting of the Wollaston Women's club of which his mother was the president. He told how his father wrote a poem, 'When Mother Joined the Club,' in connection with his mother's presidency, and he read the original poem."[96] Growing up as the son of the genteel Christian yet headstrong Mrs. Arthur Dudley Ropes, Bradford embraced an element of duality that would continue to define his career in show business.

"His Youthful Flair for Drama": The Childhood and Adolescence of Bradford Ropes

Born in Boston on January 1, 1905, as the only child of Arthur Dudley and Alice Williams Ropes, Bradford Ropes spent the majority of his childhood in Wollaston. Here, Ropes spent an upper-middle-class upbringing in an unadorned but spacious saltbox-style house at 15 Wollaston Avenue. The household included his father, mother, and a Swedish maid named Elsie (only identified by her first name on a 1910 Boston census).[97] Over the course of his youthful development as a performer and writer, Ropes grew from an upstanding young man who praised his Pilgrim ancestors and Jesus Christ to a stagestruck rebel whose work was banned by school authorities.

Ropes's early upbringing reflected his parents' convictions in the Christian values of the New Church, as well as his father's amateur interest in writing hymns and religious poetry. A 1946 profile for Ropes's Quincy High School literary magazine, the *Golden Rod*, recounted, "For the Q.H. *Golden Rod* he wrote 'Christmas in the Trenches,' of which his mother and dad are especially fond."[98] The patriotic poem, written in 1917 (the year of the United States' entrance into World War I), made a plea for Christian peace and goodwill. Ropes wrote the five-stanza poem at the age of twelve. Its last two stanzas concluded:

. . . . The flickering light of the camp-fire is dying.
The moon rises over some new-made grave:
Far away from all hate and war's brutal crying
Is the figure of Christ, come to save.

Then hail the great day of hearts all rejoicing.
When man banishes hate and ill-will.
While the figure of Christ, a figure eternal,
Sways a scarred world with His radiance, still.[99]

Three years later, Ropes may also have sought to please his parents in the bombastically patriotic tone of his 1920 essay submitted to the high school writing contest, "The Influence of the Pilgrims on the Twentieth Century, offered by the Educational committees of the Quincy Women's Clubs." Ropes's own submission won honorable mention. Ropes began his essay: "In November, 1620, a fearless band of men and women, after braving the perils of a storm-tossed sea, founded a new Plymouth on the shores of America." Later, Ropes lampooned the image of his ancestors. Here, he extolled them, arguing that "justice, the paramount virtue of this country today, began in the ideals and deeds of such upright men as William Bradford and Captain Miles Standish." At the same time, Ropes expressed the anti-Irish xenophobia that circulated within WASP culture and organizations like the DAR in turn-of-the-century Boston. Noting the "undying love between America and England" symbolized by the Pilgrims, the fifteen-year-old essayist wrote of the "Pilgrim fathers": "Are we to forget their unswerving loyalty and love and turn against our sister nation merely because a certain band known as the Sinn Feiners, who are not Americans at heart, choose to have us?"[100]

At the same time that Bradford Ropes pleased his parents with his literary talents, Christian faith, and "true Americanism," he also became increasingly stagestruck.[101] Despite the pervasive New England anti-theatrical prejudice seeded by the Pilgrims, neither of Ropes's well-traveled and literary-minded Christian parents discouraged him from pursuing his passion. "Unlike most stage-bent youths, Bradford did not have to overcome parental opposition," the *Buffalo Evening News* informed readers in 1933.[102] On at least one occasion, Arthur and Alice took young Bradford to see shows in Boston. In 1953, Ropes recounted how *The Gingerbread Man*, a musical "Fairy Extravaganza" at the Copley Theatre featuring Alfred Lunt as "The Fiery Dragon," opened his eyes to "the magic world of the theatre" when he was five or six.[103] Ropes may also have appeased any potential parental opposition by appearing in church plays.[104]

Additionally, Ropes's male gender likely eased parental support of his theatrical dreams, given the close association of actress with prostitute in the American Puritan mind. Ruth Gordon, who graduated Quincy High School seven years before Ropes, detailed contrasting experiences. The daughter of a sea captain, Gordon remembered her Aunt Ida saying that "she might as well become a harlot" as an actress.[105] In her 1947 memory play *Years Ago*, set in 1913 and filmed in 1953 with Jean Simmons as *The Actress*, Gordon recounted how she (in the guise of the protagonist, "Me") gradually wore down parental resistance to her stage ambitions. Her father in the play, a retired sea captain, gives Ruth his eventual blessing due to his own salad days as a stagehand for Lotta Crabtree and Edwin Booth. Ruth faces sterner opposition from her mother, from whom she conceals her copies of the *Theatre Magazine* within the respectable pages of a *Saturday Evening Post*. Her mother demands that Ruth dress more modestly than the actresses she strives to emulate. Hearing from her daughter that "slit skirts are all the rage!," Ruth's mother fires back:

> Well, let them be! But I'm certainly not going to have you walkin' round Wollaston in a skirt slit halfway up past all decency. . . . You can't go round dressed like Gaby Deslys. This is Wollaston, Massachusetts, please remember, not Gay Paree![106]

In his own novels, Ropes vividly captures cultural attitudes toward the stage that surrounded him growing up in Wollaston and visiting his aunts at Louisburg Square. Ropes illustrates the loosening, yet persistent, rigidity of anti-theatrical prejudice in *Mr. Tilley Takes a Walk*. In the novel, Brahmin patriarch David Endicott attempts to dissuade Katie Brannigan, a spirited Irish American girl who works as the family's maid, from going onstage. David grudgingly acknowledges his respect for Boston stage institutions like the Castle Square and Hollis Street Theaters, as well as for Boston's most aristocratic actors. Ropes writes:

> But Mr. Endicott's Puritan conscience demanded that he justify his decision, and so he embellished on his theme. "Indeed, I cherish an even warmer regard for the theatre than many of my acquaintances because that celebrated actress, Miss Charlotte Cushman, was distantly related to me on the maternal side of the family—the Saunders side. *But* . . ."[107]

Here, Ropes evokes his own formative passion for Shakespeare in alluding to the Boston-born actress Cushman: also descended from Mayflower Pilgrims and famous for her performances as Romeo, Hamlet, and Lady Macbeth. During Ropes's childhood the Bard contested with the Bible in his affections— and soon prevailed upon his imagination. In a 1933 interview with the *Golden Rod*, William Coates reported: "Mr. Ropes told me he has always been interested in acting and writing. When he was only eight, he started to rewrite Shakespeare in his own words!"[108] An even more hyperbolic 1933 *Patriot Ledger* profile also claimed Ropes as a theatrical wunderkind. John Clair Minot noted: "One of his former schoolmates . . . tells us how precocious and intense he was in his early interest in the drama and in the stage generally. Before he was 7 years old he had read all the plays of Shakespeare. . . . He had all the temperament that traditionally accompanies genius and if his audience was not duly appreciative of his rendition of Hamlet, for example, he did not hesitate to hurl a brick at it, or any other handy missile."[109]

Ropes, who later filled his movie screenplays with images of preternaturally advanced children, satirized his own youthful intellect and arrogance in his 1941 Hollywood satire, *Glamour Boy*. Here, radio whiz kid-turned-child movie star Billy Doran (played by Darryl Hickman) exasperates the adults around him with his quotations of Dickens and Einstein. When addressed as "little boy" and asked for an autograph at a diner, Billy replies, "I deplore the custom, madam, but I'd be happy to accommodate you."[110]

Beyond his prodigy adaptations of Shakespeare, Ropes also "began writing plays while in grammar school" and staged shows in a barn outside his home.[111]

Less evocative of *42nd Street* than *Babes in Arms*, the latter plays reflected the "Hey kids, let's put on a show" trope that Judy Garland and Mickey Rooney mythologized in their Hollywood musicals of the late 1930s. One 1932 interview recounted of Ropes, "His youthful flair for drama is recalled by many former associates who saw the spirited productions written and directed by him in the old barn near his home on Wollaston Avenue."[112] The *Buffalo Evening News* gave a detailed account of Ropes, as he "Started His Career in Barn." The paper noted not only young Ropes's versatility but also his interest in motifs that later found expression in Ropes's screenplays at Republic Studios, where he wrote a dozen musical Westerns for Gene Autry and Roy Rogers:

> After school hours, on Saturdays and during vacations, the children used to gather at the Ropes home. The attraction was a large barn. One day Bradford proposed erecting a stage out of old boxes and planks. Bradford was the stage manager, the script writer, the prompter, and the leading man. . . . The first few plays deal with cowboys, Indians and bandits. The girls were allowed to participate—as an audience.[113]

Ropes's theatrical barn endeavors carried over into another field, as well. When he started in vaudeville in 1923, Ropes established himself as a gifted, acrobatic dancer praised for his high kicks. Ropes started to learn the foundations of his dance technique in Quincy. Around the same time that he wrote and directed his barn plays, Ropes "received his first dance instruction at a class conducted in a building" on which Quincy's (now demolished) Strand movie theater was built.[114] Though Ropes would later write critically of the mechanized precision dancing of the troupe founded by John Tiller, his instructor was a former Tiller Girl, "one of the first dancing teachers in Quincy."[115] Ropes also brought new skills of choreography into his activities as a playwright and director.

Ropes's *The Dream Child*, written at the age of twelve and presented for his June 1917 graduation exercises at the Wollaston School, invoked the widely developing range of his interests and talents: Shakespeare, playwriting, and dance and choreography. Ropes conceived *The Dream Child* in the style of two earlier fantasy pageants he appeared in at, respectively, the Quincy Music Hall and the Wollaston School, where he attended middle school. Both *The Wishing Ring* (April 1917), in which Ropes played a "King's Imp," and *The Moon Sprites* (June 1917), in which Ropes appeared as an "Artist," drew heavily upon early twentieth-century traditions of fantasy play and pantomime extravaganza, epitomized by the long-running stage adaptations of *Peter Pan* and *The Wizard of Oz*, as well as Ropes's beloved *The Gingerbread Man*.[116]

The Quincy Music Hall and the Wollaston School mounted *The Wishing Ring* and *The Moon Sprites*, respectively, on a grand scale that suggests early twentieth-century Quincy's substantial investment in theater as a tool for education. *The Wishing Ring*, following the adventures of young Jean and Allan in "Story-Book-Land," featured "hundreds of young people." As the children encounter Simple Simon, Old King Cole, and Little Bo Peep, they also witness marvels ranging from a floral "snowdrops chorus in which one hundred little girls of six and seven take part" to the "appearance of Mrs. Pumpkin Eater (Edith Axberg) and her company of suffragettes."[117]

With the two-act *The Dream Child*, in which he also played "King of Fairies," Ropes expanded his performance experiences in *The Wishing Ring* and *The Moon Sprite* into his own musical extravaganza. *The Dream Child* channeled Ropes's love of *A Midsummer Night's Dream*, while also interpolating characters from Lewis Carroll. Ropes's dance coaching led the *Patriot Ledger*, in its profile of the play, to observe that "the graceful dancing of many of the characters deserves special mention."[118] Previously consigning girls to the audience of his barn theater, Ropes now featured them prominently in the cast, including Marion Hicks in the title role. His classmates pranced across multiple dimensions of children's literature, "admirably costumed" as such characters as Fairy of Love, Court Jester, the King of Gnomes, and Alice in Wonderland, as well as an ensemble of "Dream fairies, China dolls, Gnomes and attendants."[119]

The *Quincy Patriot Ledger* devoted ample space to detailing *The Dream Child*:

> The entire play, including the words of the many songs, the arrangements of the dances, and the working out of the pretty fairy tale which it told were entirely original and certainly reflect credit on the twelve-year old author. . . . The action of the play takes place principally at the court of the King and Queen of Fairyland in which the "Dream Child" suddenly finds herself transported, much to the delight of the King and Queen as well as of the Dream Child herself.

Amid the nationalism of the World War I era (also conjured by Ropes in the same year's poem "Christmas in the Trenches"), Ropes treated his classmates to a musical fairy play that climaxed with a magical, patriotic rescue. Placing the Dream Child at the court of the King and Queen of Fairy-Land, Ropes chronicled her "introduction to the notable inhabitants of that realm, her capture by the Gnomes, and her final rescue by 'Liberty,' in the name of the United

States of America, delight[ing] the audience who rose in a body and joined in the 'Star Spangled Banner,' which celebrated the Dream Child's return to her own country."[120] With *The Dream Child*, Ropes pleased his parents and community and demonstrated his skill with fantastical stagecraft—even as he sharpened his writing skills more trenchantly in other arenas.

"A Full-Fledged Poet": Bradford Ropes's High School Stages and Stories

As a student at Quincy High School from 1917 to 1921, Ropes continued to develop his dual passions for the stage and for dance. As a teenager, Ropes became increasingly proficient and versatile in movement. He continued his training in ballroom dancing, which became a mainstay of his vaudeville and cabaret performance career in the 1920s. The *Golden Rod* profiled Ropes in 1946, when he returned to visit his alma mater: "When in high school, Dick Hussy formed a group for ballroom dancing about which Mr. Ropes says, 'It seems like a long, long time ago, but I had a lot of fun.'"[121]

Ropes also continued to stage plays on a local, amateur level. The Deacon's Alhambra Theatre in Quincy produced the sixteen-year-old's *The Sultan of Turkey* in 1921. Drawing from the Orientalist images and narratives that pervaded early twentieth-century culture, from *Salome* to the Ballets Russes, *The Sultan of Turkey* continued the fanciful tone of *The Dream Child* but merged it with exoticism and an abundance of choreography. In the June 1921 issue of the *Golden Rod*, Ruth Kaulbeck, a classmate of Ropes, confided to her peers:

> So I went down to Deacon's Alhambra. . . . The Grand Finale was a play enti-
> tled *The Sultan of Turkey*, which was written by Brad Ropes, who is now a full-
> fledged poet. The part of the Sultan was taken by John Lane; and in his harem
> were such fair damsels as. . . . These . . . vied with one another to see who
> would be the Sultana. . . . But now entered the dark horse in the guise of John
> Laverty, the ballet dancer to the queen. He placed the Sultan in another world
> by stabbing him between the third and fourth acts; and then married the queen
> himself, and then lived scrappily ever after.[122]

The archives of the *Golden Rod* both record Ropes's adolescent writing and suggest his life at Quincy High School. Ropes's high school literary magazine leaves a complex image of Ropes between the ages of fourteen and seventeen.

He was, at once, a popular classmate, a precocious student with a saucy wit, and an introspective writer drawn to themes of melancholy and the macabre. According to one "Class History" column published in the June 1921 issue of the *Golden Rod*, a classmate (in conversational dialogue) remembers Ropes's relationship with Miss O'Neil, the school Latin teacher: "Why don't you remember the teacher in room 24 that used to give us those long Latin lessons, and with whom Bradford Ropes tried to compete (unsuccessfully) in carrying on Latin conversations? . . . As soon as you mention Ropes, I recall those funny incidents; he certainly was a clever fellow."[123] Ropes quipped epigrammatically for the "Peeks, but Not Piques" humor column of the same issue: "Ask for my pen; it governs me—I govern not it."[124]

Yet, for all of the wit he displayed to his friends, Ropes's *Golden Rod* poems and short stories conveyed a deeply reflective side, suggesting that Ropes grappled with issues of socioeconomic status. He progressed into adolescence at the start of the 1920s, when the post-World War I United States entered an era of frenzied consumerism and capitalist conservatism. In 1923, Calvin Coolidge, the former Massachusetts governor, ascended to the American presidency, boosted to national prominence for his suppression of unions during the brutal Boston Police Strike of 1919. Coolidge famously proclaimed in 1925, "The business of America is business." Although not overtly political, Ropes's *Golden Rod* writings suggest that, as a teenager, he began to question this cultural ethos. Nor would his critical attitudes fade; they transformed into Ropes's critiques of the excesses of American capitalism, as applied to the industrial contexts of Broadway show business in his backstage trilogy.

Throughout the 1920s, too, Ropes's extended family moved into closer proximity to Boston's centers of power. George Ropes II, having established a fortune in the African ivory trade, had previously married into Brahmin aristocracy in the 1880s through his union with Mary Minot Clark. If Ropes, the grandson of a New Jersey mayor and city builder, grappled with themes of money, status, and temptation in his stories and poems, this also may have been influenced by the teenager's navigation of new family dynamics. In 1915, his mother's family entered the upper echelons of Boston society, through the marriage of Bradford's cousin Edith to the lawyer and politician Malcolm E. Nichols.

An intelligent and ambitious Republican, Nichols rose rapidly in the world of Massachusetts politics. Nichols shared a similar Yankee Puritan background to David Nichols Ropes, including connections to the New Church. Like the family of Alice Williams, Nichols was born in Portland, Maine. The 1937

Who's Who in Law entry of Nichols described a trajectory from his Portland upbringing to his education at Harvard, membership in the Boston Common Council (1905-6), and career as a lawyer. Nichols then moved on to seats in the Massachusetts House of Representatives (1907-9); in the Massachusetts Senate (1914, 1917-19); and into the position of U.S. Collector of Internal Revenue (1921-25).[125] His final major role, from 1926 to 1930, was as the mayor of Boston, where he succeeded the frequently reelected Irish American populist Democrat James Michael Curley.

Born on August 8, 1892, to Fred Melvin Williams (Alice's older brother) and his wife, Ella MacDonald, Edith Marion Williams was one of the beautiful twin sisters who successively married Nichols (who wedded Edith's sister Carrie a year and a half after the former's death in childbirth). Attended by dozens of guests, including the Ropes family and ten-year-old Bradford, the opulent Nichols-Williams society wedding took place on December 16, 1915, at the Roxbury Church of New Jerusalem. The ceremony made a splashy appearance in newspapers, including the *Boston Globe*. While the *Globe* described the bride as splendidly "attired in white satin duchesse de soie," the reporter also took note of Mrs. Arthur D. Ropes wearing "nile green silk, with rose point lace."[126]

Within these larger cultural and familial contexts, Ropes's adolescent writings suggest the young man's questioning about the values of money and materialism. In *The Proper Bostonians*, Amory discusses these enduring tensions at the heart of Boston Puritan culture as the "Great Conflict."[127] As Amory describes Boston society in the mid-1800s, "The most popular lecture of the period was one entitled 'Acres of Diamonds.' In this the lecturer, Reverend Russell H. Conwell, expressed the hard-fisted philosophy of the real Yankee: 'Money is power. Every good man and woman ought to strive for power. Tens of thousands of men and women get rich honestly. But they are often accused by an envious lazy crowd of unsuccessful persons of being dishonest and oppressive. I say, Get rich! Get rich!'"[128] Yet the First Family founder and merchant-prince William Appleton detailed in his diary how the prosperity gospel also jousted with spiritual contrition, leaving "evidence of the characteristic Proper Bostonian struggle . . . between his worldly desires and his religious convictions."[129]

The tensions of the "Great Conflict," as Amory describes it, may have informed Ropes's December 1919 short story, "The Trembling Hour," as well as his June 1921 poem, "The Man Who Lost His Soul," both published in the *Golden Rod*. In "The Trembling Hour," the fourteen-year-old author blends a supernatural mystery story with a moral parable about the dangers of avarice, while demonstrating his ability to spin a tautly crafted narrative. The story's macabre sensibility and elements of gothic atmosphere also resurfaced among the vaudeville and Broadway backdrops of Ropes's backstage novels. The name "Dexter," too, given to the story's scheming protagonist, reappears in *Stage Mother* with the corrupt mayor Al P. Dexter, based upon James J. Walker.

With its shades of supernatural horror and mystery, purple-tinged prose, and ironic (if predictable) narrative reveal, "The Trembling Hour" also suggests that the adolescent Ropes may have read a fair amount of Poe, as well as Shakespeare. The story begins with the revelation of a murder. The story follows a young man named Harvy Dexter as he visits the mansion of his Aunt Kate, only to be informed by the housemaid, Lisbeth, that her murdered body had been found at midnight. Lisbeth informs Harvy: "She was stabbed in the back and when I found her, she was lying in a pool of blood with her face all twisted with fear and signs of a struggle." Here, Ropes indicates that something might be amiss with the nephew's visit: "But there was no struggle," Harvy cries.[130]

As the story progresses, Ropes intensifies the psychological horror. Harvy experiences a sense of psychic foreboding, conflicting with the anticipation of inheriting Aunt Kate's fortune. Although tormented by the feeling that someone is following him, Harvy giddily reflects "that the house was now his, and he would be rich." Yet, as the perception of "soft footsteps" intensifies in his mind, Harvy perceives "an almost invisible presence which seemed to be in his aunt's rocking chair."[131] Ropes writes, with Poe-like flourishes: "He remained cold, rigid, tense with this hideous presence of a Third."[132]

Mirrors, an essential device used by Decadent Symbolist writers to probe the depths of the subconscious, play a key role in "The Trembling Hour." Passing a mirror, the guilt-stricken Harvy cannot look away: "His own figure confronted him, almost unrecognizable. His eyes were wild and bloodshot, his hair clung damply to his forehead, his face was ghastly with the ghastliness of a man who has looked on worse than death."[133] The image of Harvy gradually transforms into that of Aunt Kate, as the clock strikes midnight:

She was standing just behind him, the slim old figure with the white hair and the gray silk dress. . . . And the eyes! The reproach in the faded old eyes! He had never thought of this, anything but this. He was a weakling, even in crime. He had detested the blood, he always detested pain. He had been thankful that she died quickly. But she had come back. She would not stay quiet in the death he had dealt her. The eyes, the eyes—blind fury assailed him. He would shut those fearful eyes forever this time, he would not be haunted. . . . The Thing must go for all time—those eyes![134]

The tormented Harvy hurls a decanter at the mirror, "crumpling into an inert heap among the piles of splintered grass."[135]

Ropes ends the story with a crafty reveal as well as a moral lesson: Aunt Kate survived Harvy's attempted murder but has staged a supernatural drama to reveal her nephew's guilt. Both a detective and a doctor converge upon Harvy, who returns to consciousness in front of the mirror. The detective exclaims to Aunt Kate, "Sneaked in here and tried to kill you to prevent you from making a new will which left him nothing and then didn't even have the nerve to find out whether you were dead or not."[136] When the detective prepares to convey Harvy to the police station, the doctor stops him: "He has left your province and entered into mine." The story ends with the doctor pointing to "the crouching figure on the floor," as the detective and Aunt Kate look on. "Harvy was playing with the shining bits of broken glass and chuckling insanely to himself, 'I've got rid of her. I've got rid of the Third in the House."[137]

Two years later, at the age of sixteen, in his narrative poem "The Man Who Lost His Soul," Ropes reprised his critical stance toward avarice, as well as the heightened gothic tone of "The Trembling Hour." Once again, Ropes gravitated toward themes of not only the temptations of greed but also identity, deception, and unmasking. In biblically moralistic tones, Ropes warned in the poem:

He stands, wrapped in the mantle of despair,
Upon his face a grotesque mask of hate;
The symbol of a man who tried to dare
To be the master of his own great fate.

But lo! off from that face there falls the mask,
Recoil in horror from the sight you see!
What phantom is that deathly skull you ask.
Friend, would you learn his bitter history?

There is a man whose only god was Greed,
A man enchained in making wealth his gold;
The anguish that he caused he did not heed,
And he has paid the price, a bartered soul.

Derisive fingers point at him with scorn,
Men mock the tortured anguish in his eyes;
There stands a man of every honor shorn,
A man whose highest goal brought but this prize.

Be warned, O friends that are of little faith,
Lest, as the seasons ever onward roll,
You in your greed become just such a wraith
As that felon, the man who lost his soul.[138]

Though ostensibly about the perils of material wealth, the poem might also be interpreted to allude to themes of sexual identity. When Ropes was coming of age in early twentieth-century Wollaston, the status of male and female homosexuality had shifted from a socially tolerated yet uncategorized under-cover practice to a pathologized disorder, as labeled by sexologists like Richard von Krafft-Ebing. In the nineteenth-century city that accommodated the conventions of the "Boston marriage" and the college-bound "Wellesley marriage," Charlotte Cushman had lived semi-openly with her partner, sculptor Emma Stebbins, and publisher F. Holland Day had printed the first American editions of the Decadent *Yellow Book* and Oscar Wilde's *Salome*.[139]

Yet, by the first decade of the twentieth century, homosexuality was increasingly criminalized, both institutionally and in psychoanalytic rhetoric. In an essay published in the *Boston Medical and Surgical Journal* in 1898, a Haverhill, Massachusetts, doctor "recommended that 'inverts,' in whom homosexuality was innate, should be sent to mental hospitals, while 'perverts,' who had acquired those tendencies, should be imprisoned."[140] In 1914, German gay rights activist Magnus Hirschfeld reprinted a letter "from an anonymous Bostonian," who observed, "In the face of Anglo-American hypocrisy, however, there is at present no chance that any man of science would have enough wisdom and courage to remove the veil which covers homosexuality in this country. And how many homosexuals I've come to know! Boston, this good old Puritan city, has them by the hundreds."[141] In writing "The Man Who Lost His Soul" within this oppressive context, and in using masks as a central image of his poem, Ropes invites its legibility as a queer text. When Ropes evokes the title character's "grotesque mask of hate," the young poet echoes Percival Lowell's condemnation of Boston Brahmin hypocrisy: "So people wore masks shocked by the sin in sincerity." When Wilde, in 1891's *Intentions*, praised the "truth of masks," he used the image to evoke the liberations of artifice, as well as the necessity of disguising male homosexuality.[142] By contrast, the "grotesque" nature of the mask worn by the title character of Ropes's poem might have called upon social condemnations of male homosexual desire as perverse and unnatural: images Ropes later critiqued in his backstage novels. In 1934's *Go Into Your Dance*, Ropes portrays the sense of refuge that chorus boys Arthur and Bobby, an open gay couple, find in the theater: "Divorced from the hectic atmosphere of backstage, they would have seemed monstrous, devoid of the slightest virtue."[143] Years after writing "The Man Who Lost His Soul," Ropes moved to reveal the sexuality of men like Arthur and Bobby and to depict American society, rather than his gay characters, as stunted by a "grotesque mask of hate."

By the time of his senior year at Quincy High School, the young writer Ropes had moved far beyond the patriotic fairy play fantasies of *The Dream Child*. Early works such as "The Trembling Hour" and "The Man Who Lost His Soul" show Ropes developing adventurousness and dexterity. He apparently continued to experiment; in 1921, administrators at Quincy High School moved to ban Ropes's senior-year class play. In its 1951 profile about *Mr. Tilley Takes a Walk*, the *Patriot Ledger* revealed: "A graduate of Quincy High School . . . [Ropes] wrote a class play, which the 'powers-that-be' decided wasn't proper for the high school body."[144]

While the newspaper did not reveal the subject of the banned play, the article indicates that Ropes had grown increasingly rebellious by 1921. From that year to 1922, Ropes attended the Thayer Academy preparatory school, in Braintree, Massachusetts, as a one-year-long "P.G." (or post-graduate).[145] Founded in 1877 by the "Father of Westpoint," Sylvanus Thayer, the school offered students a rigorous grounding in the sciences and classical humanities within its bucolic Victorian campus. Ropes, by contrast, sought to continue his studies in theater. During the academy's 1990 production of *42nd Street*, archivist Lillian Wentworth "asked the alumni at large if there was any information anyone had on Mr. Ropes."[146] An alum passed on a reminiscence from another classmate, who "remembered him vividly and [said] that he was already interested in theater when at Thayer." Although the alum recalled that new headmaster Stacy Southworth "did not entirely approve of" Ropes's passion for theater,[147] Southworth soon after warmed toward the art form, supporting a newly founded drama program at the school in the mid-1920s.[148] Ropes's love of the stage extended to more risqué performance, and in 1953, he recalled how he rearranged his class schedule at Thayer "to

Yearbook photograph of Bradford Ropes, from the 1922 edition of *The Black and Orange*, Thayer Academy. Reproduced by permission of Wentworth Archives, Thayer Academy.

permit attendance at matinees at the Old Howard," the Boston theater later notorious for its burlesque shows.[149]

At Thayer, Ropes earned the fervent admiration of his teachers and peers, as reflected in the first edition of the school's yearbook, *The Black and Orange*. Noting his nicknames as "Brad" and "Ropesy," the yearbook recorded:

The last of the Wollastonites is surely destined to make his name live in history. He is Gilbert and Sullivan rolled into one, for weren't we surprised to learn he had written a musical comedy or so, worthy of production. After looking at him, this may be hard to realize, but we vouch that this is true. Brad has only been here a year, so he really hasn't had time to show us all he can do, but we've heard it rumored he is a wonder at clog-dancing. Well, Ropesy, you can show us next year at Bowdoin.[150]

Instead of moving on to Bowdoin College, in his mother's home state of Maine, the seventeen-year-old dancer and writer heeded the call of the theater. Ropes told the *Golden Rod* in 1930: "After graduating from Quincy High in 1921 and Thayer Academy in 1922, I was slated for a business career, but the stage had been calling me since early boyhood, and during a brief visit to New York, I landed a contract on the Keith Circuit which gave me a year's experience on the vaudeville stage."[151]

As the next chapter illustrates, Ropes's reminiscence leaves out vital elements of the story of his flight into vaudeville, where he transformed into the dancer Billy Bradford. In later interviews, Ropes discussed respectably commencing his vaudeville career with the famous Gus Edwards troupe of adolescent performers. In fact, Ropes started dancing on the Keith Circuit in support of the female impersonator Alyn Mann, at a time when theatrical gender-bending (and the emerging phenomenon of the drag queen) captured the American popular imagination but also prompted deep cultural anxieties "over sexual practice and its relationship to an anchored, visible, and impermeable notion of masculinity," as Sharon R. Ullman describes.[152] Against the censorial forces of Proper Boston, Ropes climbed onto the winds of social progress that contributed both to women's sexual liberation and to the efflorescence of gay male communities in Greenwich Village and Harlem in the 1920s. As he moved into show business, the legacies of his upbringing lingered with Ropes, and in his first year as a vaudeville "trouper," Ropes also started near the top of a show business institution that in many ways emulated the hierarchical caste system of the Boston Brahmins. Dancing behind Mann, Ropes, in his first year of vaudeville, found himself performing at the world-famous Palace Theatre.

CHAPTER 2

Drag Reveals and "Strange Interludes"

BILLY BRADFORD'S DANCES ON BROADWAY

"The Mortals Who Are Allowed to Pass through the Iron Gate": From Boston into the "Big-Time"

In 1933, during the depths of the Great Depression, the conversion of B. F. Keith's Palace Theatre into a motion picture house did not prevent Bradford Ropes from conjuring the mythological grandeur that the Palace had evoked to vaudevillians in the 1910s and '20s. "The Palace Theatre has always been enthroned in the hearts of the vaudeville performer. . . . There is magic in the very word," Ropes observed of the Palace's fairy-tale lore in *Stage Mother*.[1] For Ropes and many other troupers, the Palace Theatre represented not only the most rarified heights of the "big-time" but the culmination of years of toil, tedium, and tours, of slapping on greasepaint in hard-to-reach dressing rooms, coated with "dirt, grime, filth everywhere," as Kitty Lorraine groans in the novel.[2] For troupers like Kitty, playing the Palace suggested a vision of show business in which labor was rewarded, and Broadway or Hollywood fame beckoned to the industrious variety artist.

In *Stage Mother*, Ropes portrays the Palace as "the goal for which many an artist had aspired for years": both a bastion of exclusivity and a beacon attracting a wide, international array of variety performers. Ropes evokes the theater's stage door and "backstage regions" on 47th Street as imbued with the modern air of a moated medieval castle:

> Only the performers on the bill and the representatives of the sundry theatrical sheets are permitted in the dressing rooms. . . . The average person must remain forever an outsider, gazing wistfully as the ranks of the mighty pass the

eagle-eyed guardian of the portal and walk down the sloping alleyway toward the stage door.

Ropes shows performers from across Europe flocking to the Palace's exclusive environs: "From the Wintergarden in Berlin, the Empire in Paris, the Coliseum in London they have come, these select of the theatre world; jugglers from the Cirque Medrano, opera singers from La Scala, chanteuses who charmed the tourists at the Casino de Paris."[3] For all that a booking at the Palace rewarded elite vaudevillians, the theater also marketed an ethos of meritocracy reflected in *Billboard*'s 1915 review of acts at the Palace: "Here genius not birth your rank insures."[4]

American vaudeville based these ideals closely upon its ethnic diversity. For the Anglo-Saxon Ropes, who had been, at the age of seven, president of the Children of the American Revolution of Wollaston, the demographic variety of vaudeville's performers and audiences would have delivered a dramatic change from the codes of "Proper Boston" and Puritan Quincy, even in a city with an Irish Catholic majority and the visible Black bourgeoisie later chronicled by novelist Dorothy West. If Irish Americans represented an ascendant yet disempowered majority in early twentieth-century Boston, vaudeville's melting pot ethos allowed European immigrant performers to hold sway. Headlined by stars like the Irish American George M. Cohan and the Jewish American Fanny Brice, vaudeville was "created largely by people from immigrant and working-class backgrounds who supplied both its talent and its audiences."[5]

Yet, in other ways, American vaudeville, with its illustrious headliners and unenvied "chaser" acts, evoked the stratifications of the Boston Brahmin caste system in which Ropes had grown up. Its organization, monopolized with iron-fisted control by B. F. Keith and Edward Albee Sr., promoted inequitable systems of rank and epitomized what vaudeville historian Robert W. Snyder has called "a deeply contradictory form of theatre, its meanings as elusive as the patter of a doubletalk comedian."[6] Although vaudeville was "popular in its origins," it was also "oligarchic in its distributions," as Snyder notes of the medium.[7]

The Palace Theatre's position at the top of the vaudeville theater chain replicated other hierarchies that, as depicted by Ropes in his backstage trilogy, could inspire deep envies, rivalries, and resentments among vaudeville's often underpaid performers. Vaudeville pitted the performers of the "big-time," with their enviable two performances a day, against the troupers of the "small-time," who more taxingly entertained audiences for three, four, or more daily performances. "Eager youngsters vie with seasoned performers to win first honors," Ropes observed of the Palace Theatre in *Stage Mother*.[8]

As one of those fortunate youngsters, the eighteen-year-old Bradford Ropes climbed to the Palace's heights in his first very year of vaudeville, skipping the rigors of the "four-a-day" to dance through the theater's "iron gate." Ropes's evocation of the Palace captures the excitement he likely felt when, less than a year after leaving the Thayer Academy, he joined the Keith Circuit and played vaudeville's most storied theater. In *A Whirl of Dance*, he performed high kicks behind Alyn Mann, a "terpsichorean female impersonator."[9] Over the course of his vaudeville career, which lasted through 1932, Ropes played the Palace three times: a charmed number in the terms of a fairy tale. Yet, like so many vaudevillians during the form's decline in the Great Depression, Ropes fell out of "the ranks of the mighty" only seven years after he made his Palace debut in August 1923 with Mann. Ropes's trouping on the "small-time" Loew Circuit became the impetus for his writing of *42nd Street*.

In the years between 1923's *A Whirl of Dance* and his early 1930s Loew Circuit tour, Bradford Ropes transformed into Billy Bradford and embarked on a new career as a vaudevillian and, later, a cabaret and Broadway dancer. The years 1925 through 1928 brought him his most successful years within a dance partnership. With the Seattle-raised Marian Hamilton, Billy Bradford earned acclaim for his "acrobatic dancing" and for the team's performances of the Charleston and the Black Bottom in Europe. A 1933 profile of Ropes in the *Quincy Patriot Ledger*, accompanied by his headshot, claimed that "the London papers in referring to his debut there spoke of him as the best male dancer seen on the London stage in years."[10] If his hometown paper waxed hyperbolic, London reviewers did highly praise the routines of Bradford and Hamilton. Parisian critics, too, wrote in dazzled detail about the talent of the team and of Billy Bradford as an "elastic, double-jointed man."[11] Writing of his performance in the 1926 revue *Paris, La Lanterne* marveled, "What looseness of articulations! And how happily he combines his incredible choreographic acrobatics with the delicate grace of Marian Hamilton, his partner!"[12]

This chapter explores not only the skillful metamorphoses but the concealments, reveals, and interludes that shaped the career of Billy Bradford from 1923 through 1933. During this time, he experienced the daring exposures of the 1920s revue, dancing alongside scantily clad showgirls at the London Pavilion and France's Casino de Paris. Interludes on nightclub stages and in Broadway musical comedies appeared between Billy Bradford's bookings in vaudeville, before his ultimate reinvention as a novelist. The banning in Bos-

Headshot of Bradford Ropes, ca. 1920s, published in 1933 in the *Quincy Patriot Ledger*. Reproduced by permission of M. G. Bullard.

ton of Eugene O'Neill's 1928 Pulitzer Prize-winning drama *Strange Interlude*, by Ropes's own mayoral cousin-in-law, marks another important juncture in the life and work of Ropes, who observed the controversy from the road of the Loew Circuit. Ropes alluded to O'Neill and the Theatre Guild later in his novels, which converse with O'Neill in their explorations of both theatrical hierarchies and cultural appropriation during the Harlem Renaissance.

If vaudeville, and then revue, introduced Ropes to a glittering modern world beyond Proper Boston, its many female impersonators arrived as another revelation. Ropes learned about the subtleties of gender performance from artists such as Bert Savoy and Jay Brennan at the start of the Pansy Craze, as a "popular fascination with gay culture" allowed gay men to create a veiled yet exuberantly visible public life in 1920s New York City.[13] These contexts vitally inform the world of Ropes's backstage trilogy.

In later newspaper profiles and interviews, Ropes claimed that, as Billy Bradford, he had gotten his start performing as a "Gus Edwards prodigy" in one of the impresario's youth revues.[14] A 1951 profile in the *Patriot Ledger* asserted: "While in New York, he obtained his first professional role in Gus Edwards's *School Days*."[15] Yet, while Ropes unveiled the culture of the Pansy Craze in his 1930s backstage trilogy, he also concealed the story of his first appearance on the vaudeville stage: dancing in support of Mann. The fabled portals of the Palace opened to Ropes at a time when female impersonators, popular since the early 1910s, commanded the spotlight on vaudeville stages.

"I'll Be the Champ Female Impersonator in the City": Alyn Mann and the "Reveal" of Billy Bradford at the Palace

According to Ropes, it was "during a brief visit to New York, [that] I landed a contract on the Keith Circuit which gave me a year's experience on the vaudeville stage."[16] In a 1930 interview with the *Golden Rod*, Ropes did not elaborate upon how he spent his time between his 1922 graduation from Thayer Academy and his start in vaudeville. Yet, newspaper reviews first started to mention Ropes, as a dancer in Mann's act, around March 1923.

In 1933's *Stage Mother*, Ropes captured the cultural pull of New York City through the perspective of Shirley Lorraine. Living under the care of Aunt Ida in Boston, Shirley imagines "the shining pageant of New York" as something "she scarcely dared dream of."[17] When she moves to the city with Kitty, Shirley exults in the voice of the city, expressed in the "many strange sounds that beat around her": "This was the high tide of evening, so much more stimulating than the quiet, misty nightfall which she had grown to fear in Boston. . . . Metropolis! City of Cities! New York!"[18] Ropes moved to the metropolis when the Jazz Age, if not yet in full swing, had already kicked off "New York's effulgent era."[19] "Surely this was the age of miracles," Ted Howard marvels in 1934's *Go Into Your Dance*, as his dreams for *Town Talk* blossom into fruition. Here, Ropes alluded to F. Scott Fitzgerald's elegy in his 1931 essay "Echoes of the Jazz Age": "It was an age of miracles, it was an age of art, it was an age of excess, and it was an age of satire."[20] As Stanley Walker noted, Broadway magnetized the young and ambitious from all walks of life, even if it might scarcely have occurred to Walker to place a Mayflower descendant in their mix: "Broadway remains the Mecca of the plaintive crooner . . . the hoofer who laid 'em in the aisles in Arkansas City, and all the rest of that crew of wistful hometown boys and girls who seek to overreach themselves."[21]

Joining up in New York with Mann, a "new 'find'" of the powerful, Canadian-born vaudeville producer and sketch writer May Tully, may have enabled Ropes to make a quick leap into big-time vaudeville on the Keith Circuit.[22] In a 1917 *McClure's* profile, Anna Steese Richardson wrote: "Miss Tully is known wherever 'vaudeville' shines in electric lights—big time, little time, two a day, three or four."[23] Tully enjoyed close connections to the Palace Theatre, where she had recently been the lead producer of sketches for Edward Albee Sr.[24]

The influential Tully stayed attuned to current trends. By 1923, female impersonators had firmly established themselves as an institution in American vaudeville, as the decline of Victorianism fueled their popularity at the turn of the twentieth century. As modeled by superstar Julian Eltinge, who landed endorsement deals for corsets and cosmetics, female impersonators sublimated implications of queer sexuality to a seamless performance of femininity. As the title of Eltinge's 1910 Broadway hit musical comedy *The Fascinating Widow* suggests, female impersonators traded on the beguilement of gender illusion.

While the female impersonators who rivaled Eltinge established their own performance trademarks, Mann traded upon his uniqueness as a "dancing female impersonator," noted for his "good one-foot pivots and whirls."[25] A minor star in vaudeville, the Texas-born Mann remained active throughout the 1920s, inspiring C. J. Bulliet to write in his 1928 cultural history of female impersonation, *Venus Castina*, that Mann exuded the "juvenile grace of a young high school girl." Bulliet noted Mann and Karyl Norman as among performers "who have emerged to a plane a little above the multitude of youths seriously trying to compete with girls in the matter of looking and acting like females on the stage."[26] Mann's identification as primarily a dancer set him apart from other impersonators who based their acts more so upon glamor, impressions, or comedy. He nonetheless drew ample publicity from his gowns, such as "an adorable frock of orange and silver changeable taffeta, combined with apricot georgette."[27]

The Eternal Triangle marked the start of Mann's career in vaudeville. As a "shrewd show woman" with an intimate knowledge of the vaudeville industry, Tully had a talent for "trimming and discreet maneuvering" that transformed the act from an overlong, twenty-seven-minute mini-revue into a streamlined production retitled *A Whirl of Dance*.[28] Tully cowrote the lyrics and book, while Seymour Felix, later a Hollywood choreographer for films like *The Great*

May Tully, ca. 1912.
Courtesy J. Willis Sayre Collection of Theatrical Photographs.
Public Domain through Picryl.com (https://picryl.com/media/
may-tully-vaudeville-actress-sayre-10436-80802f)

Ziegfeld, co-created the dances. After a tryout, still as *The Eternal Triangle*, at Keith's Riverside Theatre on 96th Street, Mann's new act moved to the Palace in the first week of August 1923. By then, Mann had added "a few words" to the act, since at the Riverside "he does not speak or utter a sound at any time, not even when he is uncovered."[29]

Even as *The Eternal Triangle*, Mann's act drew acclaim from *Variety*'s Jack Lait for its attractive production elements, in which "some of the sets, the cardboard announcements, and the costume of the announcer follow the triangle design in scheme." Lait described the act as a "burlesque triangle in song and dance, with Mann as a show girl between a husband and a John." *The Eternal Triangle* juxtaposed its "triangular set pieces" with the convention of the "Apache dance," in which jealous lovers tangoed in crime-of-passion scenarios inspired by stereotypes of underworld savagery. Lait observed a "Spanish tragedy triangle with stabbings and other fatalities, Mann doing a Spanish dance in a huge oilcloth skirt that whirls and flares."[30]

In *The Eternal Triangle* and its transformation as *A Whirl of Dance*, Ropes appeared as one of three "excellent male dancers" who assisted the star in going through his "three full stage pantomime and dance scenes in flashy feminine costumes." *A Whirl of Dance* billed its cast as "Alyn Mann in *A Whirl of Dance* with Jay Russell, Hal Taggart & Co., including Billy Bradford."[31] Although few reviews specifically identified him by name, later performance photos of Ropes indicate him as the performer seen "executing formidable acrobatics and high kicks."[32] At Manhattan's 5th Avenue Theatre, *Variety* gushed: "The high kicking by one [of the dancers] is the last word in that sort of thing."[33]

In addition to supporting Mann onstage, Ropes might have played versatile roles within the act as a stage assistant. Describing Ted's vaudeville work with the tango team Ramon and Noretta in *Go Into Your Dance*, Ropes both creates a narrative parallel to his debut with "Spanish-dancing" Mann and suggests that the labor of a supporting dancer in vaudeville extended well beyond the footlights. Here, Ropes describes Ted's "many and varied" duties as a "strangely hybrid orchestra director-stage hand-valet-specialty dancer-nurse maid" in *Vanities of Terpsichore*:

Ted's work began at an early hour on the opening day of each engagement. He arrived at the theater, presented the claim checks for the act's baggage to the stage manager, placed the briefcase which contained the music in the footlight trough and then divested himself of coat and shirt, so that he might be ready to assemble the cumbersome platform from which Ramon and Noretta made their entrance for the waltz and tango.[34]

Bradford Ropes
as Billy Bradford,
high-kicking in
1925 alongside later
dance partner Marian
Hamilton.
Reproduced by per-
mission of National
Portrait Gallery,
London.

Although Tully successfully streamlined *The Eternal Triangle* into *A Whirl of Dance*, she was not able to overcome critics' central reservation about the act. Reviewers repeatedly complained that Mann was insufficiently convincing as a woman ("he makes neither a ravishing girl nor a heroic man") and that the device of a "reveal" that culminated many female impersonators' acts only anticlimactically confirmed Mann's male gender.[35] Mann debuted at the Palace during an era in which gender illusionists such as Eltinge generated gasps with their "surprise" finales, in which pulling off their wigs exposed their masculinity.

Mann fared poorly at a time when female impersonation had become a common sight to New Yorker theatergoers, if still a novelty to less jaded regional audiences. "In New York the ramifications of feminine impersonations are sidewalk topics and there is no real jolt left in wig removing," yawned Jack Lait, reviewing *The Eternal Triangle* at the Riverside.[36] Though noting a favorable impression upon the Palace's audience, *Billboard* rated *A Whirl of Dance* a middling 45 out of 100 in its "percentage of entertainment" chart when the act made its debut at the Palace Theatre.

Yet, Mann's lukewarm Palace reception in *A Whirl of Dance* suffered from not only critics' biases about seamless gender illusionism but also the grim mood in the theater. When *Billboard* reviewed the act's August 6 matinee, and its bill headlined by Lou Clayton and Cliff "Ukelele Ike" Edwards, audiences were still reeling from the death, reputedly from a heart attack, of President Warren Harding on August 2, 1923. As *Billboard* noted of the acrobats Herbert and Dale, in the opening spot that followed a screening of Pathé News, the team "had the toughest position on the bill, following as they did pictures of the late President."[37]

As *A Whirl of Dance* continued along the Keith Circuit, with stops in cities including Washington, DC, Brooklyn, Boston, and Syracuse, East Coast critics expressed more approval of Mann's "reveal." By the time he returned to the 5th Avenue Theatre in December 1923, *Variety* also deemed him more convincing, observing: "Mann is a likely gal. The blonde bob is becoming and positively fooling unless advised beforehand. The unwigging was a shock, and because of the complete hoax, vastly appreciated."[38]

Performing only a "writhing business with the arms" with his "snake dance," Mann presented only a mildly scandalous act.[39] His choreography carried associations with such Orientalist dance crazes as the "hootchy-kootchy" and the "dance of the seven veils," seductively revealing the bodies of the many female, and female impersonator, performers of the early twentieth-century "Salomania" craze. *A Whirl of Dance* pleased audiences at Boston's Keith's Theatre, where Len Libbey recounted for *Variety* that Mann's act "crashed off, women in the audience screaming, and the house giving him the really only spontaneous outburst of the evening. His final bow, when he revealed that he was a female impersonator, was cleverly timed and handled."[40]

Nevertheless, Ropes's performances with a "terpsichorean female impersonator" carried the potential of scandalizing his family in Proper Boston.[41] Initially starting on the road with Mann as Bradford Ropes, the dancer adapted his Pilgrim-taunting stage name of Billy Bradford a week before *A Whirl of Dance* approached its booking at Keith's Theatre in September 1923. Although Mrs. Arthur Dudley Ropes had not discouraged her son's stage career, Alice had attained social prominence as the regent of the Wollaston chapter of the DAR. Her niece, Edith, too was now well established in her role as the wife of a public dignitary. Now an ex-state senator, Malcolm E. Nichols served Presidents Harding and then Coolidge as the U.S. collector of internal revenue.

MAY TULLY Presents

ALYN MANN

—IN—

"A WHIRL OF DANCE"

With Jay Russell, Hall Taggart and Company, Including
Billy Bradford

Music by Martin Broones—Lyrics by Leonard Fraskins and
May Tully

Pathe News—Aesop's Fables—Orchestra—Topics of the Day

Seattle Star advertisement of Billy Bradford in *A Whirl of Dance* at the
Orpheum Theatre, sharing a 1923 bill with Joe E. Brown.
Reprinted from *Seattle Star*, March 22, 1923.

Even in cities less socially conservative than Boston, female impersonator
acts could unleash sexual anxieties in the audience. In 1918, the *Vancouver
Sun* wrote that Francis Renault "disappointed most of the male attendants
last evening when he removed his feminine makeup."[42] Taking his own scantily clad "Serpent Dance" further than Mann, Bothwell Browne performed a
1913 Cleopatra act that culminated with the performer collapsing on stage
in "ecstatic agony." As Sharon R. Ullman notes, Browne "went further than
Eltinge and played on erotic imagery calculated to arouse male members of the
audience."[43] The rise of female impersonators like Browne who specialized in
blatantly erotic performances likely influenced the transformation of Bradford
Ropes into Billy Bradford, as the former may have worried what his performance in *A Whirl of Dance* might "reveal" to family members.

Billy Bradford continued to appear in *A Whirl of Dance* until June 1924,
although by February of that year he had also shifted into nightclub work in
Manhattan. Along its Keith route and extending westward onto the Orpheum
Circuit, *A Whirl of Dance* variously shared the bill with performers including
Joe E. Brown and the team of Charles Crafts and Jack Haley (later *The Wizard
of Oz*'s Tin Man).[44] Continuing in vaudeville with revues like 1926's *Blondes
Preferred*, Alyn Mann transformed by 1930 into the clearly male "Allen Mann,"

as the era of the female impersonator shifted into the racier performances of drag queens like Bert Savoy. These performers flaunted the camp effect of gender incongruity rather than an illusionistic "surprise" of their male gender.

In his writer's fame as Bradford Ropes, the former dancer never mentioned to newspaper reporters his touring with Alyn Mann. Yet, he certainly did not forget the experience. In *Go Into Your Dance*, Ropes paid tribute to his time with Mann through a farcical "strange interlude." Here, Ropes shows the heterosexual Ted narrowly escaping what might have been a deadly erotic escapade through the use of female impersonation, which Ted foils with an unintended "reveal."

The incident unfolds as Ted tours with Nora on the Orpheum Circuit. Playing a week in Detroit, Ted initiates a fling with a tough prostitute named Lilybell, who becomes dangerously obsessed with him as the hoofer tries to end the affair. Although thoroughly frustrated with Ted, Nora helps him devise a way to escape past the stage door without being shot by Lilybell, who is sitting in the front row of the theater with a poorly concealed gun. Backstage, dangling a "tumbled mass of chiffon and velvet" in front of Ted, Nora tersely informs him, "Put it on." Ropes continues the farcical scene:

> A half hour later, while Lilybell stood fuming in the alleyway below, two figures were descending the short flight of stairs which led to the stage door. One was Nora. . . . Behind her stalked a grotesque individual, liberally swathed in veils, the long cloak which enveloped it flapping mournfully at the heels.[45]

As Nora helps her veiled "Mumsie" into a taxi to the train station, Ted dangerously reveals his gender by tripping on the disguising dress: "The accident was fatal. . . . The hat from which flowed the trailing black of the veil was dislodged and Lilybell stared unbelievingly at the shorn head, which drawn from its concealment, proved to belong to her one-time boyfriend."[46] In a later chapter of *Go Into Your Dance*, Ted—in a new scrape with Chicago gangsters—contemplates, but rejects, the thought of repeating the trick: "Lissen, if I climb into women's clothes once more I'll be the champ female impersonator in the city. Besides, 'drag' wouldn't fool those Chicago babies. They'd catch on in a minute!"[47]

Anticipating the drag comedy of Billy Wilder's *Some Like It Hot*, Ropes relived his experience with *A Whirl of Dance* through the veiled revelations of his backstage fiction and, later, Hollywood screenplays. In 1942's gender-bending *True to the Army*, carnival performer Daisy Hawkins (Judy Canova) disguises herself as a man to escape the mob. She finds herself mistaken for a female impersonator in an army revue, for which she later masquerades as a male soldier and, in *Victor/Victoria* style, performs in the climactic drag fashion show number, "Wacky for Khaki." If Ropes left Mann out of his recorded history to interviewers, he found other ways to memorialize the excitements and snares of his true performance debut at the Palace, as Ted—like Mann— failed to persuade onlookers of his femininity. After the transformed Billy Bradford left Mann's act at the age of nineteen, he commenced a new stage as a nightclub dancer. He also experienced his own run-ins with New York's fabled Prohibition-era gangster culture: as much a part of Manhattan in the 1920s as Fitzgerald's flappers.

Billy Bradford at the Silver Slipper: Dancing around Gangster Culture in Jazz Age New York

In February 1924, Billy Bradford entered a world only a block away from the Palace Theatre yet far removed from the swank, respectable Keith-Albee Circuit. When the dancer started performing in a revue at the Silver Slipper, located at Broadway and 48th Street, he advanced into the enticing yet dangerous world of Prohibition-era Times Square nightclubs. Here, bootleggers like Owney Madden, rather than theatrical monopolists like Keith and Albee, called the shots—and attracted police raids. Ropes signed on to the Silver Slipper during the height of New York's "Night Club Era." Stanley Walker writes of the number of New York nightclubs by 1926: "The estimates range from the 100,000 of the more optimistic (statisticians) down to the mere 800."[48] In *42nd Street*, Ropes reminisced on the mid-1920s: "The surrender of America to Gangland was imminent."[49]

Ropes may have brought a "don't tell mama" approach to his employment at the Silver Slipper. Elected as Massachusetts president of the WCTU in 1922, Alice Williams Ropes spent much of the decade crusading against bootleggers.[50] Her son did not feel particularly safe performing among them. In 1954, he reminisced about the era to the *Berkshire Evening Eagle*, without explicitly discussing his time at the Silver Slipper: "Gangsters, he said, controlled American night clubs during the dry era and the period was a difficult one for entertainers."[51] At another time, he recalled "how [nightclub] performers earning $150 a week were compelled to pay tribute to underlords in the Capone camp in Chicago."[52]

The New York nightclubs of the 1920s conjured close association with the rumrunners who ran them. Mythologized by Damon Runyon in his stories as "the Golden Slipper," the Silver Slipper opened in November 1923, with three notorious racketeers as silent investors: Arnold Rothstein, the Harlem political boss Jimmy Hines, and Owney Madden.[53] Nicknamed "the Killer," the British-born Madden also became the proprietor of Harlem's legendary Cotton Club after his release from Sing Sing: "He was, in his way, a good deal of the salty wisecracker, a master of shockingly picturesque figures of speech."[54] Madden exerted influence on every aspect of the Silver Slipper's business: "During the period of his ascendancy, it would have been possible to pass an evening having one's cab driven by a Madden man . . . the food and drinks served by a Madden man, and the clothes brushed by a Madden man back in the washroom."[55]

Yet, if gangsters like Madden created a "difficult" environment for entertainers, Billy Bradford continued to gain experience in the kind of luxurious nightclub setting that led to his cabaret appearances in Europe. The Silver Slipper boasted "gaudy silver-and-black striped wallpaper that gave the club an air of glamour that eluded most of its competitors," observes Debby Applegate.[56] In February 1924, Bradford supported vaudeville stars Gus Van and Joe Schenck, backed by Meyer Davis's Palm Beach Orchestra.[57] Billy Bradford remained at the Silver Slipper in March, when he joined Billie Shaw's revue, featuring a "chorus of ten girls."[58] Police raided the short-lived Silver Slipper on March 27, 1924.[59] As the March 29, 1924, issue of Billboard listed Billy Bradford among the performers of the Silver Slipper's revue, the timing of the raid suggests the likelihood that he performed in the midst of it. The space reopened after its padlocking and became one of the nightclubs associated with the rise of Ruby Keeler, the club's "star entertainer" in 1927.[60]

In his backstage novels, Ropes's frequent allusions to bootleggers and their relationships to entertainers suggest parallels to the "Guys and Dolls" of Runyon, with whom Ropes shared an affinity for hard-boiled slang. Yet, Billy Bradford's time performing at the Silver Slipper suggests that Ropes's mingling of gangland culture and show business drew not only from the conventions of noir and detective fiction but also from personal experience. Gangsters and bootleggers drive key plot twists in all three novels of the author's backstage trilogy, where they appear in the forms of 42nd Street's Walt McDermott, Stage Mother's Angelo Scarlatti, and Go Into Your Dance's "the Major."

In the backstage novels, Ropes portrays New York's bootleggers as a menacing stimulant to the café society of the "Dry Era." In Go Into Your Dance, Ropes portrays Ted entering the fashionable Domino Club:

There in the dingy confines of a room which had once sheltered an American financier and his brood the more noted raconteurs and racketeers of those mad days forgathered to drink a highball or two and view with malicious eyes the parade of vanity and self-aggrandizement that swept in and out of the speakeasy.[61]

Ropes colorfully observes that notable figures at the Domino "liked this sense of rubbing elbows with the figures of a bizarre world. . . . Producers and pimps, heroines and harlots, mechanized brunettes and Mackenzied blondes."[62]

If Ropes evokes the era's blurry distinction between a racketeer and a raconteur, he also evokes show business and gangland America as topsy-turvy reflections of one another. In *Go Into Your Dance*, the Major reflects upon his experience as a backing "angel" of Ted's scandal-plagued *Town Talk* and upon his observations about the ruthless tactics of Broadway impresarios like the Wilsons (based on brothers Lee and J. J. Shubert). The Major sighs: "It's a tough game, this show business. . . . Me, I'll take a mob any time to that Wilson gang. A gangster shoots a guy in the back but the Wilsons make sure he's tied hand and foot and *then* shoot to kill."[63]

After his appearances at the Silver Slipper, Billy Bradford returned to vaudeville, having collected a range of experiences and impressions about New York's Night Club Era that later dynamically fueled his novels. As Ropes recounted, he also continued to study dancing in New York alongside "illustrious members of Michael's acrobatic school of dance: Irene Dunn [sic], Charlotte Greenwood at the bar, fledgling Billy De Wolfe (a fellow Wollastonian but unknown to him), Eleanor Powell, and James Cagney."[64] Now a twenty-year-old hoofer who had brushed shoulders with Owney Madden, he was lured in the fall of 1924 by the golden opportunity to join the family-friendly troupe of a legendary impresario and songwriter. This was Gus Edwards: known as vaudeville's "supreme discoverer of child talent."[65] Performing with the man nicknamed "Uncle Gus," Billy Bradford now made his second appearance at the Palace Theatre.

The Dance Prodigy and the Star-Maker: Billy Bradford Stops the Show at the Palace

In his backstage trilogy and in his film work as a screenwriter, Ropes evoked the life and work of Gus Edwards frequently. In 1945, Ropes used the Edwards song catalog, and standards like "School Days" and "By the Light of the Silvery Moon," in a nostalgic Republic Pictures movie musical entitled *Sunbonnet Sue*. In *Stage Mother*, Ropes fictionalizes Edwards as Mark Thorne, writing of the latter's renown as a "star-maker": "From much chaff Thorne extracted the true wheat, and it was implanted to thrive in the fertile soil of vaudeville."[66]

If the Palace Theatre represented "magic in the very word," Edwards represented "a magic name in theatrical circles."[67] By the mid-1920s Edwards, a first-generation Polish Jewish immigrant born as Gustav Schmelowsky, had risen to immense national celebrity as a Tin Pan Alley songwriter, vaudeville showman, and promoter of youthful talent. Edwards's discoveries included Walter Winchell, Eddie Cantor, Groucho Marx, Eleanor Powell, and Ray Bolger. Some of the performers discovered by Edwards rose to prominence in more risqué show business fields, such as female impersonator Francis Renault and burlesque queen Sally Rand. In *Stage Mother*, Ropes describes the Edwards-like Thorne: "He came to be known as the Columbus of the stage—and legend had it that one was really not a performer of the first water unless one had served one's apprenticeship with Mark Thorne."[68]

Yet, in his novels of the early 1930s, Ropes reflected Edwards's renown while portraying him with a cynical bite. In the troupe of the sexually predatory Thorne, *Stage Mother*'s Shirley commences her rise to stardom in a vaudeville youth revue closely resembling Edwards's *The Fountain of Youth of 1925*, in which Billy Bradford performed. Ropes also depicts Edwards's vaudeville shows as the training ground for Dorothy Brock, whose temperamental backstage behavior belies her "sweet, smilin' virgin" persona.[69] In *42nd Street*, Ropes alludes to Edwards's famous youth revue *School Days* when agent Pete Dexter exclaims of the former "child prodigy": "She didn't have nothin' but a back bend with a fan when I put her in *Happy Days*."[70]

The 1939 Paramount musical *The Star Maker*, starring Bing Crosby as a fictionalized Edwards, dramatized the producer's dealings with child prodigies and their stage mothers, eager to exchange their kids' education for *School Days* in vaudeville. The film also depicted the impresario's battles with the New York Society for the Prevention of Cruelty to Children, popularly known as the Gerry Society. This reputation prompted the *New York Times* to describe Edwards's notoriety in a profile of Billy Bradford: "He attended school at Quincy, Mass, and at Thayer Academy, after which he fell into the clutches of the inevitable Gus Edwards, at whose arrival in any given community warnings are usually sounded for mothers to hide their children."[71] In *Stage Mother*, Ropes depicts Kitty and the Gerry Society in bitter conflict, as, prior to Shirley's debut with Thorne, Kitty falsifies the thirteen-year-old Shirley's age as sixteen. Ropes observes: "Kitty's main difficulty in these days was the Gerry Society, the doughy organization which restricts the professional appearances of youngers under age."[72]

Billy Bradford joined Edwards's youth revue not as a masquerading middle schooler but as a nineteen-year-old performer with his own school days behind him. Marketed as a "Revuesical Musical Comedy in Many Vues,"[73] *The Fountain of Youth* offered audiences a revamping of *School Days*: a show that had been so successful in its vaudeville debut that it transferred in 1908 to a run on Broadway. *School Days*, and later Edwards youth revues like *Kid Kabaret*, blended sentimental Tin Pan Alley hits with performers performing the tropes of vaudevillian immigrant comedy. Extolling values of assimilation, exemplified by his patriotic paean, "When I'm an American Citizen," Edwards rivaled George M. Cohan in his flag-waving Yankee pride.

Edwards's *School Days* formula drew heavily upon what Robert Snyder describes as vaudevillians' "synthetic ethnicity formed from elements of immigrant experiences, mass culture and the stereotyped national and racial characters of the American theatre."[74] Along these lines, the *Buffalo Courier* in 1909 detailed the performance of eighteen-year-old Herman Timberg in "the leading role of Izzy Levi, a Russian emigrant, with a violin as his best love." Other characters in *School Days* included a "fighting Irish boy"; a "German youthful admirer of Limberger cheese"; "a studio youth from Boston"; and "the homeless orphan Nonnie," whose "fingers are never happy unless she is stealing something."[75]

By the time Billy Bradford joined the Edwards company, the producer had blended the sentimental immigrant comedy of *School Days* with the snappier, hedonistic ethos of the 1920s. Starring Edwards himself, *The Fountain of Youth* played, among other stops, a big-time Keith route at Keith's Bushwick, the New Brighton Theatre on Coney Island, and the Palace Theatre. *The Fountain of Youth* consisted "of a series of cameo satires of the salient scenes of current Broadway dramatic and musical comedy successes."[76]

In his efforts to update the *School Days* formula, Edwards emulated the Jazz Age's culture of commoditized feminine glamour. The male gaze steered the "Revue-sical Comedy in Many Views," which featured such numbers as "Life's One Beautiful Girl After Another" and "Ziegfeld's Going to Get You If You Don't Watch Out."[77] *The Fountain of Youth of 1925* drew upon the *Follies*, as well as the wave of beauty pageants that followed the launch of "Miss America" in 1921. Edwards's revue showcased the talents of not only teenage comedians, singers, and dancers but also "a bouquet of sub-debs" representing "the pick of beauty contests" from around the United States.[78] The marketing of *The Fountain of Youth*, with Edwards "presenting himself surrounded by a bouquet of hardy spring beauties," illustrates how the impresario commercially exploited the youth of the "sub-debs" at a time when teenage chorus girls regularly appeared in Broadway revues and in the chorus lines of nightclub floor shows.[79]

As one of the young men in the troupe, Billy Bradford returned at the end of June 1925 to the Palace Theatre, where *The Fountain of Youth* played as the headlining act. This time, Billy Bradford may have appeared as part of an unqualified hit. In *Stage Mother*, Ropes vividly describes the feelings of exultation that could accompany a Palace triumph—though he places the most ecstatic excitement in the reaction of Kitty. As Ropes describes Shirley dancing as a "blur of white and blue and gold in the shelter of [a] blue shadowed grotto," her stage mother exclaims, "Whirl, Shirley, they love you, darling! Turn! Turn! . . . . You've done it this time, my sweetheart, you've stopped the show!"[80]

Given Ropes's unflattering portrayal of Mark Thorne in *Stage Mother*, Billy Bradford's experiences with *The Fountain of Youth of 1925* could not have been all positive ones. Yet, Edwards's professional clout and savvy as a "star-maker" clearly left a considerable impact on Ropes. The latter may have experienced one of his professional highlights, as a dancer, returning to the Palace Theatre stage. Trouping with Edwards, Billy Bradford also undoubtedly encountered a multitude of stage mothers: an archetype of excessive and vicarious ambition that left a powerful legacy not only on Ropes's fiction and Hollywood screenplays but also on such subsequent works as *Gypsy*. Not unlike that musical's Tulsa with Dainty June, Billy Bradford now struck out with a dance partnership of his own, teaming up with a beautiful young dancer from Seattle named Marian Hamilton.

Enter Marian Hamilton—and a New Chapter in Europe

In later interviews, Ropes did not discuss the details of his partnership with the titian-haired Marian Hamilton. Yet, Billy Bradford most likely teamed up with Hamilton around December 1925, in a dance partnership that lasted through October 1928, when Hamilton left the stage for married life.[81] The pairing spanned London revues, the Paris music hall, cabarets in the French

Marian Hamilton and Billy Bradford, 1925. Reproduced by permission of National Portrait Gallery, London.

Riviera, and, finally, Broadway. The team specialized in a vigorous form of ball-room dancing popular in the 1920s known both as "acrobatic dancing" (as most reviews refer to the specialty of Bradford and Hamilton) and as "adagio dancing." According to Jacqui Malone, "'Adagio' dancers performed a style that consisted of ballroom dance with various balletic and acrobatics, lifts, spins and poses."[82]

After his time dancing at the Silver Slipper and in *The Fountain of Youth of 1925*, Billy Bradford may have viewed a partnership with Hamilton as a way to achieve the professional and economic stability elusive to vaudevillians, even those lucky enough to be booked on the "big-time" circuits. In his back-stage trilogy, Ropes frequently depicted the rigors of vaudeville life. In *Go Into Your Dance*, chorus boy Walt confides to Ted that he "heard you was draggin' the body around the Orpheum Circuit." Ted nods and responds: "No future, though; just coffee and cake an' prayin' to God you'll get a route for next season. Personally, I don't go for it."[83]

Whereas Ted departs vaudeville for the Broadway chorus, Ropes left his vaudeville work with Gus Edwards to team up in London cabaret with Hamilton, on whom he partially based Nora in *Go Into Your Dance*. In the novel, Ted quickly perceives in Nora the potential for a commercially successful dance partnership. Ted bases his assessment not only on Nora's background and training in dance but also upon her stage presence and beauty. Ropes details the team's rapid rise on the Orpheum Circuit: "Ted's undisputed ability and Nora's charm and good-looking legs made them an invincible combination."[84]

As Ropes's description of Nora suggests, the Broadway culture of the 1920s, watered by fountains of youth, compelled Hamilton to perform in musicals and revues that traded on feminine beauty. Born in 1907 in Leavenworth, Washington, as the daughter of the town clerk, Hamilton started in vaudeville as a dancer, singer, and harpist, performing a "harp song" in 1922 at the Pantages Theatre in Vancouver.[85] Arriving in Manhattan, Hamilton made her debut as "Ruth" and as "Dancing Specialty" in 1923's *Lady Butterfly* and then appeared as a chorus girl in *The Ziegfeld Follies of 1923* and in *The Fashions of 1924*. Prior to teaming with Billy Bradford, she had appeared in the 1925 touring musical comedy *Mr. Battling Buttler*, about a bored young husband who poses as a boxer. As one of the two female leads, Hamilton was praised for her beauty: "Polly Walker and Marion [sic] Hamilton supply feminine allure of the highest type."[86]

Reviews of Bradford and Hamilton in Europe focus less on Hamilton's "feminine allure" and more on her ability as a dancer. During a decade enamored by the multitude of male-female dance teams who followed Vernon and Irene Castle onto nightclub and Broadway stages, Billy Bradford's partnership with Hamilton allowed both the hoofer and the chorus girl to ascend the show business hierarchy even beyond the Palace. In the 1920s, the stages of London and Paris signified "class": an elusive but essential ingredient for success as a performer, as portrayed by Ropes in the backstage trilogy. "The routine ain't bad, it just hasn't got class," "Two Buddies" dancer Lou Adams informs Ted as the latter pursues his calling in *Go Into Your Dance*.

At the same time, Europe's stages also signaled sexual modernism. The years in London, Paris, and the French Riviera marked Billy Bradford's further movement away from Boston Puritan culture. In *Cochran's Revue of 1926* and *Paris*, he performed in cosmopolitan and risqué revues that brought him into close contact not only with French showgirl *vedettes* but with gay camp comedians like Douglas Byng. Ropes also encountered European modernist aesthetics, epitomized by the Cubist design of *Paris* at the Casino de Paris.

The years in London and France also marked a proximity to Black artists who experienced a greater degree of professional and economic agency than they did upon the stages of American vaudeville and Broadway. At Paris's Théâtre Apollo music hall, Bradford and Hamilton co-headlined a revue with a prominent expatriate African American bandleader and also shared an evening's bill with multiple legends of the Harlem Renaissance. First, Billy Bradford traveled to London. Performing in a cosmopolitan revue that featured interpolated songs both by Sissle and Blake and by Richard Rodgers, Bradford and Hamilton made their West End debut in a production staged by Jazz Age London's most celebrated impresario.

"They Make the Most Alarming Things Look Ridiculously Easy": Bradford and Hamilton in London

In 1921, Ropes's well-traveled mother, Alice, had delivered one of her lantern-illustrated lectures at the Ruskin Club: "Memories of England." Four years later, her son embarked upon his own journey to the United Kingdom. On November 30, 1925, the twenty-year-old Ropes arrived at Southampton from New York. Listing his profession as "Theatrical," Ropes set his bags down at Piccadilly Circus's Regent Palace Hotel.[87] Over the course of their time in London, Bradford and Hamilton performed in nightclubs and cabarets including Ciro's, the Kit Kat Club, and the Piccadilly, in performances coinciding with their run in *Cochran's Revue of 1926* from April through September 1926.

If the Silver Slipper had brought bootleggers and "butter-and-egg men" into Billy Bradford's audience, the exclusive Ciro's played to a different crowd, as "the favorite rendezvous of the Prince of Wales at that time."[88] The *Daily Sketch* praised the team as "something out of the common" among exhibition ballroom dancers: "They are both very young, about 17, I should hazard, and they certainly succeed in proving that it is possible to combine acrobatic feats with grace. In fact, they make the most alarming things look ridiculously easy."[89] While performing with Hamilton at Ciro's, Billy Bradford also performed as a solo specialty dancer, from December 1925 through March 1926, at the Gaiety Theatre in the London transfer of the Rudolf Friml-Otto Harbach operetta *The Blue Kitten*. *Variety* reported, "The acrobatic stepping of Billy Bradford scored sensationally."[90]

In a 1926 *Patriot Ledger* article about Mrs. Arthur Dudley Ropes and her sister Ellen visiting Ropes in London, the newspaper informed Quincyites that he had landed a high-profile new role in *Cochran's Revue of 1926*. The paper

Billy Bradford, in a dance pose with Marian Hamilton, 1925. Reproduced by permission of National Portrait Gallery, London.

reported: "Upon [*The Blue Kitten*'s] completion, he assumed the leading juvenile part in a musical revue produced by [Charles B.] Cochran, England's foremost producer."[91] To American audiences, Cochran's revues summoned the tantalizing image of the producer's bevy of "Young Ladies," who rivaled the American Ziegfeld Girls. Yet, Cochran's productions exuded camp sophistication and an often queer sensibility. For his revues, Cochran enlisted writers like Cole Porter, Noël Coward (whose *Private Lives* he produced), and Lorenz Hart, as well as flamboyant performers like Douglas Byng. As Patrick Newley observes, "Cochran was an English Diaghilev, an impresario with a gift for spotting new talent and for bringing established names together in exciting combinations."[92]

Starring comics Byng, Ernest Thesiger, and Hermione Baddeley among the revue's headliners, Cochran also made ample room for Billy Bradford to shine, as featured in three numbers. He appeared with Hamilton in a specialty dance for "Wedding Day"; in a burlesque of the British pantomime *Aladdin* (in which he appeared fantastically garbed as a "Black and White Door"); and in the penultimate dance number, listed in the show's program as "Billy Bradford." According to Stanley Green, Bradford and Hamilton introduced Londoners to

Richard Rodgers's "I'm Crazy 'bout the Charleston," a new version of the Rodgers and Hart song, "Maybe It's Me."[93] Although composer Pat Thayer and lyricist Donovan Parsons supplied most of the score of the revue, Cochran commissioned Parsons to add new lyrics to Rodgers's music for "Maybe It's Me," which had previously been heard in New York in the nightclub revue *Fifth Avenue Follies*.[94] As re-fitted with Parsons's lyrics, "I'm Crazy 'bout the Charleston" marked among the first of Rodgers and Hart's songs to be performed in a British show.[95] The "Billy Bradford" slot in *Cochran's Revue of 1926* may have marked the placement of this interpolated song.

Bradford and Hamilton performed songs not only by Rodgers but also by Noble Sissle and Eubie Blake, whose 1921 musical *Shuffle Along* had only recently lit the spark of the Jazz Age. Cochran co-billed Sissle and Blake with Parsons and Thayer as the revue's lead songwriters.[96] The *Shuffle Along* team, whom Cochran had recently presented to resounding success at the London Coliseum, contributed "Wedding Day" and "Tahiti" to the revue's score.[97] Bradford and Hamilton followed Cortez and Peggy, Greta Fayne, and Vera Nemtchinova and Nicolas Efimoff as the final of four dance specialty acts during "Wedding Day," introduced as a romantic duet between Elizabeth Hines and Basil Howes. "Wedding Day" appeared during a lengthy "At the Seaside" sequence that included various beach-themed numbers: in Tahiti, at Southend-on-Sea, and finally at Deauville.[98]

In addition to its racially integrated composing team, *Cochran's Revue of 1926* featured a royal flush of British, continental European, and American talent. As Baddeley recalled, "Cochran had a new gimmick—three leading ladies each from a different country," with Hines hailing from the United States, Baddeley from the United Kingdom, and Andrée Spinelly from France.[99] Former Ballets Russes star Léonide Massine choreographed the revue's three ballets, including "The Tub: A Florentine Ballet," set to music by Haydn. The revue's design team included Oliver Messel, Doris Zinkeisen, and French painter André Derain (for Massine's "Gigue" ballet).

Despite opening at the London Pavilion on April 29, 1926, during a tumultuous period of British labor history, *Cochran's Revue of 1926* quickly gained box office momentum. As Vivyan Ellacott describes, "When [the revue] came to London it was initially caught up in the problems of the National Strike, and because no newspapers were published for the first two weeks, business was somewhat patchy."[100] Yet, by May, *Variety*'s London correspondent hailed it as "the most artistic spectacle ever shown here."[101] Will Rogers further boosted sales by joining the cast in July 1926. Although Rogers's comic monologues replaced "I'm Crazy 'bout the Charleston," Ropes later recalled performing with the legendary Cherokee American *Follies* wit as a highlight of his time in London.[102]

As featured dancers in the show, Bradford and Hamilton danced "to big plaudits."[103] The great English critic James Agate additionally singled out "the altogether amazing ballroom accomplishment of Mr. Billy Bradford" within a show about which he raved: "In plain English three-fourths of this glittering revue is pure gold."[104] While the American dancer high-kicked to acclaim on the stage of the London Pavilion, he may have been tempted to socially step out with *Cochran's Revue*'s gay stars, Douglas Byng and Ernest Thesiger.

The London Pansy Craze and the "High Priest of Camp"— and an Interlude in Greenwich Village

"The homosexuals of the 1920s came out of the closet and into the drawing room. . . . They did not—or very few of them did—'come out,'" observed Noel Annan of gay life in interwar London.[105] When Billy Bradford arrived in England in late 1925, the illegal status of homosexuality necessitated meticulous social discretion. Yet, legal persecution did not prevent a vibrant gay underground from springing up, as fostered by the culture of the Bright Young Things. Of this fabled London coterie of hedonistic sophisticates, many, including Coward, expressed their homosexuality or bisexuality among themselves, while veiling their same-sex love affairs from the public.

Byng, later nicknamed the "High Priest of Camp," illuminated the London expanse of the Pansy Craze, in which New York's "gay performers moved from the margins of the city into its most prestigious entertainment district and briefly became the darlings of Broadway" in the late 1920s and early '30s.[106] A similar phenomenon swept London's West End, where Byng reigned as the queen of English cabaret with what Coward described as "the most refined vulgarity in London."[107] With Lance Lister, also a costar in *Cochran's Revue of 1926*, Byng popularized the gay innuendoes of "The Cabaret Boys," which the team recorded in 1928.[108] Signed on by Cochran in 1925, Byng "remained with Cochran for five years, playing [over one hundred parts] in *Still Dancing, Cochran's 1926 Revue, One Damn Thing After Another, This Year of Grace, Wake Up and Dream* and *Cochran's 1930 Revue*," as Newley observes.[109]

Cochran frequently paired Byng with Thesiger, who later became known as an "outrageously campy character actor" in British horror films.[110] In 1925's

Douglas Byng and Hermione Baddeley in the "Botany Babes" number from
Cochran's Revue of 1926.
Reprinted by permission of Mary Evans Picture Library. Originally published in
Eve Magazine, May 5, 1926.

On with the Dance, the Pavilion revue that preceded *Cochran's Revue of 1926*,
Byng and Thesiger appeared together in drag in a sketch written by Noël Coward. In "Oranges and Lemons," "Dougie and the eccentric, cavernous-faced
Ernest Thesiger appeared as elderly spinsters preparing for bed in a Blooms-
bury boarding house. Dougie played Grace who is 'rather set for maturity' and
dressed in slightly matronly clothes. Thesiger, was Violet, the same age but
skittishly dressed in a fringed tea-gown."[111] In *Cochran's Revue of 1926*, the performers reprised these personae. While Thesiger played an effete, parasol-toting
"Bather" in the "Roman Baths at Deauville" sketch, Byng appeared as "Gert"
opposite Baddeley's "Tilly" in the Cockney flower-girl sketch, "Botany Babes."[112]

While Bradford Ropes had appeared in support of Alyn Mann in American vaudeville, his work alongside openly gay and bisexual performers like
Byng and Thesiger opened Billy Bradford's eyes to the sophisticated, camp

London culture of the Bright Young Things. The experience in *Cochran's Revue* might also have made the twenty-one-year-old dancer more receptive to the gay culture of Greenwich Village, where a 1932 article in the *Oakland Tribune* attributed him performing after his time in London: "Between engagements in London and Paris, he appeared in Barney Gallant's in Greenwich Village and other local night clubs."[113] If Billy Bradford did indeed appear briefly at the club of Barney Gallant, the most likely date is September 1926, as he took a break in New York before returning to Europe.

If Billy Bradford felt pressure to conceal his Silver Slipper gig from his Prohibition-supporting mother, he would have felt doubly compelled to do so about Gallant, who was the first New Yorker arrested in violation of the 1919 Volstead Act after he sold alcohol at his Greenwich Village Inn. The arrest and Gallant's thirty-day imprisonment in the Tombs made the nightclub impresario "an immediate celebrity."[114] Ropes's performances in elite London nightclubs such as Ciro's might have brought him to the attention of Gallant, who operated three increasingly luxe, celebrity-filled cabarets in Greenwich Village. Although cabaret-goers associated the second Club Gallant, opened in 1924 at 85 West 3rd Street, with sophisticated sketch comedy, Billy Bradford may have performed as a dancer there. As Stanley Walker describes Club Gallant: "[Barney] built a stage, with boxes for the patrons, and he himself was a master of ceremonies. His program consisted of sketches, good vaudeville skits, and he depended strongly upon an atmosphere of intimacy."[115] Moving away from his vaudevillian origins, where he had high-kicked in *A Whirl of Dance*, Billy Bradford at the swank Club Gallant in 1926 marked a continued ascent into show business realms associated with "class."

Having appeared, either with Hamilton or solo, at a cluster of exclusive cabarets in London and Greenwich Village, Billy Bradford next found himself booked with Hamilton in not only Paris but *Paris*. An extravagant music hall revue at the Casino de Paris, *Paris* featured Maurice Chevalier in the midst of his early stardom. From Paris, Bradford and Hamilton moved on to cabaret performances in the French Riviera, which, along with Paris's music halls, inspired some of the most vivid episodes of Ropes's backstage trilogy.

"On the Steps of the Dance": Bradford and Hamilton in Paris and *Paris*

Moving on from London, Bradford and Hamilton danced in *Paris* during the heyday of the music hall revue, at the height of "*les années folles*." Most famously associated with the Folies Bergère and the Casino de Paris, Parisian music halls of the 1920s offered lavish scenic spectacle, the Art Deco designs of artists like Erté, topless showgirls, and stars like the leggy and be-plumed Mistinguett. During the *"tumulte noir"* ushered in by Josephine Baker's sensational October 1925 debut in the *Revue Nègre* at the Théâtre des Champs-Élysées, Paris's music halls and cabarets also welcomed an array of expatriate African American artists. *Cochran's Revue* had exuded a camp cosmopolitanism subject to the scruples of the Lord Chamberlain. By contrast, appearing in *Paris*, surrounded by feathered *nues*, Ropes experienced the most dramatic contrast yet with his upbringing in Proper Boston.

The team's appearance in *Paris* came about as something of serendipity. According to *Billboard*, "It looked for a time as tho [sic] America was to have no part in this revue, but at the last moment the dance team of Billy Bradford and Marion Hamilton were put in to substitute for the jazz pianists, [Jean] Wiéner and [Clément] Doucet, who were unable to appear. The Yankee dancers filled the gap and became permanent members of the cast."[116] After Billy Bradford's likely September 1926 interlude at Club Gallant, he joined up again with Hamilton in Europe sometime between October and November 1926. From December of that year through March 1927, the dance team performed in *Paris* at the Casino de Paris alongside Chevalier and his partner, Yvonne Vallée. During the run, Bradford and Hamilton built upon their London nightclub experience to dance together at a multitude of Parisian nightclubs, including the Florida Club, L'Ermitage in the Champs-Élysées, and the Théâtre Apollo on the Rue de Clichy.[117]

As a "revue in 2 acts and 45 tableaux," *Paris* offered an extravaganza intended to humble *The Ziegfeld Follies*. Featuring the "16 Lawrence Tiller Girls," as well as "The Hundred Most Beautiful Women in Paris," the production dazzled its mix of French and expatriate audiences with "400 Artists and 2,800 Costumes."[118] As written by Albert Willemetz, Saint-Granier, and Jean Le Seyeux, *Paris* demonstrated the scenic largesse of producer Léon Volterra. With "On the Steps of the Dance," "Léon the Magnificent" gave *Paris* a stunning finale, which showed "the whole scene lifting and transforming into the gigantic staircase of a trendy dance hall."[119] If London's Cochran drew audiences by tempering lavish spectacle with sophisticated wit, Volterra offered untrammeled opulence at the Casino de Paris, where he poured "on his artistic tableaux silk, feather, gold, and silver with a prodigality unknown to this day."[120]

Filled with versatile performers, the revue also contributed to the rising stardom of Chevalier. *Le Journal Amusante* observed of the boulevardier: "Chevalier is the gaiety of the evening; his verve . . . has worked wonders in skits and songs in which Miss [Yvonne] Vallée was more than a useful partner to him."[121] Alongside the couple, *Paris* showcased the Rowe Sisters, the Turkish-born comedian Alfred Pasquali, and the team of Edmonde Guy and Ernest Van Duren, known for their erotically charged dance duets. Later in the run, the show featured Yvonne Bacon: soon to be known as fan-dancing burlesque queen Faith Bacon. While Chevalier and Vallée dominated the reviews, "Monsieur Bradford and Miss Hamilton" earned a striking abundance of praise, with Parisian critics celebrating the pair as "dancers of prestigious daring, lightness, and elegance."[122]

Aside from its performances, *Paris* exemplified the French music hall's tradition of artful scenic tableaux, which *La Presse* praised for its "thousand shimmers of a rare and striking delicacy." *Paris Plaisirs* lauded the "sumptuous tableau" of "The Coral Reef," in which "the sea rises, rises, and discovers the white corals, the pink corals, purple corals, red corals," all represented by chorus girls.[123] Both "Invitation to the Voyage," described as a "dazzling walk through Morocco," and "The Coral Reef" blended scenic spectacle with Orientalist tropes and racial stereotypes.[124] In the latter number, an ensemble of "Casino Colored Boys" appeared as "the Blacks," while the North African-born exotic dancer Dahama impersonated "the Slave."[125]

If *Paris* conjured fantastical escapism through the colonialist gaze in tableaux like "The Coral Reef," the revue also pulsed to modernist visual aesthetics. *Paris* featured Cubist-inspired stage designs that glorified technology and machinery. *Paris Plaisirs* observed: "The authors have succumbed to the modern style . . . with a rare Happiness." The magazine noted one comic sketch, "Le Kouri-Kouri," as offering "picturesque Cubist costumes [that] put the public in gaiety."[126] Another Surrealist-tinged number, "The Symphony in Mauve," offered personifications of "Chromatic Fauna," "Synthetic Wisdom," and "Impromptu Ecstasy."[127]

At the same time, the revue's modernist design merged with an objectification of the female form steeped in the Paris music hall's tradition of stacking its showgirl *nues* into "living curtains" and arranging them into "living chandeliers." In *Paris*, this took the Machine Age form of costuming showgirls as the parts of a giant car in the show's prologue. According to *La Presse*, Volterra "begins with a lively and cheerful prologue, which stages the passions of motoring and introduces us to all the parts and accessories of a fashionable car."[128] *Paris Plaisirs* elaborated about the role of *Paris*'s dancers in the prologue, which "takes place under a monstrous car whose chassis serves as a roof for the stage; under this frame we have . . . a jack (Mlle. Zazani) which we

Two views of the "Prologue" in *Paris*, from *Paris Plaisirs*, 1926. Reproduced by permission of Bibliothèque nationale de France.

would no longer want to pass; headlights with luminous eyes (Mlles. Whiard, Chibaeff) . . . wheels so agile and so well-inflated . . . these are the Lawrence Tiller girls!"[129]

In his backstage trilogy, Ropes critically commented upon the standardized feminine spectacle of the Parisian music hall. Ropes also satirized how Broadway producers, particularly the Shubert Brothers (fictionalized as "the Wilsons"), skating on the edge of plagiarism, imported "sketches of old Montmartre and little ditties about Apache lovers" into extravagant Winter Garden Theatre revues like *The Passing Show* and *Artists and Models*.[130] In *Go Into Your Dance*, Ted hopes to beat the Wilsons to Paris as the first to view the new music hall spectacles. He informs Nora:

"The Wilsons have been importin' scenes for years from the Casino dee Paris and the Folies Bergère. Didn't you ever wonder why those shows at the Summer Garden are always featurin' little numbers like 'A Side Street in Old Montmartre'—'The Days of Marie Antoinette' and 'The French Revolution'? . . . Why, I learned more about French history at the Summer Garden than I did in High School."[131]

In *Go Into Your Dance*, Ropes also draws upon experience with Hamilton performing at the Perroquet, the Casino de Paris's upstairs cabaret famed for the "boudoir dolls" distributed to customers. He peers back at "the Parrot" with both vivid detail and critical distance, depicting the cabaret as a racially mixed mecca of sophistication but also as a realm of eye-popping levels of consumerist excess and transactional sexuality. In the novel, Ted follows the invitation of Gregory, a Yankee businessman abroad, to join him and his friends upstairs. Ropes describes how "the gaily colored Perroquet looked down upon the scene with a sardonic leer":

> A waiter, his arms laden with dolls, was passing from table to table, presenting a gift to each lady with a servile bow. Ted saw him pause in front of the table occupied by the Crown Prince of a Balkan kingdom and three garish ladies from a popular music hall. . . . Three Italian gentlemen were accompanying a slight, vivid Negress who seemed scarcely more than a child. Diamonds gleamed against the ebony of her flesh. . . . "They sure got the grade A customers here," Ted murmured. "I never saw so much Tiffany ice in my life."[132]

In *Paris*, Bradford and Hamilton had also appeared with members of the internationally famous Tiller Girls, a former member of whom had been Ropes's dance instructor in Quincy. Trained by the British John Tiller, and later his son Lawrence, the dance troupe appeared in revues on Broadway and in London, Paris, and Berlin. Appearing as car parts in *Paris* and in other numbers in the show, the Tiller Girls received considerable space in reviews of *Paris*. *Paris-Midi* observed of the troupe, later the inspiration for the Rockettes: "The 16 Lawrence Tiller Girls are just one body and thirty legs (I was right, the count is there) and their success was huge."[133] Ropes likely recalled the Tiller Girls car number when Marian Hamilton, in 1927, abandoned her stage career for marriage to the son of a Philadelphia automobile manufacturer.

In *Go Into Your Dance*, Nora cynically muses that the Casino de Paris, for all its color and modernism as a Parisian variety show, rejects the forces of progress: "Ten years from now Mistinguette [sic] will still be kicking above her head and the Tiller girls will form a line and imitate a train—whistle and all."[134] Yet, *Paris* left a substantial impression on Ropes as a writer. His interlude performing in France, as half of Bradford and Hamilton, informed his backstage trilogy in other ways as he and his dance partner moved on to Cannes.

"Frightfully Ostentatious, but There's Real Beauty, Too": Bradford and Hamilton in the French Riviera

If Ropes characterized the Casino de Paris's doll-strewn Perroquet as a cabaret marked by striking displays of opulence, he applied the same descriptions to much of the French Riviera's nightlife in his backstage trilogy. A 1927 *Billboard* profile, which touted Bradford and Hamilton's upcoming Broadway debut in the revue *A La Carte*, even reported the team had played before crowned heads in Europe: "They did royal command performances for the King and Queen of the Belgians, the King and Queen of Spain, and the King of Denmark. They danced before the Prince of Wales, Prince Arthur of Connaught and other royal celebrities."[135]

In performing before European royalty, Bradford and Hamilton had ample opportunity in Cannes, a pleasure resort for aristocrats as well as expat American celebrities like F. Scott and Zelda Fitzgerald. They also might have done so during their date in St. Moritz, Switzerland, where they performed at the Palace Hotel before moving on to the Riviera.[136] In *Stage Mother*, Ropes satirically contrasted the aspirational ideals of Manhattan's elite, gathering at the Mayfair Club, with the social whirl of the French Mediterranean and Swiss Alps: "If the gathering lacked the true sophistication which one might find at Juan-les-Pins or St. Moritz, it was nevertheless a definite place to see if one were socially inclined."[137]

Bradford and Hamilton's April 1927 booking at the Restaurant des Ambassadeurs casino in Cannes, with Billy Arnold's Novelty Jazz Band, followed earlier nightclub appearances in Paris, where they had danced at L'Ermitage and the Théâtre Apollo during their run in *Paris*. At the Apollo, Bradford and Hamilton appeared in the dance revue *Black-Bottom Follies*. Although touted for its "fairy-tale setting" within an opulent cabaret restaurant that suggested the "third act of *The Merry Widow*," French critics greeted the show as an "essentially American spectacle."[138] Advertisements granted Bradford and Hamilton top billing alongside the acclaimed, expatriate African American bandleader and pianist Sam Wooding, who had arrived in France in 1925 with the European tour of *Chocolate Kiddies*.[139] The show's program credited "dances arranged by B. Bradford."[140]

According to *La Presse*'s Legrand-Chabrier, Bradford and Hamilton merged a "skillful, humorous version" of the Black Bottom with "our French can-can" at the Théâtre Apollo. Chabrier compared Marian Hamilton to La Goulue, and Billy Bradford to one of the fin de siècle's few male can-can artists: "There is Valentin le Désossé [Valentin the Boneless] in this young dancer who sends his leg to touch the tip of his ear as if the joint were positively rotating."[141] Now booked at Les Ambassadeurs in *The Riviera Follies*, Bradford and Hamilton played upon their marketing as "the incontestable masters of the Black Bottom, recently arrived from America," as *Le Matin* dubiously touted their 1926 run at L'Ermitage.[142]

While Ropes devoted considerable discussion to themes of cultural appropriation in his backstage trilogy, his French Riviera performance experience also fueled his fiction. After Shirley's liaison with Mayor Al Dexter seeps into the tabloids in *Stage Mother*, she and Kitty seek refuge amid the pleasure and gambling resorts of the Riviera. These attracted revue stars like the Hungarian-born Dolly Sisters, as well as crowned heads and industrialists. Ropes details Shirley's initial excitement to perform at a string of Riviera nightclubs, as she informs Lord Geoffrey Aylesworth: "We have the Ambassadeurs at Cannes, the Negresco at Nice, and Ciro's in Monte Carlo. I'm really thrilled!"[143]

Ropes's depiction of the French Riviera reflects Aylesworth's own ambivalent commendation to Shirley: "You'll adore Cannes. . . . Frightfully ostentatious but there's real beauty, too. I envy you those Mediterranean nights."[144] In one sequence in *Stage Mother*, Ropes vividly evokes his memories of Les Ambassadeurs. He specifically incorporates a description of Billy Arnold's Novelty Jazz Band, a group of white musicians, "playing the insinuating measures of the newly imported fox trot that had taken the Riviera by storm." Ropes depicts Les Ambassadeurs, with its famous "hydraulic dancing floor," as a realm in which capitalist prosperity floated an illusion of democracy, as "kings and commoners rubbed elbows in four-four time."[145] Yet, Ropes also suggests in *Stage Mother* that Bradford and Hamilton may have had to work harder to distract their spectators from their bejeweled elbow rubbing. As Aylesworth acerbically describes Riviera audiences to Shirley: "They so emphatically refuse to be amused. Nothing thrills them, nothing pleases them. They are the world's foremost sophisticates, and they cling tenaciously to the honor."[146]

If the "frightful ostentation" of the Continent's café society left Ropes with a sense of disenchantment, he did not forget the "real beauty" of his own Mediterranean nights. If his experiences in both Paris and Cannes later furnished Ropes with fertile source material for his satiric treatment of class distinction within American show business, they also allowed Billy Bradford to market his newfound European sophistication back in the United States, as the now twenty-two-year-old dancer and Marian Hamilton returned to New York in March 1927.

From the "rainbow world" of his performances on the Continent, Billy Bradford had expanded his experiences of show business from laborious trouping to luxurious Saint-Tropez.[147] He had performed in the same cast as the "High Priest of Camp" and exposed his Puritan-bred gaze to the breasts of Casino de Paris showgirls. In London and Paris, Ropes had also observed an array of African American expatriate performers as they achieved a level of social and economic agency denied to them even within the contexts of the Harlem Renaissance and the rise of the "New Negro." When he arrived back in the United States, Ropes brought with him new perspectives about the treatment of Black performers in the 1920s.

Billy Bradford and the Harlem Renaissance at Home and Abroad

Ropes's extensive writing on race and performance in his backstage trilogy suggests that he was far from oblivious to the fact that Bradford and Hamilton had been deeply embedded in practices of cultural appropriation. Introducing "I'm Crazy 'bout the Charleston" in *Cochran's Revue of 1926* and billed for their L'Ermitage appearance as "incontestable masters" of the Black Bottom, the team ranked among the many white artists who performed and choreographed numbers inspired by the innovations of the Harlem Renaissance. Both the Charleston and the Black Bottom had originated in southern Black culture, before being popularized in New York, respectively, by African American dancer-choreographers Elida Webb and Billy Pierce. As "watered down" for ballrooms and Broadway, the dance featured a "genteel slapping on the backside, along with a few hops forward and back." Yet, the "original, black Black Bottom required the dancer to 'get down' in posture and attitude, [and] rotate the hips and articulate them in movements known as the Mooch and Mess Around," as described by Brenda Dixon Gottschild.[148]

In his explorations of cultural appropriation in his novels, Ropes also evoked the career of hoofer-turned-impresario George White, on whom he based the character of Ted Howard in *Go Into Your Dance*.[149] Starting with *Runnin' Wild*, the 1923 sequel to *Shuffle Along*, White exploitatively imported the creations of Black artists into his productions. As choreographed by Webb, the "Charleston" debuted on Broadway in *Runnin' Wild*. Placing the sensationally popular dance in the *Scandals of 1925*, White also took credit the next year for the creation of the Black Bottom, danced by Ann Pennington and Tom Patricola.[150] In 1926, composer Will Marion Cook penned a strongly worded letter to the *New York Times*: "It is doubtful if Mr. White even saw a 'Charleston' until he attended the final rehearsals of *Runnin' Wild*. Messrs. White et al are great men and great producers. Why, with their immense flocks of dramatic and musical sheep, should they wish to reach out and grab our little ewe lamb of originality?"[151]

When Billy Bradford started in vaudeville in 1923, *Shuffle Along*'s meteoric Broadway success had already launched an era in which many white theater artists, including Eugene O'Neill and George Gershwin, drew extensively from African American culture. Langston Hughes observed of the contradictions of the era's "Negro Vogue": "It was a period when almost any Harlem Negro of any social importance at all would be likely to say casually: . . . 'As I said to George—,' referring to George Gershwin. . . . It was a period when white writers wrote about Negroes more successfully (commercially speaking) than Negroes did about themselves. It was the period (God help us!) when Ethel Barrymore appeared in blackface in *Scarlet Sister Mary!*"[152]

Hughes's anecdote illustrates the pernicious persistence of minstrelsy into the 1920s, despite African American artists' social and economic advancements. Like many of his peers, Billy Bradford interacted with blackface performers along segregated American vaudeville circuits, where African American performers confronted the "widespread practice of putting only one black act in a show."[153] In September 1923, the *Brooklyn Standard-Union* promoted Moran and Mack at Keith's Bushwick, where *A Whirl of Dance* shared the program. The paper announced: "George Moran and Charles Mack, 'Two Black Crows,' will be seen in their ludicrous burnt-cork comedy and lazy, shuffling steps."[154]

Yet, Billy Bradford danced on top of fault lines of cultural and racial contradictions. If *A Whirl of Dance* shared a bill with the white minstrels Moran and Mack, Mann and his troupe also followed the comic song-and-dance act of Rufus "Rah-Rah" Greenlee and Thaddeus "Ga-Ga" Drayton at the Palace Theatre during the first week of August 1923. Greenlee and Drayton "pioneered the 'class act' tap style, which combined grace and elegance with precision soft-shoe tap dancing." Eschewing the stereotypes of the American minstrel stage, Greenlee and Drayton "were among the few African Americans to play at the Palace Theater in New York on the vaudeville circuit during World War."[155] In the United States, Ropes observed Greenlee and Drayton navigating an era of increasing self-determination. Now in Europe, he danced to the songs of venerated touring and expatriate African American musicians, including Sissle and Blake.

Additionally, in December 1926, Billy Bradford shared a Parisian performance bill with a superstar trio of Black artists. At the annual banquet of the Anglo-American Press Association at Paris's Claridge Hotel, featuring a lineup of revue and cabaret performers, Bradford and Hamilton appeared in the same gala as the American-born "Queen of the Nightclubs" Ada "Bricktop" Smith, as teamed with the Grenadian British singer and pianist Leslie "Hutch" Hutchinson. Josephine Baker, holding "the attention of the assembly for forty consecutive minutes," headlined the gala, "adding to the belief already current that this American star is not only unique but indefatigable."[156] While Ropes incorporated multiple allusions to Baker in his novels, he suggested a more sustained acquaintance with Bricktop. In *Go Into Your Dance*, Ropes alludes to both the red-headed Black nightclub hostess and "Chez Florence" proprietress Florence Jones when he describes how Ted and girlfriend Eunice "went on rides in the Bois toward sundown, to tea in the shops along the Rue Royale, [and] made nocturnal visits to the haunts of Florence and Bricktop."[157]

In *Stage Mother*, Ropes depicts patronage at Bricktop's as a sign of cultural modernity and racial mixing. In the novel, Shirley expresses to Aylesworth her desire to return to Chez Bricktop, where patrons enjoyed the hostess-entertainer's sophisticated performances of songs by her great friend (and Hutch's lover) Cole Porter. By contrast, Ropes characterizes Shirley's mother as hampered by bigotry. Kitty had spent her youth in segregated American vaudeville, where Ropes depicts Kitty uttering ethnic slurs about the Japanese acrobats opening the bill.[158] When Aylesworth politely attempts to invite Kitty with them to Chez Bricktop during their stay in Paris, Shirley responds: "Don't be silly. She hates Bricktop's."[159]

Along with exploration of Black artists and modernism, themes of appropriation and cultural transfer between Black artists and white imitators pervade the novels of Ropes, who shows white hoofers benefiting from the labor of Black performers. In *Stage Mother*, the teenage Shirley learns her craft as a tap dancer from a Black instructor. Ropes writes: "When the ballet instruction was over, she packed her clothes into a satchel and walked four blocks north to the studio where a grinning Negro presided over classes in buck and wing and tap dancing. She was not so adept at that style of work; her body, accustomed to the mannerisms of formal ballet, did not respond easily to this less stylized art, but she managed well enough."[160]

In both *42nd Street* and *Go Into Your Dance*, Ropes conjures the staggering influence of Bill "Bojangles" Robinson, already legendary for his staircase routines, on white tap dancers of the 1920s, including Fred Astaire. In *42nd Street*, Terry defends his choice to not "flash much o' my stuff around the theatre." He explains to Peggy how many dancers have "copped" routines from Robinson: "Boy, you work years gettin' a good routine an' then everybody uses it. Look at Bill Robinson. He done more to help the staircase business than all the house building booms combined."[161] Similarly, in *Go Into Your Dance*, young Ted asserts: "I want to go to dancin' school. I'd like to get some o' these guys like Bill Robinson to teach me a knockout routine."[162]

Ropes's critical focus upon cultural appropriation in dance extends to his fictionalization of George White in *Go Into Your Dance*. Here, Ted and Eunice attend a late 1920s revue at the Casino de Paris, where Ted is dazzled by the performance of Josephine Baker, whom he hopes to bring to Broadway.[163] Using racial slurs and stereotypes, Ted confesses his plans to Eunice, as Ropes alludes to Baker's 1925 Paris breakout in the *Revue Nègre*:

> "I'd like to import that dinge girl. She'd sure knock 'em for a row on Broadway. . . . I'd build a great Harlem number around her. She's primitive, that gal, they're keeping her under wraps here. I'd like to've seen her a coupla years ago when they let her wiggle that cute little fanny of hers wearin' nothin' but a string of bananas and a 'G' string."[164]

Back in New York, after the disastrous "Living Trellis of Girls" production number injures his performers, Ted decides to interpolate a "Harlem number" into his new *Town Talk*. Here, Ropes alludes to White's own appropriation in the *Scandals* and *Runnin' Wild*, as Ted informs Nora of the trellis sequence: "I fixed up a hot Harlem number in its place."[165]

While White did not publicize his Austrian Jewish heritage, Ropes's backstage trilogy also provides insights into the thorny issues of collaboration, cultural synthesis, and theft that marked the relationship between African American and Jewish artists in the 1920s. David Savran details how the ethos of "jazz cosmopolitism" negotiated a complex cultural relationship between Black artists and Jews. Savran observes, "During the 1920s, Jewish musicians and vaudeville entertainers . . . were constructed less as thieves than as the primary intermediaries and popularizers of a musical vernacular that indisputably began as an African American form but of which, for biological and cultural reasons (it was reasoned), Jews have a deeper understanding than any other ethnic group."[166] On the other hand, Jews participated with other white Americans in what Savran describes as "a sublimation of minstrelsy, a radical rechanneling and elevation of blackface performance."

The cultural relationship between Black and Jewish artists in the Jazz Age played out strikingly in the work of Gershwin. As Savran observes, "Gershwin especially, 'more than any other composer (or critic or historian) of his time, constantly sought out black musicians and listened to the widest possible range of black music."[167] Gershwin believed that "the American soul . . . is a combination that includes the wail, the whine and the exultant note of the old mam(m)y songs of the South. It is black and white. It is all colors and all souls united in the great melting-pot of the world."[168]

Ropes incorporates the figure of Gershwin, directly and through roman à clef narrative strategies, into *42nd Street* and *Go Into Your Dance*. In *42nd Street*, Ropes incorporates the music of Gershwin directly to comment upon the cross-fertilization between Jewish and African American musicians. At the Greenwich Village party attended by Peggy and Pat, the two view an impromptu recital by a "small, dark-eyed Jewess" named Gertrude. Ropes embeds his description of Gertrude's playing with racial signifiers that suggest Gertrude's synthesis of Black blues and spirituals and Eastern European Jewish klezmer into her own "jazz cosmopolitanism." Gertrude's playing of "some old Polish tune pregnant with sorrow and death" transforms into Gershwin's *Rhapsody in Blue*, even as Ropes depicts the pianist's evocation of "no melody, no form, just savagery ground out by white hands." Ropes describes the powerful effect the music has on its audience:

> Gertrude sat down and presently a strange jargon of notes began to weave their tortured spell. . . . At last, like a paean of modernity the beauty of Gershwin's *Rhapsody* crashed through the room and the concert was over. They applauded wildly and demanded more, but Gertrude explained that her hands were numb. Pat could well believe it; the wonder was that such power could dwell in the slight frame of the little Jewess.[169]

Here, Ropes links Gertrude's Black and Jewish influences as a pianist with Andy Lee's emulations of Harlem Renaissance dance. During rehearsals of *Pretty Lady*, Peggy watches Andy instruct the chorus in the number "Manhattan Madness." Ropes conveys Peggy's thoughts as she gazes at Andy, finding his "artistry no less thrilling than Gertrude's music. It was an outpouring which found its medium in Gertrude's fingers and in Andy Lee's feet. The slouch, the gaucherie of the Negro were introduced to perfection."[170] Ropes describes how the innovations of Harlem dancers have elevated Andy along a show business hierarchy: from "unsavory East Side streets" to vaudeville stages and, finally, to prestige in Broadway musical comedy:

> "Watch me," Andy Lee commanded. Hat pushed far over his eyes, he simulated the slow writhing dance of the Harlem negro. The middle part of his body gyrated with effortless ease, first one foot shuffling back, then the other. His audience was entranced. In the turmoil of rehearsal they had lost sight of the fact that Andy Lee was probably the greatest dancer the Ghetto had produced.

Ropes depicts the *Pretty Lady* ensemble's realization that Andy had "danced until the art became his God, and, like a bountiful God, it was now repaying him."[171]

In his backstage trilogy, Ropes expresses contradictory attitudes toward themes of cultural appropriation. Celebrating Andy's choreographic apotheosis from New York's mean streets, Ropes does not explore the significant disparities between Black and white dancers and performers in terms of the "payment" afforded by their art. Ropes perpetuates the mainstream white attitude, in the 1920s and 1930s, that Black art provided fertile "raw material" for Jewish American artists like Gertrude and Andy to export and reinterpret.[172] Ropes also draws upon stereotypes of African American dance as "gauche" and "primitive" rather than meticulously studied and crafted.

At the same time, Ropes points out dissonances and contradictions between the rampant appropriation practiced by white artists and their demeaning treatment of African Americans. In *42nd Street*, for example, Ropes contrasts Terry's casual racism with the chorus boy's respect for Bill Robinson as a dance innovator. After trading shoptalk pleasantries with George, the affable elevator man and "recipient of confidences from the majority of guests" at the Hotel Columbia, Terry issues a racial slur under his breath. "Pretty good guy for a monkey chaser," he remarks to his friend Harry.[173]

Ropes's allusions to American slavery, in connection with the often grueling labor conditions of show business, also stand out in his backstage novels.

In 1850s New England, Ropes's grandfather David Nichols Ropes had offered his home in Portland, Maine, as a "hiding-place" on the Underground Railroad.[174] His grandson was also attuned to discourses and iconographic images of slavery. Yet, Ropes divorced them from the realities of systemic racism. Dorothy complains to Andy in *42nd Street*, "You're the most conscientious slave driver I've ever met."[175] Using a third-person omniscient voice that carries *42nd Street*'s narrative weight, while weaving in and out of individual character psychology, Ropes observes the labor of chorus dancers, who spend "soul-racking day[s] of tapping feet and swinging arms." Ropes elaborates: "Someday the *Uncle Tom's Cabin* of the chorus girl will be written."[176]

Ropes's writing also conveys an awareness that the white performers can only wanly simulate the authenticity of Black performance styles. When Shirley studies dance with her Black studio dance instructor in *Stage Mother*, Ropes specifies that Shirley's "soft shoe dance lacked authority," even if "it was nonetheless a praiseworthy simulation" of her teacher's steps.[177] In the same novel, at a party at the Park Avenue Plaza, an orchestra blasts out "the latest Harlem fox trot and drunken couples tottered over the floor in a none too successful emulation of the Lenox Avenue dance."[178]

To Ropes, the innovations of the Black performers and artists of the Harlem Renaissance represent a "paean to modernity" that he contrasts starkly with American Puritan culture. In *42nd Street*'s "Ticka Tacka Toe," Ropes opposes "red hot rhythm" to his upbringing: "You'll find a movement that's most entrancing / Something a Boston cop just couldn't call dancing."[179] As an improper Bostonian who had danced the Charleston and the Black Bottom across the cabaret stages of Europe, Ropes portrays Broadway dance and musical performance, as derived from Black artists, as vital expressions of cultural modernism. He represents this variously through the choreographic appropriations of Andy Lee, the musical synthesis of Gertrude's piano, and the interracial mixing at Chez Bricktop. When Billy Bradford returned to New York in August 1927, he performed once again in the contexts of commercial American show business. This time, Bradford and Hamilton were bound for Broadway.

Bradford and Hamilton *A La Carte* on Broadway

Bradford and Hamilton's well-received partnership in Europe boosted their acclaim back in the United States, enabling the team to make their Broadway debut. Hamilton informed the *Brooklyn Standard-Union* that their command performance before King Albert and Queen Elisabeth of Belgium "made such a reputation that when she returned, she found many offers to go into shows in New York."[180] Newspapers also profiled Billy Bradford more regularly, a few mentioning him as the cousin of Malcolm E. Nichols, recently elected in November 1925 as Boston's mayor.

By now, Bradford and Hamilton's European experiences allowed them to be touted as a "class act," as the latter returned to the Broadway stage and the former made his debut. *Brooklyn Life and Activities of Long Island Society* reported on the team's appearance in George Kelly's 1927 revue *A La Carte*: "With his charming partner, Marian Hamilton, a Seattle, WA girl, he has been appearing for the past year in the smartest revues, night clubs and at the most exclusive watering places abroad."[181] In their elite social backgrounds and sardonic comic wits, Ropes may have found considerable common ground with the Irish American Kelly, the vaudeville sketch writer-turned-Pulitzer Prize-winning dramatist of *The Show-Off* (1924) and *Craig's Wife* (1925). Kelly's upbringing within a socially prominent, conservative Main Line family, the "Philadelphia Kellys," prompted him to conceal his longtime romantic relationship with his "valet/secretary/traveling companion" William E. Weagly.[182]

Featuring a book and sketches by Kelly, and "peopled for the most part by vaudevillians," *A La Carte* played August 17 through September 24, 1927, at the Martin Beck Theatre.[183] The show belonged to the genre of the sophisticated intimate revue, exemplified by *The Garrick Gaieties* rather than the spectacular revues of Ziegfeld and White. Along with "sartorial splendor" and comic sketches, producer Rosalie Stewart showcased dance. While Kelly staged the book scenes, Sam Rose choreographed such "elaborate ballets" as the first-act finale "The Fairy Doll," based on the "old idea of a toy shop where the playthings come to life after closing hours."

Although critics viewed *A La Carte* as an admirable misfire, Bradford and Hamilton attracted praise. Rowland Field praised an "excellent team of dancers in the persons of Billy Bradford and Marian Hamilton, [who perform] some amazing acrobatic gyrations a la Russe." *A La Carte's* choreography kept both dancers busy, with Billy Bradford appearing as a Neapolitan dancer in "Italy"; as "Baby Blue" performer and harlequin in "The Fairy Doll"; and as a "Kangaroo" performer and third caddy in "Daisies on the Green."[184]

After *A La Carte* closed in September 1927, Bradford and Hamilton returned to what Ropes later described as "the strange and hectic business of vaudeville."[185] Now, they used their Broadway cachet as billing, appearing as "Twin Stars in a Single Setting" in an act entitled "Dancers a la Carte."[186] Supported at the piano by Phil Sheppard, they performed in this act from October 1927 through August 1928 on a Keith-Albee route that included dates in Philadelphia and Chicago, where they "scored a big hit" at the New Palace Theatre.[187]

In his backstage trilogy, Bradford Ropes devoted considerable space to describing both the excitement and tedium of life on the road. In *Stage Mother*, describing Kitty's impressions as she tours with Shirley and the Thorne troupe, Ropes observes the 1920s as a period of increasingly palatial vaudeville theaters, swelling audiences, and a glamour that could sometimes overshadow exploitative working conditions within an oligarchic institution. Ropes narrates:

> The thrice familiar towns passed in rapid kaleidoscope: Syracuse, Rochester, Pittsburgh, Cleveland, Grand Rapids. . . . The great stone pile of the Palace Theatre in Cleveland reared its imposing stories before the amazed eyes of the local burghers. . . . Much has been written against the regime of Mr. Edward F. Albee, but it was the hey-day of his power that the vaudeville entertainer was first recognized as a human being.[188]

Equally, Ropes describes vaudeville trouping as bursts of excitement enclosed in long stretches of boredom. In *Go Into Your Dance*, Ropes describes how Ted, crossing the country by train with Ramon and Noretta, experiences the reduction of great cities to tired peeks through the window, between card games: "There was little space in his letters devoted to the industries from which these cities derived their being. A grain elevator was a drab-colored shaft set in the midst of some uninviting mid-Western landscape, a cotton field a far-reaching expanse of white to which his eyes strayed when she was tired of looking at the succession of kings, queens and aces which were dealt him from the pinochle deck."[189]

The respectability of Bradford and Hamilton's success on Broadway and in big-time vaudeville drew increasing admiration from his hometown. In June 1928, the *Golden Rod* profiled Ropes in one of their alumni notes: "Bradford Ropes, class of 1921, is well known in theatrical circles. . . . He was met in the South Station a few weeks ago by one of our teachers. He told her that he had just returned from a six weeks' engagement in a London theatre and was to perform at Keith's in Boston. After a week's engagement in Boston, he was to go to New York for an indefinite stay."[190] Back in New York, Bradford and Hamilton jumped back in the musical comedy pool, and in October 1928, the team opened in their most high-profile American pairing to date. They played featured roles and appeared as a dance specialty act in *Billie*: a new musical comedy by no less than "The Man Who Owns Broadway."

"Not a Libido in a Wagon Load": Bradford and Hamilton in Cohan's *Billie*

In 1917, twelve-year-old Bradford Ropes, in his World War I-era graduation show for the Wollaston School, had concluded *The Dream Child* with a flag-waving finale. The pageant had culminated in Fairy-Land with the title character's rescue "by 'Liberty,' in the name of the United States of America."[191] The jingoism of Ropes's finale could have found no more fitting embodiment than the Irish American, vaudeville-honed George M. Cohan. After transforming American musical theater at the turn of the twentieth century with his frenetic, dance-filled, patriotic musical comedies, such as *Little Johnny Jones*, Cohan had continued his career as a librettist, playwright, and producer.

After his time amid the cosmopolitan modernism of London, Paris, and the French Riviera, Billy Bradford might not have disagreed with reviewers who found *Billie* "quaint" if not puritanical. "Some of it has the stamp of 1910 upon it," observed Arthur Pollock in the *Brooklyn Eagle*.[192] Indeed, Cohan based *Billie*, for which he wrote the book, music, and lyrics, upon his 1912 comedy *Broadway Jones*, Yet, if Cohan no longer captured the pulse of the Jazz Age, dancing in a Cohan show would have been an opportunity all but impossible to turn down for an ambitious young dancer.

A moderate hit at Erlanger's Theatre, *Billie* belonged to the multitude of 1920s musical comedies that extolled the joint "liberties" of the American flag and Wall Street by setting loose a varied cast of characters on the estates and pleasure resorts of East Coast millionaires. In *42nd Street*, Ropes may have been satirizing *Billie*, as well as 1920s musical comedy more generally, when Andy Lee instructs his ensemble: "Y'see, the set is the garden of a Long Island home and you girls are on the verandah."[193] By contrast, *Billie*'s action straddled Jackson Jones's home in "Havenford, Connecticut" and the Jones Chewing Gum Plant, to which he is the heir.

Billie's dancing, primarily choreographed by Edward Royce, earned particular praise from critics. In the title role, *Billie* starred Polly Walker, the actress who had shared "feminine allure" with Hamilton in *Mr. Battling Butler*. The *New York Times* observed of *Billie*: "Principally it is an exhibition of dancing. With hardly an exception everybody in the cast dances at one time or another—even including the villain."[194] Once again, Bradford and Hamilton, playing characters named "Will" and "Marion," earned praise as "a youthful and clever dancing team."[195]

Yet, critics found *Billie*'s dancing the freshest element of a musical comedy by a theatrical institution struggling to keep up with 1920s youth culture. "The jazz babies will think it slow," Pollock quipped of *Billie*. The critic elaborated:

> *Billie* is jolly and gentlemanly and romantic, a story of pleasant, bright-eyed people with not a libido in a wagon load. . . . His heroine is a nice girl, too. . . . Not exactly a ginny heroine. Where has she been since Prohibition and the Padlock Law?[196]

The Wales Padlock Law, implemented in March of 1927, in fact clamped around Mae West's *Pleasure Man* at Broadway's Biltmore Theatre the very same night that *Billie* opened at Erlanger's Theatre. As authorized by Mayor James J. Walker, New York police raided *Pleasure Man* on October 1, 1928, arresting West and all fifty-six cast members, many of whom masqueraded in its second-act drag ball scene (West was eventually acquitted, in a legendary 1930 trial). The homophobic anxiety that greeted West's "gay plays" also pervades Pollock's review. Jibing at the absence of "fairy" chorus boys, a community highly visible within Ropes's backstage trilogy, Pollock cracked of *Billie*: "You may know how quaint and of yesteryear it is when I tell you that the chorus men act manly."[197]

By contrast with *Pleasure Man*'s single, interrupted performance at the Biltmore, *Billie* ran for a respectable 112 performances, playing through January 1929. Yet, during that run, Billy Bradford experienced the breakup of his professional partnership with Marian Hamilton. The dancer may have regarded marriage as more secure than even success on Broadway, in which women's careers were closely intertwined with the commercial imperatives of youth and beauty. Subtitling its article on the wedding "Marian Hamilton Wants a Full-Time Marriage to Rich Youth," the *Brooklyn Standard Union* quoted her: "I finally decided that if I had to choose between marriage and the stage, I'd give the stage the air. . . . Marriage, to me, is something that requires all the time a woman can give to it." The newspaper editorialized: "When the chance to dance in *Billie* finally came, Marian thought she was finally achieving her dreams. But Mr. Ludlum changed all that and now Marian is about to start on 'the biggest career of all.'"[198]

In November 1928, Evelyn Martin replaced Hamilton in *Billie*, after the latter married David S. Ludlum Jr. on October 30, 1928. The son of the former president of the Autocar Company of Ardmore, Pennsylvania, Ludlum worked in the publicity office of the company when he married Hamilton, whom he had met in 1924. In a newspaper photo, Hamilton looks beautiful in her wedding gown, veil, and bouquet, but also pensive—perhaps ambivalent about the prospect of leaving her stage career, despite her earlier comments to the *Standard Union*. In a piece entitled "Cupid Wins on Broadway," the same newspaper reported that "Miss Hamilton declares she will continue her dancing" after her marriage to Ludlum.[199] Yet, Hamilton does not appear to have returned to the stage, and 1940 census records show her living with Ludlum and a young daughter in Syracuse, New York.[200]

If Hamilton accrued no further professional stage credits, she left a considerable mark on Ropes's backstage fiction. Bradford and Hamilton had performed together in London, in Paris, in St. Moritz, in Cannes, on Broadway, and around the United States from 1925 through 1928. Inscribing *42nd Street* "To Mary," it's likely that the dedication paid tribute to Hamilton, who had, like Peggy Sawyer, started in the chorus and reached her Broadway dream, though not the upper echelons of stardom enshrined in the film and stage versions. Hamilton's influence can be read into the characters of both Peggy and Nora Wayne. The latter character's partnership with Ted Howard suggests a composite portrait of Bradford and Hamilton, as well as George White and the *Scandals* star Ann Pennington. Hamilton also informs Ropes's picture of Shirley in *Stage Mother*, where he alludes directly at one point to Ludlum's courtship of the stage beauty.[201]

The marriage of his dance partner may have thrown Billy Bradford for something of a loop. The dancer took some time off before returning as a solo act to vaudeville: a faltering institution as the "talkies" revolutionized the entertainment industry. At some point between the end of *Billie*'s run in January 1929 and his return to American vaudeville, Ropes returned briefly to Europe, perhaps to reconsider the direction of his career as Billy Bradford. On July 19, 1929, Ropes sailed from Cherbourg back to New York City.[202]

"But with Vaudeville in Such Lousy Shape": Billy Bradford's Third Time at the Palace

Returning to vaudeville, Billy Bradford performed on its stages from the end of 1929 to 1932, when he also contributed sketches for acts ranging from Rosetta

Duncan to aviatrix Marion Eddy.[203] At first, he clung to the remnants of the "big-time" during vaudeville's period of rapid decline. In *42nd Street*, Ropes depicted the era's professional threat to vaudevillians, as Danny remarks, "But with vaudeville in such lousy shape a guy's gotta do something. What the hell, it ain't a perfession now, it's a job."[204] Yet Billy Bradford had experienced his first success performing with Alyn Mann, with whom he now reunited for his third time performing at the Palace Theatre. As more brazen drag performers rose to prominence during the height of the Pansy Craze, Allen Mann now showcased his skill as a dancer. In an act called "Personalities" that played across the country, Bradford and Mann teamed up with ex-Ziegfeld Girl and dancer Dorothy Van Alst. The act consisted of "Mann doing tap dancing and Miss Van Alst and Bradford precision kicking while all three are said to take a turn at the piano and sing songs mostly of a humorous vein."[205] The trio also performed a selection of "dirty jokes."[206]

Bradford, Mann, and Van Alst played the Palace and RKO Circuit (as the Keith-Albee Circuit had been renamed) during a time of upheaval in the entertainment world and mergers among vaudeville circuits and motion picture companies. "Talent's getting pretty scarce, I guess. All the big names are goin' into picture houses," comments Danny in *42nd Street*.[207] As Snyder observes, "By 1928, there were only four theaters in the United States offering vaudeville without films. One of them was the Palace in New York."[208] When Bradford, Mann, and Van Alst played the Palace (now the RKO Palace) in October 1930, it was still a vaudeville house: a status it relinquished by November 1932 to show only motion pictures.

New York reviewers conferred mostly raves upon Bradford, Mann, and Van Alst in "Personalities." At Seattle's Orpheum Theatre, too, the trio's dancing was praised as "outstanding."[209] By contrast, the December 1930 issue of *Exhibitor's Herald* suggested that Billy Bradford, playing Detroit's Hollywood Theatre, now danced outside of his comfort zone, as no longer paired with Hamilton. Noting that "this particular audience does not care for ballroom stuff," the magazine reported: "Allen Mann, with Billy Bradford and Dorothy Van Alst, are the flash act, with Allen doing a dance which the reviewer believes would be hard to equal. Billy should stick to his piano, for as a dancer he is a total failure."[210]

Ironically, Ropes's depictions in *42nd Street* of the vaudeville era being rapidly eclipsed by Hollywood talkies inspired the 1933 film that regenerated the movie musical after several years of box office decline, as well as codified the genre of the backstage musical. As Billy Bradford arranged a risqué new trio with Mann and Van Alst during the twilight of the Keith-Albee Circuit, he likely paid close attention to events unfolding back in Boston and Quincy in the fall of 1929. In a controversy that may have fueled Ropes's later critiques on the suppression of free sexual expression, Malcolm E. Nichols presided over the banning of Eugene O'Neill's *Strange Interlude*.

"An Infinite Sojourn in the Age of Innocence": Eugene O'Neill and the Theatre Guild in the "Battle of Boston Morals"

In *42nd Street*, Ropes satirically summons both the Theatre Guild and the American playwright the Guild had raised to saint-like status after his earlier successes with the Provincetown Players. In an early scene of the novel, chorus girls Ann and Flo dine by the door of the British Tea Room, regaling Peggy with theatrical gossip as a cavalcade of show people walk in. Evoking the cultural hierarchies that Gilbert Seldes influentially catalogued as "highbrow" and "lowbrow" in 1924's *The Seven Lively Arts*, Ropes dramatizes the cliquishness dividing the show folks and the "legitimate" actors:

> At a table near the door an earnest young group of "Theatre Guilders" had gathered, their youthful faces puckered with the burden of carrying the weight of the theatrical world on their shoulders. These disdainful youngers were apart from the motley; the fancy that they were torch bearers to a newer and better regime intrigued them, and so one heard murmurs of Eugene O'Neill and St. John Ervine (with the "Sin Jen" precisely articulated) wafting from their nook.[211]

In *42nd Street*, Ropes humorously characterizes his fellow vaudevillians as "an easy-going band of performers who murder the King's English, talk shop from morning to night, and who are cheerfully ignorant of the fact that such men as Mencken, Freud, Kant and Pater exist. Eugene O'Neill they know because *Variety* tells them that his plays are invariably box office winners."[212] Flo and Ann associate O'Neill with the elite modernist literary drama produced by the Theatre Guild. By contrast, the vaudevillians know that, in O'Neill's plays, sex universally sells—and scandalizes.

Six years after Ropes first appeared with Alyn Mann in *A Whirl of Dance*, the banning of O'Neill's 1928 Freud-inspired, Pulitzer Prize-winning drama

Strange Interlude from Boston's Hollis Street Theatre marked one of the decade's most highly publicized theatrical controversies. Backed by a coalition of Catholic priests and Baptist ministers, Mayor Malcolm E. Nichols condemned *Strange Interlude* as glorifying "an indefensible standard of conduct and an abject code of morals."[213] In response, Ropes's hometown welcomed the production into Quincy's Capital Theatre in October 1929. As the Theatre Guild, the New York producers of *Strange Interlude*, defended the play, the case made headlines nationwide, as it fueled the decade's ongoing debates about theatrical free speech and censorship, as well as tightened the connection between Boston and cultural Puritanism in the national imagination.

A five-hour, nine-act epic, *Strange Interlude* broke formal and thematic ground as a "thunderous psychodrama" that explored such taboo themes as sexual promiscuity, abortion, atheism, and the Oedipus complex.[214] After opening at the John Golden Theatre on January 30, 1928, with Lynn Fontanne as Nina Leeds, *Strange Interlude* provoked both satire and awe. The play's stream of consciousness soliloquies inspired parodies, such as Groucho Marx's famous address in the 1930 musical comedy *Animal Crackers*: "Pardon me while I have a strange interlude." By contrast, Robert Benchley observed, "*Strange Interlude* is a highly important play, probably a great one, and one which is bound to make a turning-point of one sort or another in dramatic history."[215] The play earned O'Neill his third Pulitzer Prize for Drama, after those for *Beyond the Horizon* (1920) and *Anna Christie* (1922).

Strange Interlude's critical accolades in 1928 accompanied an international box office hit for the Theatre Guild. As Neil Miller details, "By the time it was scheduled to open in Boston, it had been seen by an estimated one-and-a-half million people across the country. It had played for eighteen months in New York—resulting in the greatest financial profit ever made by a Theatre Guild production—and in state theaters in Stockholm, Vienna and Budapest, with London and Berlin productions planned."[216]

Yet, *Strange Interlude* opened on Broadway against a context of increasing censorship in both New York and Boston. Enabling the raid of West's *Pleasure Man* on the same night that Cohan's *Billie* opened, the 1927 Wales Padlock Law gave New York City's licensing commissioner "the power to revoke a theatre's license for up to a year if an offending production were convicted of obscenity under prevailing city statutes." Broadway reached its most sensationally censorious peak in New York on February 9, 1927, when "in a sudden burst of activity . . . police squads descended on three productions": Édouard Bourdet's lesbian drama *The Captive*, William Dugan's *The Virgin Man*, and West's *Sex*.[217]

Pollock's review of *Billie*, with its lack of a "ginny heroine," spoke to the increasingly risqué nature of Broadway theater in the 1920s. From the opposing corner of Little Theatre Movement-inspired art theater, O'Neill joined forces with the Broadway commercialism of West in disregarding the objections of censors. The *Strange Interlude* controversy continued O'Neill's own history of escaping the wrath of New York's reformers, who had been inflamed by the "miscegenation" plot of 1924's *All God's Chillun Got Wings*, in which white leading lady Mary Blair kissed the hand of African American star Paul Robeson. Censors had also (unsuccessfully) dispatched a Play Jury committee, of reform-minded citizens, to the Broadway production of *Desire Under the Elms* in November 1924.[218]

Plays by West and O'Neill alike played into the disdain for Puritanism that marked Jazz Age intellectual culture and the culture of 1920s modernism. In a 1914 essay for the *Smart Set*, H. L. Mencken had satirically railed against cultural expressions of "Comstockery," as inspired by the New York Society for the Prevention of Vice founder Anthony Comstock. Whereas earlier American Puritanism had emphasized individual penitence, Mencken found the new version "not ascetic but militant. . . . Its supreme manifestation is the vice crusade, an armed pursuit of helpless outcasts by the whole military and naval forces of the Republic, a wild scramble into Heaven on the backs of harlots."[219] Despite the implementation of the Wales Padlock Law in New York theater, Mencken's disdain of "Comstockery" prevailed in Jazz Age Manhattan.

By contrast with New York's theatrical libertinism, the censorship of the New England Watch and Ward Society drew notoriety for more consequential Puritan severity. As Cleveland Amory notes, "In its founding year of 1878, the Watch and Ward Society had banned Walt Whitman's *Leaves of Grass*. Yet, its banner year was 1927, when Boston saw no less than sixty-eight volumes impaled," including works by H. G. Wells, Sinclair Lewis, Ernest Hemingway, and John Dos Passos.[220] As Miller observes of the Watch and Ward Society, in which Godrey Lowell Cabot served zealously as its longtime treasurer, it represented "almost a roll call of the Brahmin aristocracy" as dues-paying members.[221]

The infamy of the Watch and Ward Society spawned the phrase "Banned in Boston" as a national punchline. In an article on Nichols's *Strange Interlude* ban, the *Chattanooga Daily Times* connected the O'Neill and Theatre Guild controversy to the city's culture of banning modernist books: "Boston persists in making itself ridiculous before the country with its extreme measure of censorship of books and plays. . . . The authorities there ban books and plays that the rest of the country enjoys without harm."[222] The Watch and Ward Society, focused on books, largely avoided the theater. Yet its ethos contributed to formal theatrical censorship officially handled by Boston's mayor, the police superintendent, and the chief justice of the municipal court.

As the Republican mayor of Boston from 1926 to 1930, Nichols mixed his cultural conservatism with some economically liberal policies, as he expanded municipal services, increased city worker salaries, and established the Boston Port Authority.[223] A baseball lover, Nichols thwarted "Puritanical religious restriction" as he signed an 1929 ordinance allowing Sunday sports.[224] At the same time, Nichols upheld the cultural standards of the Watch and Ward Society, whose goals dovetailed with guardians of Irish Catholic moral conservatism. Nichols's denial of a theatrical license for *Strange Interlude*'s scheduled September 1929 production at the Hollis Street Theatre stemmed from the play's sexually charged themes of infidelity and abortion, as well as O'Neill's skeptical portrayal of Christianity. As Miller recounts of Nichols, "In this decision, he was aided by the city's unofficial censor, John M. (aka 'Little Rollo') Casey, a former drummer in burlesque pit bands and kettle-drummer for the Boston Symphony Orchestra. . . . His theatrical standards were summed up in his statement, 'Nothing should be placed upon the stage of any theatre anywhere to which you could not take your mother, sweetheart, wife or sister.'"[225]

Before the cancellation, the Theatre Guild had looked forward to *Strange Interlude*'s Boston production scoring another box office success. As Miller details, "The touring company was to begin its Boston production on September 30, 1929. The Theatre Guild had been advertising it since May and had sold 7,000 advance tickets. . . . On September 16, two weeks before its scheduled opening, city censor Casey, acting on orders from Mayor Nichols, informed the Hollis Theatre that *Strange Interlude* would not be permitted to be performed in Boston."[226]

Resolving to allow Nichols to amend O'Neill's script, the Theatre Guild then attempted to appeal Nichols and Casey's decision in what the *North Adams Transcript* called "the Guild's battle of *Strange Interlude* vs. Boston morals."[227] Yet, Nichols rejected the Theatre Guild's concessions in his letter to its directors Theresa Helburn and Lawrence Langner. Nichols wrote to both:

> Last Friday evening, you were good enough to send me the so-called stage version which is the printed book sparingly penciled. This stage version I have examined and could of course suggest deletions copious and without number, but none that would leave a play that in my official capacity I could defend.[228]

Helburn and Langner once again attempted, to no avail, to reach Nichols through the swaying of public opinion. Teaming with critic Walter Prichard Eaton, they "took to the radio to try to persuade the mayor to change his mind. Eaton, a member of the panel that had nominated O'Neill for the Pulitzer, organized a Citizens' Committee of approximately 300 who inundated the mayor with appeals to recant. The Guild's board of directors even retained counsel to prepare an appeal to the federal Court of Appeals challenging the mayor's constitutional right to suppress a play before it had been performed."[229]

With Nichols refusing to bend and court action ineffective, Thomas McGrath, the Republican mayor of Quincy, stepped in. McGrath sought an influx of funds to fuel commerce and industry into Quincy, now struggling in the weeks before the Wall Street Crash. Mayor McGrath welcomed *Strange Interlude* into Quincy's thirteen-hundred-seat Capitol Theatre at the end of September. To appease Quincy's ministers, he previewed the drama before an eighteen-member citizens' play jury. *Strange Interlude* not only passed the review on to the mayor's full approval but opened as a substantial commercial hit that economically revitalized Ropes's hometown.[230] As the Old Colony Railroad, connecting Quincy and Boston, added extra trains for the play's opening night, Bostonians flooded in to see the play, which received fourteen curtain calls.[231] *Billboard* opined that "everyone else gains and only Boston loses by its determination to sojourn infinitely in the 'Age of Innocence.'"[232]

The censorial objections toward *Strange Interlude* may have stemmed not only from O'Neill's portrayal of Nina Leeds's sexual promiscuity and her abortion. O'Neill also included implications of homosexuality in the character of Charles Marsden, a novelist whom O'Neill introduces as having "an indefinable feminine quality about him, but it is nothing apparent in either appearance or act."[233] Among his eight-point "Code of Morals" for theatrical productions (a list that also forbade such acts as "all forms of 'muscle dancing'"), Casey forbade "the portrayal of a moral pervert of sex degenerate, meaning a homosexual."[234]

By contrast with many writers, including Ropes, O'Neill eschewed a full embrace of gay culture despite his association with Greenwich Village in the 1920s. In *Strange Interlude*, O'Neill depicts Marsden, who cares for Nina in a possessive yet nonsexual sense, as "always having loved" Nina "in some queer way of his own."[235] While Nina's virile lover, the scientist Edmond Darrell, describes Marsden as "one of those poor devils who spend their lives trying not to discover which sex they belong to!," Nina articulates her thought, "Pah! ... how limp his hands are!'"[236] In his portrayal of Marsden, O'Neill draws from

the many 1920s discourses that attributed male homosexuality to the influence of overbearing mothers. When Nina's husband, Sam, asserts he wants his
son Gordon "to grow up like a real he-man and not an old lady like Charlie,"
Sam speculates, "That's what's made Charlie like he is, I'll bet. His mother
never stopped babying him."[237]

For all their differences, Ropes and O'Neill wrote upon some convergent
ground. In satirizing both the Theatre Guild and O'Neill in *42nd Street*, Ropes
resisted the rigid cultural hierarchies erected around both institutions by critics like Eaton, who called the Theatre Guild "the true theater of the spoken
drama."[238] At the same time, *42nd Street* illustrates how Ropes shared much of
the modernist project of the Theatre Guild and O'Neill in the author's defense
of free speech and sexually oriented artistic expression throughout his backstage trilogy. While Ropes never referred directly to the banning of *Strange
Interlude* in his novels, the event nonetheless informs the author's strategies,
references, and themes. "Boy, how my detective's report would sell in Boston
until the censors got hold of it," Amy taunts Andy Lee in *42nd Street*.[239]

In Quincy, Mayor McGrath welcomed *Strange Interlude* just before the onset
of the Great Depression, which devastated both the American economy and
vaudeville. Miller observes, "*Strange Interlude* continued in Quincy for another
month, closing two days after the stock market crashed on October 24 [1929]. . . .
It was replaced the night after it ended by a vaudeville revue called *On with the
Show*."[240] Ropes, too, persisted in Depression-era show business, reaching the
highest peaks of his celebrity not as a vaudevillian hoofer but as a novelist.

"On with the Show":
The Return of Bradford Ropes and the Writing of *42nd Street*

As Billy Bradford, Ropes returned to a vaudeville industry whose demise looked
less like an interlude than a worsening blight, if not an "infinite sojourn." In
1928, Billy Bradford, with Mann and Van Alst, had played the big-time RKO
Palace. Two years later, he slipped into the small-time Loew Circuit. In a profile
boosting the publication of Ropes's first novel, Gilbert Swan noted, "Bradford
Ropes, author of *42nd Street*, is a stage dancer and did his writing on a road tour
over the Loew Circuit."[241] In a 1951 interview with the *Patriot Ledger*, Ropes
spoke more generally about writing *42nd Street* amid the rigors of small-time
vaudeville: "In fact, it was while doing the usual 'four a day' on the circuit that
I wrote *42nd Street* which Warner Brothers produced."[242]

Encompassing many theaters in New York's outer boroughs but also stretching out nationally, the circuit of vaudeville and movie theater impresario Marcus Loew represented the most extensive vaudeville route of theaters associated with the "small-time." In *Go Into Your Dance*, Ramon speaks to Ted about the reliability of small-time vaudeville work in the early 1920s: "Soon's we come off the Interstate [circuit] we get back to New York, play all them houses again an' then I'm gonna take the act over the Loew time. It's three an' four a day, but it's steady work an' that's something you can thank God for in show business."[243]

Yet, even before the onset of the Depression, the "Loew time" also represented a drop in status and considerably reduced salaries.[244] A 1910 cartoon in the *Player* "showed performers climbing up into a water tank labelled 'The Goal—Big Time' and then falling straight through it onto rocks labeled 'small-time.'"[245] Snyder notes how "big-time acts booked at Keith theatres in New York in February of 1919 averaged $427 a week," compared with the $20 for a 1918 solo performer at Loew's Royal Theatre in Brooklyn.[246] As suggested by one article, Ropes played vaudeville theaters around the Midwest in 1930. That year, Billy Bradford, performing in St. Paul, adopted a female Scotch terrier whom he named Hobo. The *Buffalo Evening News* reported of Ropes, then a successful novelist, "Medium in height and slight in stature, his build is that of a dancer. . . . His eyes light up when one mentions his dog, Hobo. Hobo, a Scotch terrier, was picked up by Ropes three years ago, when was he appearing in vaudeville in St. Paul. The little gray and white dog followed him to his hotel, and was adopted as a mascot. . . . Hobo has traveled across the country twice."[247]

Accompanied by a dog whose naming suggests the realities of the Depression, as well as the vagabond life of the vaudevillian, Ropes may have created *42nd Street* from a complex blend of economic exigencies and narrative impulses. The *Patriot Ledger* reported that Ropes, knowing show business as well as he did, "decided to give the public an authentic account of how the members of the theatrical profession live."[248] Yet, certainly the conception of the backstage novel equally drew from the financial needs of vaudevillians scraping by in a declining industry. Ropes may have conceived of the novel's cinematic prospects right away, given how quickly he sold his novel to Hollywood, making the sale to Warner Brothers in August 1932.

If Ropes conceived of *42nd Street* as a viable option for Hollywood adaptation, the movies may have equally inspired him in the plotting of *42nd Street*. The immense popularity of early talkie Hollywood backstage musicals exerts a strong narrative influence on *42nd Street*. Though drawing extensively upon Billy Bradford's experiences in vaudeville, cabaret, and musical comedy, *42nd Street*'s story of a stagestruck ingenue going on for the star was hardly an original one in 1932. In the 1929 Hollywood musical *On with the Show*, Sally O'Neill's ambitious usher Kitty replaces Betty Compson's diva Nita French after the latter's fit of temperament leads to her withdrawing from the musical comedy *Phantom Sweetheart*. A plethora of popular theater fiction also inspired hit movie musicals, including *Applause* (1929) and *Show Girl in Hollywood* (1929). Although the form had been labeled box office poison by 1931, due to overproduction, Ropes might have sensed that the time was ripe for its comeback.

Ropes may also have embraced a return to the literary activity that had defined his youth as equally as theater and dance. Although the demands of the Loew Circuit taxed him, Ropes wrote *42nd Street* during "odd moments" of trouping. The *Golden Rod* reported in 1933: "Touring on a vaudeville circuit keeps one pretty busy, but Mr. Ropes found spare time for writing. . . . For [*42nd Street*] he drew his material from the stage life around him. Through a friend who introduced him to a literary agent, the book was published."[249] This agent was Grace Morse.[250] A former stage and silent film actress who shared Ropes's Proper Bostonian background, Morse "ran away from home because her people did not consent to her becoming an actress."[251]

In July 1932, newspapers touted the publication of *42nd Street* as a book in which "all the color and excitement of show business, from casting day to opening night, is dramatically revealed."[252] In August 1932, as Ropes worked on his second novel, *Stage Mother*, newspapers announced that Ropes had sold the motion picture rights of *42nd Street* to Warner Brothers. According to journalist Gilbert Swan, after placing his novel, Ropes "got $6,000 for the movie rights, which is plenty change for an actor in these times."[253] Matching his own sensibility with the novel's hard-boiled style, Warner executive Darryl F. Zanuck bought the novel in galley proofs.[254]

A May 1933 profile in the *Golden Rod* gives more insight into the hot-streak sequence of writing, publishing, and selling movie rights that absorbed Ropes in 1932 and '33:

One day, Mr. Ropes returned to New York from Trenton, where he had been playing, to learn that Warner Brothers had bought the motion picture rights to his book. Immediately he bought a car and motored out to Hollywood to write the dialogue for the picture. He was there eight weeks. Then he returned to New

Grace Morse, 1922. Courtesy J. Willis Sayre Collection of Theatrical Photographs. Public Domain through Picryl.com (https://picryl.com/media/grace-morse-stage-actress-sayre-7800-0b67cc)

York to write his second novel, which is to appear this month. He plans to write a third, for which he already has a contract, while cruising in South America this spring.

According to the profile, "*42nd Street* was rewritten twice, and it wasn't until the rewriting that he realized the possibilities in it."[255] Ropes's novel was published by Alfred H. King in September 1932 and then again in a 1933 "Photo-Play" edition by Grosset and Dunlap.[256]

The marketing of *42nd Street* touted the novel as a lurid theatrical exposé of sex and labor. Alfred H. King also framed *42nd Street* as something of a theatrical answer to the Austrian novelist Vicki Baum's 1929 literary sensation *Grand Hotel*. Influenced by the "New Objectivity" movement, Baum's novel had applied a panoramic approach to a cross-section of Weimar Republic Berlin society. Portraying the hotel as a capitalist institution impervious to the lives of its occupants, Baum anticipated Ropes's own depiction of a Broadway musical comedy rumbling on "with a sort of Olympian inevitability," presided over by a deity-like director.[257] Critic John Selby described *42nd Street* as "Bradford Ropes' clever combination of [the play] *Burlesque* and the ubiquitous *Grand Hotel*."[258]

42nd Street received largely positive reviews from critics. Informing readers that *42nd Street*'s "author, Bradford Ropes, is the Billy Bradford who has been dancing in musical shows and restaurants in New York for the last ten years," the *Oakland Tribune*'s reviewer aptly identified *42nd Street* as a perceptive record of Broadway as an industry: "Patrons of musical comedies and revues will close *42nd Street* with a deeper appreciation of the work done by chorus girls, with a sounder understanding of the problems of the gambling showmen, and with a clearer viewpoint of the theater of today and its hazards."[259] Yet, Ropes's success in selling *42nd Street* to Hollywood led to the eclipse of his own novel as it moved into production.

Conclusion: *42nd Street*, from the Show as Star to the Star of the Show, and Concealing Bradford Ropes in *The Gold Diggers of 1933*

Warner Brothers' reshaping of Ropes's cynical backstage novel into a more conventional commercial shape resulted in both a critical and a box office smash, as well as the film's Oscar nomination for 1933's Best Picture. The *Motion Pic-*

ture Herald reported *42nd Street* as the "top box office attraction for the first half of 1933," and the anticipation of its success sparked the rapid production of its follow-up, *The Gold Diggers of 1933*, at Warner Brothers.[260] The *New York Times*'s Mordaunt Hall called *42nd Street* "the liveliest and one of the most tuneful screen musical comedies that has come out of Hollywood."[261]

Warner Brothers positioned the film as one of national import. A week after sending its "42nd Street Special" train to Roosevelt's inauguration in Washington DC, where *42nd Street*'s stars and chorus girls marched in a parade auguring "Better Times," Warner Brothers released the film across the United States on March 11, 1933.[262] Ropes worked on an early draft of the screenplay, which was eventually credited to Rian James and James Seymour.[263] (The process of *42nd Street*'s novel-to-film adaptation and its minimization of Ropes's queer content, themes, and characters will be discussed more extensively in the next chapter).

Warner Brothers rerouted Ropes's novel into a narrative of American Dream individualist aspiration, within the larger context of New Deal collaboration. In his book, Ropes had critically examined show business hierarchies. Warner Brothers reinscribed them with what *The New Yorker*'s John Mosher called "as pretty a little fantasy of Broadway as you may hope to see."[264] The film transformed Peggy Sawyer from a self-aware young woman proficient with a wisecrack into a doe-eyed naïf, as played by Keeler, and converted Billy Lawler from the calculating and cynical young lover of Julian Marsh into Peggy's affable love interest. Whereas Ropes had critically reflected and demystified the Cinderella myths of the 1920s, the film version treated Peggy's rise to Broadway stardom as a more familiarly feminized Alger story.

By contrast with the Hollywood adaptation, Ropes's narrative approach had been more collectively driven, along the lines of Baum's *Grand Hotel*. By comparison, the *Oakland Tribune* wrote of Ropes's *42nd Street*: "He has assembled a believable group of persons within the four walls of theater and followed them in *Grand Hotel* fashion to their temporary homes and back again."[265] The *Tribune* observed of the role of Peggy in the novel *42nd Street*: "In Ropes's tale, Peggy takes her proper place. She is useful merely as an agency by which the story may be threaded together."

The *Oakland Tribune* shrewdly predicted how Hollywood would reshape the focus of the book. Its reviewer observed: "In the motion picture version, no doubt, the adventures of Peggy Sawyer the chorus girl, fresh from the sticks who becomes a prima donna in her first flight on Broadway, will be the accentuated point. The persons with whom she is concerned will either be dropped from the tale entirely or so softened that their importance will be lost."[266] Warner Brothers' *42nd Street*, now set amid the urgency of the Depression rather than the late 1920s, in fact preserves much of the caustic tone and systemic critique of the novel. Yet, Ropes's *42nd Street* also became a little less *strange* in its Hollywood adaptation: both less queer and more amenable to individualist mythmaking.

For a brief interlude in Ropes's career, Warner Brothers' more conventional Broadway fairy-tale treatment of *42nd Street* elevated him to literary stardom, as he no longer was the "eager youngster" staring starry-eyed at the Palace. In the spring of 1933, Ropes had earned sufficient recognition that William Coates, a student interviewer at the *Golden Rod*, approached him "feeling a little nervous" during the author's visit to his parents in Wollaston, where Ropes had traveled to attend the film's opening at the Strand Theatre. Coates recounted: "I rose as he entered, a young man of medium height, wearing a dressing gown. His pleasant manner set me at my ease, and we were soon chatting like old friends."[267]

Indeed, when Mayor Charles A. Ross celebrated Ropes at the Strand Theatre screening, Quincy now hailed its prodigal son as an accomplished "hometown boy." The *Patriot Ledger* covered the event: "Bradford Ropes, the first Quincy man to write a book that has been adapted to the screen, was given a standing ovation last night at the Quincy Theatre. . . . Mr. Ropes wore a broad smile as he held the autographed volume of the city's history," presented to him by Mayor Ross.[268] Yet, at the Strand, Ropes chose not to exploit his growing fame or reveal too much of himself to audiences. He "quietly accepted their encomiums" and reminisced about directing *The Dream Child* at the Wollaston School."[269]

Later, Ropes also declined to boast about a remarkable distinction. His novel galvanized the revival of Hollywood musicals after the early 1930s box office lull. In 1951, the *Patriot Ledger* interviewed the author: "Mr. Ropes, a gracious and unpretentious person, was too modest to state that this film started a whole new series of film musicales."[270] Although the *Oakland Tribune* had predicted of the novel that "its success [in the cinema] is equally as dubious as its luck on the stands is certain," *42nd Street* revived the movie musical, as well as launched a chain of backstage musicals at Warner Brothers, including *The Gold Diggers of 1933*. As Louella Parsons recounted of the film *42nd Street*: "Up to that time musicals were a drug on the market. Then along came Bradford Ropes's sparkling, sprightly story with worthy songs. . . . [Warner Brothers] were pulled out of a financial hole and everybody was happy."[271]

If Ropes had started his vaudeville career with a concealment, as he morphed into Billy Bradford, he may have consequentially repeated the feat in Hollywood. Textual evidence suggests that, during his contract with Warner Brothers, Ropes helped the studio beyond his roles as the original novelist of and early screenplay contributor to *42nd Street*. Newspaper profiles of Ropes imply that he resided in Hollywood between November 1932 and March 1933: a timeline that aligns with the screenplay drafts of *The Gold Diggers of 1933*.[272] Elements of Ropes's life story appear, in coded form, in the masquerading character of Brad Roberts/Robert Treat Bradford. The very high likelihood that Ropes worked as an uncredited ghostwriter on the screenplay of *The Gold Diggers of 1933* explains these striking biographical confluences.

At first glance, *The Gold Diggers of 1933* suggests that its credited screenwriters, and particularly the Boston-born, Harvard-educated James Seymour, knowingly invoked Ropes's life story.[273] Featuring additional dialogue by Ben Markson and David Boehm, Warner Brothers billed the screenplay as the work of Erwin S. Gelsey and Seymour, also the co-screenwriter of *42nd Street*. Ropes's biography has never been cited as an influence on the film's plot, which placed a backstage putting-on-a-show framework around Avery Hopwood's *The Gold Diggers*. Directed by Mervyn LeRoy, the film incorporates the play's central stratagem of the three showgirls Polly Parker (Keeler), Carol King (Joan Blondell), and Trixie Lorraine (Aline MacMahon) as they outwit the staid J. Lawrence Bradford to pull off Polly's marriage to Brad. In Hopwood's source comedy, the ingenue chorus girl, Violet, finds romance with a young man named Wally, who defies a family of Manhattan millionaires rather than Boston Brahmins—and does not himself go into show business. Yet, Ropes appears to have left a Rosetta Stone of clues for future historians to arrive at the conclusion that, as ghostwriter, he contributed to the screenplay of *The Gold Diggers of 1933*. Like many writers in Hollywood, Ropes worked within a system of uncredited dialogue contribution; at First National/Warner Brothers, he performed unknown work on the screenplay of 1932's *Frisco Jenny*.[274] The fact that Ropes had ghostwriting experience illuminates the uncanniness with which portions of dialogue in *The Gold Diggers of 1933* evoke Ropes's voice in his novel *42nd Street*. In *The Gold Diggers of 1933*, Trixie assures Polly of Brad: "There's more to that kid than I thought. He's regular. He belongs in the show business." Similarly, in Ropes's *42nd Street*, the working-class dancer Terry informs Peggy, an unusually genteel chorus girl: "I knew you was regular the moment I saw you."[275]

Beyond the dialogue, numerous character names and references in *The Gold*

Diggers of 1933 reflect Ropes's consistent use of roman à clef strategies and strategically coded nomenclature throughout his backstage novels. In *The Gold Diggers*, Hopwood had introduced a chorus girl named Trixie Andrews—whose name reappears in *The Gold Diggers of 1933* but with the surname changed to "Lorraine."[276] Just two weeks before the May 27, 1933, release of *The Gold Diggers of 1933*, Ropes had published *Stage Mother*, featuring Kitty Lorraine as its title character.

Suggesting specific allusions to Ropes's family history, other names and references in *The Gold Diggers of 1933* add to the many details specific to his life and work. Brad's "Back Bay Boston friends" believe "him to be following technical studies at the Stevens Institute." In this, the Hoboken, New Jersey, institution of technology alluded to the alma mater of Ropes's engineer uncle, Albert Barrett, even as his father, Arthur Dudley, attended MIT. Ropes may have left his most personal calling card and clue in Trixie's response to aspiring sugar daddy Faneuil H. Peabody (Guy Kibbee), when he asks if "she had a mother whose name was Eunice." Trixie responds: "I did have a mother. Whose name was Gertrude." Gertrude was the middle name of Ropes's own mother, Alice. Ropes also irreverently alludes to the name—and Alice's temperance activism—in *42nd Street*, as Jack Winslow exclaims: "One more drink and we'll give our right names. . . . Mine's *Gertrude!*"[277]

The critical success of Ropes's novels following *42nd Street* might have granted him more open gratification than his probable work on *The Gold Diggers of 1933*. The novels and film adaptations of *Stage Mother* and *Go Into Your Dance*, respectively published in May 1933 and January 1934, followed quickly after *42nd Street*. Signing Ropes to cowrite the screenplay with John Meehan, MGM purchased *Stage Mother* in April 1933.[278] Opening to glowing reviews, its film adaptation starred Alice Brady as Kitty and Maureen O'Sullivan as Shirley. In 1935, without the direct participation of Ropes, Warner Brothers embarked on a less faithful adaptation of *Go Into Your Dance*. The movie musical starred Ruby Keeler and Al Jolson, who performs in his signature blackface makeup in multiple numbers, including the title song.

Ropes also ventured, unsuccessfully, into writing musical comedy. Yet, the failure of 1935's *Home Town Boy* to arrive on Broadway, coupled with Ropes's rising profile in the movies, may have sealed the conviction of the now thirty-year-old Ropes to remain in Hollywood. Newspapers described *Home Town Boy*, pairing book and lyrics by Ropes with music by Philip Charig, as "a metropolitan affair, with literary and New York allusions."[279] Hearing a preview of the musical's score, Walter Winchell wrote in one 1934 column that both the

Bradford Ropes, at the time of writing *Preview*, 1940.
Reproduced by permission of Thomas Crane Public Library, Quincy, MA.

music and the lyrics "are grand and the critics should rave about them."[280] However, *Home Town Boy*'s financing fell through.

Ropes did not publish any other backstage novels until 1951's *Mr. Tilley Takes a Walk*. Yet, in 1940, Ropes worked on a Hollywood-set show business novel called *Preview*. Once again, Ropes cited Baum's story as an inspiration, in writing collectively about an industry. The *Patriot Ledger* reported, "*Preview* 'is just a novel of Hollywood,' according to Mr. Ropes, who briefly described it as done on the *Grand Hotel* style in loose form, 'very effective in a certain type of story because it gives you the whole picture of a community.'"[281]

Drawing inspiration from collective models of storytelling that revealed "the whole picture of a community," Ropes hardly wrote his backstage trilogy within a literary vacuum. *42nd Street* drew substantively upon both the gay male novels of the Pansy Craze and the genre and form of the backstage novel, which proliferated throughout the 1920s. As both "one of the most recent of the dozens of novels about Broadway" and one of a number of groundbreaking novels centered on the lives of gay men, *42nd Street* broke out from among not one but two vibrant literary chorus lines.[282]

CHAPTER 3

"This Is Not a Book to Give to a Maiden Aunt"

THE INFLUENCE OF BACKSTAGE NOVELS AND PANSY CRAZE NOVELS

"Never Wont to Take Her Seriously": "Light Amusement" versus Literature

From 1932 to 1934, over the course of publishing his backstage trilogy, Bradford Ropes drew critical praise for his skill with show business argot, back- stage authenticity, and the atmosphere of his "entertaining and idiomatic sto- ries." Clifton Cuthbert of the *New York Sun* observed of 1933's *Stage Mother*: "[Ropes's] people come to life and breathe in a manner that is rare in stories of the theater."[1] The next year, the *New York Times* enthused of Ropes's writ- ing in *Go Into Your Dance*: "He has the Broadway patter of hoofers, actors and producers down pat. . . . It's a lively, swift-moving, hard-boiled chronicle with a true professional tang."[2]

The positive receptions of *Stage Mother* and *Go Into Your Dance* expanded the accolades that Ropes had received in 1932, as he debuted as a novelist with *42nd Street*. At the same time, *42nd Street*'s review in the *New York Times* reflected an ambivalence on the part of many book critics to engage with Ropes's gay-themed backstage novel as a work of popular fiction with serious themes and intentions. In *42nd Street*, Ropes strategically frames the circula- tion of backstage gossip as a means of theatrical survival as well as sustaining camaraderie and pleasure for "show people." As such, Ropes's use of dialogue constitutes an essential part of his realism in *42nd Street*, and the *Times's* critic lauded "the sure touch of a writer thoroughly at home with his theme."[3] Yet, the same reviewer qualified his praise for Ropes's authenticity by conflating the writer's strategies and style with that of a tabloid journalist: "This is not a book to give to a maiden aunt, nor can one relish it as a clever, naughty *jeu d'esprit*. Anecdotes, allusions and conversations are, for the most part, of an excessively vulgar, gossipy nature."[4]

The review sharply illustrates a shared predicament between backstage novelists and writers of Pansy Craze fiction: the failure of early 1930s critics to take either form seriously. These perceptions were conditioned variously by modernist anti-theatrical prejudice, misogyny, homophobia, and the perception of both genres as light, frivolous, and "gossipy." As such, backstage novels have long eluded literary canonization, even as LGBTQ/queer studies have only in the twenty-first century enabled ample space for the recognition of Pansy Craze novels, and particularly gay-themed novels driven by the camp aesthetic, as substantive and ambitious works of modernist literature.

The *New York Times*'s review of Ropes's *42nd Street* exemplifies how generic dismissal of the New York stage as a "light subject" qualified critical admiration during the boom in backstage novel publication during the 1920s and early '30s.[5] Comparing J. P. McEvoy's *Show Girl* (1928) to "a glass of champagne," the *Brooklyn Times Union* observed, "It is nonsense—simple, absurd, frothy, slapstick comedy, fermented in the night clubs of the Gay White Way—but never literature."[6] Forty years after *Show Girl*, Mario Puzo (writing as a book critic for the *New York Times*) reiterated the perceptions of earlier reviewers in his piece on James Baldwin's *Tell Me How Long the Train's Been Gone* (1968): "Unfortunately, the novel next moves into the phony milieu of the theatrical world. . . . The theater as background for a serious novel so earnest in tone is simply not right."[7]

In reducing Ropes's theater chronicle to a fictional tabloid, the *Times*'s critic also used a critical feint that slighted not only backstage fiction but the novels of the Pansy Craze. "The Princesse's friends were never wont to take her very seriously," writes Max Ewing of the eccentric, bibelot-collecting Princesse Angele de Villefranche in *Going Somewhere*, a camp escapade that masks currents of Lost Generation futility within its surface frivolity.[8] Ewing himself described his novel: "At bottom it is a very MORAL book. . . . The Philadelphia review is superb in the way it points out my serious attacks under all the froth on top."[9] Overlooking Ewing's satiric use of bohemian banter as social portraiture, the *New York Times* observed (in a review that reflects that of *42nd Street*): "Very occasionally Mr. Ewing produces an amusing bit of nonsense;

but on the whole *Going Somewhere* is a dreary, labored transcription of remarks which can be heard any day in certain drawing rooms and studios."[10]

Received, respectively, as backstage and café society novels, *42nd Street* and *Going Somewhere* subordinated overtly queer themes to settings of Broadway and New York bohemia. By contrast, of the "flurry of gay-themed novels [that] appeared between 1930 and 1934," many drew critical condescension as works of vulgarity and salaciousness, if not downright degeneracy.[11] Critics viewed only a small minority of Pansy Craze novels as works falling upon "respectable" terrain. For instance, *Strange Brother* (1931), by the female anthropologist Blair Niles, "was written by a published author who was simply describing another exotic milieu with as much insight and understanding as she could," as Roger Austen describes.[12]

The scandalous allure of backstage novels, some of which (e.g., *Show Girl* and Beth Brown's *Applause*) were adapted into talkie musicals, contributed to their authors obtaining major publishers despite their status as "light entertainment." By contrast, the writers of the Pansy Craze, whose books were considered part of "an embarrassing genre," endured rejections from the publishing giants, despite exceptions like the splashy critical reception afforded Ewing's *Going Somewhere*.[13] Dr. Jeannette Foster of the Kinsey Institute remarked: "No other class of printed matter except outright pornography has suffered more critical neglect, exclusion from libraries, or omission from collected works than variant *belles lettres*."[14] In this, Foster anticipated Sarah Schulman's analysis of "the equation of queer literature with pornography" that has persisted into the twenty-first century.[15] Yet, for all the critical dismissal and sometimes contempt that greeted their work, the novelists of the Pansy Craze published over two dozen novels in the early 1930s, and, in multiple examples, blended gay fiction with theatrical themes and settings.

This chapter illustrates how Ropes left his mark as an exemplary novelist among the writers mixing the influences of the backstage novel and the fiction of the Pansy Craze. Ropes joined the vitality of his voice to a remarkable collective. Drawing upon their experiences on Broadway and in Hollywood, J. P. McEvoy and Beth Brown distinguished themselves as perceptive and distinctive writers of novels about theater. McEvoy's *Show Girl* and Brown's *Applause* (both 1928) can be considered substantial influences upon Ropes's backstage trilogy. The playwright and revue composer Max Ewing, too, drew upon his own varied show business career in his 1933 novel *Going Somewhere*: a book that can be productively compared to *42nd Street* in its style and strategies.

The scarcity of interviews with Ropes about his habits as a reader precludes a definitive account of which backstage and Pansy Craze novels he encountered and absorbed. Textual evidence suggests Ropes's familiarity with both *Applause* and *Show Girl*. Outside of backstage fiction, Ropes also favored books by gay writers. In one 1932 interview, Ropes identifies Noël Coward and W. Somerset Maugham's *Of Human Bondage* as, respectively, his favorite playwright and novel. Ropes elaborated that Coward "is the one playwright whom I admire more than any other. . . . His crisp, direct dialogue is scintillating."[16] While Ropes did not discuss his reasons for preferring *Of Human Bondage*, he may have identified both with its queer but heterosexual-passing author Maugham and with the novel's rebellious protagonist, Philip Carey, who drifts away from his early Christian faith, path in business, and conventional English morality to pursue a bohemian life in Paris.

Given their movements within overlapping social circles, Ropes and Ewing, who also venerated Coward, may have crossed paths. Ewing's *Going Somewhere* received wide publicity among "sophisticated" New Yorkers in 1933: a group with which Ropes identified. While taking account of these likely inspirations, this chapter seeks less to provide a conclusive survey of Ropes's direct influences than a topography of the literary-theatrical landscape that generated the books of his own backstage trilogy as distinctive hybrids of backstage and Pansy Craze novels.

"No Business Like . . ."? The Place of Backstage Novels within the Realm of Theater Fiction

With their intense focus upon the structures of commercial show business, *42nd Street*, *Stage Mother*, and *Go Into Your Dance* can be productively discussed as examples of the backstage novel, which I consider as a specific subset of the "theater fiction" and "theater novels" theorized by Graham Wolfe. As Wolfe describes in his foundational scholarship on theater fiction, these works "typically focus on actors, playwrights, directors, audiences, critics, and other theatre-types, and they take theatres, stages, or other performance spaces for dominant settings."[17] Wolfe situates theater fiction and theater novels within a thematically and historically wide-ranging expanse of theatrical territory, encompassing the European Romantic Nationalist stage (e.g., Johann Wolfgang von Goethe's *Wilhelm Meister's Apprenticeship*, 1795) and amateur theatricals (e.g., Virginia Woolf's *Between the Acts*, 1941), as well as works about commercial theater and the variety stage. Within this capacious terrain, I propose the backstage novel, as it appeared between the late nineteenth and twentieth centuries, as a vernacular modernist form particularly concerned with the industrial contexts of *theater as show business*, which Ropes often considers materially and metaphorically as a "machine."

More so than any other branch of theater fiction, backstage novels parallel the genre of the backstage musical on Broadway and in Hollywood and such paradigmatic examples as Cole Porter's *Kiss Me, Kate* (1948). As theorists of the stage and screen backstage musical have demonstrated, the form engages in intense formal self-reflexivity. Scott McMillin writes, "Backstage musicals are about putting on musicals, so that the plot is about the means of its own production. . . . Since the characters are show people whose job is song and dance, much of the singing and dancing is called for by the book."[18]

Backstage musicals, too, have also held intertextual mirrors to their own production histories, in which *42nd Street* has held a prominent place. Oscar Micheaux's 1938 movie musical *Swing!* filtered elements of the 1933 Warner Brothers film through the perspective of a working-class Black female protagonist played by Cora Green. *Swing!* parallels *42nd Street*'s Peggy with domestic worker-turned-singer Mandy Jenkins (Green); Dorothy Brock with diva Cora Smith (Hazel Diaz), who breaks her leg in a fit of drunken temperament three days before opening night; and Julian Marsh with Broadway-bound Harlem producer Ted Gregory (Carman Newsome). Like Marsh, Gregory delivers rousing pep talks to his cast. Yet, a gentler impresario than Marsh, Gregory gears his perfectionism toward not only producing a hit musical but proving to the gatekeepers of the "Great White Way" that they have more to offer than "just another colored show":

> You know and I know . . . that while a colored show may be and is supposed to stay within a certain prescribed scope, we must, if we hope to get anywhere, deliver something within that scope, that the public will like and come to see. . . . So I want all of you to do your best.[19]

Blending self-reflexivity with industrial reflection, backstage musicals also draw upon images of theatrical performance as assimilation, as Andrea Most has written of the myriad backstage narratives historically crafted by Jewish American immigrants, including musicals like 1927's *Show Boat* and 1946's *Annie Get Your Gun* (with its iconic Irving Berlin anthem "There's No Business Like Show Business").[20] Most describes how backstage musicals, along with dramas, "emerged to articulate this new ethos": "With the entrance en masse of first- and second-generation Jewish writers, directors, and producers into the world of American entertainment, however, attitudes toward the theater and theatricality in America underwent a radical shift. Theatrical life was transformed from the 'wicked stage' to a celebrated, respectable, and quintessentially American cultural mode."[21]

The backstage novel shares significant similarities with, but also notable distinctions from, its analogues on-screen and onstage. Like the Broadway and Hollywood backstage musical, the backstage novel focuses its narrative "concentration on behind-the-scene preparations and the relationships between show people," as Martin Rubin describes.[22] Yet, if stage and screen backstage musicals tend to focus upon the *show*, backstage novelists intensify the focus on the *business*. By contrast with their counterparts, backstage novelists look past the utopian rainbows at the finale of many backstage musicals; they use strategies of demystification and "a Naturalist ecology of dirt and vice" indebted to the influence of Émile Zola and his peers.[23] The novels of Ropes and his peers celebrate the lure of costumes, music, and lights and the resilience of show people. Yet, by contrast with musicals like *Kiss Me, Kate* and *Annie Get Your Gun*, backstage novels also explore issues of labor, commerce, and exploitation that suggest reasons *not* to "go on with the show."

The immense popularity of the backstage novel between the 1910s and the 1970s attracted a wide range of authors, from respected "serious" writers like Edna Ferber and James Baldwin to critically disparaged "pulp" writers like Jacqueline Susann. As Wolfe notes, many writers, performers, and artists with stage experience gravitated to theater novels, "as a way in which theatre-makers themselves engage further with that medium's complexities, challenges, and potentials."[24] Famous American theater artists who created significant backstage novels include playwrights like Elmer Rice (1949's *The Show Must Go On*) and directors like Elia Kazan (1974's *The Understudy*). In the United States, the subgenre of the summer stock novel flourished, as exemplified by Sinclair Lewis (1940's *Bethel Merriday*) and Herman Wouk (1955's *Marjorie Morningstar*). In England and France, respectively, J. B. Priestley and Colette too wrote about their experiences in the commercial theater, with the latter weaving her experience as a variety performer into *L'Envers du Music-Hall* (1948).

Portraying a wide array of theatrical backgrounds, professions, and positions within theatrical hierarchies, backstage novels also suggest various motives of creation, ranging from petty to profound. With its infamous caricature of Ethel Merman as Helen Lawson, Susann's *Valley of the Dolls* illustrates the roots of some backstage novels as enmeshed in score-settling impulses. Yet, many novels offered searching, ambitious meditations on the theatrical process and movement between creative mediums. Wolfe observes theater fiction's "paradoxical ability to proffer more theatre than theatre itself." He notes that novels about the stage can "bring forward what is out of sight to most audiences," ranging from "business operations to backstage feuds," as well as the hidden props and objects that form "the medium's materiality."[25]

Additionally, many backstage novelists created books steeped in industrial critique. In this way, the backstage novel can be compared to the parallel form of the Hollywood novel. Starting with such books as the anonymous 1915 *My Strange Life: The Intimate Life Story of a Motion Picture Actress*, the Hollywood novel "opened up the space for cultural critique of the film industry at a time when the industry lacked the capacity to critique itself," as Justin Gautreau observes.[26] The Hollywood novel sought to bypass the Hays Code censorship that surveilled Hollywood productions. By contrast, the backstage novel braced the "unspeakable" truths omitted from Hollywood and Broadway commercial discourses, even as the American stage faced less institutionalized censorship measures than the movies. Subjects of the backstage novel's industrial critique encompassed the sexual exploitation of actresses, systemic racism in Broadway casting, and the artistic limitations and compromises of the commercial Broadway theater.

Given its impetus in artists' personal experiences in the theater, the backstage novel might be productively compared to theatrical memoir. Yet, the propensity toward roman à clef gives the former a veracity that might contrast with the frequent self-flatteries of the latter. The function of backstage novels can again be compared to the Hollywood novel, which prompted journalist, screenwriter, and *The Skyrocket* novelist Adela Rogers St. Johns to describe "writing about Hollywood in fiction as 'the only way in which you could print the truth.'"[27] Like the theatrical memoir, backstage novels have also eluded literary categorization and, with rare exceptions, canonization. However, a small group of novels, including Ferber's *Show Boat* (1926), Susann's *Valley of the Dolls*, and Garson Kanin's *Smash* (1980), joined *42nd Street* in attaining enduring recognition through theatrical and cinematic versions.

"Good Novels about Show People Have Been Rare": Theater or Literature?

If alluring to Hollywood and Broadway, backstage novels nonetheless occupied an amorphous cultural position, often falling between the cracks of theater and fiction. In his review of *Stage Mother*, Cuthbert reflected upon the generic challenges of writing theater fiction: "Good novels about show people have been rare, curiously so considering the glamour usually considered to attach to the stage. Writers of distinction, turning from their cultivated lives to examine the theater, have lacked authority, and those who have lived in the intimacy of performers have seldom known how to write."[28] Cuthbert considered Ropes one of the few authors able to skillfully straddle the worlds of fiction and theater.

Modernist discourses of anti-theatricality, and anxiety around theater's proximity to labor, contributed to the relative exclusion of backstage novels from twentieth-century literary canons. Detailing "a sense of 'something wrong' with theater in the period of modernism," Wolfe (drawing from Martin Puchner) describes the "notion of 'modernist anti-theatricalism,' developed with reference to writers such as Mallarmé, Stein, and Joyce, all of whom were attracted to theater yet eager to keep it 'at arm's length.'"[29] As Wolfe observes, modernist resistance to theatricality stemmed from both Platonic skepticism toward representational mimesis and anxiety toward the stage's "collaborative manyness."[30]

Modernist writers also sought to distance themselves from the marketplace, which they associated with theater as a commercial form. In his 1928 backstage novel *The Great Bordello* (posthumously first published in 2011), playwright Avery Hopwood evokes a modernist cultural hierarchy that valorized the solo-authored integrity of the novel above the collaborative commercialism of the theater. The book's protagonist, playwright Edwin Ensleigh, castigates himself as a Broadway sellout for whom the deferred vision of novel writing offers the promise of artistic redemption: "Then he would retire from the theatre . . . and devote himself, at last, to writing the 'something big'— his novel—good fiction."[31] If *The Great Bordello* can be read as a self-reflexive bildungsroman about the writing of Edwin's novel, then Hopwood undercuts modernist anxieties in Edwin's production of "good fiction" intensely focused upon the stage.

In his review of *Stage Mother*, Cuthbert had singled out Ropes as a writer able to produce "good novels about show people."[32] Yet, joining writers like Brown and McEvoy, Ropes by no means stood alone in his gift. By the early 1930s, the backstage novel had already developed into a form with recognizable tropes, conventions, and thematic preoccupations: namely, the perception of the actress as sexual object and the reality of her status as worker.

"Creatures from Fairy-Land": Chorus Girls, Actresses, and the Development of the Backstage Novel into the 1920s

The commercially oriented backstage novels of the 1920s drew upon a long history of theatrical fiction that placed actresses at center stage. Georgian and Victorian novelists gravitated to the actress's navigation of changing gender roles enabled by the Industrial Revolution. Yet, as Wolfe notes, many of these novelists sought to "construct theatre and theatricality as a foil . . . to the inscription of proper feminine gender roles, centered around interiority and domesticity."[33] Yet, as early as 1858, Anna Cora Mowatt challenged New England society's "deep-rooted repugnance for the theatrical profession" in *Mimic Life; or, Before and Behind the Curtain.*[34] Tapping into her experiences as a commercially successful playwright (most famous for 1845's *Fashion*), Mowatt both celebrated the colorful world backstage and accentuated the capacity of theater fiction "for exposing concealed injustices and brutal working conditions."[35]

The progression of the nineteenth century unleashed a proliferation of American and British novels about actresses and chorus girls. Cultural anxieties about the New Woman and her entrance into the urban industrialized workforce and about the relationship of feminized labor and prostitution fueled these works in both Edwardian England and the Progressive-era United States. At the same time, readers' voyeurism into the unveiled sexuality of the theater world corresponded to the decline of Victorianism. As Wolfe observes, "Theatre-novels rise with the diminution of anti-theatrical prejudice in Britain, with a broadening interest in the stage and its people, [and] with the theatre's enhanced suitability for the middle-classes."[36]

Sending literary shockwaves beyond France, Émile Zola's 1880 novel *Nana* also fueled a rise in books about female performance and spectacle, on- and offstage. In Zola's morality tale, the eponymous Parisian showgirl-courtesan successively destroys a chain of wealthy men obsessed with her near-nude appearances at the Théâtre des Variétés in *The Blonde Venus*. The impact of *Nana* extended into Anglophone countries, with many works of actress fiction appearing in the United Kingdom, ranging from Harriett Jay's *Through the Stage Door* (1883) to Compton Mackenzie's *The Vanity Girl* (1920). In America, Kenneth McGaffey's *The Sorrows of a Show Girl: A Story of the Great "White Way"* (1908) offered more lighthearted variations upon the themes of sexual exploitation and prostitution explored by Theodore Dreiser in his epochal

1900 Naturalist novel *Sister Carrie*, which recounts the fall and rise of Carrie Meeber from factory worker to courtesan to chorus girl and actress in turn-of-the-century Chicago.

In the United States, African American novelists joined white writers like Dreiser in exploring the cultural position and subjectivity of the actress. Yet, writers like Paul Laurence Dunbar (with 1902's *The Sport of the Gods*) and Wallace Thurman (with 1929's *The Blacker the Berry*) explored the wider scope of racism, colorism, and sexism navigated by Black women working in theater. New to Harlem and "enchanted" by the women like "creatures from fairyland" she sees onstage during her first time at the theater, Dunbar's Kitty Hamilton resolves: "How I'd like to be an actress and be up there!"[37] Yet, Kitty faces multiple obstacles, including the internalization of W. E. B. Du Bois's "double consciousness." From producers, she encounters pressure to "practice the detestable coon ditties which the stage demanded" (she later finds work as a chorus girl in *Martin's Blackbirds*).[38] Kitty's mother also objects that the self-display of actresses looks "right down bad to me."[39]

As T. Austin Graham notes, the many novels at the turn of the twentieth century, driven by "the public's ever increasing interest into the private lives of chorines and actresses," incorporated a close engagement with the cultural trope of the chorus girl as socially ascendant Cinderella (and, often, as gold digger).[40] Graham places Ropes's *42nd Street* within the context of a multitude of early twentieth-century novels exploring the exploitation of chorus girls, including John Dos Passos's 1925 modernist novel *Manhattan Transfer*, in which *The Zinnia Girl* chorine Ellen Thatcher features as a major character. As Graham observes, Ropes's *42nd Street* exposes "the theater's mechanical heart with much the same pitilessness" as *Manhattan Transfer*.[41]

The public's fascination with chorines and actresses only intensified in the early twentieth century. Social controversy about the actresses' theatrical exposure and their vulnerability to backstage predation accompanied Progressive-era discourse of the "stagestruck girl," whose perceived "lack of experience and single-mindedness unwittingly invited moral hazard, economic ruin, and a miserable end," as described by Ann Folino White.[42] The 1919 Actors' Equity Strike (and the same year's Chorus Girl Strike) further exposed to the public gaze the vulnerability of young women to backstage harassment, even as an exploding media and celebrity culture expanded the ways in which the public might gawk at show people. As Graham observes, "The institutional voyeurism associated with modern celebrity culture reached new heights in the years when Dreiser was honing his craft. The century's turn saw a florescence of publications—*Billboard* (founded 1894) and *Variety* (founded 1905) being the most remembered today—that covered the stage world."[43]

Graham inversely parallels the backstage reader's desire to "get over" into Broadway's wings, dressing rooms, and feminized private spaces with that of the actress to "get over" the footlights in her appeal to the audience. As such, voyeurism constituted an essential allure of the early twentieth century's surge of actress novels and theater fiction, which expanded into the Hollywood "extra girl" novel of the 1920s.[44] As Graham observes, "*Sister Carrie* is the prototypical chorus girl novel, the first significant literary adaptation of the musical Cinderella narrative, and one of the earliest American novels to 'get over' into Broadway's backstages."[45] Graham speculates that Dreiser "could not have anticipated in 1900 just how frequently audiences in later years would 'know the marvel' of Broadway backstages that *Sister Carrie* had revealed."[46]

The readers' impulse to "get over" carried into the literary convention of the "backstage tour." Describing the device as one of theater fiction's "key attractions," Wolfe observes: "Showcasing the varied operations and jobs involved in mounting theater's spectacles," as well as providing peeks into dressing rooms, "such chapters evoke and respond to the many same desires as actual backstage tours, which, in Alice Rayner's words, offer 'a sense of privileged access to the secrets of the 'real thing' . . . the truth behind the illusion of the stage space."[47]

In the backstage novels of the 1920s, novelists depict even American Puritans fascinated by their theatrical peeks behind the curtain. At the start of Fannie Hurst's 1921 *Star-Dust: The Story of An American Girl*, one of the few backstage novels to feature a female protagonist who works in offstage theatrical production, Carrie Becker disapproves of the ambitions of her stagestruck daughter Lilly. Yet, after Lilly progresses from a vaudeville booking agent to the coproducer of a hit Broadway crime drama, Carrie itches to "visit behind the scenes between acts." "I want to get a look-in on what goes behind there," Mrs. Becker exclaims "through a sniff." She then clarifies that she will continue to disapprove: "Fine mess!"[48]

The curiosity about backstage space, as evoked by novelists and shared by the readers and characters of *Star-Dust* and *Applause*, extended into discourses of the casting couch. In 1921, writing on *Star-Dust*, critic Heywood Broun remarked upon the trope of the actress at the prey of managers: "Several of the obligatory scenes of the novel dealing with stage life are present. Yes, there is a scene in which a manager tries to seduce a young woman. No novel of the theater can do without that."[49]

From Zola's 1880 portrayal of the theater as brothel in *Nana*, backstage novelists regularly critiqued sexual exploitation in the commercial theater industry as a real and pervasive "system" as much as a set of narrative cliches. In *Star-Dust*, in which Lilly succumbs to advances by vaudeville producer Robert Visigoth out of financial urgency, Hurst depicts sexual harassment as a ubiquitous obstacle for young women desiring to work in the theater. Similarly, in Hopwood's *The Great Bordello*, actress Julia Scarlet retreats to a Midwestern stock company after her refusal to sleep with powerful Broadway impresario Daniel Mendoza costs her a starring role in New York. In Kansas City, Julia confronts the repeated harassment of Daniel Mendoza's brother Moses, also a theater manager. When Moses pushes, "Julia Scarlet—have you never loved—passionately?," Julia staggers back, as "a sudden impulse to laughter almost overcame her. Good Heavens, she thought, he says the same things that Daniel does. They must have learned it together. It's a system!"[50]

Early twentieth-century novels about actresses and chorus girls led to the immense popularity of the backstage novel in the 1920s, as concerns about the self-display of the actress fed into broader exposures into the mechanisms of commercial theater. If novels like *Sister Carrie* focused most upon the rights and roles of the actress, the backstage novel of the interwar era extended into a wider range of concerns about labor and exploitation, affecting both male and female theater workers. Examining show business structures and systems, interwar backstage novelists critically exposed the theater's prevailing myths.

"It's Painstaking, Heartbreaking Work": Demystification and the Backstage Novel as a "Blue-Collar" Form

The backstage novel's intense focus on labor and commerce distinguishes the form from its corollaries in film and theater, and particularly the Broadway and Hollywood backstage musical. While models of backstage narrative across media dramatize working conditions for actors, creative teams, and technical crews, the backstage novel views them with more sustained and unsentimental scrutiny. As Wolfe describes the theater fiction of the British writer of *The Good Companions* and *Lost Empires*: "[J. B.] Priestley's most provocative contribution to the genre may consist, however, in his spotlighting of a motif that hovers in the wings of many theatre-novels: the stage's relation with *labour*. One of the genre's peculiar features is its capacity to accentuate the work typically concealed behind proscenium arches, a world of prompters, scene-shifters, technicians, and dressers."[51] In their detailed attention to the commercial stage as an industry, these writers anticipated Elizabeth L. Wollman's call for theater historians to bring the history of Broadway into sharper focus through "closer attention to the ways its machinery influences its artistic output."[52]

In portraying the nuts and bolts of theatrical labor, the backstage novel contrasts most starkly with the golden age Hollywood backstage musical. Film theorist Jane Feuer details how the traditional backstage film musical exposes "the world backstage" in order to narratively parallel "the success of the couple and the success of the show."[53] As Feuer details, "From the 1929 *Broadway Melody* there emerged a combination with some modification that would become the means of identifying the backstage species . . . the perfect doubling of the world off the stage and the world of the stage as dual comic universes." Feuer describes how the Hollywood backstage musical creates utopian harmonies through this doubling of real-world couple and show couple, evoking "the parallel between love and work that only the theater can provide."[54]

The romanticizing process of mystification, as theorized by Feuer, arranges the "perfect doubling" of the "real" and the show worlds.[55] As such, it works in dialogue with the processes of demystification that invite audiences to satisfy their curiosities about the mysteries of backstage activity. Rick Altman describes "the show musical as a functioning system" rather than merely as a backstage setting, as "the show musical camera becomes an agent of voyeurism. When we go to a backstage musical, we lift a veil."[56] Yet, even in Hollywood backstage musicals like *A Star Is Born* that expose the hidden stains of show business, the seams are stitched back together by the end of the narrative; the veil once again drops. Feuer elaborates, "In this way, demystification is always followed by a new mystification, the celebration of the seamless final show or placing back on her pedestal of a disgraced performer. No matter how much the seamier side of entertainment has been exposed, it is always 'Mrs. Norman Maine' by the end."[57]

By contrast, the backstage novel, as exemplified by Ropes and his contemporaries, more consistently pursues strategies of demystification. From the perspective of cultural materialism, Rick Altman considers the classic Hollywood "show musical" as a "white-collar form" that "rarely shows the work of production." Altman argues that "providing a strikingly middle-class view of the process of producing and marketing a commodity (the show), the show musical takes for granted most of the activities normally performed by a working class. The backstage musical rarely shows the work of production (sets are not built, they appear; lighting is not planned, it is as natural as the stars; curtains aren't cracked open, but rise on their own)."[58]

Backstage novelists, including McEvoy and Brown, anticipated Ropes in unmasking "the blue-collar work of production." Brown focuses extensively on backstage workers in *Applause*, in which costume artisan Alice Roseboro lifts the veil for April Darling, working as a seamstress in Alice's Theater Arts Warehouse:

> "Now you can see for yourself, April, how very ordinary these girls are. But what a contrast on opening night! And to think that the astonishing trans- formation is accomplished with the aid of greasepaint, mascara, clothes and lights! . . . But the audience has no notion of our share in that. . . . They haven't the least idea of all the work that goes into a costume before the performer even puts it on. . . . It's painstaking, heartbreaking work."[59]

In portraying the dedication and dignity of technical workers like Alice, novels like *Applause* challenge a theatrical system that, as Christin Essin argues, has historically "position[ed] backstage workers as the 'also rans' to their onstage colleagues.[60]

McEvoy and Brown joined a corps of backstage writers, including the prodigal Puritan Ropes, in exploring the mundane blue-collar work under- pinning the theater's magical transformations. All of these writers, too, gravitated toward consistent thematic motifs and images connected to the unsavory or unseen sides of theatrical labor: the acrid smell of greasepaint; the grime and dirt of dressing rooms; costumes' seams and the "seamy kinds of things."[61] In many ways, the backstage novels of the 1920s stemmed from developments in the literature and drama of the nineteenth and early twen- tieth centuries.

"You Always Did Have a Good Memory for Dirt": Naturalism and the Backstage Novel

In 1966, in an interview with the *New York Times*, Jacqueline Susann observed, "If you think critics have vilified me, you should see what they did to Zola."[62] The comparison may have surprised the many critics who considered *Valley of the Dolls* a lurid soap opera fantasy pitched to housewives' fantasies. Yet, Susann was determined to expose the abuses of "a story she knows well—the seamier side of show business."[63] She "never stopped writing about or discussing [show business] as particularly devastating to women."[64] In this, she aptly connected herself to the "muckraking" impulses of nineteenth-century literary Naturalism, telling the *Times*: "They considered [Zola] a yellow journalist."[65] Influenced by the forces of Positivism and Darwinism, Zola and his followers pioneered a literary and theatrical movement concerned with the effect of environment and heredity upon human behavior and sexuality, as well as with the survivalist battles of "the human beast."

Writers, including Zola, placed images of dirt and contamination at the center of this new *"litterature putride."* As Jessica Tanner observes, "Zola used dirt to brand his fiction and brand himself as a writer. . . . Critics denounced Zola throughout his career for peddling literary filths both material and moral."[66] In this tradition, images of dirt, grime, filth, and putridity abound in the backstage novel. In his 1948 backstage novel, *The Show Must Go On*, Elmer Rice portrays the interactions of director Leroy Thompson, producer Claire Weir, and stagehand Harry Baumrack as they walk through the "reeking" alley outside a Broadway theater. As Leroy reminiscences about the rarely cleaned "Farow Theatre," Claire collides metaphorical and material inferences, replying: "Yes, you always did have a good memory for dirt." Harry, the house carpenter, adds: "I don't know where all the muck comes from, but I never yet saw the theayter that you could keep the dirt out of."[67]

In reviewing backstage novels, critics also suggested literary Naturalism as a strong influence upon writers exposing theatrical "dirt." A 1928 ad for *Show Girl* in the *Times Herald* quoted Walter Wanger on McEvoy's champagne-froth comic inversion of the grim, materialist aesthetic: "Theodore Dreiser wrote the American Tragedy. J.P. McEvoy wrote the American Comedy."[68] In the 1920s backstage novel, writers connect "muck" and "dirt" not only to the exposure of corrupt and harmful labor practices but also to women's treatment in show business.

In its focus upon these themes, Ropes's backstage trilogy can be compared to J. P. McEvoy's *Show Girl* and Beth Brown's *Applause*. Both novels appeared in 1928: a year in which backstage narrative saturated stage and screen markets and that also entertained sophisticated reading publics accustomed to the influence of Zola and Dreiser. In the Naturalist tradition of Zola's *Nana*, both *Show Girl* and *Applause* focused critically on themes of the sexual exploitation and objectification of women as theatrical workers: a concern that Ropes would integrate into his critique of the homophobia faced by gay men working on Broadway.

"That's What We Need in This Sentiment Business":
J. P. McEvoy's *Show Girl* (1928)

While drawing upon the themes explored by Naturalist writers, J. P. McEvoy buoyed his *Show Girl* with fizzy Jazz Age slang and tabloid lingo. McEvoy extended the backstage novel into what Steven Moore describes as "avant-pop" formal experimentation, as *Show Girl* recounts the rise of Dixie Dugan, whom McEvoy introduces as "the hottest little wench that ever shook a scanties at a tired business man."[69] Corresponding in a popular comic idiom to the fragmentation and collage of writers like Dos Passos, McEvoy's *Show Girl*, first serialized in *Liberty Magazine* in 1928 and released by Simon and Schuster in July of that year, debuted as one of the author's six "multimedia novels." These "unfold solely by way of letters, telegrams, newspaper articles, ads, telephone transcriptions, scripts, playbills, greeting card verses, interoffice memos, legal documents, monologues, song lyrics, and radio broadcasts."[70]

In writing his Dixie Dugan backstage trilogy, which also includes *Hollywood Girl* (1929) and *Society* (1931), McEvoy drew upon his varied background both in Chicago and in Broadway revue. In Chicago, McEvoy had worked as a sports journalist and comic strip writer, as well as at the P. F. Volland Greeting Card Company. He then moved on to become one of the successful librettists of 1920s Broadway revue, including with several editions of *The Ziegfeld Follies*. McEvoy channeled his expertise in writing revue into *Show Girl*, whose structure incorporates both the variety stage and *Variety* magazine. *Show Girl's* juxtaposition of media shapes the novel into a literary vaudeville show even as its focus on tabloid culture and entertainment magazines connects it to *Variety*. As Dixie opens on Broadway in *Get Your Girl*, McEvoy includes a medley of press clippings that allude to the trade paper as both stylistic source and foil: "*Get Your Girl*—A Wow! . . . a sock in the nose! . . . a kick in the pants!"[71]

In *Show Girl*, McEvoy bombards the American "Cult of Sentimentality," which he depicts as the driving force of both the greeting card and the tabloid newspaper industries. McEvoy satirizes these interests through two of Dixie's suitors: Indiana-based greeting card salesman Denny Kerrigan and *New York Evening Tab* columnist Jimmy Doyle. Denny's doggerel for the Gleason Greeting Card Company reflects his desire to lure Dixie into picket-fence domesticity. Denny's sales manager applauds his "sediments" about hearth and home: "You ought to sell Greeting Cards all the better for that. That's what we need in this Sentiment business—more sentiment."[72]

McEvoy places Broadway at the crossroads of a sensationalizing tabloid media and the puritanical circulation of maudlin feeling. Near the beginning of McEvoy's satire, Dixie finds herself at the center of a near-murderous crime of passion. Here, the Argentinian Alvarez Romano (depicted stereotypically by McEvoy as "a sun-kissed tango dancer from the coffee belt") stabs a lecherous Wall Street broker in a duel over Dixie.[73] In *Show Girl*, which the *Evening News* compared to Maurine Dallas Watkins's 1926 play *Chicago*, "sob sister" Beatrice Heartease picks up the scandal, hypocritically selling sex while sobbing over threats to feminine "virtue."[74] Before long, the *Evening Tab* offers "Dixie Dugan's Own Story." Ghostwritten by Dixie herself (who has gone into hiding with Jimmy in a staged kidnapping), the story recounts "how a young girl who leaves her home to find fame and fortune in the wicked maze of Broadway becomes involved in a scandal which is rocking New York's social and financial structure." While bewailing the degeneracy of Flaming Youth, *The Evening Tab* ballyhoos: "Don't miss the first installment of this epic of night club life which Dixie Dugan has called with amazing simplicity 'Ten Thousand Sweet Legs.'"[75]

McEvoy juxtaposes the commodified sentimentality of 1920s newspaper publicity with that of 1920s Broadway musical comedy, as represented by fictional titles like *Sentimental Susie*. Throughout *Show Girl* (and anticipating similar strategies by Ropes), McEvoy satirizes the 1920s "Cinderella musical." In one of the novel's many letters, Dixie informs her friend Sunshine about the plans of Milton: "As for the show he's going to put on, we haven't named it yet but it's all about me starting poor and winding up rich."[76] As *Get Your Girl* transforms into its final shape from incoherent incarnations such as *The Girl from Woolworth's*, *The Girl from Tiffany's*, *The Girl from Childs*, and *The Girl from the Rio Grande*, Broadway producer Eppus explains to librettist Jimmy his decision to cut the original first act finale, which had showed the heroine "happy and having a good time." Eppus explains that "you've got to have her crying. . . . That's the secret of successful musical shows, knowing just when to break the little girlie's heart."[77]

If the Broadway patriarchy represented by Eppus intends to portray Dixie as a broken-hearted "little girlie," McEvoy depicts his heroine shrewdly capitalizing upon her avalanche of publicity after the Milton-Romano scandal. Instead of tabloid tales like "Ten Thousand Sweet Legs" sinking her show business career, Dixie finds herself flooded in offers from cosmetic and lingerie companies and from big-time vaudeville impresarios. Here, McEvoy includes "Theatrical Notes" from the *New York Herald Tribune*: "Pretty young things who get entangled with the law usually use the front page as the springboard into the Two-a-Day . . . Dixie Dugan's vehicle, in what is euphemistically called Variety, in a new sketch called *Night Club*. . . . It will have a tryout out of town and then come into the Palace."[78]

In *Show Girl*, McEvoy depicts Broadway "sex scandals" as veiling the truly scandalous behaviors within Broadway's normalized culture of sexual harassment. McEvoy portrays scenes involving the coercion of women in show business. In one scene, banker Jack Milton, seeing Dixie dancing in a nightclub floor show at the *Jollities*, nearly rapes the dancer at a house party after the show. Previously, Dixie had written to her sister Nita: "The boss wanted me to join some friends of his at the table the first night but I says to him, 'There are no gorillas in my contract.'"[79] Yet, Dixie capitulates to her boss's pressure to join Jack and his Wall Street friends, writing later to Nita: "I tried to get out of the room several times but he headed me off and finally I began to scream. . . . He clapped his hand over my mouth, carried me over to the elevator, slammed the door shut and whisked up to the next floor, paying as little attention to me as if I were a rag doll. He carried me into the library and dropped me on the divan, still holding his hand over my mouth."[80]

That Dixie later works with Milton as the "angel" backer of *Show Girl* and allows him to continue to make advances to her might strain a contemporary reader's credulity. Yet, McEvoy portrays Dixie's resigned disgust with Jack, as the novelist critiques a show business industry that pressures economically vulnerable women to work with, or play up to, their abusers and harassers. McEvoy, too, satirizes an American culture steeped in the mythology of "how to marry a millionaire." Although the sob sisters of the media shame famous gold diggers like Peggy Hopkins Joyce, Dixie's Flatbush family pressures her to marry Jack Milton. Dixie laments to Nita: "What with . . . the family on my neck for coming home late and looking like hell and not marrying a millionaire I'm rapidly going nuts."[81] Yet even the sister in whom Dixie confides colludes with the family. Nita writes of Milton: "Wading around in money up to his adenoids and if you play your cards right he'll marry you and eat out of your hand."[82]

In *Dixie Dugan*, a serialized illustrated story and later a comic strip, McEvoy and cartoonist John Striebel modeled Dixie after the Ziegfeld Girl-turned-film star Louise Brooks, whom McEvoy had admired while writing for the *Follies*. If a less cerebral beauty than Brooks, the streetwise Dixie conveys the icon's fierce independence: "I'm young and full of the devil and want to stay that way for a while."[83] Jimmy sings the praises of an intelligence that Dixie underplays in a culture that derides "dumb chorus girls." He writes: "Besides being cute and all that she's got a quick mind, a keen sense of humor and says just what she thinks. And she really thinks."[84]

As though confirming the ironic insights of McEvoy's novel, the media characterized Dixie as a gold digger in publicity surrounding *Show Girl*'s adaptations. These included Ziegfeld's stage version, *Show Girl* (featuring Ruby Keeler as Dixie), and *Show Girl*'s October 1928 radio adaptation for the Ever Ready Hour, emceed by McEvoy himself. For the latter, the *Brooklyn Times Union* advertised a search for "America's Perfect Show Girl" to find the young woman who best resembled the "sparkling, vivacious and gold-digging Dixie."[85] If McEvoy worked complicity within systems of publicity as they objectified showgirls and actresses, he incisively examined the mechanisms of "the sentiment business" in his Dixie Dugan novels. In *Applause*, Beth Brown, too, explored the publicity mechanisms used to reduce and commodify the feminine image.

"She Told Her Burlesque Was Made for Men": Beth Brown's *Applause* (1928)

Released by Horace Liveright in October 1928, Beth Brown's *Applause* reflects the influence of McEvoy in recounting Kitty Darling's experiences in burlesque, from what the *Brooklyn Citizen* called its "high honky-tonk days on the Bowery and in small-time stands in the hicks to the stock burlesque every big town has now."[86] In 1944, Brown enjoyed her biggest literary success with the children's book classic *All Dogs Go to Heaven*. Yet, as a young woman, Brown established herself as a racy literary prodigy in commercial fields: a prolific novelist and screenwriter known for the closely observed detail of her work, much of which she set in show business.

If less formally experimental than *Show Girl*, *Applause* also drew heavily from tabloid and media culture. Brown blended Fannie Hurst's sentimental fiction of maternal sacrifice with the urbane slang of *Variety*, for which she had briefly worked as the editor of the literary page.[87] In fact, Brown dedicated *Applause* to Sime Silverman, *Variety*'s legendary general editor. She salutes the trade paper in *Applause*, in a scene set in a theatrical hotel: "The showfolk came like children to a class-room with a textbook under their arms. The textbook was *Variety*—that bible of the theatrical profession."[88] At the same time,

Brown, both a novelist and a Hollywood screenwriter, critically explores the workings of publicity in relationship with show business's commodification of women's bodies.

Like McEvoy, Brown draws from literary Naturalism in *Applause*. The *Brooklyn Citizen* praised Brown's writing: "Burlesque is crude, rude, raw, red, hot and spicy. So is this book—all but hot. It is not sensational, but human and even matter-of-fact."[89] Zola's *la litterature putride* inflects *Applause*, in which Brown describes the reactions of Kitty's daughter, who has left her convent schooling to join her mother on the road: "To April she seemed to be struggling as one struggling in mud. The mud was everywhere, not only at the theater, on the stage, in the dingy dressing rooms, but on the streets and at the hotels."[90]

Brown earned critical praise for the authentic detail of *Applause*, which drew upon her own show business background and ethnographic research. The *Atlanta American* averred, "Nobody but a trouper could have written *Applause*."[91] Brown's upbringing resonated with that of Ropes, as she told *Screenland*: "I was on the stage long before my kindergarten days (my father was a showman). But my mother, who is a blue-blood, yanked me off and sent me away to school."[92] By 1925, Brown had found success dividing her "time equally between writing fiction and writing for the screen."[93] "Such a little girl . . . and such a big check!," *Screenland* exclaimed of Brown's salary for the film version of *Ballyhoo*.[94] For the latter novel, Brown worked briefly in a circus, and then she toured with a burlesque troupe for *Applause*. As the *Syracuse American* described of Rouben Mamoulian's 1929 film adaptation: "The character of Kitty Darling, which Miss [Helen] Morgan so capably portrays, is a composite of three girls whom Beth knew during her own experience in burlesque, for this childish looking author put in three grueling years with 'turkey shows' just to gather material for a book about a subject which she considers one of the most colorful extant."[95]

Applause demystifies show business myths while exposing misogynistic discourses around burlesque and women in show business. In an editorial about Brown's *Applause*, Gilbert Swan overlooked the author's critiques to opine about burlesque's "tragic grandmothers": "I know of no more pathetic picture in the long lane that is lit with bright lights than these queens of yesteryear who keep hanging grimly on year after year—who keep hanging on when their hands have grown too feeble to cling."[96] In confronting the ageism and sexism directed at women like Kitty Darling in *Applause*, Brown drew from her own experiences. In an interview with the *New York Post*, Brown confided of her "pug nose and funny face": "Why, I had a hard time once making an editor

"She's five-foot nothing and does not look like an author! Her latest book is *Applause*": Beth Brown in *Screenland*, 1929. Reproduced from *Screenland* (August 1929).

believe I had actually written the book I was trying to sell him. He thought I looked too childish to be able to write a book."[97]

Brown assertively promoted her feminist convictions to the press. In a 1934 column for *Screenland*, entitled "Man-Made Movies for Women!," Brown transforms a humorous essay into a stinging editorial. In the essay, Brown's narrator converses with "George," the driver on a Hollywood tour bus, and inquires into the contents of his "Blue Book" directory. "Tell me, George, who are the women producers in pictures? I was thinking of the legitimate theatre with its Eva Le Gallienne, its Elizabeth Miele, its Peggy Fears." George replies successively about the extreme scarcity of "women supervisors," directors, interior decorators, cameramen, electricians, technicians, and dressmakers. Listing the contributions of women working in fields ranging from aviation and science to arts and letters, Brown's narrator concludes: "Women everywhere—but behind the scenes in Hollywood."[98]

Brown connects her understanding of show business as a boys' club to her critiques of publicity as a function of patriarchal gatekeeping. As Kitty relates to April: "She told her that burlesque was made for men."[99] Brown frames some of burlesque's publicity events as benign, even magnanimous. At the Gayety Girls Burlesque Company, press agent "Rubbertongue" Farley suggests a benefit "corset ball" to raise money for the pregnant Kitty. Yet, as April matures backstage with her mother's many burlesque troupes, the teenage girl finds herself at the center of gimmicks that demean and humiliate her. At a "Garter Night" hosted by Kitty's boyfriend, the juggler Hitch Nelson, the latter instructs "twelve beauties, each wearing a garter" to present their garters to raffle-ticket holders. Each time a number is drawn, Hitch removes an article of clothing from April's body. Hitch ballyhoos: "Since there are only twelve girls on this stage and our little lady is wearing only eleven pieces, you can judge for yourself what the evening promises."[100] Hitch neglects to tell April that the stage lights will dim before the twelfth girl's garter is removed. When April feels Hitch's hands upon the clasp, she turns and strikes Hitch "across the face with all her might." As Brown describes, "She ran from the stage in a skelter of fear, shame, and trembling and—into her mother's arms."[101]

In *Applause*, Brown deploys strategies of demystification to show the distance between image and reality in an ageist burlesque industry premised, like Hollywood, on the commodification of feminine youth. Illustrating Kitty's slide down the ranks of burlesque, Brown conjures the discrepancy between Kitty's body and her posters. Unlike Gilbert Swan, Brown treats the figure of the ageing burlesque queen with empathy. In the novel's first sequence, in Oil City, Oklahoma, at the turn of the twentieth century, Brown describes the beautiful, young Kitty as a "poster come to life," as Oil City turns out with "its eyes agog" to see "that alluring, amazing, astounding Queen of Burlesque!"[102] Kitty's poster still promises a degree of verisimilitude at a stock burlesque theater in Newark some years later, as April runs "to a life-sized poster standing in its tarnished frame."[103] By the time a middle-aged Kitty plays the Venus Stock Burlesque Company, "a life-size lithograph," picturing the burlesque queen in a "costume little more than a string of beads," shows only "the Kitty of ten years ago. The age of a burlesque performer was always the same. So was her lithograph."[104]

Like McEvoy, Brown unflinchingly portrays the normalization of sexual harassment in show business. Brown depicts Kitty as both a loving mother and a naive and self-deluded woman who turns a blind eye to Hitch's predations on her teenage daughter during their dance lessons. Describing how Hitch's "hands touched April at the slightest pretext," Brown portrays the juggler ignoring the girl's pleas to leave her alone. He continues to come "carelessly into the room where April was undressing or dressing," although Brown (like McEvoy in *Show Girl*) stops the narrative short of a sexual assault.

For the thematic inspiration of her backstage novel, Brown juxtaposes the "lure of applause" with the cocaine to which Kitty becomes addicted. Kitty's self-delusion leads her to cling first to the abusive Hitch and then desperately to April, who has fallen reciprocally in love with an upper-crust Princetonian named Ronny Delacourt. As Kitty tumbles down the ladder of burlesque, Brown observes: "True, Kitty was being beaten, but she tried to shut her eyes to defeat. She clung desperately to her illusions."[105] Having always desired for her daughter the life of a "real lady" over the degradations of a burlesque stage "made for men," Kitty eventually supports the marriage. In a melodramatic ending that evokes *La Dame aux Camélias*, Kitty induces a cocaine overdose to free April from the stigma of a burlesque queen mother.

In depicting applause as a narcotic conduit to self-delusion, Brown, on one level, indulges the anti-theatricalism that surrounded backstage narrative. In the most affecting scene in the novel, Kitty takes April to the Old Actors' Home outside Manhattan to visit Alto Birmingham. A former burlesque colleague who started as a Shakespearean actor, Alto had once warned Kitty, "The stage takes all and gives nothing."[106] Kitty and April are struck by the sight of the elderly actors, forgotten by the public. With some bitterness, Alto describes the group: "They have given all they had to give—And the reward? Well, Miss Kitty, over the door outside the threshold to this place, the builders should have carved, "*Applause is the artist's reward!*" "None of that for April!" vows Kitty, in response to her visit to the Old Actors' Home.[107]

Yet at the same time that Kitty vows to take her daughter out of show business, Brown demonstrates the backstage novel's potential "to proffer more theatre than theatre itself."[108] In the scene, Alto and his friends discuss the long history of American burlesque, as Brown demonstrates the value of the backstage novel as a repository of theater history. The actors not only recall facts; they also wax poetic over past roles, debate whether *The Black Crook* was the first burlesque show, and comb through the "long yellowed" pages of their memories. Here, Brown depicts the "old-timers" as "growing younger in the telling of the old tales. All were onstage again, and memory was the stage-hand."[109]

At the end of the sequence, Alto shows Kitty and April a library of props and artifacts. These include "a faded waxed rose, a tarnished sword, horse-hair rings, age-brown programs, blurred manuscripts . . . the stub of an old-style lime-light."[110] One of the actors insists that Alto have time alone with Kitty and April: "Give Mr. Birmingham time to see his visitors. . . . It would take us weeks to tell all there is to be told about burlesque!"[111] In this way, Brown pushes against anti-theatrical prejudice by positioning the backstage novel as an inviting affective archive of theater history. Along with *Show Girl*, the appeal of *Applause* likely extended an irresistible call to Ropes.

The Influence of *Show Girl* and *Applause* upon Bradford Ropes

Starting with their commercial show business settings and *Variety*-influenced stylistic flourishes, *Show Girl* and *Applause* can be closely compared to Ropes's backstage novels. While McEvoy centralized nightclub floor shows and Broadway musical comedy in *Show Girl*, Brown explored burlesque's circuits in *Applause*. McEvoy, in particular, circulates the stylistic influence of tabloids and nightclub culture, which, along with the slang and gangster characters of Damon Runyon, Ropes absorbed into his novels. McEvoy's conception of his Dixie Dugan books as a trilogy, too, appears to have influenced Ropes. The latter's *42nd Street*, *Stage Mother*, and *Go Into Your Dance* share crosscutting of characters, as Julian Marsh appears in *Go Into Your Dance* and Dorothy Brock in *Stage Mother*.

Show Girl and *Applause* also share overlapping themes with Ropes's backstage trilogy. Like Ropes, McEvoy and Brown explored the effects of anti-theatrical prejudice, the circulation of gossip, and cultural hierarchies between variety theater and the "legit." Like these backstage novelists, too, Ropes focused his critical gaze upon sexual exploitation in the commercial theater. In *42nd Street*, Richard Endicott premises his backing of *Pretty Lady* upon an exclusive sexual relationship with star Dorothy Brock, while Ropes depicts *Stage Mother*'s Mark Thorne and *Go Into Your Dance*'s Ted Howard making repeated advances on chorus girls.

Beyond thematic commonalities, *Applause* suggests specific narrative influence upon Ropes's *Stage Mother*. *Stage Mother* overlaps with Brown's novel in a number of plot points. Both Shirley Lorraine and April Darling are "born in a trunk" after their mothers' acts, spend genteel adolescent upbringings away from the theater, and engage in romances with aristocratic young

New Englanders whom they fear will disapprove of their show business backgrounds. A more caustic writer than Brown, Ropes drew from his own teenage experiences with Gus Edwards to steer the trope of self-sacrificing actress into ruthless stage mother in his 1933 novel.

In endowing *Stage Mother*'s Kitty Lorraine with the same first name as Kitty Darling, Ropes may have been inviting intertextual comparison to the novel's predecessor by Brown. However, Ropes appears to critique the theatrical tropes of maternal sacrifice used by Brown and, before her, Hurst in *Star-Dust*. In *Applause*, Brown depicts Kitty Darling's possessiveness as inspired by a deep love for, and indissoluble bond with, her daughter. By contrast, Ropes portrays the erosion of Shirley's love for Kitty. In *Stage Mother*, the title character's relentless drive for show business success and for prostitution of Shirley to rich and powerful men pushes her daughter beyond emotional reach.

The extent of Ropes's direct inspiration by Brown and McEvoy remains a matter of conjecture. Yet, their backstage novels can be regarded as influential models of show business demystification, which Ropes enriched with his own insights as a gay man working in vaudeville and on Broadway. The Bostonian writer added to these previous models a distinctive camp sensibility that infuses every aspect of his novels. This ranges from his wise-cracking dialogue and farcical interludes to his centralization of gay male characters. Ropes shared the latter feature of his work less with McEvoy and Brown than with the novelists of the Pansy Craze.

Strange Brothers, Twilight Men, and Scarlet Pansies: The Novels of the Pansy Craze and Hybridization with Theater Fiction

The backstage novels of Ropes's predecessors also dovetailed with the proliferation of novels by gay male authors, spanning 1931 through 1934, enabled by the Pansy Craze. If critical gatekeepers largely dismissed gay novels, their authors nonetheless created a robust body of fiction during these years that allowed their authors "to depict the gay world and publically articulate a gay sensibility."[112] A number of cultural milestones, including the 1928 appeal of Radclyffe Hall's *The Well of Loneliness* after its conviction for obscenity, enabled the publication of gay novels in the late 1920s and early '30s, including Andre Tellier's *Twilight Men* and Robert Scully's *A Scarlet Pansy*. Pansy Craze fiction also encompassed the gay novels of the Harlem Renaissance, such as Wallace

Thurman's 1932 *Infants of the Spring*. It ranged in style from the sophisticated popular fiction of Carl Van Vechten's 1930 *Parties* to the "high modernism" of Charles Henri Ford and Parker Tyler, whose 1933 *The Young and Evil* vividly portrays a stream-of-consciousness drag ball. As Chauncey describes the contradictions of Pansy Craze fiction:

> Some portrayed the gay world in unflattering terms, but several provided remarkably detailed descriptions and defenses of gay speakeasies, drag balls and other institutions. Most ended with the death or suicide of the gay protagonist, but only a few made this end seem inevitable; in the other novels the ending is obviously nothing but an obligatory bow to convention, transparently intended to disarm the moralist who might otherwise have tried to suppress the books.[113]

The Pansy Craze novels appeared despite institutional obstacles that extended from publication to critical reception. The majority of books found release on "pulp-paper presses" or private printings, with Niles's *Strange Brother*, at Liveright, the only explicitly gay book of the early 1930s to be released by a major publisher.[114] As Austen observes of the early 1930s, alluding to the gay-coded female characters of Marcel Proust: "The options for gay novelists were still limited; they could write an honest novel and put it in a drawer, camouflage the gayness through the Albertine strategy, write a sensationalized exposé and send it to Godwin or Castle, or arrange to have a candid novel published privately or abroad."[115] In *Go Into Your Dance*, Ropes suggests his familiarity with the latter category of novels, published for Continental distribution by the German Tauchnitz company and restricted from traveling to the United Kingdom and the United States. Ted jokes to a reporter, at his dockside arrival in New York from Paris: "No dirty post cards or Tauchnitz editions, buddy."[116]

The novelists of the Pansy Craze contended not only with the homophobia of publishers but with that of writers and critics. In a 1992 foreword to Robert McAlmon's *Sophisticated Air* (1925), a collection of "Grim Fairy Tales" about gay life set in Weimar Republic Berlin, Gore Vidal bluntly speculated: "McAlmon was not particularly open about his sex life but everyone knew, and he was treated with some disdain by Hemingway and Fitzgerald, two sissies in terror of being thought fairies. . . . After all, they wanted to be Great Writers, and every American knew then as they know now that no Great Writer can be a fag."[117]

Yet, gay men widely discussed the novels of the Pansy Craze. Anticipating the fervent reception of lesbian pulp fiction in the 1950s, published on imprints like Fawcett Gold Medal and exemplified by Ann Bannon's *Beebo Brinker Chronicles*, the novels of the Pansy Craze offered reassurance and recognition to gay male readers. According to Kim Clarke, Forman Brown (under his pen name of Richard Meeker) received a multitude of letters from his readership after the publication of his 1933 novel *Better Angel*. A man in Memphis, Tennessee, confessed to Brown, "I have thought for a number of years that I would like to write a book and give to the world a true picture of the thoughts and experiences of an invert who had education, culture and a genuine depth of character. You have done that for me."[118]

Strikingly, a number of the earliest novels of twentieth-century American gay fiction incorporated theatrical settings or characters working as actors and playwrights. These included early works like Charles Warren Stoddard's *For the Pleasure of His Company* (1903) and Henry Blake Fuller's *Bertram Cope's Year* (1919). Carl Van Vechten, too, infused his gay high-society novels with unabashed theatricality. In the writer's camp escapade *The Blind Bow-Boy* (1925), the Duke of Middlebottom decides to stage "Fernand Nozière's libertine drama in one act, *L'après-midi Byzantine*."[119]

If many gay-themed novels invoked the stage as a location, multiple Pansy Craze authors hailed from theatrical backgrounds. These included *Better Angel*'s author Forman Brown, a songwriter and librettist who innovated as the writer of the puppet revues of the Hollywood Puppeteers and, later, LA's Turnabout Theatre. Through the movements of his protagonist Kurt Gray, who composes the music for a Gilbert and Sullivan-style comic opera called *The Duchess Decides*, the author used theatrical settings and characters to explore the performance of gender and sexuality as an intricate process of masking and unmasking. By comparison, the versatile Max Ewing shared with Ropes a background of work in revues, composing songs for *The Grand Street Follies*.

The abundance of gay men writing theater fiction in the early twentieth century suggests that at a time when their sexuality may have placed a glass ceiling on their commercial success in American entertainment, novels provided a "second stage" for theatrical artists to express queer sensibilities. The tradition has since been carried on, into the post-Stonewall era, by such celebrated authors as the playwrights Robert Patrick (with 1990's *Temple Slave*) and Charles Busch, whose 1993 roman à clef *Whores of Lost Atlantis* transforms the East Village performance space, the Limbo Lounge, into the decadent "Golgotha." The censorship-defying pages of the backstage novel, then, might be productively compared to nightclubs and cabarets: illicit stages that, often more so than Broadway, welcomed flamboyantly gay artists like Ewing.

"*Matelot*-Mad": Max Ewing's *Going Somewhere* (1933)

In *42nd Street*, Ropes portrayed the cultural divide between Broadway and vaudeville, while weaving in the speakeasies that both welcomed and threatened performers during Prohibition. Even more so than Ropes, Ewing focused upon the "illegitimate" nightclubs, performances spaces, and cruising grounds that made up the queer underground of early 1930s New York. Costume pageants and drag balls abound in *Going Somewhere*, in which Ewing parallels poses of gay male self-presentation with cultural forms of masquerade. Ewing's carnivalesque novel flips artistic hierarchies while slyly celebrating homosexual "inversion."

Ewing basks in "sequined and scintillating" surfaces in *Going Somewhere*, published in January 1933 by Alfred Knopf.[120] Ewing's novel flaunts an exuberant dandyism greatly influenced by the novels of Van Vechten and Ronald Firbank (from whose *Parties* and *Vainglory*, respectively, Ewing prefaces his novel with epigraphs). Like these writers, Ewing steeps *Going Somewhere* in self-aware "camping," which, as Kate Hext argues in her essay on the correspondence and novels of Van Vechten and Firbank, "had [by 1922] already acquired much of the self-conscious performativity, effeminacy, and humor that would feed into [Susan] Sontag's definition of camp style forty years later."[121]

With *Going Somewhere*, Ewing drew from a theatrical background, as positioned within his wide-ranging body of work as a "poet, novelist, composer, pianist, photographer, and man-about-town."[122] After attending the University of Michigan, Ewing moved to New York City as an aspiring concert pianist. In 1927, a finger injury playing George Antheil's "Ballet Mécanique" at Carnegie Hall redirected Ewing toward songwriting for New York revues. Ewing contributed songs to the 1925, 1928, and 1929 editions of the satiric *The Grand Street Follies* at the Neighborhood Playhouse. The *Follies* represented only one outlet for his queer artistry. At Ewing's "Carnival in Venice" photo exhibition at the Julien Levy Gallery in 1933, "some of the gentlemen sitters, for instance, were but lightly attired."[123] As the writer of two unproduced plays, *The Golden Girls* and *Return Ticket* (written for Tallulah Bankhead), Ewing had embarked upon a new chapter at the time of his 1933 suicide, when, despondent at his mother's death, he drowned himself in his hometown of Pioneer, Ohio.

The publication of *Going Somewhere*, which debuted under the mainstream banner of Alfred A. Knopf, contrasted with the private and small-press printings of most other Pansy Craze novels. The book premiered to critical accolades, even if sales were hindered by the worst period of the Great Depression. While *Going Somewhere* was arguably one of the most strikingly original gay novels of its time, its high-profile critical reception drew upon Ewing's "concealed" rather than explicit handling of male homosexuality. Critic John Selby praised the "savage criticism" of Ewing's "1933 model Oscar Wilde prose."[124] At the same time, Ewing suffuses his novel with camp allusion and frequent references to homoerotic desire, cruising, and drag balls. Along with his fictional portraits of modernist icons Marchesa Luisa Casati (as the Duqusea Barocca) and Muriel Draper (as Aurora Overauhl), among others, Ewing shows his characters giddily reading works by European pioneers of queer and camp modernism, including Wilde, André Gide, Colette, Jean Cocteau, and Radclyffe Hall.

Suffused with flamboyantly theatrical personalities, theater also wends its way through *Going Somewhere*, although Ewing largely avoids the convention of the "backstage tour." Early in the novel, Ewing introduces the Duquesa Barocca as she plans a costume as a skyscraper for one of her famous pageants, a "Fall Fête" in Paris displaying the "Capitals of the World": "She (the Duquesa) had become, without having appeared on stage, one of her century's greatest theatrical creations. . . . The Duquesa made her most casual excursions into the streets in highly fanciful attire. . . . The almost constant motif was concealment."[125]

The Duquesa's offstage masquerades inspire Ewing's own strategies in *Going Somewhere*, as he creates an intensely theatrical promenade through Manhattan entertainment at the end of Prohibition and the hungover first years of the Depression. *Going Somewhere* traverses Broadway revue but also movie palaces, dance marathons, radio, Times Square flea circuses, and, most extensively, Broadway and Harlem nightclubs. Ewing portrays early 1930s Manhattan as an Aristophanic "Cloudcuckooland" of frenzied escapism and ballyhoo: "It was a city of lunar paradox . . . a metropolis where everything was topsy-turvy, vulgar and purposeless, grandiose and mad."[126] At the novel's climactic moment of satire, Aurora Overauhl, tiring of New York, "climbs into her autogiro and faces toward a new planet."[127] Here, Ewing parallels Aurora's attempted escape to Pluto with the polyamorous desire of dilettante-composer Napier Knightsbridge to marry beautiful fraternal twins in the country of "Trans-Urania."

Anticipating José Esteban Muñoz's concept of queer futurity as the "rejection of a here and now and an insistence on potentiality or concrete possibility for another world," Ewing blasts the characters away from the conformity of Broadway's stages.[128] At the same time, Ewing draws upon his theatrical background in the novel's engagement with West End and New York revues. Napier contributes a song to the revue *Get Up and Rest* that boasts distinctly Cowardesque lyrics of gay innuendo: "I love to be around where lots of *matelots* abound, / So let me know if any ship of battle goes aground, / I rave about a *matelot*, / I crave a naval battle, oh, / I'm absolutely *matelot*-mad!"[129] Satirizing two Cochran-produced revues (Coward's 1928 *This Year of Grace* and Cole Porter's 1929 *Wake Up and Dream*), *Get Up and Rest* moves to Broadway after playing the London Pavilion (where Billy Bradford had performed in 1926).

Ewing's elevation of nightclubs and cabarets above Broadway's more "legitimate" stages might itself suggest a queer representative strategy, as the Pansy Craze enabled the flourishing of drag performance at Times Square venues like the Pansy Club rather than in Broadway plays and musicals. Yet, the queer performance culture of the 1920s also embraced revues, including Ewing's own work with *The Grand Street Follies*, where the drag comedian Albert Carroll convulsed audiences with his impersonations of Fanny Brice and Anna Pavlova. Fittingly, the *New York Sun* commented on Ewing's theatrical influences: "Everything succeeds by excess and mounts to a fantastic climax. It manages to be as expansive as a circus and as smart as an intimate revue."[130] Sharing strategies with McEvoy's *Show Girl*, which was also "characterized as a 'novel [revue] . . . ,'" *Going Somewhere* merged gay themes with Ewing's subversive brand of theatricality.[131] In it, Ewing used the stages of theater fiction to pose nightclubs, drag balls, and pageants as defiantly queer—and definitely theatrical—stages.

"Sinister Ladies" and Subordination: The Influence of Pansy Craze Theater Fiction on Bradford Ropes

If the "straight" backstage novelists of the late 1920s inspired Ropes in his settings and subject matter, Ewing and other Pansy Craze novelists like Forman Brown joined Ropes in centralizing the lives of gay men working within Times Square's varied performance spaces. Weaving Broadway's neon and glitter into the texture of his prose, Ropes displays a stylistic flamboyance that strongly links him with Ewing. Ropes animates all three of his novels with the effervescent wit of the chorus boys and dancers stereotyped as fairies, pansies, and nances. The gay male theater novelists of the Pansy Craze also share with Ropes an ambivalent portrayal of lesbian culture substantially less nuanced than their portrayal of gay men. In Kennilworth Bruce's *Goldie* (1933), the gay rights activist Shaw proposes for his "Twilight League": "We've got to let the Lesbians in. We can't advocate freedom for men and not for women."[132] By contrast, Brown and Ewing largely elide lesbian culture. Despite his own personal friendship with Gertrude Stein, Avery Hopwood, too, variously portrays gay women characters in *The Great Bordello* as officiously hovering, sexually predatory upon straight women, and unattractively "manlike."[133]

Ropes echoes these negative depictions of lesbians in *Go Into Your Dance*. In Ropes's third backstage novel, Ted starts a Paris affair with socialite-turned-songwriter Eunice Goddard. Ted perceives Emmy, the chaperone masquerading as Eunice's "distant cousin," as the biggest threat to the romance. To Ted, Eunice describes how her bankrupted family trusted Emmy to provide for her: "They thought Emmy was a good sort. . . . But I can't bear going on like this. . . . She's mother, father and husband combined into one." Yet, Eunice tries to deflate Ted's suspicions, even as Ropes confirms that Emmy is a "sinister lady": "Oh, I don't think Emmy's a Lesbian—but she has all the instincts and impulses of the breed."[134]

In the mid-1930s, Hollywood columns chronicled Ropes's friendships with multiple prominent lesbians in show business, including Peggy Fears and Patsy Kelly. Later, in the early 1950s, he also collaborated with the songwriter Dana Suesse, the partner of writer-editor Virginia Faulkner. Ropes's numerous relationships with lesbian women, coupled with his sensitive portrayals of male homosexuality, suggest unfortunate blind spots in his backstage trilogy, if also the likelihood that he exploited lesbian stereotypes to deflect his bold portrayals of gay men.

If Ropes shared a negative portrayal of lesbians with other gay male writers, Ropes and Ewing overlapped in their strategies of subordination. As Austen observes: "Another variation of playing the game during the 1930s was the inclusion of gay motifs in novels that were principally concerned with other themes . . . so long as the gay angle was sufficiently subordinated to grander themes, allowing all to escape the stigma already being attached to the gay novel."[135] Positioning *Going Somewhere* as a sophisticated satire of Manhattan café society, Ewing sailed away with bounteous risqué gay puns and references to cruising at the St. George Hotel pool. Similarly, in *42nd Street*, Ropes subordinates the many strands of gay male relationships to the main narrative through line of putting on *Pretty Lady*. The reluctance of critics to fully engage with the gay themes, characters, and subtexts of *Going Somewhere* extended to the critical reception of *42nd Street*, which in turn led to the diminishment of Ropes's vision in Hollywood.

Queer Diminution in the Critical Reception and Film Adaptation of *42nd Street*

The 1932 reviews of *42nd Street* demonstrated critical minimization, if not erasure, of the gay subject matter of Ropes's backstage trilogy. In addition to the long neglect of backstage novels as a serious form and the persistent out-of-print status of his books, the reluctance of 1930s literary critics to delve into the novels' gay themes illuminates why Ropes has so long escaped canonization. At the same time, the production history and the gay context and subtexts of Warner Brothers' 1933 film adaptation have attracted more sustained critical attention from scholars of LGBTQ+ film.

Though most reviews of *42nd Street* avoided discussion of Ropes's gay subject matter, a few reviewers alluded to it through euphemism: some with ambivalence and some with disgust. The *Oakland Tribune* referred to "the decision of the producers to hire the famous Julian Marsh, whose private life may not be above scruple but whose professional career is respected."[136] Similarly, the *St. Louis Globe Democrat* considered "kept men and chorus boys" among the elements running "through a narrative of shady affairs." In its allusions to *42nd Street*'s homosexual characters, the *New York Times* inferred homosexuality among the reasons not to "give the book to a maiden aunt." Responding inversely to Ropes's intentions of portraying Peggy as an ally to gay men, the critic described her as "the good girl of fiction who passes uncontaminated through moral vileness to virtue's reward."[137]

The reviews and reception likely influenced the minimization of the gay subject matter in the film version of *42nd Street*, in which "as early as the skeleton outline, Julian Marsh was reengineered as straight." Yet, as Leonard J. Leff describes, "Various drafts of the treatment and screenplay—including an undated version credited to Bradford Ropes and Rian James—contained traces of the character's gay sexuality." Leff notes that "in the first draft screenplay (September 6, 1932), for instance, Julian agrees to direct *Pretty Lady* because he needs money and not because, he tells the producers, 'I've any flaming passion for you two boys.' One of the two boys may be gay."[138] These lines originated in Ropes's novel, from which the transformation of *42nd Street*'s screenplay involved a thirty-eight-page first treatment by Whitney Bolton and then an outline treatment and two screenplays by Bolton and James Seymour. As Rocco Fumento writes, "Then Bolton was dropped and Rian James coauthored the third and final screenplay."[139]

In numerous ways, queerness subtextually ghosts the films, offering coded appeals to gay male spectators in 1933. Leff discusses numerous examples of how Julian Marsh, as played by Warner Baxter, evokes the character in Ropes's book, despite the conversion of Billy Lawler into Peggy's heterosexual love interest. The film depicts Julian as an effete, almost "danfidied" bachelor who lives alone; charges him with an unspecified, feminizing "illness"; and, in the final scene, shows Julian alone in the theater's alley: a common site of gay assignation on Forty-Second Street.[140] Leff also discusses a scene in which the seemingly tireless Marsh, letting down his guard after a particularly arduous rehearsal, tacitly propositions Andy Lee (played by George E. Stone): "Come home with me, will you? I'm lonesome."[141]

Other scenes in the film circulate the queer affects and desires expressed in Ropes's novel. In the *Pretty Lady* number "You're Getting to Be a Habit with Me," a bevy of loose-limbed chorus boys exchange flirtatious glances at one another, neglecting their ostensible romantic focus on Bebe Daniels's Dorothy. As *Pretty Lady* moves from rehearsal to opening night, the production number "Young and Healthy," centered on Dick Powell's Billy and a nameless, toothsome blond played by Toby Wing, boasts lyrics that "so overstate his male libido that they may have produced laughter in 1930s moviegoers who had read the novel, recalled the singer's sexual roots, and understood why he had to pop vitamins to boost his 'nature.'"[142] That Hays Code censor Joseph Breen, a virulent homophobe, denied the movie musical reissue in 1936 suggests the preservation of queerness in *42nd Street*'s early drafts.[143] Despite its heterosexual reorientation, *42nd Street*'s iconic film version reflected Ropes's daring blend of backstage fiction and the novels of the Pansy Craze—all while safely playing to "maiden aunts" in movie theaters across the country.

Pansies Backstage:
The Synthesis of Forms and Influences in Ropes's Novels

As a cultural topography, the collective influence of Beth Brown, J. P. McEvoy, and Max Ewing should be strongly considered in discussing Ropes's backstage trilogy. Yet, these writers' influence is by no means exhaustive. Ropes blended the more critically respectable influence of Naturalism with genres not taken seriously by literary critics. This included not only theater fiction and gay literature but also women's popular magazine fiction, as well as pulp and gangster narratives. *42nd Street*, *Stage Mother*, and *Go Into Your Dance* also evoked the adjacent Times Square milieu of Runyonland.

Only a few critics in the early 1930s fully appreciated Ropes's particular blend of influences. Among them was Clifton Cuthbert, who, writing on *Stage Mother*, picked up on Ropes's innovations as a demystifying writer of backstage bromides: "Mr. Ropes is a master of the argot used by staged people for purpose of communication, and a skillful creator of character." Cuthbert also identified Ropes as something of a Naturalist, writing a yarn that "rings true in every particular whether it is unpleasant or cheerful." Considering "the author's abilities as superior to his material," Cuthbert observed, "*Stage Mother*, while without technical originality, is as carefully done as a good naturalistic novel of twenty years ago, and several times livelier."[144]

The influence of Naturalism can be extended into queer discursive contexts as well. In his backstage trilogy, Ropes transforms the Zola-esque impulse to expose the "filth" of society's flaws into the camp idiom of "dishing the dirt." In Ropes's backstage trilogy, gay show people exuberantly wield "anecdotes, allusions and conversations of a vulgary, gossipy nature," as the author continued to challenge their exclusion from both "serious" literature and the mainstream of American life.

CHAPTER 4

"Light Hearted and Damned"

ANTIGAY DISCRIMINATION AND CAMP DEFIANCE IN ROPES'S BACKSTAGE NOVELS

Stepping Out of Line:
Bradford Ropes's Dancers and Chorus Boys

In *Stage Mother*, Bradford Ropes continued to expand his literary and theatrical canvas, as fueled by works like *Show Girl, Applause*, and his own *42nd Street*. The marketing for the latter had aptly touted the book as "epic in scope . . . and enormously rich in the pageantry of its detail."[1] Nonetheless, Ropes had confined the action of his first novel to the theatrical vortex of Times Square and its large ensemble to the making of *Pretty Lady*. By contrast, *Stage Mother* juxtaposed the genteel Boston of Ropes's youth with the "Manhattan Madness" of Prohibition-era New York. Describing the scene outside Boston's South Station as one of "Mayflower descendants moving disdainfully through the motley," Ropes dramatically contrasts Boston with Broadway.[2] He populates this on-the-make Times Square with hustlers, bootleggers, and political bosses no less relentlessly ambitious than Kitty Lorraine.

Kitty commands star billing in *Stage Mother*, with her "juggernaut determination" to make Shirley a Broadway star.[3] Yet, juvenile lead Jack Thomas also plays a substantial role in the book's narrative, as Shirley's dance instructor, friend, and confidante. She immediately appreciates Jack, whom Ropes describes as "a tall dapper youth with slim languid hands and a manner of ineffable boredom. Shirley liked him instantly, liked him for the bland way in which he flaunted his abnormality directly under the tip-tilted noses of the righteous, for his magnificent sense of humor that neither rebuff nor downright indignation could dull." Jack unleashes his risqué, impudent wit when he first meets Shirley, coding his introduction with a simultaneous dirty joke and allusion to D. H. Lawrence. Accused in 1921 of the "glorification of homosexuality" in *Women in Love*, Lawrence created a sensation with 1928's *Lady Chatterley's Lover*, to which the author had given the suggestive earlier title, *John Thomas and Lady Jane*.[4] Ropes refers to this in *Stage Mother*, where the chorus boy introduces himself to Shirley: "I'm Jack Thomas. . . . Jack's short for John—John Thomas, get it, dear? Lady Chatterley, please write!"[5]

Yet, the gossip-prone Jack, with his "unflagging wit," meets a tragic ending as he gets caught in the political machine. Jack is murdered by goons at the behest of Jack Reilly, the ruthless strategist behind the ineffectual mayoral curtain. Ropes portrays Reilly's thoughts on the killing: "Anyone who threatened the present regime must go. And so, light hearted and damned, Jack Thomas passed from the scene."[6] Framing the crime as a suicide, Reilly explains to Dexter that Jack talked too much, unable to restrain himself from publicly joking about the affair. Yet, Ropes supplies the men who kill Jack with their own hateful motivations. Bootlegger Angelo Scarlatti assents enthusiastically to the crime: "He was a degenerate, a pervert. It was mercy in the sight of God to rid the world of him."[7]

Although Jack Thomas doesn't make his first appearance until the last of *Stage Mother*'s three sections, the character, in a sense, upstages Kitty in his role as the novel's defiant camp conscience. Jack's truth-telling presence and "critical gaze" are vital to the themes of the backstage novel, which Ropes pervades both with a trenchant critique of American cutthroat capitalism and with the ironic and parodic aesthetics of camp. If American society insists on damning Jack, Ropes insists on asserting Jack's right to be "light hearted" in the face of its puritanical social attitudes. Ropes connects Jack's lightness of heart to his looseness of tongue: his refusal to stay silent before the corrupt and patriarchal ruling class of 1920s New York.

Throughout his backstage trilogy, Ropes repeatedly summons the figure of the gay Broadway dancer and, particularly, the icon of the chorus boy. These characters include not only Jack Thomas in *Stage Mother* but *42nd Street*'s Jack Winslow and *Go Into Your Dance*'s Bobby Rogers. Ropes depicts their lives as circumscribed by the social discrimination rendered into violent threats by *Stage Mother*'s macho gangsters. Bobby and Jack Thomas meet tragic ends, respectively, by suicide and murder. Only the unabashed "fairy" Jack Winslow escapes the tragedies of the other chorus boys. A character of disarming vitality, Winslow exclaims, "I'm a great big gorgeous camp, and I don't care who *knows* it!," even as his authenticity is likely to cost him his professional mobility on Broadway.[8] Unsurprisingly, the 1933 Hollywood and 1980 Broadway adaptations of *42nd Street* eliminated the character of Winslow, who is unwilling to be censored or assimilated to heterosexist norms.

This chapter shows how, through the vibrant voices of Jack Winslow, Jack Thomas, and Bobby Rogers, Ropes portrays camp as a liberating and libidinal life force that metaphorically enables his gay dancers and chorus boys to step out of line. Camp irony functions alternately as armor and weapon in the backstage trilogy of Ropes, who indeed controls the salvos of his writer's pen, despite his earlier *Golden Rod* quip: "Ask for my pen; it governs me—I govern not it."[9] In *42nd Street*, *Stage Mother*, and *Go Into Your Dance*, Ropes channeled discursive energies that challenged and disrupted the era's persisting homophobia and American society's "grotesque masks of hate" (a phrase Ropes called upon in his poem "The Man Who Lost His Soul").[10] Like the damned but defiant Jack Thomas, Ropes cannot help but to "dish the dirt."

"They Took Life as a Huge Joke": Camp as a "Strategy for a Situation"

Ropes threads his backstage trilogy with allusions to camp, at the same time that camping stylistically suffuses his novels. In *Go Into Your Dance*, Ropes introduces Bobby and Arthur as both close friends and likely on-and-off lovers: "Their friendship had been one of those Damon and Pythias affairs which carried them from show to show and scandal to scandal." Ropes portrays the irreverent "good humor" of Arthur and Bobby thawing Ted's homophobia after he joins the Broadway chorus of *Sweet Sally*. Ropes observes of the pair: "They took life as a huge joke. Morals were fabled possessions which they scorned to own. The world to Arthur and Bobby was a 'great big camp.'"[11] In this, Arthur and Bobby deploy camp as a "strategy for a situation," as Esther Newton detailed in her influential 1972 study *Mother Camp: Female Impersonators in America*. Here, Newton conceptualized the irony, incongruity, and theatricality of camp as a defense against the poisonous currents of "self-hatred and lack of self-esteem" circulated by a homophobic American society.[12]

The camp sensibility that pervades Ropes's novels emerged in dialogue with Billy Bradford's personal experiences, relationships, and travels throughout the 1920s. Ropes had performed with Alyn Mann in vaudeville and at Barney Gallant's nightclub in Greenwich Village. Ropes's work on the West End had, in all likelihood, introduced him to the gay London subculture associated with his *Cochran's Revue of 1926* costars, as well as Noël Coward. The novelist refers to Coward's 1930 comedy *Private Lives* in *42nd Street*, where the romance between Peggy and Pat sharpens itself on a shared appreciation of epigrams. Seemingly alluding to *Private Lives*, Pat quips to Peggy: "Isn't it damning how good music stirs up a sense of futility, Miss Sawyer?"[13] As their flirtation deepens, Pat and Peggy discuss the relationship between sincerity and artifice. When Pat asks Peggy, "In other words, you like an epigram in its proper place—behind the footlights?," she responds: "Yes, a stage setting gives a certain truthfulness to wit that is lacking when the same remark is made in everyday surroundings."[14]

Ropes's self-reflexive discussion of epigrams in *42nd Street* expresses only one of the camp devices that coruscate throughout his backstage novels. Here, Ropes centralizes the performance of frivolity through the camp poses and postures of his gay dancers and chorus boys, who aim their sardonic laughter at the insults of a hostile outside world that seep into the safer spaces of the Broadway theater. Ropes's backstage novels abound in repartee, innuendoes, gossip, and wisecracking, which the author places upon the tart tongues of showgirls, vaudeville troupers, and chorus boys alike. Ropes identifies camp repartee as the basis of backstage gossip, although not all slingers of "show talk" participate in gay culture. In *Stage Mother*, as the widowed Kitty reunites with friends from the Orpheum Circuit, Ropes describes her pleasure in theatrical language: "Conversation buzzed ceaselessly, shop talk, show talk, music to the starved soul of Kitty Lorraine. The kind of laughter she had known since childhood, the ready quip, the coarse jest, the malicious innuendo."[15]

The quip, jest, and innuendo weave themselves intricately into the fabric of Ropes's prose and dialogue. Navigating a fiercely competitive industry, Ropes's show people cling to their proficiency with an ego-preserving jest. In *42nd Street*, these wisecracks fuel the backstage rivalries dividing *Pretty Lady*'s industrious chorus girls and "orchidaceous" showgirls.[16] Sizing up the monocle-sporting showgirl Diana Lorimer, who likes to boast of her Park Avenue penthouse, Flo explains to Peggy: "Just one of Broadway's whorified girls."[17]

Such innuendoes equally flavor the acidic camp wit of Ropes's gay chorus boys. At the same time, Ropes shows the close proximity of verbal frivolity to the threat of homophobic violence and danger. For flamboyant chorus dancers like *42nd Street*'s Jack Winslow, a well-aimed wisecrack can mean the difference between diffusing antagonism and staving off physical assault, which George Chauncey describes as an "abiding threat" to effeminate gay men.[18]

"Who says I can't fight back? . . . I'll lay him to rest in forty shades of lavender," Jack jousts against a posturing, macho hoofer in the cast of *Pretty Lady*.[19] Jack had already been threatened by heterosexual chorus boy Terry: "Any more of your nance comedy and you'll go out the door."[20]

If Ropes describes the tragic Jack Thomas in *Stage Mother* as "light hearted and damned," the author connects his own camp aesthetic to, as for many gay men, the internalization "of the anti-homosexual attitudes pervasive in their society."[21] Despite the partial liberations of the Pansy Craze, gay men in the 1920s faced the criminalization of their sexuality and, culturally, the persecutions of vice squads. The irony, theatricality, and purposeful frivolity of camp served as a powerful strategy of survival for men contending with the cultural assault to their self-images and with the institutional threat to their livelihoods and lives. Early twentieth-century policing of gay male sexuality by a private state of vice squads and "social purity groups" (such as the Committee of Fourteen) increasingly interacted with American police and court systems. During World War I, a "discourse of urban degeneracy," concentrated on both female sex workers and gay men, gripped reformers, who feared that "the war had resulted in a substantial growth in the scale and visibility of gay life in the city."[22]

The loosened social mores of the Prohibition era precipitated some relaxing of discrimination, making it "possible for the gay world to expand and become considerably more visible than it had been during the war."[23] Nevertheless, as Chauncey describes, "hundreds of gay men were arrested in New York City every year in the 1920s and 1930s for cruising or visiting gay locales."[24] In 1923, the New York state legislature passed a statute that "for the first time, specified homosexual solicitation (a person 'frequent[ing] or loiter[ing] about any public space soliciting men for the purpose of committing a crime against nature of other lewdness') as a form of disorderly conduct."[25] The hundreds of gay men arrested before and after the passage of the 1923 statue on charges of "degenerate disorderly conduct" faced imprisonment at Welfare Island (now Roosevelt Island).

Anthony Comstock's New York Society for the Suppression of Vice, founded in 1872, reinforced the 1923 legal statue with theatrical censorship. Succeeding Comstock as vice commissioner in 1915, John Sumner established himself as a key player in the persecution of gay men, and "in 1920-21, his agents assisted in the arrest of two hundred men on charges of degenerate disorderly conduct by leading the police to movie theaters, subway washrooms, and restaurants where they had learned gay men congregated."[26] In 1927, Sumner switched his tactics to the cultural front, as the New York Society for the Suppression of Vice galvanized the passing of the Wales Padlock Law.

Mae West's "gay plays," *The Drag* (1927) and *Pleasure Man* (1928), challenged the framing of gay male sexuality as "degenerate" moral illness. West critiqued these discourses through the character of Dr. James Richmond, a "physician" who has been attempting to apply conversion therapy treatments to the "outcast" David Caldwell. Unbeknownst to the doctor, David has been the lover of Dr. Richmond's son-in-law, the heir to an ironworks; this revelation triggers the climactic murder of the play. Contrasting with Ropes's *Stage Mother* description of Jack Thomas as "light hearted and damned," West portrays David in unalleviated torment. He explains to Dr. Richmond, "I'm one of those damned creatures who are called degenerates and moral lepers for a thing they cannot help. . . . Oh, God!—Doctor, I can't explain."[27]

Yet, with its third-act drag ball scene, alternating specialty nightclub turns with exchanges of dirt dishing, *The Drag* buoyantly and bawdily subverted Dr. Richmond's framing of gay men as "misfits of nature." In this play and *Pleasure Man*, West celebrated and appropriated the camp subculture that flourished in the gay enclaves of Greenwich Village, Times Square, and Harlem, where the interracial Hamilton Lodge Ball drew thousands of spectators. The 1923 disorderly conduct statue had attempted to "criminalize the assembly of gay men in a public place or in their adoption of distinctive cultural styles."[28] Yet, many men, gathering in restaurants and cafés, defiantly cultivated an expressive subculture of camping. In his novels, Ropes evokes 1920s gay culture's coded argot that included feminine signifiers and pronouns, often used by Ropes's characters to flaunt their effeminacy. Both gay and in-the-know straight characters frequently allude to "belles" in Ropes's novels. In *42nd Street*, Abe Green watches Billy Lawler make his first appearance onstage: "There was a smattering of applause from a few oversexed matrons and three or four Park Avenue homosexuals. 'The belles stick together on a night like this,' thought Abe."[29]

By the late 1920s, the self-conscious camp sensibility that developed in the police-surveilled spaces of restaurants and cabarets had established itself visibly, if not centrally, on the Broadway stage, as well as in the pages of Pansy Craze novels. If *42nd Street*, and then *Stage Mother*, celebrated "the ready quip, the coarse jest, the malicious innuendo," as well as the Coward-esque epigram, Ropes also filled his backstage trilogy with the discursive pleasure of dirt dishing. In *42nd Street*, Jack Winslow exclaims, "Dearie, the woman that don't like dirt, don't live! . . . I've kept my lips sealed long enough. I'm just a girl that has to dish."[30] In particular, this circulated through the vaudevillian comic routines of Bert Savoy, a performer deeply influential on Ropes.

Bert Savoy and the Circulation of Dirt Dishing in Novels and Plays of the Pansy Craze

To the 1932 readers of *42nd Street*, Jack, with his effusions of "nance comedy," would have channeled specific cultural references, with particular resonance for gay male readers. In particular, Jack evoked the expressive culture brought into the mainstream by the drag queen Bert Savoy, whose "'flaming' performance style made an indelible mark on early-twentieth-century queer culture."[31] On June 26, 1923, Savoy was tragically struck by lightning while walking along Long Island's Long Beach with friends. Reportedly camping until the end of his life, Savoy mythically remarked during the storm, "Mercy, ain't Miss God cutting up something awful?"[32]

Records of Ropes's early vaudeville career leave no doubt that he was familiar with the work and persona of Savoy, who also hailed from Boston. From February 1923, when Ropes most likely relocated to New York, to Savoy's death five months later, Ropes would have had a window of opportunity to encounter the drag queen in New York, where he and his partner, Jay Brennan, headlined two editions of *The Greenwich Village Follies* between 1920 to 1923. Additionally, in support of Mann, Ropes shared a *Whirl of Dance* bill with Brennan in Washington, DC, the week of August 22, 1923. By then, Brennan had reteamed with Stanley Rogers, stepping into the gowns of Savoy's iconic vamps and sirens. As the *Evening Star* detailed, "Stanley Rogers, who has assumed the Savoy characterization, is spoken highly as a mine of slangy, raucous, garrulous, smart, and quite frank femininity."[33]

Whether Ropes saw Savoy perform toward the end of his fabled career or merely absorbed a colorful simulacrum of his act through Rogers on the Keith Circuit, the novelist paid consistent tribute to Savoy in his writing. Ropes's backstage trilogy draws upon discourses of dirt dishing that, as closely associated with Savoy, became conventionalized and celebrated in Pansy Craze literature and drama. Savoy's garrulous "frank femininity" strongly inflects work not only by Ropes but also by Robert Scully, Robert McAlmon, and, most famously, Mae West.

These writers drew upon practices of dirt dishing and of "letting one's hair down," which allowed gay men to construct a veiled yet boldly visible expressive culture in the midst of "the public and private agencies of social control, as well as popular hostility."[34] As Chauncey describes: "Gay men turned many restaurants into places where they could gather with gay friends, gossip, ridicule the dominant culture that ridiculed them, and construct an alternative culture." At Louis's Restaurant, on West Forty-Ninth Street, one writer in 1924 described how the "fairies dish the dirt there the same as they would if they were in a hovel in the Village or in Gertrude Stein's bizarre salon."[35] Ropes alludes to comparable banter in *Go Into Your Dance*, in which Bobby and Arthur allow Ted into their confidence and their repartee: "You're nice to have around, dear. . . . A girl likes to let her hair down in front of a real man, now and then."[36]

Savoy emerged out of this culture of bawdy gay badinage. Sporting a flaming red wig and Gay Nineties frippery, Savoy (born Everett McKenzie) played "an overdressed and exceedingly gabby female" opposite Brennan.[37] Edmund Wilson eulogized Savoy: "When he used to come reeling on to the stage, a gigantic red-haired harlot, swaying her enormous hat, reeking with corrosive cocktails of the West Fifties, one felt oneself in the presence of the vast vulgarity of New York incarnate and made heroic."[38] Savoy steered the female impersonator tradition of the 1910s, as exemplified by Julian Eltinge (also raised in Boston), into the more confrontational queer persona of the Jazz Age drag queen. As Laurence Senelick details, Savoy's offstage persona conjured the flamboyant guise of the "fairy": a figure who also appeared as a limp-wristed, lisping stereotype in the burlesque figure of the "nance" and the "pansy." Nevertheless, Savoy used the icon of the fairy to sport a "kind of clown costume that warded off serious opprobrium by raising mirth."[39]

"The most quoted comedian of his time," Savoy coined a number of iconic catchphrases, including "You don't know the half of it, dearie"; "Whoops, my dear!"; and "You must come over." Many of Savoy's raucous routines centered on Savoy's gossipy banter to Brennan about her shameless friend, Margie. In "The Mutterings of Margie" (published in *Variety* in 1917), Savoy's character asserted that she planned to change her ways with a more loquacious act: "I am going to take the opportunity to make a camp of this an' tell the past, present and future." Savoy's character concludes her conversation with Margie: "Goo-bi, dearie! Come up and dish the dirt again."[40] In his mutterings with Margie, Savoy often appeared in the persona of Maude: a drag alter ego that Savoy had introduced "on stage in a concert-hall in Deadwood, South Dakota, after the fit-up company in which Mackenzie served as a chorus boy was stranded."[41] According to his *Variety* obituary, Savoy had previously performed suggestive routines as a "chair dancer" at a Boston curio museum.[42]

Before reaching the writing of Ropes, Savoy's influence upon Pansy Craze literature extended from Robert McAlmon's 1925 story "Miss Knight" to the riotous strange interludes of Robert Scully's 1932 *A Scarlet Pansy*. The latter recounts "the sexual adventures of its transgender protagonist, Fay Etrange, to whom it refers throughout as 'she,' as she triumphantly makes her way in the world." In both works by McAlmon and Scully, the authors' gay male and transgender main characters find inspiration in Savoy's persona. An ex-chorus boy and expatriate female impersonator in Berlin, Miss Knight remarks to a friend: "I wuz at the Y.M.C.A—in drag you know—some outfit I had too, stars and spangles and jewels all over me, Mary. Whoops my dear, you must come over, ah come on, come over an' call on me some afternoon."[43]

Even more so than in the McAlmon story, the transformations of Bert Savoy mold the carnivalesque world of *A Scarlet Pansy*. As Robert J. Corber describes, "Whereas Miss Knight enables McAlmon to document camp and other queer practices, Miss Savoy functions in the context of *A Scarlet Pansy* to foreground the performative aspects of gender and sexual identities." Corber elaborates, "Fay learns from Miss Savoy how to perform her sexual identity. . . . She increasingly imitates Miss Savoy, repeating phrases like, 'You don't know the half of it, dearie,' made famous by the impersonator, and following her advice when cruising for trade."[44] In his narrative, Scully portrays "the ebullient Miss Savoy" as a "fairy godmother" to Fay, a medical student and part-time female impersonator who increasingly emulates Miss Savoy's brazenness.[45] When a landlady, at an apartment building drag party, impugns Miss Savoy as a "woman of the streets," the latter quips: "You flatter me! I've never done it yet, but now that you encourage me I shall go right out and try as soon as I have attended the party."[46]

If Savoy entered the pages of Pansy Craze literature, he also deeply influenced the drag plays of Mae West, who "onstage probably owed more to Bert Savoy than any woman in the theatre before 1920."[47] While the practice of dirt dishing infuses *The Drag*, it propels the plot of *Pleasure Man*, which also includes a cast party with "queens next door, campin'."[48] In West's 1929 backstage comedy, which critiques the intersecting forces of homophobia and misogyny in show business, the playwright portrays the female impersonator Paradise DuPont, known as an "awful gab," informing on the bisexual libertine Terrill. Terrill has conducted a secret affair with "the Bird of Paradise" while practicing a hypocritical, toxic masculinity that results in a chorus girl's botched abortion. Paradise indicts Terrill: "And if you're a man, thank God, I'm a female impersonator."[49]

Ropes exuberantly wove the dirt-dishing discourses popularized by Savoy, mythologized by Scully, and appropriated by West into his own backstage trilogy. In *42nd Street*, Ropes summons the famous persona of Savoy when he introduces Maud, a voluble "buxom blonde lady of a certain age."[50] Though writing the character as a woman, Ropes characterizes Maud, an "urbane" vaudevillian performer and friend of Jack Winslow, as a figure who blends gay patois with wisecracking camp allusions. Maud's quips draw upon a strand of ageism that inflects Ropes's wisecracks, even when spoken by female characters. Here, Maud "shrills" her derision of Dorothy Brock: "That belle! . . . Why, my God, she's got callouses on her fingers from sewin' sweaters for the Rough Riders."[51]

Maud reappears in the Philadelphia tryout sequence of *42nd Street*. Here, at the elaborate party in Terry and Harry's hotel suite, Ropes evokes Mae West's theatrical drag balls. None of Ropes's characters appear at the party in drag. Yet, Jack shows up at the party not with Maud but with Mae Morton and Sophie Gluck, two louche *Pretty Lady* chorus girls. Jack introduces the pair: "That's Gluck and Morton. . . . I knew those belles would be along the minute they smelled liquor." Ropes describes how, as Terry opens the door, "two young ladies with predatory eyes and coarse manners burst in a frenzy of greeting."[52] Ropes's naming of the chorus girls evokes not only West but the racy vaudevillian "Last of the Red Hot Mammas," Sophie Tucker.

The cast party sequence moves forward the plot of *42nd Street*, as the ebullient vulgarity of the party pushes the genteel Peggy away from her working-class suitor Terry, whom she later dismisses as a "roughneck."[53] At the same time, through the ribald dirt dishing of Jack, Mae, and Sophie, Ropes also swerves his narrative into a disruptive vaudeville turn full of Savoy-esque repartee, with Ropes coding the two chorus "belles" as drag queens not unlike those of West's gay plays. Mae tells Sophie and Jack that she's infatuated with a collegiate sax player. When Sophie retorts to Mae that he "has no money. An' you can't *blow* your way through life," Jack Winslow inquires: "Who *says* so?"[54]

Throughout the party scene, Jack, Sophie, and Mae engage in baldly risqué banter that repels Peggy, despite her own proficiency with a polished epigram. Although the most tolerant of the *Pretty Lady* cast toward homosexuality, Peggy dislikes the flamboyant "fairy" comedy that fueled Savoy's routines. When Sophie informs Peggy that Terry and Harry are "a couple of yesmen that want yeswomen," Jack interjects with a wisecrack that later became famous in the 1933 film version of *42nd Street*, as directed upon Ginger Rogers's Anytime Annie. "Sophie only said 'no' once an' then she didn't understand what the man asked her."[55]

In *42nd Street*, Peggy Sawyer demonstrates an ambivalence toward the outré fairy comedy of Jack Winslow that evokes the reticent values of her own, and Ropes's, New England upbringing. Peggy's preference of the "queer" juvenile Billy Lawler over the "fairy" persona of Jack plays a vital role in the narrative of *42nd Street*, in which the impulses of dirt dishing must be suppressed in order to achieve assimilation and success on Broadway. Commenting upon the stigma centered upon the figure of the Broadway chorus boy, *42nd Street* also celebrates what José Esteban Muñoz and Jack Halberstam theorized in the twenty-first century as "the queer art of failure."[56]

"People Like That Can't Get You a Thing": Fairies and the Queer Art of Failure in *42nd Street*

Drawing from Savoy's popularization of dirt dishing on the Broadway and vaudeville stages, Ropes made the practice central, both stylistically and thematically, to his gay backstage novels. Ropes disperses Jack's flair for dirt dishing into every aspect of *42nd Street*. In the book, it functions as a means of gay self-expression and community building and also extends to backstage culture, where gossip serves as a strategy for self-preservation amid the precarious circumstances of Broadway life. Yet, in *42nd Street*, the queer discursive practices of Jack Winslow and his friends represent not only the allure of authenticity but a defiant challenge to gay men seeking concealment and assimilation. Peggy, the "company's Cinderella," strategically distances herself from Jack to ally herself with the poised and cautious Billy, who casts himself, with self-aware irony, in the role of her fairy godfather.[57]

Yet Ropes casts Jack, a "fairy" known for his shameless dirt dishing, as the animating spirit of *42nd Street*, as he embodies the "queer art of failure."[58] By contrast with Billy, Jack proudly insists that he doesn't care "who *knows*" that he's a "great big gorgeous camp."[59] Writing about the contemporary drag performance artist Jibz Cameron (aka Dynasty Handbag), Muñoz observed in 2009: "This is a modality of being off script, off page, which is not so much a failure to succeed as it is a failure to participate in a system of valuation that is predicated on exploitation and conformity. The queer failure of Dynasty Handbag and countless other queer performers is a failure that is more nearly a refusal or an escape."[60]

Cut from the 1933 film and the 1980 Broadway musical adaptations of *42nd Street*, Jack plays a vital role of utopic resistance in Ropes's novel. *42nd Street* drives itself upon the discourse of "queers" and "fairies" that George Chauncey detailed in 1994's *Gay New York: Gender, Urban Culture, and the Making of the Gay Male World, 1890-1940*. Highly conversant with this influential discourse, *42nd Street* adds further illumination to the interwar world of *Gay New York* through the lens of backstage narrative. In his novel, Ropes suggests how Jack's exuberant excess hinders his assimilation into the American success myth, which in its masculine incarnation models itself after affluent virility rather than the flamboyant example of Savoy. By contrast, Billy Lawler performs the persona of the "queer": a more discreet performance of sexual identity adapted by upwardly mobile middle- and professional-class men seeking to distance themselves from the coded working-class "vulgarity" of fairies like Winslow.

Ropes's *42nd Street* demonstrates just how much the subsequent adaptations, mimicking Billy, suppressed the queer spirit of Jack. The tensions that propel Ropes's *42nd Street* very likely draw from the autobiographical contexts that shaped the author's life and career. Beginning in church plays and school pageants in Proper Boston, Ropes flouted respectability in his vaudeville days dancing with Alyn Mann. Moving away from drag acts, he then ascended into increasingly elite spheres as a dancer on the stages of London, Paris, and, finally, Broadway. Given these experiences, Ropes keenly understood the conflicts of ambition, self-concealment, and authenticity that polarize Billy and Jack in *42nd Street*, despite their shared identities as gay men working on Broadway.

The novel, film, and stage versions of *42nd Street* all position Peggy as a feminine embodiment of the American Dream. Yet, Ropes's framing of Broadway success varies considerably from later adaptations. Ropes does not predicate Peggy's rise on the providence of "sheer luck and talent" that Warren Hoffman attributes to the film and stage musicals.[61] Instead, Ropes attributes Peggy's ascent to her open-mindedness coupled with her shrewd navigation of backstage politics. Ropes depicts the pervasiveness of homophobic attitudes, exacerbated by Broadway's winner-takes-all capitalism, as a significant shaper of professional alliances. Ropes frames these as key determinants in the Broadway success narratives that the public consumes as tabloid romances. In Ropes's novel, Peggy rises less because of meritocratic virtue than because her tolerance toward gay men in the theater earns her a devoted ally in Billy. *Pretty Lady*'s juvenile lead tells Peggy that she'd never have stayed in the chorus: "You were bound to rise." To this, Peggy retorts: "Thanks, Mr. Alger!"[62]

Aspects of gender presentation and class status, drawing upon the early twentieth-century discourse of queers and fairies, as well as the cultural stigma of the chorus boy, deeply inform Ropes's portrayals of *42nd Street*'s gay characters: Julian Marsh, Billy Lawler, Jack Winslow, and the bisexual Pat Denning. Ropes's delineation of this spectrum aligns with the cultural types detailed by Chauncey. In the early twentieth century, "gender status superseded homosexual interest as the basis of sexual classification." This created a hierarchy that conferred higher social status upon "queers" as "conventionally masculine males, who were regarded as men" than on "effeminate males, known as fairies or pansies, who were regarded as virtual women, or more precisely, as members of a 'third sex' that combined elements of the male and female."[63] Rooting the tension between queers and fairies as heavily a "*class* antagonism," Chauncey observes that "many queers were repelled by the style of the fairy and his loss of manly status, and almost all were careful to distance themselves from such men."[64]

Ropes's distinction between queers and fairies in *42nd Street* overlapped with depictions by novelists and playwrights, including Forman Brown. In 1933's *Better Angel*, Brown portrays the "sensitive but not otherwise feminine" Kurt protesting "the strange vindictiveness the normal man has toward our sort. We're all, to him, like the street corner 'fairy' of Times Square—rouged, lisping, mincing . . . a streetwalker."[65] The character conforms to Chauncey's insight: "Many queers not only refused to endure the indignities suffered by fairies, but resented the men who did, for they believed it was the flagrant behavior of the fairies on the streets that had given the public its impression of all homosexuals."[66]

Popular media of the 1920s and '30s closely connected the stereotype of the fairy, and his vaudevillian variants as the nance and the pansy, with the stigma of the Broadway chorus boy. As Senelick observes, cultural "indignation was directed at the 'offensive, disgusting, effeminate male or 'fairy' impersonator.'" He belonged to a "roster of effeminate males [that] included the chorus boy, now classified as a distinct species, as well as the 'tango pirate' or 'lounge lizard,' too dependent on women, overly concerned with their grooming and feminine in their attention to clothing."[67] West, who further cemented the association between the fairy and the male ensemble dancer in filling her cast of *The Drag* with forty chorus boys, candidly discussed their casting obstacles: "All the chorus boys (in those days) were gay. But the producers never gave speaking parts to homosexuals! So I helped a lot of gay boys along. I gave them parts."[68]

In *42nd Street*, Ropes keenly details the social stigma and professional obstacles that faced the Broadway chorus boy. Ropes undoubtedly knew and befriended many men in the "merry merry" (as early twentieth-century vernacular dubbed the institution of the chorus), even as Ropes himself appeared on Broadway as a featured dancer. Using the third-person omniscient voice that carries the narrative weight of 42nd Street but weaves in and out of individualized character psychology, Ropes observes:

> The chorus boy is much maligned. He is pointed out as the degenerated, effeminate male whom all normal boys should avoid. . . . His haughty sisters [in the chorus] have small use for the companionship of a chorus man, the boss regards him as a necessary evil, and so he is forced by an unfriendly world to become a solitary segment in the well-appointed structure of the modern musical comedy.[69]

In 1934's *Go Into Your Dance*, Ropes reiterates the low status and "arduous" labor of the "chorus man," describing it as "one of the most thankless roles in the world." The author contrasts the role of the Broadway chorus boy with the more glamorous icon of the chorus girl. Ropes details, "The chorus girl was a much-feted individual whose accomplishments and escapades were the subjects of great press comment. But silence was the lot of the chorus boy. He appeared at designated intervals, sang his bit of song, capered about in the series of absurd steps which the dance director had evolved for him and retired to the obscurity of his dressing room without the benediction of applause or admiration."[70]

Ropes depicts the world of the chorus, despite its relative sexual openness, as beset with homophobic anxiety, partially due to gay men's interactions with "normal boys": straight or closeted dancers wary of being associated with the male chorus dancer's "doubtful standard."[71] "Goodness knows the chorus boy has had few defenders in his time," observed Gordon White in *Billboard*.[72] Writing of the large numbers of gay men who "worked as chorus boys, actors, stagehands, costume designers, and publicity people; waiters and club performers; busboys and bellhops," Chauncey asserts that the "theatrical milieu did offer them more tolerance than most workplaces." At the same time, Chauncey qualifies his discussion of gay men's relative freedom in the Broadway theater industry with the assertion that "gay men did not enjoy unalloyed acceptance" in the work environment of the 1920s Times Square theater district.[73]

In *42nd Street*, Ropes establishes a Broadway industry in which the chorus serves as a metaphor for the condition of gay men in show business. They constitute a strong presence within its ranks yet must navigate an environment marked by homophobic anxiety. Ropes first introduces his readers not to Jack but to Terry and Harry, who view the chorus as a professional stepping stone from vaudeville. The men share their fear that they will be tainted with the queer stigma of the chorus boy: a concern confirmed by Terry's and Harry's rivals, the O'Malley Brothers, who greet them outside of the Palace Theatre: "Hey, Terry; hear you're one o' the girls!" and "Harry, how does it seem to be with all them fairy nice boys?"[74]

Ropes demonstrates Terry and Harry as eager to establish a veneer of hetero-masculinity, in the midst of a *Pretty Lady* chorus conspicuous with the presence of fairies. Terry and Harry first allude to Jack as a possible source for Harry to pay off a debt. When Terry suggests to Harry, "How about that fagot in the show? He's got a yen for you, maybe he'd come across," Harry bristles. Ropes describes the character's shoulders squaring "with a sense of outraged virility": "Lissen! I ain't putting myself under obligation to no fag. He won't keep his hands offa me now. Someday, I'm gonna sock that guy!" Terry responds with logic that reflects *The Drag*'s Dr. Richmond: "He ain't a bad egg, that Winslow, and them guys can't help themselves. . . . Why I palled around with a nance for a whole season an' he never even tried to touch me."[75]

Ropes contrasts Jack's ill repute as a fairy, and the anxiety it evokes in men like Terry and Harry, with the queer self-presentation shared by Billy Lawler and Julian Marsh. Whereas Winslow is open about his gay sexual orientation, Billy and Marsh are not. Yet, the *Pretty Lady* company receives their affair as an open secret. Deftly, Ropes shows how the power dynamics of the *Pretty Lady* production shape the unequal share of animus directed against the powerful Marsh and his younger lover. The company perceives Billy as having landed the juvenile lead role in the *Pretty Lady* company due to sexual politics. Only Si Friedman dares to confront Julian about the scabrous scandal the affair has unleashed: "You drag that young punk Lawler everywhere. . . . Don't people's talk mean nothing to you?"[76]

Ropes portrays the Broadway of the 1920s and early '30s as an industry that accepts, and even condones, the pervasive reality of the casting couch when it exploits women. Pointing to a pernicious double standard, Ropes shows how the *Pretty Lady* company views Billy through the double stigma of prostitution and homosexuality. Ropes portrays the character contending with resentment fueled by homophobic discrimination, as well as status anxiety about the blurring of Broadway's hierarchies. The company resents that the young juvenile, despite still projecting the appearance of a "glorified chorus boy," sways Broadway's most powerful impresario.[77] Speaking to Maud, Danny Moran rails: "Ritzy kid, too. Thinks he runs the show. I'd just as leave tell him that he can't boss me just because he's Julian Marsh's mistress."[78] Later, copro-ducer Abe Green muses on "something sickening and unholy in the alliance" between Marsh and Billy.[79]

Describing "Billy Lawler striding disdainfully by, disliked by principals and chorus alike," Ropes sympathetically, yet unsentimentally, portrays the social ostracizing that exacerbates Billy's self-defensive posture of snobbery.[80] Ropes locates the source of the gossip about Marsh and Billy as Jerry Cole, the company's music director. At one rehearsal, Ropes describes Billy, at Julian's side, having "no wish to converse with Jerry," as "the instigator of the rumors which had been started about Marsh and himself."[81] Throughout 42nd Street, various Pretty Lady cast members spitefully refer to Billy as "that bitch" and "that dame."[82] After her replacement of Dorothy, Peggy similarly defends Billy against the jibes of her chorus girl friend Flo. The latter remarks that Peggy's rise, aided by Billy, is "no balloon ascension as far as I'm concerned. More like an undersea voyage." Peggy snaps back: "Still harping on Billy's sins aren't you? . . . I just get so terribly annoyed at the attitude everyone in this company takes toward Billy Lawler. He's human like the rest of us, isn't he?"[83]

By contrast, Ropes depicts Julian Marsh, the feared, autocratic director of Pretty Lady, as treated with almost godlike deference by the company but mocked resentfully behind his back. In both Ropes's novel and the 1933 film musical, Marsh embodies Chauncey's concept of the queer as a gay man able to channel the codes of a "sophisticated" yet straight-passing white-collar masculinity.[84] Writing of Marsh's film representation, Leonard J. Leff describes the impre-sario's appearance as a "normal" man: "In short, if Julian's no sissy, he *must* then be straight. . . . He must adhere to middle-class standards of heterosex-ual manhood, since, otherwise, especially in Hollywood in 1933, what the fairy represents—freedom from a rigid middle-class identity—may taint all men."[85] It is only the outing of the sexual affair between Billy and Marsh by Jerry Cole that pushes the queer presentation of the two men closer to the spectre of the fairy, represented by Winslow. The spilling of the secret leads to backstage dirt dishing and catty references to the director as "Madame Marsh."[86]

Ropes inducts Peggy into these complex backstage dynamics. Ropes also explores the role of social class in shaping relationships among gay men and their straight, female friends and allies. Although Peggy expresses kindness to both Jack and Billy, she finds herself offended by Jack's fairy outrageousness at the Philadelphia cast party. By contrast, Peggy expresses more sympathy toward the refined and discreet Billy, who lauds her "thoroughbred" dedication to the Protestant work ethic.[87]

Ropes draws Peggy and Bill's relationship into *42nd Street*'s pervasive dialogue about the performance of social class. In the backstage novel, theater makers and performers covet the illusion, if not the substance, of "class." Ropes depicts this as both an ineffable charismatic quality and a concrete arbiter for Broadway success in the 1920s, as connected to the marketable polish of "showmanship." Terry discusses his ideas with Peggy as he helps her with her dance routines:

> "an' you gotta get class, too, because dancin' don't mean nothin' if you don't got the showmanship to sell it. Look at the kid we got in our show; prob'ly a lousy hundred a week is all she gets an' she can bend like a pretzel, while there's girls like Evelyn Law can't do half the stuff, but they pull down five hundred or more cause *they* got the class."[88]

Hungry for the "atmosphere of Sutton Place and the Mayfair," Ropes shows Billy gravitating to signifiers of class status.[89] Billy admires the "gentility" of Peggy, whom Marsh later refers to sardonically as "Little Miss Boston."[90] Billy appraises the minister's daughter even as she struggles with her time step: "Heretofore she had been one of a conglomerate mass of be-rompered dancers. Now he saw an attractive youngster who bore herself with a certain distinction that the average chorus lady woefully lacked."[91]

Despite her New England Puritan background, Peggy is characterized by Ropes as the most tolerant heterosexual member of the *Pretty Lady* company in regard to gay rights. Peggy mingles with friends in Greenwich Village and dips into modernist literature of the sort banned in Boston. Anticipating the *Lady Chatterley's Lover* allusion made by Jack Thomas in *Stage Mother*, Ropes shows Peggy sharing a secret pleasure with Billy when the latter sees her, at Penn Station, carrying "a novel with a bright yellow jacket" given to her by Pat Denning.[92] Jesting that the unnamed novel is "bad reading for good little girls," Billy feigns indignation: "Whoa, there, child. . . . Too much traffic for light reading!"[93]

Among the men in *Pretty Lady*'s company, Peggy finds her closest rapport with Billy. When Peggy, to Terry, compliments Billy's "sweet" encouragement, the chorus boy "checks himself" against uttering a homophobic slur: "Huh . . . That—." Peggy objects: "I suppose you don't believe all those tiresome rumors. . . . I don't. Anyway, what business is it of ours?"[94] As the relationship between Peggy and Terry dissolves, the latter intensifies his animosity against Billy, as well as Marsh. He sneers, "Marsh! Keepin' a young punk like Billy

Lawler! I hope you don't think a guy's worthwhile because he's queer and don't chase women."[95]

In the final sequence of the book, Ropes illustrates how Peggy's alliance with Billy results in the trajectory that the 1933 film musical famously mythologized as "going out a youngster and coming back a star." Ropes does not exonerate Peggy of calculation. Even before Dorothy's injury, Peggy hopes that Billy can help her advance in the *Pretty Lady* company. Ropes observes, "She was learning to be shrewd; there are politics in all professions. Billy Lawler was her friend—she'd coax Billy to put in a good word for her."[96] At the same time, through the evocation of interior monologue, Ropes portrays the powerful force of Billy's gratitude to Peggy after "long weeks of snubbing and innuendoes":

> Peggy Sawyer alone had disregarded the hatred and contempt of the others and had greeted him pleasantly. In his heart of hearts, he was not convinced of her great ability, but he felt that her treatment of him should be rewarded and here was the opportunity.[97]

As the musical comedy prepares for its Philadelphia opening night, Billy uses his powerful influence with Marsh to argue for Peggy as the new star of *Pretty Lady*: a show whose title satirizes the fungibility of many 1920s musical comedy ingenues. Ropes ironically invokes the era's dominant Cinderella narrative in the reaction of Abe Green, who resents the interference of Billy, and the romantic infatuation that he perceives as turning Marsh into a "doddering, fatuous old man" rather than a cunning Broadway showman. Abe scolds Billy: "What do you think this is? A Paramount Picture, bring in the kiddies and let 'em hear about Cinderella? . . . Not one of those chiselin' gold diggers knows the first thing about showmanship."[98]

To this appeal to showmanship, Billy evokes Terry's earlier disquisition on "class," in arguing his case for Peggy. When Marsh objects, "But Billy, the girl's an amateur. . . . It took years of training to perfect the coyness that dear Dorothy's public is so mad about," Billy maintains, "And which Peggy Sawyer possesses naturally." Billy elaborates: "She's decent, she's civilized, she's no more a chorus girl at heart than I am." Yet, Ropes caustically clarifies that Billy, no less than Peggy, is driven by professional self-interest as well as feelings of genuine alliance. He negotiates, "Julian, if we put this deal through, I want the dance I do with the girls put in the second act." When Marsh concedes to Billy with a vulnerable confession—"You know my life means nothing to me if I can't make you happy"—Billy draws back with an allusion drawn from gay slang. He urges the older showman not to out himself with feminine senti-mentality: "For Christ's sake, stop acting like an old auntie. . . . You talk like this when we're alone, but it's a different story if I try to get a better opportu-nity in the show."[99]

As Peggy prepares for her Philadelphia opening night, Ropes reintroduces Winslow, absent from the narrative since the Philadelphia cast party. As Billy and Peggy re-encounter Jack, Ropes subtly critiques the ways in which the homophobia practiced against Billy has become harmfully internalized by the young juvenile as well. Ropes observes that while Billy "had managed to weather the storm, it had not left him unscathed."[100] In his characterization of Billy, Ropes reflects Chauncey's observations of the interactions among queers and fairies: "While most [queer] men could elaborate the ways in which they were different from fairies, they needed to do so only because the similarities seemed so frighteningly apparent."[101] Billy's self-distancing from Jack occurs outside the elegant, "self-conscious gentility" of the Ritz Lenox Palm Court. To Peggy, Billy affirms his conviction that "you never belonged in the chorus. . . . I could tell that the first time I spoke to you."[102] He successively urges her to relinquish her relationships with Flo, Terry, and Pat. Billy coldly remarks of Flo: "She's been in the merry merry for about six years. Never will get any further. You can't afford to be too friendly with people like that."[103] When Peggy frowns, "Billy—you're not trying to make a snob out of me?," her friend responds, "Far from it. I'm merely advising you to look out for number one." Billy then sug-gests to Peggy that they enter into a lavender romance engineered for career advancement—and for Peggy to avoid entanglements with "Park Avenue play-boys." Peggy considers Billy's request, reflecting on its "mutual benefit" to the both of them:

> Obviously, Billy felt that such a companionship would serve as a smoke screen for his relations with Julian Marsh. She knew that Lawler was incapable of gen-uine admiration for her. . . . But it served his purpose to be seen about town with a comely young woman who was a figure on the Broadway scene and he was not averse to taking that means of stopping gossip. Well, two could play that game.[104]

As Ropes critically portrays Billy's Hobbesian opportunism, he pulls Jack back into the narrative. As Billy and Peggy leave the Palm Court and stroll along Broad Street, they encounter Jack, whose flamboyant gait attracts crude sidewalk harassment (and a mocking allusion to Savoy's "Whoops, my dear!" catchphrase):

> Peggy noticed a languid figure walking ahead of them, his hips swaying in a sort of rhythmic undulation. Two sidewalk hangers-on, lounging in front of a cigar store, sighted this person in the same moment. One of them emitted a derisive laugh and the other called, "Whoops, dearie, mind all the bad men or they'll change your name to Brown!"[105]

Ropes depicts Jack responding to his harassers in terms that express proud dignity, as well as his irreverent camp wit. Jack turns to them "regally" and turns a "withering glance on the hecklers," saying with "startling distinctiveness": "Lissen, girlie. . . . Don't think you're fooling anybody just because you've got hair on your chest. Every time you get a lump in your throat you start sewing baby clothes!" The chorus boy sails on, "leaving two discomfited hoodlums in his wake."[106]

As Jack leaves the scene, Ropes suggests that Billy has absorbed a scathing cultural message: that the only way for a gay man to succeed on Broadway as a leading man—and, by metaphorical extension, to lead as a "man" in mainstream American society—is to vilify and banish the signifiers of homosexuality that will mark him as a fairy. To the litany of friends whom Billy has advised Peggy to drop or avoid, Billy now adds Jack. Billy nods in the direction of the vanished chorus boy, fuming to Peggy: "That's what you want to get away from. . . . Cheapness! Nastiness! Never mind what people do so long as it's accomplished with an air. But a boy like that—! And I'll wager my last dime that you've been on parties with him, had to laugh with him and treat him like an equal." When Peggy replies, "rather feebly," that "Jack means well," Billy storms that Jack can be of no use to her: "People like that can't get you a thing. If you must know immoral folks like that get those who have graduated with honors, not dirty little failures who are bound straight for perdition!"[107]

Anticipating his description of Jack Thomas in the next year's *Stage Mother*, Ropes illustrates Billy's self-harming conviction that to express an openly gay identity, in the lighthearted manner of Jack Winslow, is to damn oneself to the "perdition" of failure in the commercial American theater. Yet, Ropes portrays Jack in terms of a redemptive pride and a virtuosic sense of self that embraces queer failure as "a rejection of normative protocols of canonization and value," as described by Muñoz.[108] If Jack knows that he risks Broadway "perdition," he also evokes the theorist's observation about "queerness itself as being filled with the intention to be lost": "To be lost is not to hide in a closet or to perform a simple (ontological) disappearing act; it is to veer away from heterosexuality's path."[109]

Although Ropes somewhat draws from the stereotypes of hysterical effeminacy that characterized the 1920s stage "pansy" in his depiction of Jack, he sympathetically portrays the chorus boy as a character whose courageous authenticity and lack of shame distinguish him sharply from the more conformist Billy. In Ropes's nuanced portrayal of the cultural tension between queers and fairies, Billy, in sublimating an authentic identity to his winner-takes-all concept of assimilation and success, has relinquished some of the moral imperative embedded in Peggy's defense of him: "He's human like the rest of us, isn't he?"[110] By contrast, Jack embraces the "queer art of failure," which, as Halberstam observes, "turns on the impossible, the improbable, the unlikely, and the unremarkable. It quietly loses, and in losing it imagines other goals for life, for love, for art, and for being."[111]

In the conflict between Billy and Jack, Ropes may have been playing out the tensions in his own private and public lives: discreet and "modest" in the pages of newspaper profiles but personally flamboyant and possessed of an irrepressible camp wit linking him with the working-class icon of the fairy and Winslow's "nance comedy." Aligning with the codes of Boston Puritan culture, Ropes shied away from talking about his personal life in interviews with local and New York newspapers, avoiding the café society notoriety eagerly courted by gay male contemporaries like Coward and Cole Porter. On the level of his public persona, Ropes may have identified personally with the "queer" self-concealment of Billy (who shares a first name with the author's vaudeville alter ego). At the same time, Ropes's refusal to tame his own luxuriantly bawdy style in the pages of his backstage novels connects him even more closely to Jack.

Through the stylistic centralization of Jack's voice in *42nd Street*, Ropes denies and defies Billy's denunciation of Jack: "People like that can't get you a thing."[112] From Jack, Ropes "gets" a great deal: the camp comic dirt dishing that provides the fuel of *42nd Street*'s interlocking industrial machines. In *42nd Street*, Ropes leaves little doubt that Jack, unlike the Cinderella-like Billy, will not be promoted to the stature of a leading man. Yet, "sailing off" against a last torrent of homophobic abuse, Jack will continue to authentically be who he is: an artist of queer failure camping riotously in front of his audiences, backstage with the chorus boys, and in the pages of Ropes's definitive show business novel.

"I'm Miss Pathé Weekly When It Comes to News": Stage Mother's "Teeth of the Machine" and the Loose Tongue of Jack Thomas

42nd Street portrays dirt dishing not only as a central force of gay culture but also as the grease in the cogs of the Broadway machine, which Ropes uses as a pervasive metaphor for both Pretty Lady and the Broadway industry. Jack Winslow may not rise to the pinnacle of Broadway success like Peggy Sawyer, whose surname evokes the wholesome adventuring of Mark Twain's boys. Yet, Jack demonstrates a proud and defiant ethos of survival in 42nd Street. By contrast, in Stage Mother, Ropes demonstrates the dangers of dishing the dirt for gay men, particularly those moving closer to the centers of political power. Book reviews of Stage Mother in 1933 overlooked the character of Jack Thomas, just as reviews of 42nd Street had largely done with Jack Winslow. Like Winslow, too, Jack Thomas was cut from Warner Brothers' 1933 film adaptation of Stage Mother, cowritten by Ropes.

With Stage Mother, Ropes created a literary succès d'estime, drawing upon a variety of generic sources. The New York Times praised Ropes's infusion of urban realism and pulp storytelling into Stage Mother, observing: "Not a very sensible or elevated story, it is yet sure-fire entertainment for those who like their fiction rough, raw, riotous and gaudy."[113] The New York Mirror's critic probed deeper into the author's intentions, observing: "Bradford Ropes has written his best novel in this strange and merciless story—strange because it gets behind the lights and beneath the pavements of Broadway; merciless because under the professional dignity lies hunger for truth and ultimate humanity."[114]

In 42nd Street, Peggy had functioned less as the protagonist of the novel than as a plot catalyst for a Grand Hotel-like collective of characters representing Broadway as a culture industry. Similarly, Kitty galvanizes the events of Ropes's wide-lens canvas of Prohibition-era Broadway in the 1920s. In this world ruled by crime and graft, Ropes portrays Kitty's implacable show biz ambition, driven by years of battling the combined forces of ageism, classism, and sexism, as less reprehensible than the grindings of a Tammany Hall-like political machine. Drawing from his teenage experience performing with the Gus Edwards troupe, Ropes perpetuates the enduring negative stereotype of the stage mother as "among the most obnoxious pests in the theatre business."[115] At the same time, Ropes critically details the objectification and exploitation of women within and outside the walls of the theater.

In *Stage Mother*, Ropes links the intimidation of female sex workers, under the administration of New York's "Jazz mayor" James J. Walker, to the persecution of gay men. The criminalization of their sexuality closely connected gay men and female prostitutes. With the character of Jack Thomas, who dishes the dirt while blowing the whistle on mayoral corruption, Ropes critiques the intersectional misogyny and homophobia institutionally enabled by systems like Tammany Hall but also reflected in American culture at large despite the licenses of the Jazz Age. In Ropes's portrayal of Jack, the author links the forces of American Puritanism with those of political corruption, enabling gangsters, bootleggers, and bosses to prey upon female sex workers and gay men alike.

The Cultural and Political Contexts of *Stage Mother*

Ranging in action from the 1910s through the late 1920s, *Stage Mother* represents a Depression-era novel reflecting upon the excesses of the Jazz Age. The circumstances leading to Walker's resignation in the 1930-32 Seabury Investigations provide an essential "key to the city" for understanding Ropes's contexts for *Stage Mother*, as well as his critique of the Walker administration's treatment of prostitutes and gay men. Mayor Al Dexter in *Stage Mother* strongly suggests a roman à clef portrait of Walker and the political bosses who operated Tammany Hall's machinery. At the same time, Ropes's background as the grandson of David Nichols Ropes, a mayor of Orange, New Jersey, in the 1860s, as well as his close family relationship to Malcolm E. Nichols, inspired a knowledge of mayoral politics that also informs the dynamics of *Stage Mother*.

Prefacing *Stage Mother* with a disclaimer that "all characters and incidents in this novel are fictitious," Ropes displaces Dexter's mayoral seat from New York to a large city outside New York, whose descriptions most closely evoke Newark.[116] Nevertheless, in his characterization of Dexter, Ropes creates unmistakable parallels between the character and Walker, who drew acres of publicity as a Prohibition-flouting playboy-politician of mythic proportions. As a "debonair prophet of gaiety and extravagance and glitter," "Beau James" epitomized New York City's defiance of Prohibition and disdain for the Puritan ethos that continued to hold sway in Boston.[117] Yet, Walker, known equally for his weak resolve, fell increasingly in thrall to Tammany Hall corruption. Reporter Milton Mackaye described Walker as "glib, vain, prodigal, luxury-loving, and amazingly indifferent to the rules of common honesty."[118]

Set in the 1920s but published in May 1933, *Stage Mother* draws upon the recent newspaper sensation of the Samuel Seabury corruption trials that, in 1932, precipitated Walker's resignation from mayoral office after his two wildly popular terms. As Miller describes, Judge Seabury's court "unearthed massive graft and incompetence in the Walker administration and in the municipal courts it oversaw," as well as the revelation that Walker "had received, under the table, over one million dollars in 'beneficences,' as he cagily called those handouts from well-heeled friends." As Miller recounts, on September 1, 1932, Walker "was forced to resign, pushed out of office on suspicion of rank corruption by members of his own party, led by his political sponsor ex-Governor Al Smith and current Governor Franklin Delano Roosevelt."[119]

In Ropes's portrayal of Al Dexter's affair with Shirley, *Stage Mother* also draws substantially upon the poorly concealed affair of Walker and Betty Compton, who became Walker's second wife after his resignation. Starting as a Broadway chorus girl, Compton rose rapidly to featured roles in shows like the Gershwins' *Oh, Kay!* (1926) and Cole Porter's *Fifty Million Frenchmen* (1929). In 1933, when Stanley Walker published *The Night Club Era*, the mayor's scandalous affair with the "apple-cheeked chorus girl" had become public knowledge, with Walker dirt dishing of his mayoral namesake: "Was he seen with Betty Compton at prizefights on nights when his wife was either at their home in St. Luke's place or in Florida? Very well. Good for Jimmy."[120]

Finally, *Stage Mother* draws upon Walker's relationship to the political institution of Tammany Hall. In the nineteenth century, Tammany Hall "quickly evolved into the most powerful urban political machine in the country," drawing from a base of Irish American Democratic loyalty.[121] In the early twentieth century, a succession of unscrupulous political bosses ran Tammany Hall. These included Charles Francis Murphy, whom Miller describes as "the shrewdest and most powerful overlord in Tammany History," and John Francis Curry.[122] As Ropes dramatizes in *Stage Mother* through the relationship between ruthless political boss Reilly and Dexter, Walker demonstrated his loyalty successively to the bosses from whom he drew political support in return for allowance to commit acts of corruption and graft.

The bosses commanded the loyalty of the twenty-three Tammany Hall district leaders who presided over New York's boroughs. As Miller observes, "For doing the work of the people, the district leader expected iron loyalty and generous kickbacks—the sources of Tammany power."[123] Walker held a particularly close relationship to the ruthless Harlem district leader Jimmy Hines, one of the three lead investors of the Silver Slipper. As Debby Applegate notes,

"Walker was the front man of the show, but Hines, with his army of voters and gangland backers, was the closest it had to a real boss."[124]

In his portrayal of the Hines-like Reilly in *Stage Mother*, Ropes also critiques Walker's turning a blind eye to corruption in the police system, under the feckless police commissioner Grover A. Whalen. Although Walker framed himself as the adversary to moral reformers, he nonetheless gave free reign to police officers to harass and extort sex workers. Stanley Walker recounts the investigation of these frame-ups, eventually exposed in Seabury's court. These inquiries "unraveled the tangled, sordid situation under which stool pigeons had framed innocent women, policemen had assaulted and robbed and taken bribes from women of the street and honest old households. It smelled to Heaven."[125]

The Vivian Gordon murder case of 1931, in which a sex worker-turned-crime moll was found strangled to death, led not only to sensational tabloid stories but to an investigation into police practices that contributed to Walker's indictment. Rachel Shteir describes how Franklin Delano Roosevelt, then New York's governor, "suspected there was a connection between Gordon's murder and police 'frame-ups.' . . . He had already empowered former judge Samuel Seabury, a crusader against Tammany Hall, to investigate corruption in the magistrates' courts, where police and judges framed innocent women as prostitutes."[126] Further investigation by the Seabury Commission revealed sordid and damning details. Seabury learned that Detective Andrew McLaughlin "had deposited $35,800 in his bank account over a period of two years when his salary was $3,000 a year" and that he had "made as many as 1,200 vice arrests in ten years, roaming up and down Broadway arresting women, working through his lunch break. . . . While interrogating witnesses, [he] pummeled them with their previous crimes until they confessed to imaginary new ones."[127]

"The Women Our Vice Committee Imprisoned"

On the surface, the police frame-ups of female sex workers that flourished under Walker's mayoral administration might have little in common with the portrayal of gay male culture on Broadway that Ropes centers around the loose-lipped Jack Thomas. Yet, in his political backstage novel, Ropes subtly connects the persecution of female prostitutes with the criminalization of gay male sexuality. After Jack's murder in *Stage Mother*, Ropes depicts Dexter rationalizing Jack's death by expressing his conviction that Jack deserved to die. Initially amused by Jack's wit, Dexter is relieved that Shirley has a companion of whom he "won't ever have to be jealous."[128] Dexter's deep-seated homophobia emerges as Ropes portrays his mental state:

> That men were being murdered to keep him in office, that women were forced to endure the vilest degradation so that the empty title "His Honor" might be bestowed upon him—of these things Al Dexter was not ignorant, but he contrived to excuse the methods of his employers with the phrase, "It is all for the public good." A man like Jack Thomas is better off dead. He was a degenerate, a pervert. It was mercy in the sight of God to rid the world of him. And those women our Vice Committee imprisoned. Suppose they weren't guilty of the charges. They've probably done things far worse.[129]

In linking the Vice Committee's frame-ups of sexually transgressive women (who may or may not be prostitutes) and the framing of gay men as "degenerates" and "perverts," Ropes demonstrates the close relationship between prostitutes and gay men as targets of vice squad persecution. Chauncey observes that both fairies and prostitutes, both of whom were visible denizens of Times Square, "congregated in many of the same locales and used some of the same techniques to attract attention; the fairy's most obvious attribute, his painted face, was the quintessential marker of the prostitute."[130]

Like Jack Winslow, Jack Thomas disdains convention with "his magnificent sense of humor that neither rebuff nor downright indignation could dull."[131] Unlike the irreverent Winslow, however, Jack Thomas steps not only out of line but across the nebulous boundaries that separate backstage gossip from political scandal. In *Stage Mother*, Ropes illustrates the danger, as well as the liberation, that dirt dishing could pose to gay men during an era that flourished in tabloid gossip in magazines like *Broadway Brevities*. Specializing in camp argot, *Brevities* illustrated how this discourse straddled the gay underground culture and more mainstream circulation to Manhattanite insiders. As Hugh Ryan observes, "Although its articles were disapproving or salacious, the writers of *Broadway Brevities* clearly had intimate knowledge of New York City's queer scene," with headlines like "Third Sex Plague Spreads Anew! Sissies Permeate Sublime Social Strata as Film Stars and Broadwayites Go Gay."[132] In *Stage Mother*, the luridly repackaged queer dirt dishing that spread to the pages of *Brevities* also poses a threat to political insiders, should gossip jump from the nightclub into the media. As John Reilly observes in *Stage Mother*, "It's only a short jump from speakeasy gossip to the editorial pages of the newspapers."[133]

In *Stage Mother*, Ropes aims his most direct critique not at his complexly rendered, eponymous stage mother but at the authority figures who enabled hate crimes against fairies and sexually transgressive women alike. Ropes pointedly alludes to the hypocrisies of a Walker administration that flouted its Jazz Age hedonism while punishing "degenerates" to appease vice squad reformers who threatened district bosses. In 1928, while running for reelection, Walker authorized and took credit for the Wales Padlock Law raid upon West's *Pleasure Man*. As John P. Houchin describes, "While claiming he was a liberal and a supporter of theater, [Walker] drew the line when blatant homosexuality was displayed." Walker vowed to voters that "we shall not have disgusting or revolting degenerate plays for public exhibition in the city. The efforts of the police and what they will do have my hearty support."[134]

In *Stage Mother*, Ropes illustrates that gay men in 1920s New York were far from safe, even in the relatively permissive atmosphere of the Broadway theater industry. The "magnificent" camp humor with which Ropes endows Jack Thomas frames the dancer as the paradoxical moral id of the novel—but also precipitates his murder. Using the tools of crime and pulp fiction in *Stage Mother*, Ropes shows how "dishing the dirt" functions as an essential aspect of gay male expressive culture. At the same time, Ropes explores the dangerous risk of self-disclosure for gay men in 1920s and early '30s New York, despite the rationalizations of their oppressors: "It is all for the public good."

Stage Mothers and Stag Mayors:
Gossip and Scandal in Ropes's Jazz Age New York

The introduction of Jack Thomas into *Stage Mother*'s narrative expands upon Ropes's allusions to the recent Seabury trials and Walker's resignation. It also builds upon Ropes's critique of 1920s Broadway as an industry dependent upon the sexual exploitation of actresses and chorus girls. Alluding to the camp comedy of Bert Savoy at a pivotal narrative moment, Ropes subtly links the forces of misogyny and homophobia in his backstage novel.

As Dexter visits Manhattan from the neighboring city over which he presides, Ropes describes Dexter in terms that evoke Walker's fabulous appearances in tabloid media. Ropes writes:

The story of Al Dexter, genial good fellow, had struck the front pages of the New York journals with a resounding whack. His predilection for graft and handsome ladies of the theater had set him amazingly apart from the humdrum succession of sour-visaged reformers and coarsely predatory ward heelers who were his immediate contemporaries.[135]

Ropes's depiction of the Dexter-Lorraine relationship draws closely from the scandalous relationship of Walker and showgirl Compton. Hardened by Kitty's sabotaging of her romance with Warren Foster, Shirley cynically enters into an affair with Dexter. "Playing around with Dexter sets you in the money," her agent Louis Hearn bluntly informs the Lorraine women.[136] Backstage, Hearn announces to Shirley and Kitty that a distinguished visitor has come to see *Adam and His Eves*: "Waiting downstairs for Miss Shirley Lorraine is Alfred P. Dexter, the play-boy mayor." At a party after the show, Dexter woos Shirley with jokes about his reputation for luxury and laxity: "Fortunately, my Board of Estimate is laid away in mothballs from Saturday until Monday, so I seize opportunity by its forelock and find time for a little private sinning."[137]

In using the Walker-Compton affair as the inspiration for the Dexter-Lorraine liaison in *Stage Mother*, Ropes also critically portrays an industry that commoditized women as part of the system of erotic capitol that Will A. Page, in 1927, labeled the "Broadway Beauty Trust." Press agent Jack Lait had queried in his preface to Page's chorus girl exposé, which sought to reveal the secrets of revue showgirls: "What, in brief, is the actual truth about Broadway's hothouse flowers and the men who make them bloom?"[138]

With their *Behind the Curtains of Broadway's Beauty Trust*, Page and Lait luridly exploited the public's hunger for titillation involving cultural myths of gold-digging chorus girls and Wall Street sugar daddies. Ropes also pulls open Broadway's curtains for revealing views backstage. Unlike Page and Lait, Ropes indicts the systemic sexual exploitation of women working in commercial theater industries. The author critiques Broadway show business, and, particularly, the forms of the Broadway, West End, and Paris music hall revue, as a "showmart" of women's bodies.[139] Ropes observes omnisciently in 1933's *Stage Mother*: "A lean day has fallen upon the theatre, but a comparatively few years ago the glamorous showgirls were bejeweled and maintained in the best traditions of the 1920s. Men of affluence and power grew humble in the presence of these stately goddesses. Titans of finance drooled with envy when a rival captured the blonde prize of the hour."[140] Here, Ropes evokes backstage novel predecessors Émile Zola and Avery Hopwood in exposing the Broadway theater industry of the 1920s as a "great bordello."

Ropes poses the showgirl as the major factor driving the revenue of the Jazz Age revue, which depended in no small part on the expectation from the "titans of finance" that economically vulnerable women in the chorus would consent to affairs. Although Shirley has bypassed the chorus, rising from a "subdeb" in a vaudeville youth revue to romantic ingenue in *Adam and His Eves*, she too finds herself constructed as an erotic commodity whose image is used to both subsidize and sell the musical to the "army of brokers and wealthy play-boys hammer[ing] at the portals of the stage door."[141]

In *Stage Mother*, Ropes sets the Dexter-Lorraine affair within the larger context of the "Broadway Beauty Trust." Kitty overlooks her initial trepidation about encouraging her daughter's affair with Dexter in deference to its potential for financial gain. Ropes observes: "Kitty had known of this state of affairs for many years. She was fully cognizant of the influence which those who flourish under Park Avenue patronage may wield in the theatre."[142] Such critiques may have had an autobiographical impetus: Billy Bradford's own vaudeville and cabaret dance partnership with Marian Hamilton had ended in 1928 after Hamilton left the stage to marry David Ludlum Jr.[143] In *Stage Mother*, Ropes alludes directly to the marriage as Shirley considers the propositions of multiple affluent suitors. A gossip column notes: "Walter Bigelow, Jr. whose dad makes those cars, and the lovely toe-tantalizer, Shirley Lorraine, are torching it."[144]

Stage Mother introduces Jack Thomas as an irreverent, dirt-dishing threat against the secrecy that shrouds Shirley and Dexter's relationship. At the same time that Ropes depicts Dexter plucking Shirley out of the Broadway "showmart," he depicts the furtiveness that surrounded Broadway affairs at the most elite levels of power. Hearn had strictly counseled mother and daughter that they must keep the affair out of the newspapers: "Not publicity, I mean, after all a guy who's mayor don't want too much of that kind of three-sheeting, but he sure will shell out the berries if Shirley acts nice."[145]

If Hearn advises Shirley against tabloid exposure, he cannot prevent Shirley's fast friendship with the effeminate Jack. Possessed of a "gauche effortless dancing style" alongside his "easy familiarity" and "florid mannerisms," Jack signs on to *Adam and His Eves* to "instruct Shirley in the rhythmic dances which were becoming the rage."[146] When Shirley meets Jack, she likes him immediately for his wit—and as the one friend to whom she can dish about an affair kept scrupulously out of the tabloids. Kitty disapproves of Jack as an "unfit companion for her daughter." Yet, Dexter—at first—is "highly delighted" that Shirley has a companion who is not a sexual rival. Shirley appreciates Jack's encouragement of her dancing, as he exclaims: "Now listen, girl friend, loosen up. Fling those hands; don't try to pull a Pavlowa on your old Aunt Jessie. . . . And show those legs! Mistinguette [sic] in her best days never boasted a pair of pins like that."[147]

A wryer, more literate wit than Jack Winslow, Jack Thomas shares with the *42nd Street* character a distinct camp sensibility, as well as an insistence on dishing the dirt. As well as helping Shirley in her dancing, Jack accompanies her to parties, dispensing "acid commentaries on the follies of mankind which passed before his critical gaze." At this, stage mother Kitty registers alarm: "Privately she thought this cultivation of the notorious young man rather dangerous. Jack, in his cups, was prone to gossip and he never suffered from too great a degree of reticence."[148]

Ropes depicts Jack's flair for gossip as an essential part of the fabric of not only gay camp culture but backstage "show talk." At the same time, *Stage Mother* allegorizes the threat that dirt dishing, as a discursive form of gay male carnivalesque, posed to hierarchies of patriarchal power in the 1920s and '30s. When Jack's loose tongue conflicts with Dexter's political machine, the results turn deadly for the juvenile dancer, whose murder is countenanced both on the grounds of political expedience but also because all of the powerful men involved and implicated in the crime despise gay men.

Ropes reflects James J. Walker's loyalty to Tammany Hall's political bosses and district leaders in the relationship of Al Dexter and his boss, John Reilly: the adversary who determines to stop Jack Thomas from dishing the dirt. Ropes describes Reilly as the "nominal head of the organization which kept Al Dexter in power; Reilly, the Voice behind the Voice, the true ventriloquist from whose brain emanated the policies which Dexter successfully mouthed." When an inebriated Jack accompanies Shirley to a gin-soaked party at the Central Park Casino, he inadvertently gossips about the affair to none other than Reilly. Jack boasts: "Baby, I'm Miss Pathé Weekly when it comes to news about Shirley an' the Mayor. . . . Grand kids the both of 'em. I love 'em—God how I love them."[149]

Ironically, Jack Thomas seals his fate by revealing his camp truth telling to a perilous enemy of its expression. Here, Ropes subtly brings in the fairy persona of Savoy, whom he links to the character of Jack. Pointing to Dexter and Shirley, Jack unwittingly whispers in Reilly's ear at the party, before swaying and falling against the political boss: "Get those two. . . . The dirt I could dish if my lips weren't sealed. Come up to my place, boy friend, and maybe I'll open up over a bottle an' a bird."[150] "Come up to my place" alluded not only to Savoy's most famous catchphrase, "You must come over," but to West's iconic transformation of the line, addressed to Cary Grant, in the 1933 Paramount film *She Done Him Wrong*: "Why don't you come up some time, and see me."

References to Savoy recur in the next sequence, in which Ropes portrays the alliances among district bosses and bootleggers that flourished in Walker's New York. At the elegantly appointed speakeasy of Angelo Scarlatti, Reilly finds Jack drinking a succession of whiskey sours. At Angelo's, Reilly discusses Jack with the "ex-convict" Scarlatti, a practiced killer. Scarlatti confirms that Jack is a regular patron: "You know, the juvenile! Plays in a lot of shows. He's queer, but he gets 'round plenty.'" Reilly responds to the gangster: "A bad boy, that Thomas! . . . Talks too much!"[151] Scarlatti informs Reilly that Jack's stories about Dexter and Shirley sharing a hotel suite at the Savoy Towers have reached the ears of tabloid reporters: "Why, a coupla reporters nailed him the other night an' he spilled a yarn about the mayor bein' locked out of his room at the Towers an' runnin' up an' down the corridors like a maniac until Lorraine let him in her bedroom. . . . An' him meetin' a lot of important political guys the next morning." In choosing a "Savoy" hotel as the site of Jack and Shirley's dirt dishing, Ropes—consistently strategic in the naming of his characters and locations—appears to once again allude to the influential *Greenwich Village Follies* star as he invokes the drag queen's troubling of moral authorities.

Ropes portrays the conspiracy between Reilly and Scarlatti to "attend to Mr. Thomas" as fueled by the men's shared homophobia, as well as the compulsion to keep Dexter and Shirley's affair from reaching additional reporters. When Jack approaches Reilly and Scarlatti's table, the two men deceptively invite him for a drink. Ropes portrays the eagerness of the men to kill Jack. Scarlatti nods his assent to Reilly with the admission: "Okay! . . . I never *did* like faggots!"[152] Scarlatti then arranges with Mike, the bartender, to poison Jack's highballs. As the "room [becomes] a slow shifting mass of color," Jack continues to spin out witticisms, taunting the political boss as "Mr. Grafter." He maintains his "high spirits" shortly before falling unconscious to the floor: "But don't keep me up here too long—there's some gorgeous looking things downstairs an' I want a crack at them. Come on down an' watch Thomas do his stuff."[153]

The aftermath of Jack's murder occupies much of the third section of the novel, as Ropes continues to demonstrate how homophobia fuels the corruption within Dexter's administration. Armed with an alibi, Reilly, Scarlatti, and Mike place Jack's body into a car outside the speakeasy and prepare to drive toward the Hudson River. As they rearrange Jack's corpse into his clothing, they cruelly mock his dandyism. Mike jibes, "Kinda lightweight for such a tall feller. . . . Dresses well, though. Christ, did youse get a load of the shoes that punk is wearing!" Ropes does not spare graphic details of the results of the men's hate crime, which the newspapers report as a suicide: "Three days later the corpse was recovered—a hideous object whose water-bloated torso and mutilated face caused the onlookers to shudder."[154]

Portraying Jack Thomas as the riotous, if unrestrainable, camp conscience of *Stage Mother*, Ropes frames the dancer's death as the impetus for Shirley's moral awakening. She increasingly becomes aware that Dexter's charm masks a rotten center. Here, Ropes calls upon his adolescent writing in the *Golden Rod*. He reprises the last name of the greed-crazed, homicidal nephew "Harvy Dexter" from "The Trembling Hour," while revisiting the themes of his poem "The Man Who Lost His Soul." Believing Jack's death a suicide, Shirley mourns to newspaper reporters: "He was a peculiar chap, very melancholy at times, at other times sitting on top of the world. It's too bad. Jack was unfortunate, but he was a grand trouper and a good friend." Ropes's inclusion of alcoholism as a significant factor in Jack Thomas's death might seem to ally Ropes with the reformist concerns of his WCTU-leading mother. At the same time, Shirley's reflection to the newspapers—"It must have been in a moment of drunken despondency"—links the character's drinking less to his own moral failure than to his condition in an American society that condemns him for his sexuality.[155]

Ropes uses the device of interior monologues throughout the third book, "Enter a Lady," of *Stage Mother*. In doing so, Ropes illustrates the homophobic motivations that impel not only Reilly but Dexter to justify Jack's murder. Ropes depicts Reilly's thoughts on the "ghastly truth" of Jack's killing: "If the dying cry still rang in his ears . . . it was destined to be; at all costs the organization must remain in power. Anyone who threatened the present regime must go. And so, light hearted and damned, Jack Thomas passed from the scene."[156] Confronting Dexter with the question, "Is it true about Jack Thomas?," Shirley already knows the answer. She reflects that Dexter must have been "sick to death of Reilly and his schemes, but he was inextricably caught in the machine of which he was such an important cog. . . . Jack Thomas had hurled himself into the teeth of the machine and was removed from its path. Dexter saw these things and remained helpless."[157]

Finally, Dexter admits to Shirley that Reilly's goons have killed Jack. The mayor exclaims to his mistress: "After all . . . Thomas was no good, he had it coming to him, sooner or later some rough-neck would have stuck a knife in his back." Again, Ropes opens the curtains on Dexter's psyche with an interior monologue: "It'll teach the others. They'll learn that they can't talk about the mayor and get away with it. One and all they'll remember what happened to Mr. Jack Thomas."[158] Lamenting the loss of her friend, Shirley realizes the scale of the moral turpitude that has subsidized her affair with the "spineless" playboy mayor.

Reviewers of *Stage Mother* viewed Ropes's story as revolving around its "juggernaut" title character. Nevertheless, Ropes's critique of Broadway show business, as an industry driven by the ruthless imperatives of capitalism, vitally intersects with the story of Jack Thomas. In *Stage Mother*, Ropes illustrates the subversive potential of camp discourse. Jack's truth telling and "ready wit" threaten the political and economic hierarchies that have also scathed Kitty Lorraine. Through the character of Jack Thomas, Ropes reframes the fabled hedonism of Jazz Age New York as only a partial liberation fueled by interlocking currents of misogyny and homophobia.

Although drawing from the same tabloid energies that animated the scurrilous *Broadway Brevities*, *Stage Mother* suggests Ropes's overarching moral vision. "He did talk too much for his own good," reflects Shirley, sadly, of her murdered friend, who had dubbed himself "Miss Pathé Weekly."[159] In the figure of the *Lady Chatterley*-reading Jack, who also evokes the "nance comedy" of Savoy, Ropes once again thwarts the cultural Puritanism and censorship exercised by the New England Watch and Ward Society. Alluding to the Seabury trials, Ropes imagines an alternative history in which a fairy's dirt dishing exposes the crimes of the vice squads enabled by Walker's administration. "But the hue and the cry had not died with Thomas," Ropes writes, as the revelation of Jack's murder leads to the exposure of Dexter's corruption.[160] Through his portrayal of the damned, loose-lipped, yet resolutely lighthearted Jack, Ropes adds memorably to his gallery of Broadway dancers and chorus boys: a figure he once more returned to in the pairing of Bobby and Arthur in 1934's *Go Into Your Dance*.

"It Was Strange That Bobby Should Die So Tragically": Camp and the Macabre in *Go Into Your Dance*

From the blend of Broadway show business and Tammany Hall-style politics that Rope had explored in *Stage Mother*, the novelist stepped back into the "fascinating back-stage world" of vaudeville and Broadway musical comedy in *Go Into Your Dance*.[161] At the same time, echoing the pulp-noir elements of *42nd Street* and *Stage Mother*, the novel also portrays show people mixing with the gangster underworld of the 1920s. The proximity of Broadway's scandals to newspaper tabloids fuels *Go Into Your Dance*, much as it had in *Stage Mother*'s Jack Thomas subplot. In *Go Into Your Dance*, the same sex-and-crime saga that threatens Ted's production of a new musical revue (based on *George White's Scandals*) also propels it at the box office when the story leaks about his sister Ellen's role as the mistress of a murdered racketeer.

Ropes fuses this world of show business and crime to his portrayal of a darkening cultural landscape for gay men. In *42nd Street* and *Stage Mother*, respectively, Jacks Winslow and Thomas had supplied the camp consciences, as well as stylistic impulses, of Ropes's hard-boiled backstage chronicles. By contrast, in *Go Into Your Dance*, the lives of gay male characters, informed by Ropes's reflection of an intensifying homophobic backlash in 1934, directly propel the plot of his novel. In a work written at the twilight of the Pansy Craze, Ropes once again highlights the paradoxical tension between a "lighthearted" camp persona and the condition of cultural damnation that necessitates its performance. As before, Ropes explores the lives of gay men on Broadway through the figure of the chorus boy.

The aftermath of the suicide of Bobby Rogers drives a pivotal plot reversal in Ropes's novel. This occurs during the Staten Island Ferry sequence of *Go Into Your Dance*, in which Arthur, after Bobby's suicide, enlists Ted's help in scattering Bobby's ashes over New York Harbor. Here, Ropes juxtaposes the fortuitous meeting of Ted and Nora Wayne with the tragedy that befalls Arthur and Bobby, whom Ropes suggests are both great friends and a sometime couple. The meeting of Ted and Nora on the Staten Island Ferry results in their successful show business career as a dancing team and Ted's continuing "climb up the rungs of his ladder" as a Broadway producer.

In *Go Into Your Dance*, Ropes draws with unflinching realism the tragedies that could upend the lives of gay men, whether working on Broadway or in other industries. Ropes creates a scene of incongruous satire on the Staten Island Ferry as he intermixes black comedy with the tragedy of Bobby and Arthur, curiously, the first name of Ropes's father, Arthur Dudley Ropes. The adolescent Ropes had indulged a macabre literary streak in stories like "The Trembling Hour," with its shades of Poe. In *Go Into Your Dance*, the grotesque and gothic also tint Ropes's camp comedy, which anticipates Jack Babuscio's concept of "bitter-wit." As Babuscio observed in 1977, bitter wit stems from a comic vision of the world that deals "with the painfully incongruous situations of gays in society" through "laughter, rather than tears."[162]

In *Go Into Your Dance*, Ropes uses registers of macabre camp to allegorize the social situation of American gay men in the 1920s and early '30s. In Ropes's satire, which expresses the irreverent "bad taste" so often associated with the camp aesthetic, the desperate tragicomic attempt to find a safe home for Bobby's ashes serves as a metaphor for the great difficulty that gay men had in finding intimacy and sexual freedom in public spaces. The shocking final moment of the scene, involving the men's room on the ferry, comments upon the police-persecuted culture of cruising, in parks and "tearooms," established by urban gay men.

Go Into Your Dance explores a social context of increasing censorship and criminalization in 1934. As Chauncey details, the mid-1930s marked something of an unofficial end to the Pansy Craze.[163] Muffling the bawdy wisecracks of Pre-Code Hollywood, the movie industry more stringently invoked the censorship of the Hays Code. The exigencies of the Depression as well as the repeal of Prohibition enabled a return to moral sobriety and sexual conservatism, alongside Roosevelt's New Deal.[164] Fiorello LaGuardia's 1933 election as New York's mayor, following the resignation of Walker, also led to the 1937 closure of New York's burlesque theaters, under Vice Commissioner Paul Moss.[165] A new slate of laws targeted gay men, along with the transgressive women of Minsky's. "The revulsion against gay life in the early 1930s," as a backlash to the Pansy Craze, led to an oppressive new regime of laws that denied liquor licenses to any bar or nightclub serving visibly self-identifying gay men.[166]

Although set in the 1920s, *Go Into Your Dance* powerfully evokes the landscape navigated by gay men during an era of increasingly restricted civil liberties. The Pansy Craze had enabled Ropes to dish the dirt on the relationships and communities constructed by gay men, particularly those working on Broadway. That Ropes would settle in Hollywood after 1934, for a long and versatile career as a screenwriter, cannot be surprising given that his freedom as a backstage novelist would soon be dramatically minimized. Yet, with *Go Into Your Dance*, Ropes placed the gay male experience, through the voices of Broadway chorus boys, at the very center of the narrative, as much as the book's title evokes the persona of Ted Howard as the novel's skirt-chasing, dance-driven protagonist.

As he had done in *42nd Street*, Ropes portrays a show business shaped by the forces of homophobia, even as the Broadway industry provides a relatively open environment for gay male theater workers. The figure of the "fairy" chorus boy, once again, allows Ropes to explore these tensions. In *Go Into Your Dance*, Ropes shows Ted's trajectory, as he moves from "four-a-day" vaudeville into the chorus of a musical comedy, as one of increasing tolerance toward (if not quite outright comfort with) the gay men who dance with him in the ensemble.

Ropes initially characterizes the Bronx-born, Irish American Ted as anxiously defensive toward the preservation of heterosexual masculinity. Ropes depicts Ted's discomfort at his first lessons in stage makeup. Preparing for his amateur night performance at the Regent Theatre, Ted ties "his wardrobe together in a small bundle, the shoes, the jar of Vaseline which he would use to slick down his hair, even, much to his secret shame, the powder puff that Lou Adams had advised him to use."[167] Here, Ropes depicts Ted's struggle to preserve his hetero-masculinity as embodied in an imbroglio with the powder puff. As Ted stands holding a passenger rail on the subway: "The loosely tied bundle crashed to the floor, opened like a malevolent flower and revealed its shameful contents."[168]

Ted's entrance upon the Broadway stage allows Ropes to dramatize the homophobic anxieties centered on the figure of the chorus boy. Though hoping to join the moderately well-paid ranks of a Broadway ensemble, Ted resolves: "If it's gotta be the merry, merry, I'll try anything. . . . But only for a year, because, God, how I hate it!"[169] As Ted rehearses for *Sweet Sally*, Ropes shows the "languid" Walt Milburn challenging Ted's prejudices; he initiates Ted into the world of the Broadway chorus and lessens the anxieties that propelled the subway powder puff incident. Ted starts to find "the companionship of the chorus men . . . both stimulating and amusing. Lazy, shorn of ambition, they were, nevertheless, a breezy, impudent race apart, laughing good-naturedly at the world which often condemned them."[170]

As Ted becomes assimilated into the chorus of *Sweet Sally*, Ropes portrays the growing friendship of Ted with the vivacious blond chorus boys Arthur and Bobby, to whom Arthur refers affectionately as "Miss Rogers." Ted not only develops respect and affection toward the gay men in the Broadway chorus but is able to befriend "the belles in the show" that he might formerly have scorned.[171] Ropes describes how Arthur and Bobby regale Ted "with stories of their conquests and their narrow escapes from those individuals who frown upon their rather brazen advances. . . . And, listening to them, Ted found his attitude of freezing intolerance melting in the fire of their good humor."[172] Arthur and Bobby focus their camp satire on exaggerated femininities: "a

spinster hurrying with mincing stride past the entrance to a burlesque theatre" and a "Broadway sister team, hats, dresses, curls and make-up identi-
cal, rushing along Seventh Avenue, their music and practice clothes carried in
absurd little satchels." Bobby exclaims of the latter: "Get Mona and Lizzie, the
Happiness Girls. . . . Aren't *they* a camp?"[173]

Ropes describes how Arthur and Bobby, as a united pair, find some degree
of safety in the more permissive atmosphere of 1920s Broadway theater,
even while drawing attention to the "narrow" nature of their escapes. Ropes
observes: "The two chorus boys, Arthur and Bobby, were quaint characters.
Their talk, their mannerisms, were a part of the crazy-quilt pattern of the
theater. Divorced from the hectic atmosphere of back stage, they would have
seemed monstrous, devoid of the slightest virtue. Here, behind the protec-
tive wall which performers throw about their private lives, they were not only
accepted, but quite admired."[174]

Ironically, Ted's growing admiration of Bobby and Arthur and, by extension,
his increasing tolerance of gay culture take him into the human dimensions of
a tragedy, the realities of which had been masked to Ted by the chorus boys'
"gay laughter." Previously, Arthur and Bobby had "always emerged unruffled,
each golden stand of hair in its proper place, ready to face the next emergency."
Yet, Bobby commits suicide during rehearsals for *Sweet Sally*. Ropes's portrayal
of Ted's thoughts about Bobby, after learning of his death, evokes Shirley's
public statement about Jack in *Stage Mother* as "very melancholy at times, at
other times sitting on top of the world." In *Go Into Your Dance*, Ted puzzles: "It
was strange that Bobby should die so tragically. Ted had never known anyone
in whom the sheer joy of life flowed more abundantly."[175]

If Ted can scarcely believe that Bobby would take his own life, Ropes
powerfully depicts Arthur's despair. The suicide occurs during a cast party,
where Bobby appears to be in good humor, as he exchanges "comments on the
behavior of various members of the company" and dances with a guest. Ropes
describes Arthur's running to Ted, "inarticulate, half-mad with grief," after
Bobby jumps from the roof:

> "Bobby, he—oh, God—he fell—off the roof. They jus' found him." Arthur crum-
> pled to the floor. Ted bent over him stupidly. He wanted to say the right thing,
> now was the right time for him to be masterful, poised, certain of his ground. . . .
> "It—it's all right!" The puny, meaningless words hurled so ineffectually into
> the awful chasm of Arthur's grief. He began to laugh, not pleasantly, but with
> short stabbing gasps which ended on a note of hysteria.[176]

Arthur continues to confront the magnitude of his grief, as policemen enter the party and transport Bobby's friend away from the room.

If Ropes portrays Arthur, in the aftermath of the suicide, succumbing to a despair to which it is impossible "to say the right thing," Ropes also shows the chorus boy returning to the bitter-wit camp sensibility that has sustained his relationship with Bobby. If Arthur and Bobby had "let their hair down" in front of Ted, Arthur now speaks with unmasked openness about "Miss Rogers," whose feminine name Ted accepts, due to being "accustomed to the bewildering confusion of genders so often employed by this specie of male."[177] Also portrayed by Ropes as effeminate, Arthur frequently refers to Bobby in feminine-gendered terms. Arthur explains to Ted, "A moody girl that one. Laughing and carrying on most of the time, but she had her moments, poor kid."

In a sequence that morbidly parallels the spilled contents of the powder puff, Arthur charges a highly conflicted Ted to help him scatter Miss Rogers's ashes into the harbor: a request that Bobby had previously made to Arthur. Discarding the first masculine pronoun for feminine ones, Arthur recounts to Ted:

> "He told me what he'd like to have happen if he ever—ever died. We was cock-eyed, the two of us, an' I thought he was kiddin,' but drunk or no, she made me pull myself together an' promise one thing. She was bound to be cremated—that one—an'—here's the payoff—she wanted her ashes scattered over New York harbor. Said she spent so many hours on the waterfront the ferry boats wouldn't rest easy unless she was with them in spirit."[178]

Arthur explains to Ted that a heterosexual man will allow him more safety from "Lily Law," as well as "moral support," in carrying out Bobby's wish: "Imagine me flying my hips up an' down on the deck of a ferry boat with a mess of ashes under my arms. I might get pulled in."[179]

As Ted and Arthur, aboard the Staten Island Ferry, frantically attempt to "scatter Miss Rogers's ashes to the breeze," Ropes portrays the chorus boy performing his grief as a "great big camp." Ted, viewing the "sinister secret" of the parcel in Arthur's arms, asks, "Don't they give you somethin' better to carry him—it—in? . . . An—an urn or something?" Arthur responds, "It don't look so pretty—but it's still Bobby!"[180] As passengers start to board the ferry, Ted urges Arthur to scatter the ashes. Arthur shakes his head: "No. . . . The wind would carry the ashes right back onto the pier and poor Miss Rogers distinctly said that she wanted her remains sprinkled on the water. Water! An' her with the best champagne taste of any chorus moll in the state!"[181]

Over the course of the scene, Ropes seriocomically depicts Ted and Arthur's task as thwarted by a lack of privacy. Here, Ropes metaphorically suggests that, even in death, society denies gay men their ability to achieve freedom and authenticity in conducting their relationships in public space. High winds and an inescapable stream of passengers on the upper deck scuttle the men's efforts, as a "puff of wind . . . stirs the ashes to vindictive life. They swirled from their hiding place, for all the world like a scattering of cigarette ashes, and raced playfully across the deck," causing a "large, red-faced man" to reach for his handkerchief.[182] Attempting to find a more sheltered spot in the leeward cabin, they attempt "a second emancipation of the ashes."

Into this scene of morbid farce, Ropes introduces Nora. When an eight-year-old boy, accompanied by Nora, his older sister, interrupts the attempt and inquires about the contents of the bag, Arthur hisses: "*That* is none of your business, *dear*. . . . Run along and let a lady admire the scenery!" When Tommy, the little boy, scoffs, "Huh, you ain't a lady," Arthur recoils.[183] Perhaps now fearing "Lily Law," he leaves Ted alone to scatter the ashes and to make conversation with Nora. When Nora realizes Ted is carrying ashes, he explains to the disapproving young woman that he has agreed to help with Bobby's "last wish," even though he doesn't like the task: "They—they're really a friend of ours. I guess that sounds kinda nutty."[184] Yet, in his deepening conversation with Nora, Ted also convinces her to team up with him in vaudeville. Here, Ropes creates a startling juxtaposition of heartbreak for his gay characters with incipient Broadway triumph for the heterosexual characters, who proceed to produce the *Scandals*-like *Town Talk* revues.

The astringent farce of the Staten Island Ferry scene concludes with Ropes making barbed, coded allusions to the illicit and stigmatized, yet sexually liberating, institution of "tearooms" in gay culture. Chauncey details the irreverently named spots: "Of all the spaces to which men had recourse for sexual encounters, none were more specific to gay men—or highly contested, within the gay world and without—than New York's public comfort stations and subway washrooms. . . . If 'tearoom' normally referred to a gracious café where respectable ladies could meet without risk of encountering inebriate males, it could ironically name the less elegant locale where so many gay men met." Though the police's "enforcement efforts were only sporadic," tearoom "arrests could have catastrophic consequences. Conviction often resulted in a sentence of forty to sixty days in the workhouse, but the extralegal sanctions could be worse."[185]

As Ropes alludes to the compromised public privacy offered by tearooms, the Staten Island Ferry scene climaxes with Arthur flushing Miss Rogers's ashes down a public toilet. Interrupting Ted's rapt conversation with Nora, Arthur opens the door off the inner cabin and floats "languidly into view. No longer was he chafing under his irksome burden. The paper bag with its gruesome contents was gone." Moving out of earshot of Nora, Arthur greets Ted, "I've been lookin' for you behind water coolers an' everywhere! Well, it's done. Miss Rogers is finally in the harbor!" When Ted gasps, "Where? How?," Arthur responds: "Well, with that wind an' all. . . . I couldn't see throwin' ashes right and left. . . . I was tryin' to find some real appropriate place, so— . . . There!" Arthur nods to the door opposite, as Ropes ends the scene with a bitter punchline about the only place that Arthur and Bobby can, for the last time, be alone together: "Ted read the word inscribed on the panel: "Men."[186]

In the juxtapositions of Go Into Your Dance's Staten Island Ferry scene, Ropes mordantly suggests that Broadway's narratives of the American success myth in the 1920s and '30s not only excluded gay men but thrived upon their marginalization. Ropes underscores this point in the novel's final scene, as Ted tells Nora, without mention of Arthur and Bobby: "I guess we were meant for each other. . . . Ever since that day on the Staten Island ferry."[187] Ropes declines, too, to provide a single explanation for the suicide of Bobby Rogers, whose initials, incidentally, mirror the author's own, even as Bobby's last name evokes that of female impersonator Stanley Rogers. Ropes might have intended to allow heterosexual readers in 1934 to identify with Ted's shock and to come to a deeper empathy with Bobby and Arthur, as Ted moves beyond "taking their lives as a joke." For gay readers, the death of Miss Rogers likely, through the coding of a particularly macabre strand of camp, portrayed layers of culturally inflicted shame and sadness navigated by gay men through strategies of defiant bitter wit.

Although Ropes returned to elements of the backstage novel in Mr. Tilley Takes a Walk, Go Into Your Dance marked the conclusion of his 1930s backstage trilogy. It also signaled the beginning of his enduring career as a screenwriter in Hollywood, where he prospered under the restrictions of the Hollywood Production Code despite finding its regulations onerous. The Quincy Patriot Ledger reported in a 1940 interview: "He has found scenario writing more difficult than novel writing because of the many rules that must be followed."[188] As a contracted screenwriter for Republic Studios starting in 1936, Ropes wrote multiple singing-cowboy Westerns starring, first, Gene Autry and, later, Roy Rogers. Ropes later quipped of the "taboos encountered in writing westerns: no drinking, no drawing of a gun-first, and naturally no acting for the great stone faces adorning the sagebrush."[189]

Bradford Ropes, with dog, during his Hollywood screenwriting career.
Reproduced by permission of M. G. Bullard.

Despite his frustrations with Hollywood censorship, Ropes proved a versatile screenwriter specializing in musical comedies. He worked with composer Jule Styne, during the latter's Hollywood period, on seven films between 1940 and 1942: *Sing, Dance, Plenty Hot*; *Melody and Moonlight*; *Melody Ranch*; *Angels with Broken Wings*; *Hit Parade of 1941*; *Ridin' on a Rainbow*; and *Ice Capades Revue*. Freelancing with the major studios, Ropes wrote films such as the drama *Lord Jeff* (MGM, 1938) and *Nothing But Trouble* (MGM, 1944, with Laurel and Hardy). With Val Burton, he also created comic blockbusters for Abbott and Costello, including *The Time of Their Lives* (Universal, 1946). Ropes self-effacingly wrote to a Hollywood columnist in 1947 that he had "typed off many a screenplay, some good, some stinkers."[190] Yet, Ropes's screenwriting proved frequently inventive, topical, and sometimes influential. *The Hit Parade of 1941*, set in the world of early television, featured a scene of revealed lip-syncing that foreshadows 1952's *Singin' in the Rain*.

As newspaper columns indicate, Ropes also stayed active in Hollywood's gay subculture of the 1930s and early '40s, when the Cold War intensified discrimination and concealment. Ropes's 1940 gay camp Western *Melody Ranch*, starring Autry, Ann Miller, and Jimmy Durante, featured dialogue and songs that, flying under the noses of censors, drew from the spectacularly bawdy nightclub routines of Ropes's friend Bruz Fletcher. Hailing from a famous Indiana banking dynasty, Fletcher wrote and performed "party songs" such as "My Doctor" and "She's a Nympho-Dipso-Egomaniac." Starting out in New York's gay underground nightclubs, Fletcher became associated with Hollywood's Club Bali until his 1941 suicide. The performer's "Wide Open Spaces," with its coded allusions to anal sex in both its title and its lyrics, makes a remarkable reappearance in the film's "Torpedo Joe" number (with music by Styne and lyrics credited to Eddie Cherkose).[191] "Where did you learn that deplorable song?," Barbara Jo Allen's Veronica Whipple interrupts Mary Lee's Penny, after she sings such apparently innocuous lyrics as "Torpedo Joe, he don't know nothin,' nothin' / Nothin' about hustlin' or cattle rustlin' / Nothin' about ridin' or the great dividin.'"[192]

From his 1933 arrival in Hollywood into the early 1940s, Ropes also lived with a man who was very likely his lover. Roswell Jolly Black's 1942 suicide, after his World War II military draft, tragically echoes the themes of Ropes's novels, as well as the author's preoccupation with telling the stories of gay men despite censorial efforts to keep them silent.

"Ill-Timed Jocularity": The Probable Hollywood Romance of Bradford Ropes and Roswell Jolly Black

If the coded language and lighthearted strategies of camp fueled Ropes through his backstage trilogy, the writer also expressed an equal knowledge of the limitations of "gay laughter" within a damning American society. In the painfully funny Staten Island Ferry scene of his 1934 novel, Ropes illustrates how the use of camp armor might find itself at least temporarily impotent in the midst of grief. "His jocularity was ill timed," writes Ropes in Go Into Your Dance, describing Nora's annoyance at Ted's macabre humor on the ferry, as he tells her about the plot for Miss Rogers's ashes. "Once was enough," quips Ted, after Nora shares that she had an aunt "who was cremated once." Nora snaps, "I don't think it's funny at all. There's nothin' about dying to make me laugh! Living's tough enough!"[193]

In 1942, Ropes's probable ten-year-long romance with a man named Roswell Jolly Black ended with the death of his lover. Black's 1942 suicide in a jail cell in San Clemente, California, after his draft into the army near the start of the United States' entry into World War II, concluded a relationship that probably began around 1932. A combination of newspaper articles, census reports, and draft cards can only suggest the outlines of a relationship that may forever elude historians. Yet, it is hard to doubt that, whatever the details of the relationship, Black's death at the age of thirty-four must have deeply grieved

Ropes. The final section of this chapter represents my attempt to reconstruct the larger shape of the relationship, while acknowledging that its particular intimacies belonged solely to Ropes and Black.

Appearing in the pages of Hollywood gossip columns from 1936 to 1938, Roswell Black masqueraded his identity. *Los Angeles Times* columns in 1938 described Black, spotted at nightclubs with Ropes, as an "eastern society man" and as "Roswell Black III."[194] Given Ropes's own background, perhaps this represented a private joke at the expense of blue-blooded Boston society. In actuality, the remarkably named Roswell Jolly Black hailed from a middle-class West Coast background in Sumner, Washington (close to Tacoma), where his father, Alonzo, worked as a salesman in a general store.[195]

Three years younger than Ropes, Black, born on October 8, 1908, shared a Christian background with Ropes. As a high school student, Black served as an "active member" in the "Sumner Chapter of De Molay": the same Masonic youth society for whose female chapter Arthur Dudley Ropes had written hymns. Black's 1929 Sumner High School yearbook described the organization: "Its members must be between the ages of sixteen and twenty-one; the purpose of the Order is to 'create and build up better types of Christian character, and to develop better citizens by coming into contact with other students in school life by better, cleaner and higher planes of living.'"[196]

Black's early background suggests that he was on track to leading a "clean" and respectable life within his community, with a particular focus on music. By 1930, the twenty-one-year-old Black had found work as a pipe organist, and in September of that year he married a twenty-year-old Tacoma woman named Eleonore L. Jackson at the Evangelical Lutheran Church in Mount Vernon, Washington.[197] Historical records for Black become scanter between 1930 and 1932. That year, the *Quincy Patriot Ledger* identified Roswell Black as Ropes's "secretary" and noted that Black accompanied Ropes from the East Coast to Hollywood after the motion picture sale of *42nd Street*.[198] While newspaper records do not reveal the location or date of the pair's first meeting, one possibility is January 1931, when Billy Bradford toured with "Personalities" to Seattle.

By 1933, Roswell Black's name became regularly connected with Ropes in newspaper items, as Ropes reached the peak of his fame with the film adaptation of *42nd Street*. Referring only to Black as Ropes's "secretary" or "friend," newspapers never connected the men as romantic partners. One November 1933 article also suggests that Ropes, now under contract to Warner Brothers, had adapted Black into an active social life, as the two visited friends in Syracuse, New York.[199] The same month, for a Wollaston screening of *Stage Mother*, Ropes, "motoring from New York," brought Black to his home in Wollaston for the Thanksgiving holiday. Here, Ropes introduced Black to his mother and father. The *Patriot Ledger* noted: "Accompanying the young author was his friend, Roswell Black of Seattle, Wash, and Miss Flora Williams of Orange, NJ, sister of Mrs. Ropes."[200]

However Black and Ropes may have conducted themselves back in Wollaston, the men appear to have fully embraced Hollywood's gay subculture in the mid- to late 1930s. Columns in the *Los Angeles Times*, published between 1936 and 1938, connect Ropes and Black to an active social group, centered at the Club Bali, that included many gay and lesbian artists. The circle included not only Fletcher but also Ziegfeld Girl-turned-Broadway producer Peggy Fears (who later developed the Fire Island Pines); Patsy Kelly and her partner, Wilma Cox; *Citizen Kane* costume designer Edward Stevenson; movie milliner Robert Galer; and set designer Casey Roberts (also the partner of Fletcher). Ropes also became close with Cary Grant, whose relationship with Western star Randolph Scott, echoing the gay subtexts of *Melody Ranch*, Hollywood insiders received as an open secret in the 1930s. According to a 1937 *Golden Rod* interview, Ropes counted Grant along with actors Alice Faye and Mary Brian and bandleader Ranny Weeks as "some of his best friends."[201]

Gossip columns also linked Ropes romantically with musical comedy star Queenie Smith, famous for her skill as a dancer and stage persona as a comic soubrette. From headlining Jazz Age musicals like the Gershwins's *Tip-Toes* (1925) and *The Street Singer* (1929, with Grant, as Archie Leach, joining her for the 1930 national tour), Smith had moved on to work as a character actress in Hollywood. Here, after divorcing drama critic Robert Garland in May 1937, she joined a lesbian clique that included Kelly and Helen "Cupid" Ainsworth (also a good friend of Ropes).[202] A former vaudeville and movie comedienne who presented a butch persona in films like *Big News* (1929), Ainsworth left her performing career to establish herself as a top Hollywood actors' agent. She appears to have coaxed Smith into the profession. Smith, with whom Ainsworth went into business from the late 1940s through the early 1950s, had previously been appointed the West Coast talent representative for the Theatre Guild in 1946.[203]

Whether or not Smith was romantically involved with Ainsworth, she and Ropes played out a "smoke screen" relationship not unlike that of Peggy and Billy in *42nd Street*. From December 1937 through March 1938, the *Los Angeles Times* rumored romance, and even "an early marriage," between Ropes and Smith: "It wouldn't surprise any of their friends if Bradford Ropes and Queenie Smith decided to get married, judging by the way they held hands and looked at each other at Bruz Fletcher's Club Bali."[204] Given that the romance unfolded at a nightspot closely connected with Hollywood's gay subculture, columnist Read Kendall may have enjoyed the irony of his reporting. In July 1939, Louella Parsons also commented on Ropes's social circle at the Club Bali: "Venita Varden and Peggy Fears at the Bali highly amused over Bruz Fletcher's new songs. Bradford Ropes and Queenie Smith, who used to be a twosome, that way again."[205]

While publically appearing with Smith, Ropes lived for years with Roswell Black in Hollywood. A 1940 census record listed the men as the two "household members" of an apartment on Fountain Avenue in Beverly Hills. A 1942 voter registration identified Black as Ropes's secretary—and both men were registered Republicans.[206] The conservative Christian background that Ropes shared with Black may have distanced the men from Hollywood's more progressive, Popular Front-era circles, even as Ropes's backstage novels consistently critique the exploitations of American capitalism and its intersections with misogyny and homophobia. Yet, by the late 1930s, Ropes had entered a glamorous California "smart set" far removed from his black sheep vaudevillian days. He socialized with Black and other friends at nightspots like the Beverly Glen Lodge and at parties such as the "Antibes Ball at the Yacht Club and Casino in San Clemente."[207]

The motivations for Black's suicide, on March 29, 1942, may never be known to historians. Circumstances suggest that Black became deeply distressed when he was drafted into the U.S. Army on January 5, 1942, less than a month after the country entered World War II. Only a scattering of newspapers covered the suicide of Black, described both as Ropes's secretary and roommate. These reveal details of the tragic sequence of events on March 29, 1942: an hour after the thirty-three-year-old Black was arrested for drunk driving, he hanged himself in a jail cell in San Clemente, an hour north of San Diego. Shortly before his death, Black had told Police Chief Floyd Cowger that "he was to be inducted into the Army next week and that he was having a 'last fling' before his entry into the service."[208] The *Los Angeles Times*, the same newspaper that had chronicled Ropes's and Black's nightclub sightings in its gossip columns, now reported:

> When arrested, Black was driving an automobile registered to Ropes. He told police that he had been visiting his employer, who was vacationing at La Jolla. San Clemente police yesterday were attempting to find relatives of the dead man.[209]

Black was laid to rest in his home state of Washington, his ashes interred at Seattle's Acacia Memorial Park and Funeral Home, in an ornate mausoleum of marble and stained glass.[210]

Given the scarcity of newspaper coverage of Black's life and relationship with Ropes, contemporary readers and historians can only conjecture on how Black's lover of ten years received the tragedy and what "chasms of grief" he navigated. Ropes himself served in the U.S. Army, although he was not assigned the active military service that may have alarmed Roswell Black. According to Ropes's 1966 obituary, "During World War II, Mr. Ropes served with the First Cavalry division at Ft. Bliss, Tex, and wrote technical and training films for the Army."[211] After his honorable discharge in 1943, he resumed his prolific Hollywood career.[212] As the repressions of the Cold War era closed in, Ropes now focused on entertaining mass audiences. However, with Burton (his regular screenwriting partner since 1938), he returned to a coded discussion of gay and lesbian culture in 1951's *Mr. Tilley Takes a Walk*.

Ropes's insistence on exuberantly dishing the dirt in the pages of his 1930s backstage trilogy, through dancers and chorus boys like Jack Winslow, Jack Thomas, and Bobby Rogers, comes into stark conflict with the fact that media narratives did not disclose the authentic details of the lives of gay men. With only a fragmented historical record of his life and his relationship with Ropes, Roswell Black "passed from the scene." The scarcity of biographical material illuminating the relationship between Ropes and Black reinforces the novelist's urgency in detailing the lives, in all their comic and tragic variety, of gay men in show business. Ropes boldly stepped out of line to do so at a time when newspapers, stages, and silver screens largely distorted, concealed, or withheld their narratives.

Camp, as a strategy for a situation, allowed Ropes a means of telling such stories with defiant humor and in contradiction to Nora's protest: "There's nothin' about dying to make *me* laugh! Living's tough enough!" Lighthearted in his style, Ropes thoughtfully considers, but ultimately dismisses, such damnation of camp's jocularity and irreverence. Ropes's work makes nods not only to Bert Savoy but also to Oscar Wilde and his dialogue-writing idol Noël Coward, whose 1932 *Design for Living* ends as the merry ménage à trois of Gilda, Otto, and Leo "break down utterly and roar with laughter."[213] In his backstage trilogy, Ropes redeems "gay laughter" not only as an artful mode of queer failure but as a completely serious approach to life.

CHAPTER 5

"Your Blood Responds More Eagerly to the Lure of the Theatre"

THE BACKSTAGE TRILOGY,
THE PURITAN ETHOS, AND
THE MYTH OF "THE SHOW MUST GO ON"

"You Can't Get Show Business out of Your Blood"

If *42nd Street* endures as Ropes's most iconic backstage novel, *Stage Mother* suggests his most personal evocation of the tensions between his genteel upbringing and the "irresistible" glamour of the footlights. In the 1933 novel, straightlaced "Ma" Lorraine rebukes her daughter-in-law Kitty: "I have failed to win you over to my way of thinking, your blood responds more eagerly to the lure of the theatre than to the saner, quieter call of the home which might have been yours and Frederick's."[1] The charged exchange illustrates a theme to which Ropes repeatedly returned not only in his backstage novels but in his Hollywood screenplays: the pull between the heritage of "blood" and of home and the siren call of the stage.

In fact, Ropes frequently explores the various meanings of "blood" in his backstage novels. In the Swedenborgian New Church in which Ropes grew up, blood represented a "meeting ground" between the corporeal and the spiritual, according to Jane Williams-Hogan.[2] By contrast, in the backstage trilogy, Ropes conceptualizes blood as a conduit between ideas of genealogy, labor and ambition, and the undeniable lure of the stage. Ropes calls upon the image of stage lure as blood tonic when he describes Kitty's powerful longing to attend a Boston cast party held by touring vaudevillian friends: "Trouper! That's what she was, all right. With every drop of blood in her she wanted to attend the party tonight, wanted to saturate herself with the shop talk which features at all such gatherings."[3] Ralph Martin tempts Kitty to return to the stage before it's "too late": "You can't get show business out of your blood. An old war horse always hears the bugle call, you know."[4] Later, Kitty tells Mark Thorne: "I've sweated blood to help make [Shirley] a success; I've been willing to ruin my own life so's she could get ahead."[5]

For the Mayflower-descended performer formerly known as Billy Bradford, theater possessed a compelling power able to transgress and transcend the taboos of a blue-blood family tree. Dancer-turned-agent Lou Adams repeats Kitty's mantra in Go Into Your Dance: "Funny how this show business gets in your blood."[6] If theater compels stagestruck aspirants on a blood-deep level, Ropes externalizes its liquid lure through the smell of greasepaint, with its distinctive admixture of zinc, ochre, vermilion, and lard. Ropes establishes that the theatrical life, however exciting, invites more bittersweet sensations in Go Into Your Dance, as Ted Howard follows the "Two Buddies" into a hoofer's life. In a backstage corridor, Ted is surrounded by "the acrid, unforgettable odor of greasepaint. . . . This was the life he had chosen."[7]

At the same time, Ropes's novels reflect the author's deep awareness that entering show business necessitated a difficult existence. Consistently, Ropes critically questioned the relationship between "the lure of the theatre" and what might lie concealed beneath its myths. In Go Into Your Dance, Ropes describes the obligations of performance intervening with Ted's burgeoning acquaintance with the "Two Buddies": "the show which, according to song and story, must go on."[8]

In framing "the show must go on" as a cultural trope rather than a moral mandate, Ropes critiqued the culturally powerful pull of the "trouper." Andrea Most connects the myth to the communitarian ethos of Jewish liberalism: "In the unwritten but universally acknowledged laws of the theater, all members of the company are obligated to do what they can to make sure that the show goes on."[9] While exuberantly celebrating theatricality throughout his back-stage trilogy, Ropes examines trouping from another angle: as an embodi-ment of the extremities of the Protestant work ethic. In his backstage trilogy, Ropes questioned imperatives that theater workers should uncritically "go on with the show" despite often meager salaries, a normalized culture of sexual harassment, and sometimes hazardous working conditions. Ropes depicts an industry that affords little room for human fallibility. In 42nd Street, Abe Green insists to a doctor that Dorothy Brock, as part of the community of "show folk," must go on in the Philadelphia premiere of *Pretty Lady* despite her concussion: "We can't be sick, we can't die, because there's always the show to consider."[10]

Using strategies of demystification in his backstage trilogy, Ropes exposed the taxing labor conditions underlying the public's misconceptions of "show people" as shiftless and dissolute. Ropes shows the pervasiveness of anti-theatrical prejudice across religions and regions, as Joey Howard, the more conservative brother of the stagestruck Ted and Ellen, chastises them as "lazy" in *Go Into Your Dance*: "Lookin' for the easiest way to put your hooks on some dough without really workin' for it."[11]

Ropes demonstrates how, by contrast with the myths of the Protestant work ethic, the intervention of providence does not necessarily reward the labor of show people. In *The Business of the Theatre* (completed in 1928), Alfred L. Bernheim conceded the gamblers-luck rarity of a successful Broadway run. At the same time, he reaffirmed New York's commercial theater as a well-functioning meritocracy, observing, "Almost overnight an unknown author can become a national figure. An obscure young man or woman can attain stardom. . . . Of course there usually is a long and weary apprenticeship, but extraordinary brilliancy can find a quick reward, and sound talent combined with perseverance, and a fertile field to till."[12] In the rise of Peggy, the Warner Brothers film version of *42nd Street* exemplified Algeresque narratives of trouping and triumphing against the odds. By contrast, Ropes depicts success in show business as frequently contingent upon luck and professional connections. This includes the alliance, sealed by a mutual disdain for the industry's homophobia, between Peggy and Billy. In his novel, the author frames the "quick rewards" extolled by Bernheim as random harvests arising from economic scarcity as much as from fertile fields of talent.

This chapter explores how the tensions of Ropes's Puritan upbringing and his deep stagestruck intoxication interact in the backstage trilogy's themes of labor and commerce. Often using roman à clef techniques, Ropes critiqued the exploitations of the self-elected "gods" of commercial Broadway show business and questioned enduring stereotypes about the immorality of show people, as well as the trope of "the show must go on." Ropes placed Broadway's fables into probing dialogue with the cultural myths and anti-theatrical prejudices circulating through the Mayflower-descended bloodline that, in another life, would have prohibited his own entrance upon "the wicked stage." Ropes does this in *42nd Street* and *Stage Mother*, respectively, through the semi-autobiographical characters of Peggy Sawyer and Kitty Lorraine.

"They Don't Want Puritans in Show Business": Peggy Sawyer and the Topsy-Turvy Social World of *42nd Street*

With the sharply contrasting characters of Peggy and Kitty, Ropes most concretely explored the tensions between Proper Boston and profane Broadway. Ropes portrays both the refined Maine minister's daughter-turned-chorus girl and the brash vaudevillian-turned-maternal menace as reflections of his native Boston. Through the character of Ann, Ropes wisecracks of his hometown in *42nd Street*, "Boston isn't so bad because you can always feed the pigeons on the Common and avoid the facts of life."[13]

Drawing autobiographical parallels to himself with Peggy, Ropes depicts the chorus girl moving incongruously among show people who do not recognize her as one of their own. Peggy's dilemma suggests keen resonances with tensions that Ropes, as Billy Bradford, likely experienced in the 1920s in vaudeville after leaving behind his mother's milieu of the Ruskin Club, the WCTU, and the DAR. The author unflinchingly catalogs social distinctions in *42nd Street*. In one scene, Peggy accompanies Terry to a greasy-spoon diner patronized by show folks: "Peggy watched him, amused, and faintly disgusted. In New England, nicety of table manners was inborn."[14] In the eyes of *42nd Street*'s streetwise and often immigrant-descended New Yorker characters, Peggy paradoxically represents an upper-class, Anglo-Saxon Other. Whereas much of WASP society shunned show people as vagabonds in the early twentieth century, Ropes illustrates how the topsy-turvy world of *42nd Street* inverts these dynamics. Here, the Puritan plays the pariah.

Throughout *42nd Street*, Ropes shows how the cast and creative team of *Pretty Lady* associate Peggy with her New England background. When Peggy confirms that she's "not a New York girl," but instead "comes from New England," Terry responds: "I thought so. . . . I can spot that damn 'A' every time."[15] Other characters assume that Peggy comes from Boston, which they view as a synecdoche for New England. Whereas Julian Marsh refers to Peggy as "Little Miss Boston," Flo also assumes Peggy will go "high hat" after her debut as *Pretty Lady*'s star: "Sure you won't drag the Boston accent outta mothballs and ritz the old gang?"[16]

Yet Ropes also contrasts Peggy's theatrical experience against his own. Whereas Ropes had plunged into vaudeville after his year at the Thayer Academy, Peggy doesn't recognize the names of the variety stage's most famous impresarios. Ropes observes, "She was unfamiliar with Mr. [Edward F.] Albee's reputation, having confined her attentions to the legitimate end of the show game."[17] When quizzed by Marsh about her previous experience, Peggy elaborates that she has acted back in Maine in "one or two amateur shows and four months in the local stock company."[18]

If Ropes establishes biographical distance between himself and Peggy, the character also allowed the author to reflect upon the contradictions of his own paradoxical position in show business. At the Philadelphia cast party, Peggy's reactions to Terry's carousing lead her to acknowledge some truth in his damning statement: that Puritans are not wanted in show business.[19] In an earlier scene, set at a party in a Greenwich Village atelier, Ropes establishes Peggy as a character who enjoys the liberations and libations of the Jazz Age— but with scruples. With customary self-awareness, she warns Pat that he had "better not" fill her glass: "The good folk of Paris, Maine aren't educated to such rare liquor. It's apt to go to my head."[20] While Ropes himself later confronted alcoholism, the exchange underscores Ropes's position as the son of one of his state's most prominent temperance reformers in the 1920s.

Ropes extends Peggy's inhibitions to the Philadelphia cast party sequence. Here, Terry assumes that the bawdy dirt dishing of Jack, Sophie, and Mae offends Peggy. Yet, after fleeing the hotel room, Peggy reveals that it's Terry's hedonism that most repels her. Chastising him for his excessive "drinking—gossiping—gambling," Peggy rebukes Terry, "Don't you want to get anywhere?"[21] By contrast, Peggy, dedicated to the Protestant work ethic's myths of toil rewarded by providence, praises Marsh's unswerving dedication to his work. She exclaims to Terry, "The successes of the world weren't made by loafers!"[22]

Here, Ropes vividly dramatizes Peggy's conflicts between Jazz Age modernity and genteel tradition. Ropes contrasts Peggy's desire to fit in socially with her castmates with the more powerful compulsion to hold herself apart: the quality that appeals to Billy Lawler as "decent," "civilized," and worthy of his intervention with Marsh. As Ropes describes Peggy's reflections at the raucous cast party, she experiences "some inner rebellion at the character of this gathering" and thinks of Terry and his friends "like hogs swilling up all they can hold." "I suppose you're disgusted," Terry exclaims, as Peggy admits the truth of his accusation: "But please don't tell the others. They'd claim I was high-hat."[23]

Ropes portrays Peggy's Puritanism and Terry's hedonism as not fully reconcilable. The hoofer regretfully tells the chorus girl: "I guess we weren't meant to mix, but I'm nuts about you jus' the same."[24] While sharing a comparable background with Peggy, Ropes suggests that Terry's ethos better aligns with the realities of show business. Emboldened by liquor, Terry tells Peggy: "I treated you like the lady you was, but you might as well get wise to this; *they don't want Puritans in show business* an' if you think we're a lot of bums because we get tight once in a while you better scram for New England."[25]

While Ropes likely understood Peggy's discomfiture at the Philadelphia cast party, the author also points to the complex realities comprehended by Terry. Ropes does not deny that the rigors of the trouper's life inclined many performers toward alcohol abuse: "The bigger the artist the bigger the drunkard," Terry exclaims. At the same time, Ropes suggests that Peggy's Puritanism also carries the danger of perpetuating attitudes of anti-theatrical prejudice. Enjoining Peggy to "act regular" to be popular in show business, Terry explains to the chorus girl: "After a show we gotta have our liquor an' all the pro'bition in the world won't change that. It's snobs like you that make trouble for people in show business. They see us take a coupla drinks an' then spread the word that we're no good."[26]

Suggesting keen autobiographical resonance, Ropes portrays both Peggy's incongruity and her "inner rebellion" as a Puritan in show business. At the same time, both the characters of Peggy and Dorothy Brock also allow Ropes to critique misogyny in the entertainment world. Peggy's inclination toward temperance collides with Terry's steam-blowing carousing. Yet, Ropes also aligns Peggy's reserve with her dignity and self-respect as she encounters the sexual politics behind Broadway "angeling" in the 1920s, in which additional backers bolstered the investments of the main producers. As Bernheim observed, "Untold thousands of angels' money always stand ready to pour into theatrical productions."[27]

A few of these angels hailed from Boston Brahmin backgrounds. In his memoir, producer John Murray Anderson recounted his memories of Ronald T. Lyman, an "aristocratic gentleman" who lived on Beacon Street: "He invested, quite moderately, in several of my shows, but without much reward. Yet he never complained and seemed happy enough merely to be able to attend rehearsals and meet the players, with whom he was very popular. . . . Ronald was the best type of 'angel' in the Theatre's Golden Era."[28]

Yet, Ropes and other backstage novelists depicted some backers investing in Broadway shows with the intention of obtaining sexual favors from female cast members. Ropes may have envisioned badder "angels" than Lyman in the Brahmin character of Richard Endicott, the playboy from a "very first family" who serves as an all-demanding sugar daddy to Dorothy Brock.[29] In dramatizing Dorothy's unfaithfulness to Endicott as a potential crisis to the funding of

Pretty Lady, Ropes critiques a Broadway patriarchy premised in prostitution. Ropes illustrates how the "heavy sugar for the outfit" provided by Endicott (transformed into Abner Dillon in the 1933 film version) relies upon Dorothy's compliance to his sexual demands. When Dorothy replies that she prefers to finish rehearsing for *Pretty Lady* before she can consider Endicott's marriage proposal, he (only half-jokingly) threatens to yank Dorothy's scenic effects on opening night: "Technically, I'm your boss. No 'yes,' no feather curtain."[30]

Ropes connects Endicott's behind-the-scenes behavior with a normalized culture, within Endicott's exclusive socioeconomic milieu, of predatory droit de seigneur attitudes toward chorus girls. Ropes also introduces Warren Standish and Mark Ames, two Columbia fraternity boys who lure Peggy, along with Ann and Flo, to an expensive dinner at El Mirador. Ropes depicts Standish, with his "irritating combination of superiority and sensuality," as entitled and sexually proprietary in his interactions with Peggy, whom he regards as a "cheap little gold digger."[31] When Warren propositions Peggy, she indignantly berates him. Ann defends her friend: "Why I'd like to crown that funny-looking mug of yours with the Standish coat of arms you're always yelping about."[32]

Notably, Ropes calls upon the names of two of his Mayflower Pilgrim ancestors: Miles Standish and Richard Warren. If Peggy faces her own conflicts as a greasepaint Puritan, she also rejects the connections of patriarchy, class snobbery, and lineage embodied by Endicott and Standish. Here, Ropes distances himself ideologically from the Pilgrims whom he had extolled at the age of fifteen as "sturdy, God-fearing men."[33] Ropes expresses his outrage at the claim of Standish and Ames to the superiority of their "blue blood" and their presumption upon women's bodies. In the next year's *Stage Mother*, Ropes continued, from a different perspective, to explore tensions between the lure of the stage and the call of home, while once again focusing upon the lives of women in show business.

"They Couldn't Understand Show Folks in a Million Years": Scandalizing "Proper Boston" in *Stage Mother*

On the surface, the character of the domineering Kitty might appear to have little in common with the self-possessed Peggy. Yet once again, in *Stage Mother*, Ropes used the character of Kitty to negotiate the complexities of his relationship to Proper Boston. As with *42nd Street*, where Ropes appears to split his identifications among Peggy, Billy, and Jack Winslow, *Stage Mother* does not suggest literal autobiography in its portrayal of family and religion. In the novel, Ropes depicts stagestruck Bostonians who are estranged from, or antagonistic to, their families. By contrast, Ropes appears to have remained close with his mother, Alice, despite their differences. Similarly, Ropes portrays the upper-class family in *Stage Mother* as Catholic rather than Protestant, the religious milieu in which he grew up.

Nevertheless, *Stage Mother* shows the author intricately exploring the cultural tensions that had informed his upbringing. These included his staunchly Christian background, his precocious attraction to the theater, and his defiance of the culture that expected him to follow family tradition instead of fleeing to the Keith Circuit. As Shirley starts a clandestine romance with painter Warren Foster, Ropes observes: "She listened while he told her of the staid New England family from whose loins he had sprung."[34] By contrast, Ropes might have described his own family less as "staid" than as colorfully respectable, not unlike Alice's travel lectures at the Boston Public Library. By contrast with those of Warren, Ropes's parents did not impede his artistic ambitions. At the same time, the writer conveys in *Stage Mother* his veiled recollections of growing up in a conservative culture notorious for its anti-theatrical prejudice.

42nd Street had variously incorporated Ropes's New England background through the characters of Peggy, as well as the Brahmin "angels" and playboys Richard Endicott, Mark Ames, and Warren Standish. *Stage Mother* incorporates Boston much more extensively into its setting and narrative. Ropes summons Proper Boston through the character of Frederick Lorraine, who ran away from an elite school to go onto the Orpheum Circuit as a cyclist. Reflecting his characterization of Peggy, Ropes depicts Fred's incongruous fit in vaudeville before his untimely onstage death. When Kitty later reveals to her friend Ruby that Fred hailed from Boston, Ruby jibes, "I always knew he was kinda diff'rent. A regular guy, you know, but sort've funny an' stand-offish at times, an' he talked real elegant for a trick bicycle rider."[35]

With keen detail and empathy, Ropes portrays the obstacles faced by Kitty, still very much lured by the theater, as she enters into the "staid" dominion of Fred's Boston family. As Kitty arrives at the house and meets the assembled relatives, Ropes describes the Lorraines' living room with gothic detail. Ropes writes, "Portraits of former Lorraines lined the walls—ship captains of the eighties, one or two grim visage merchants and the somber, brooding women who had been the wives and mistresses of their homes."[36] Although Ropes establishes the Lorraine women as Catholic, he leaves no doubt as to the women's anti-theatrical Puritanism as "church people" who disdain stage performers. The most zealous of the Lorraines, Ida attempts to convince young Shirley that "the friends of your mother are godless and wicked."[37]

In *Stage Mother*, Kitty faces her most bitter conflict with Ida: a less three-dimensional if no less vivid character than Kitty. Using grotesque caricature, Ropes satirizes Ida's Puritanism, as Kitty muses: "Why the old gal's such a pink-an'-pure babe she's even afraid to talk about improper fractions." The women prohibit Kitty from returning to the stage. Conflating vaudeville with burlesque, Mrs. Lorraine appeals to Kitty's maternal virtue to give up her work in variety theater: "Perhaps burlesque performances may not seem revolting to you, but, surely, you don't want your daughter to grow up in that atmosphere."[38]

As years pass in the novel, Ropes returns to the tension between the lure of the theater and the call of home. The author paints Kitty's desire to return to the stage with vivid sensory detail, as she visits her friends backstage when they pass through Boston on the Orpheum Circuit. Ropes writes, "Kitty stared hungrily into the succession of dressing rooms which they passed. The old make-up shelves, the uncomfortable, rickety chairs, the wash bowl, the strip of dirty carpet—this was Heaven."[39] As Kitty and Ralph Martin roam the "narrow streets" of her adopted city after a cast party, he urges her to leave the Lorraines. To Ralph's suggestion that Kitty is "smotherin' to death" in Boston, she responds, "I'd make out fine here if it wasn't for Ida an' Ma Lorraine. . . . They couldn't understand show folks in a million years."[40]

As Shirley launches into her affair with Warren Foster, Ropes parallels the painter's story with that of Fred Lorraine, as black sheep rebels from Proper Bostonian backgrounds. Ma Lorraine had lamented to Kitty that "Fred and I did not talk the same language." She informs Kitty: "I insisted on a thorough schooling for all my children. Fred alone rebelled and I have never quite forgiven him."[41] By contrast, Ropes characterizes Warren, the Back Bay scion of one of Boston's wealthiest families, as similarly rebellious to Fred (traits also reflected by Brad Roberts in the same year's *The Gold Diggers of 1933*). Evoking Ropes's own trajectory in the early 1920s, when he was bound for Bowdoin and the business world, Warren explains to Shirley: "I was destined for Harvard and bonds. . . . There has never been any other course for the Fosters. They were born with that bondish look."[42]

Determined to keep Shirley away from men who might interfere with her stage ambitions, Kitty confronts Mrs. Foster at her home on Commonwealth Avenue. Entering "the most majestic of Boston thoroughfares," Kitty schemes to blackmail Mrs. Foster with an intercepted erotic letter from Warren to Shirley.[43] Paralleling the "somber" home of Ma Lorraine with the "grim-lipped, solemn-visaged" ancestral portraits of Mrs. Foster, Ropes depicts Kitty's motivations as fueled by disdain for Puritan conventions and the "saner, quieter call of the home" represented by both families. At the same time, Ropes portrays Kitty's contempt of the anti-theatrical prejudice that has halted her stage career. Staring up at the portraits, she reflects, "Always I must fight people like this. The good, the proper, the safe kind of people who don't understand me and never will."[44]

Ropes empathetically paints Kitty's embattled lure to the theater throughout *Stage Mother*. Ropes shows Mrs. Foster's snobbish reduction of Kitty to a "noisy common woman." Ropes does not exonerate Kitty from the shortcomings of her ignorance. By contrast with the cultivated Peggy, Ropes implies his own distance from the coarse Kitty, whom he depicts as homophobic in her view of Jack Thomas, as well as resistant to Modernism's interracial mixing. Ropes observes: "To the world at large, Kitty was a shrew, a harridan whose bleached hair and over-rouged cheeks were the time-honored insignia of the despised creature—the stage mother."[45]

Ropes nonetheless etches the character of Kitty with nuance as he illustrates the forces of ageism and sexism that transform her into the trope of the stage mother. Building upon previous representations of the stage mother in works like Edna Ferber's 1928 story "Mother Knows Best," Ropes had himself perpetuated the type in the character of *42nd Street*'s Mrs. Blair. Ann comments of Mrs. Blair: "Stage mothers. . . . God damn every one of 'em! That old bat'll have her pride an' joy in the grave in about five more years."[46]

By contrast, in *Stage Mother*, Ropes depicts Kitty's complexity. When Kitty (now implied to be in her early thirties) attempts to book "forty weeks in burlesque" for herself, agent Abe Levey pulls no punches about her marketability.[47] He fumbles, "Personally, I'd get you set in a minute . . . but time ain't the best friend a woman's got."[48] In *Stage Mother*, Dorothy Brock reappears as the older rival to Shirley in *Adam and His Eves*. Ropes writes of the audience's impressions: "Dorothy Brock was a well-liked figure, but time had staled her none too infinite variety and the spectators welcomed the opportunity to hail this new ballerina."[49]

Ropes characterizes Kitty as a "battle-scarred warrior" who takes arms against the forces of institutionalized theatrical patriarchy and the "masters of show business."[50] Yet, Ropes shows Kitty's warfare ultimately dehumanizing her as she pursues Shirley's success at the cost of human empathy. Kitty informs Shirley, "Show business isn't the place to be sentimental. First come, first served—that's always been my motto."[51] At the same time, Ropes suggests the figure of the stage mother as a grotesque distortion of the misogyny fueling show business. Kitty defends herself to agent Lew Hearn: "They say stage mothers are tough. Well, look who they're dealing with—gorillas, gangsters, bad old boys who should've learned to behave years ago."[52] The stage mother's old friend Ruby sighs to her, "Kitty, you used to be a human being once." To this, Kitty shouts, "Yeah—an' what did it get me?"[53]

In the figure of "Kitty the implacable," Ropes creates a character deeply resonant with Rose Hovick, memorialized by Gypsy Rose Lee in her 1957 eponymous memoir and in the classic musical it inspired: 1959's *Gypsy*, with music by Jule Styne, lyrics by Stephen Sondheim, and book by Arthur Laurents. The Seattle-born Louise Hovick, who transformed into the legendary ecdysiast, recalled that her mother "in a feminine way, was ruthless."[54] Ropes characterizes Kitty similarly. He observes that Mark Thorne "secretly feared this woman. . . . Kitty's determination was a juggernaut crushing the obstacles which stood in her path."[55]

Ropes's 1933 novel and Lee's 1957 memoir, which depict both Kitty and Rose, respectively, booking their daughters on the Orpheum Circuit, evoke the overlapping entertainment worlds through which Lee and Billy Bradford criss-crossed in the mid-1920s. As a child performer with the "Baby June and Her Newsboys" act managed by Rose, Louise Hovick played Elks and Shriners lodges not unlike those conjured by Ropes as stages for the teenage Shirley in *Stage Mother*. "That'll go swell at the Elks banquet," Kitty gloats of Shirley's patriotic costume. In her memoir, Lee also reminisced of crossing similar paths with the Gus Edwards "kiddie revues": both Edwards and Rose Hovick faced judges' fines for breaking child-labor laws.[56]

Beyond the parallels with Lee's 1957 memoir, *Stage Mother* converses on numerous thematic and textual levels with *Gypsy*, whose composer Styne contributed songs to seven early 1940s movies with screenplays co-written by Ropes. In *Stage Mother*, Kitty's slangy bravado anticipates that of Rose, as she assures Shirley, "Darling, you're going to be swell—*swell!*" Kitty promises her daughter, "You're going up and up till you hit the top with a bang. . . . Mumsie's gonna make you one of the biggest stars on Broadway, wait an' see."[57] The acerbic tone of Laurents's libretto in *Gypsy* also finds a precedent in the Ropes novel, as a bystander views Shirley and Kitty "from a distance," darkly quipping, "In ten years that kid will either be a star or a corpse."[58]

Ropes's satiric portrayal of Kitty as exploitatively "alive to the demand for patriotic entertainment" during World War I also anticipates Rose. In *Stage Mother*, Kitty fashions "a red-white-and-blue costume shot with stars" for the teenage Shirley's early performances at lodge halls. Ropes had performed on Broadway in 1928 in *Billie*. Both *Stage Mother* and *Gypsy* satirize flag-waving Cohan-esque bombast—and, in the heightened pages of her memoir, Lee also recalled stage guinea pigs playing "Stars and Stripes Forever" as part of Baby June's act.[59] In *Stage Mother*, Ropes shows a rival young dancer to Shirley donning an "Uncle Sam hat for the tap dance."[60] By comparison, *Gypsy* depicts Baby June and Her Newsboys, in "Let Me Entertain You," pulling out all the stops in vaudeville. Backed by the boys in military costumes, June (transforming into costume as the Statue of Liberty) twirls batons and enjoins the audience to give thanks to "an uncle of mine—and an uncle of yours. The Greatest Uncle of Them All."[61]

Like Rose, Kitty dominates *Stage Mother* as a complex character who conflates her ambition for her daughter's career with her own hunger for success. Ropes shows Kitty's drive as indivisible from her blood-deep love for the stage, denied by both the "smug world of the Puritans" and the "masters of show business." After Shirley achieves her mother's dream of Broadway stardom, she seeks to distance herself from Kitty, who lashes out: "So this is what you get! . . . You plan for everything to come out diff'rently and this is what you get. You run their lives, you sacrifice the best years of your life and they want to pay you for the trouble—one hundred a week!"[62] By comparison, Rose charges Louise (now famous as Gypsy Rose Lee): "All the working and pushing and finagling. . . . What'd I do it for? You say I fought my whole life. I fought *your* whole life. So now tell me: what'd I do it for?"[63] Both Kitty and Rose redefine cultural tropes of maternal sacrifice in terms of self-serving material reward. However, *Stage Mother* might be considered a bleaker and more cynical work than *Gypsy*; only Rose, of the two stage mothers, demonstrates the impetus for growth.

After her "eleven o'clock number" recognition scene in *Gypsy*, "Rose's Turn," Rose demonstrates an openness to healing her relationship with Louise. She concedes, "I guess I did do it for me."[64] By contrast, Kitty remains in a state of self-delusion to the end of *Stage Mother*, which Ropes concludes with a powerfully ironic gesture: Shirley's denial of Kitty and her explanation to Lord Geoffrey Aylesworth that Kitty is only her chaperone "stage mother." Ropes concludes his novel with Kitty's devastating line, "Thank God I've made her happy!," as the stage mother convinces herself that the wealth and fame she's brokered for Shirley are the means to her daughter's contentment.[65]

Like Rose, Kitty vicariously seeks her "turn" upon the vaudeville stages of Ropes's Jazz Age America. In *Stage Mother*, the author collides the tensions of Proper Boston and the pressures of Manhattan cosmopolitism to raise challenging questions about tradition and modernity, as well as women's roles within industrial capitalism and Broadway show business. Kitty joins Peggy as a layered female character through whom Ropes negotiated the interlocking circuits of his family history, his Quincy and Boston upbringing, his performances in vaudeville, and his writer's calling. At the same time, Ropes persistently explored the image of Broadway as "machine."

"Who Said 'The Show Must Go On'?":
Defying the Machine in Ropes's Backstage Trilogy

Throughout his backstage trilogy, Ropes consistently questioned the myths of show business, including its most sacred mantra. After a particularly dispiriting rehearsal of *Town Talk of 1926*, Ted faces the queries of his own Broadway "angel" in *Go Into Your Dance*. Here, racketeer-turned-show business financier the Major demands: "Where's all this enthusiasm I been hearin' so much about? Who said 'The show must go on'?"[66]

The Major's discontent stems from his anxiety as a first-time Broadway backer.[67] By contrast, Ropes asks the question "Who said 'the show must go on'?" from the perspective of Broadway's stage workers. In his backstage trilogy, Ropes suggests some producers' use of the "lure of the theatre" as a means of perpetuating harmful working conditions. At the same time, Ropes also questions the relationship of "on with the show" tropes to the industrial imperatives of the Protestant work ethic. Ropes's backstage trilogy, then, suggests a powerful paradox. On one hand, Ropes shows how Puritan suspicions about actors as "loafers" fuel anti-theatrical prejudice. Equally, Ropes illustrates how the ethic fuels the mythologized ethos of show business "trouping," even at the expense of performers' health. When the pangs of pregnancy tempt Kitty to miss a show in *Stage Mother*, Fred (before his tragic accident) tells the doctor that Kitty should not miss the evening show: "Kitty's a dyed-in-the-wool trouper—she'll get by!"[68]

In *42nd Street*, characters extol the trouping Peggy as the apotheosis of the Protestant work ethic at the same time that her Puritan ethos renders her a misfit with Terry. Before learning of her star casting in *Pretty Lady*, Peggy imagines Marsh promoting her from the chorus to a "small part" as "a reward for persistent endeavor."[69] Yet, Ropes also connects Peggy's embodiment of the ethic to her purposeful, if ambivalent, ability to assimilate into Broadway's "vast machine."

In his backstage trilogy, and most prominently in *42nd Street*, Ropes critically questions the relationships between the theater and Fordist industrialization. Ropes found this connection epitomized in the lockstep high kicks of the Tiller Girls, with whom he had shared the stage at the Casino de Paris in the same *Paris* revue that transformed its chorus girls into cars. Writing his backstage trilogy from 1932 through 1934, Ropes may have encountered discourses informing Siegfried Kracauer's influential 1931 essay "The Mass Ornament." Here, the German theorist observed that the Tiller dancers were "no longer individual girls, but indissoluble female units whose movements are mathematically demonstrated."[70] The dancer-choreographer Gertrude Hoffmann, too, instructed her Hoffmann Girls to work "against the mechanical rhythm" of the Tiller Girls through choreographic syncopation, as Sunny Stalter-Pace observes.[71]

Ropes's allusions to the Tiller Girls, in both *42nd Street* and *Go Into Your Dance*, reveal similar anxieties about Fordist standardization. In *42nd Street*, Andy Lee rebukes the chorus girls: "A little style; you're not working for Tiller. You can afford to act human."[72] In *Go Into Your Dance*, Nora's "bored" view of the Casino de Paris's shows contrasts with Ted's eager appraisal: "They were so dismally alike, these Paris shows with their displays of nude flesh, their bovine chorus girls, their troupes of thin, mechanical dancing girls imported from London, their adagio dancers, flinging themselves from one corner of the proscenium arch to the other."[73]

If Ropes depicts the Tiller Girls dancing with automaton-like precision, he also pervasively portrays Broadway musicals as machines throughout his backstage trilogy. In *The Business of the Theatre*, Bernheim noted the industrial nature of "the combination system" of Broadway's legitimate theater: "Still another feature . . . worth noting is that the producer, like the automobile manufacturer, to some extent runs an assembling plant."[74] At the same time, Ropes's use of *machinal* metaphors connects him to a wide Modernist discourse during the 1920s. David Savran writes of the Theatre Guild's productions of writers like Elmer Rice (*The Adding Machine*): "Expressionism was welcomed into the American theatre in the early 1920s in part because of its skill at addressing the many anxieties of the new middle class about standardization, Fordism, and consumerism."[75]

Ropes consistently confronts these tensions in his novels. At the same time, he demystifies the lure of the theater by analyzing "the cogs" in its "complicated machines." In *42nd Street*, Ropes captures the tension between quixotic aspiration and grinding human labor in the musings of Abe Green.

Ropes shows the producer reflecting: "Without laughter and applause for fuel, the machine would stop and these cogs would be separated and lost. What it takes a hundred brains three months to conceive, one audience can tear down in a night. There is the romance of show business, the eternal wish to tilt at windmills." Ropes comments: "No wonder Abe Green stood in the rear of the orchestra, tearing at his fingernails."[76]

Ropes portrays how the engineering of Broadway musicals toward profitable perfection can distort the self-identity of their performers. Of a fourteen-hour *Pretty Lady* rehearsal led by Andy Lee, Ropes observes: "It was said of Lee that he got results. On opening night, he never failed to present a well-trained machine." Resentful of Andy's rigorous standardization, Peggy longs to be cast in a "real play." She reflects, "In the chorus you are part of a machine, except for the fact that instead of coils and wires you possess joints and muscles which ache when you exert them too much."[77]

As depicted by Ropes, "the show must go on" myth hinges on the concept that performers can transcend their human frailty, sublimating it for the larger good of the show. Ropes writes in *42nd Street*, "In the stifling August heat such activities breed madness, yet the show must go on. They were not human beings with whom Andy Lee was dealing, but a well-ordered row of dancing shoes strangely vitalized."[78] In *42nd Street* and *Go Into Your Dance*, Ropes uses specific incidents in the plot to extend his critique of Andy Lee's treatment of the chorus. In both novels, Ropes shows how Broadway "trouper" myths fuel the self-sacrificial "romance of show business." At their extreme end, Ropes suggests that they also threaten the safety of performers, placing human bodies under the profit motives that spin the wheels of the machine.

"Nothing Must Stand in the Way of the Show": Death in the Rose Garden and Disaster on the Flower Trellis in *42nd Street* and *Go Into Your Dance*

Two scenes in the backstage trilogy particularly illustrate Ropes's critical examination of "the show must go on" trope, as connected to his demystification of Broadway musical production processes. In *42nd Street*, Ropes portrays how the commercial imperatives of show business diminish human rituals of grieving. In one startling scene, elderly character actor Lionel Crane dies upon the idyllic set of a Long Island rose garden. In *Go Into Your Dance*, by contrast, Nora survives the collapse of a flower trellis set in an onstage accident. In both incidents, Ropes collides utopian images of musical comedy artifice and abundance with the realities that producers spend fortunes to disguise. "Yes, musical comedy was a bed of roses, thorny side up," vaudevillian Danny Moran muses in the novel.[79] This contrasts with Julian Marsh's more famous hosanna in the 1980 stage musical: "Think of musical comedy, the most glorious words in the English language!"[80]

During *Pretty Lady*'s out-of-town tryout in Philadelphia, Ropes depicts Marsh using "the show must go on" tropes to rhetorically rally his cast into opening night. At the same time, Ropes shows Marsh privately subordinating the death of Crane to *Pretty Lady*'s profits. Ropes observes that, for Marsh, "the play was the thing. . . . The show must always be the main consideration, each tragedy lost some of its force because the show was dominant."[81] Tragedy strikes the company during the show's Philadelphia dress rehearsal, as Crane suffers a fatal heart attack onstage while playing a sheriff. To avoid an inquest, Marsh, Green, and Friedman arrange a cursory onstage Catholic memorial service and then bribe a doctor to move Crane's body offstage and issue a certificate "swearing Crane died in the ambulance." Ropes writes, "The doctor knew his show world. Its members were not calloused, but they had learned a thousand times over that phrase, 'The Show Must Go On.'"[82]

Ropes imbues the scene with a sense of the incongruous and the surreal, as Crane's "body lay prone, giving a macabre note to the gay scene of the rose garden." Ropes depicts the *Pretty Lady* cast struggling to balance their trouper ethos with their grief and confusion: "No one knew what to do. On the stage was a dead man—a member of the cast who had departed with appalling swiftness."[83] As Marsh, Green, and Friedman bring in Father Reilly to "commend the soul of this poor player," Ropes describes the performers' unease: "Chorus boys awkwardly clutched their silver-colored top hats and tried to step lightly so that the metal cleats nailed to their dancing shoes would make as little noise as possible. . . . All hovered over the prostrate figure of a man past seventy who had answered his last cue."

Ropes ironically underscores the tension between Marsh's private pragmatism and his public rhetoric to *Pretty Lady*'s cast. Ropes portrays Marsh's internal calculations dominating his authentic sadness. Ropes observes, "Marsh began to speculate as to Crane's successor. The thought came mechanically welling above the sorrow which had risen in his heart. A man has duties; an investment of one hundred thousand dollars cannot wait upon the passing of one human being."[84] Without villainizing Marsh, whose philosophies Ropes connects systemically to Broadway's box office operations, Ropes portrays the impresario's total subscription to his credo: "Nothing must stand in the way of the show."[85]

Ropes, who had read many of Shakespeare's works in his youth, may have called upon *Julius Caesar* in his characterization of Marsh. Evoking the oratory of Mark Antony, Marsh issues a unifying speech to the cast of *Pretty Lady*, who have forgotten lyrics and dance routines in the midst of their loss. Marsh implores, "No one grieves for that poor man more than I do. But we must leave the dead to Providence." Ropes shows Marsh, with an actor's rhetorical brilliance, harnessing the "romance of show business" toward his investment. He appeals to the cast of *Pretty Lady* to view the musical as their "monument" to Crane: "Mr. Crane was a gentleman and a trouper. He wanted this play to succeed. . . . Don't fail him now. It is a fitting tribute to a great man that we can bear up under calamity and finish the work which he had hoped to see completed."[86]

The Lionel Crane scene in *42nd Street* allows Ropes to portray the complexities around Broadway's machinery, as applied to natural human processes of mortality and mourning. Strikingly, the erasure of the Crane scene from early drafts of *42nd Street*'s 1933 screenplay echoes Marsh's cover-up of Crane's death. Cast as the elderly actor, silent film veteran Henry B. Walthall "was reduced to playing a nonspeaking bit role" in the film.[87]

By comparison, a stunning sequence in *Go Into Your Dance* allows Ropes to explore the hazardous potentials of Broadway's profit motive, as not only cauterizing grief but endangering human life. During the Atlantic City tryouts of Ted's new *Town Talk*, his lax safety protocols result in a near-tragic accident. In the sequence, a towering flower trellis set climbed upon by florally costumed chorus girls collapses and injures many of the women, including Nora. Ropes depicts the horror of the accident while indicting the behavior of Ted, who, overlooking the urgent warnings of his stage manager Friedman, wants to produce the splashiest number possible.

Here, Ropes draws upon the excesses of a Broadway culture in which its impresarios competed to produce the most spectacular Broadway revues. These "Mastodons of Musical Extravaganzas" (as Jonas Westover has described the Shuberts' *Passing Shows*) attracted both awe and criticism. In 1928, Bernheim lamented that the extravagant revue, seeking to emulate the movies, created "waste" through an "over-elaboration" that was "injurious to scenic art"—as well as potentially dangerous to performers. Bernheim wrote of one unnamed production: "There is the case of the solid india rubber tree. . . . The tree yielded gracefully enough and safely deposited our heroine [from a twenty-foot elevation], but when the bough was free of her weight, it jumped back with such vehemence that it tore through the set and knocked it ten feet off stage."[88]

In setting Ted's perilous production number upon a giant flower trellis, Ropes also draws critical inspiration from the "living curtain" and "human chandeliers" that sprung first in the Paris music hall and increasingly in Broadway extravagant revues. These numbers, which reflected "the trend toward depicting people as objects," suspended scantily clad showgirls above the stage, decoratively stacking the women on top of each other or strapping them to lighting fixtures. Westover observes that *The Passing Show of 1923* "had three spectacles: an 'Animated Curtain,' a 'Jeweled Curtain,' and a 'Living Chandelier.'"[89] In *Go Into Your Dance*, a "living curtain" dazzles Ted at the Casino de Paris, where he vows to import it to Broadway.

Ropes critiques both the objectification and the danger of "living curtain" numbers and the "over-elaboration" of the Paris and Broadway revue. Vowing to outdo the *"Passing Revues"* of the Wilsons (based on the Shuberts) and Lane's *"Frivolities"* (based on *The Ziegfeld Follies*), Ted decides to import an acclaimed Parisian number into his new *Town Talk*. Ropes describes Ted's brainstorm: "The first-act finale of the new revue was to be a carbon copy of that lavish interlude in the Casino de Paris which was fulsomely entitled 'The Living Trellis of Girls.'" Ted orders the construction of a "huge latticework" extending from the ground "high into the flies of the theatre."[90]

Ropes contrasts the mounting terror of the chorus girls with the saccharine trappings of the number, in which they parade across the stage "in wisps of tulle and long trains of silken wisteria blossoms." Ropes sardonically describes how the number unfolds while "Nora and the show's inevitable tenor sang fervidly about the joys of 'Wistaria Time.'" Ropes depicts the sixteen women making the climb up the latticework due not only to fears of job scarcity but also to the mandates of the "trouping" ethos. Ropes writes, "The chorus girls balked at the nerve-tightening climb to the summit of the huge screen, but, with true Broadway philosophy, they gradually accepted the feat as one of the day's tasks and pulled themselves up hand over hand to the very top of the device."

Illustrating the connection between "over-elaboration" and impresarial hubris, Ropes depicts Ted, a Broadway Icarus who himself doesn't have to venture close to the sun, flagrantly ignoring Friedman's concerns.[91] Ted ignores his stage manager's initial warnings of the set as a "source of great danger to human lives unless each bolt was in its proper place."[92] In defiance of Friedman, Ted decides to send Nora up the trellis to "be framed in the center of the girls." Ted snaps: "It's safe enough. . . . It'll sort of complete the picture."[93]

Once again revealing the flaws in Broadway's profit-driven machines, Ropes shows Friedman sublimating his conscience to his job security, as the stage manager becomes increasingly obsequious to Ted and withdraws his petition to halt the number.

From the point of view of Nora and the chorus girls, Ropes vividly describes the fear of the *Town Talk* dancers. When the women "cling wide-eyed to their perilous perch," terrified to look down, Ted barks at the girls: "And for God's sake don't look like you were scared out of your wits."[94] Suddenly, one of the women shrieks as the dancers plunge to the stage:

> There was a horrible ripping noise, the agonized scream of the metal as it tore loose from its foundation, buckled and curved in a sickening arc. . . . The impact of their bodies was terrifying. . . . The moans of the injured girls who were pinned beneath the wrecked framework shot through the theater.[95]

Nora, too, falls to the stage when her silk train is ripped from her shoulders. To the alarmed Ted, Nora retains her acerbic character. Smiling "painfully," she whispers to Ted that he has outdone himself: "What a finale. . . . The Wilsons can never top that one."[96] At the hospital, Nora learns from a glib Ted about the condition of the other women: "No real damage. A busted arm for Helen Fields. . . . There was more smoke than fire. Only you, you old so-and-so, with that broken leg." Unrepentantly, Ted jokes about Nora being irreplaceable: "you out there looking trim and sweet in one of those Kiviette dresses, hoofin' your dear life away."[97] In Ted, Ropes created a compelling yet distinctly unpalatable antiheroic protagonist. "That partner of mine—he's a no-good, egotistical rat," admits Nora, with whom Ted unites at the end of the novel, in a conclusion that suggests Ropes's sour complication of a Hollywood ending.[98]

Indicting Ted's negligence as symptomatic of larger commercial theater structures, Ropes illustrates the potential of a bucolic "Wistaria Time" to become a disastrous spectacle that asks performers to potentially hoof away their lives. Having himself been part, as a featured dancer, of "mastodon musical extravaganzas" like *Paris* at the Casino de Paris, Ropes reaffirms the anxiety behind Peggy's observation: "In the chorus you are part of a machine."[99] In his backstage trilogy, Ropes demonstrates the moral transactions that underlie the pragmatism of Marsh's reflection, "the play was the thing," as the author reaffirms the dignity of human life as a "true Broadway philosophy." To deliver his critical points, Ropes also draws upon the satirical, and not always discreet, storytelling devices of roman à clef.

Broadway Keyholes: Ropes's Romans à Clef and Impresarios as the Gods in the Machines

Among the pages of Ropes's backstage trilogy, 1930s readers encountered a cavalcade of fictionalized reflections of celebrities and their affairs. On one level, these blind item-like disclosures allowed Ropes to write tantalizing novels that, like New York's tabloids, allowed readers to peek at "Broadway through a keyhole" (as a 1933 pre-Hays Code film inspired by Walter Winchell's columns promised audiences). Yet, beyond this surface sensationalism, Ropes's use of roman à clef strategies illustrates the potential of backstage novels to illuminate hidden corners and affective dimensions of theater history, including the lives of gay men and women on Broadway.

The shapes of Ropes's narrative "keys" varied. The writer often spliced his celebrity sources with performers from his personal history. For instance, Shirley Lorraine in *Stage Mother* variously suggests Marian Hamilton; showgirl Betty Compton; and Adele Astaire, who married into the British aristocracy in 1932. Ropes channels Astaire's wedding to Lord Charles Cavendish in the marriage between Shirley and Lord Geoffrey Aylesworth. Even more specifically, Ropes conjures Cole Porter in *Go Into Your Dance*. The Newport-dwelling Dodo Meehan appeals to Ted as a possible songwriter for his new *Town Talk*. Ropes describes Dodo as "skillful in the wording of ditties that were miles above the below-sea level of the average Tin Pan Alley output. He dared to rhyme words of more than three syllables and did so to the delight and amazement of the little producing band."[100]

Ropes's fictionalized characterization of George Gershwin also stands out in *Go Into Your Dance*. Although Ropes does not identify the character as Jewish, he leaves no doubt as to the source of composer Johnny Bartels. Whereas Gershwin's one-act jazz opera *Blue Monday* (a prototype for *Porgy and Bess*) electrified *George White's Scandals of 1922* before it was cut by White, Bartels demonstrates a similar, Harlem-themed opus for Ted. Johnny plays a "number of his more provocative tunes" for the "rapt" Ted, Nora, the Major, and his moll Laura Whitney. Ropes observes: "He played a number of his more provocative tunes for them . . . the incendiary blues, born of dark torment, of Harlem nights, of the age-old plaint that man is never faithful."[101] Indeed, Ropes likely knew Gershwin personally, as the writer and the composer shared a literary agent in the rebellious actress-turned-manager Grace Morse.

Yet, while Ropes's backstage trilogy stands out as a "Broadway through a keyhole" landscape portrait of Jazz Age theater, the writer focuses his roman à clef characterizations most stingingly upon Broadway's impresarios, producers, and managers. Using these strategies, Ropes explores how Broadway's producing class perpetuated show business as a "machinery" fueled by both performers' dreams and scarce, often exploitative working conditions. Ropes shows actors laboring in what Sean P. Holmes calls an "occupation characterized by huge inequalities of wealth and status."[102]

In Quincy, Ropes had grown up staunchly Christian, if increasingly apostate, among the congregants of the New Church. This background informed the frequently religious iconography he drew upon in characterizing Broadway's impresarios, whose imposing commercial power he had witnessed during his dancing days as Billy Bradford. Throughout his backstage trilogy, Ropes characterizes impresarios as the gods in the machine, including *Stage Mother*'s Mark Thorne, whom Ropes describes ironically as a "man who walked and talked with gods." Similarly, in *42nd Street*, Ropes observes of Marsh: "Again his likeness to a mighty god struck Marsh forcibly. . . . He and only he could breathe life into the creature of his own making."

As David Armstrong has compellingly suggested, Ropes likely based the Oxford-accented Marsh at least partially on the English-born Hassard Short, who conducted a semi-public relationship with the chorus boy Billy Ladd.[103] The *Greenwich Village Follies* showman John Murray Anderson, with his innovations in New Stagecraft, suggests yet another inspiration for Marsh, who skillfully weds his "unerring instinct for business" to a "sense of the artistic."[104] Yet Marsh aligns even more closely with Short, who was "variously referred to as 'Broadway's master magician,' and the 'master of color and movement.'"[105] Broadway insiders in the 1920s considered Short's homosexuality an open secret, though the director himself "shunned publicity."[106] As Kevin Winkler describes, "The always impeccably attired Short frequently traveled to Europe looking for ideas and inspiration, and newspaper notices remarked on his departures or returns, often with [Moss] Hart or the Berlin family. However, none mentioned that he traveled with his companion, Billy Ladd, a slender chorus boy with bleached blond hair. Mrs. Irving Berlin later remarked that Bobby and Billy's 'was the happiest marriage of the group.'"[107]

Like Billy Ladd, Billy Lawler destabilizes Broadway hierarchies by intervening in the casting of Marsh's shows. According to Winkler, Ladd wielded considerable influence over his director-lover, despite his status as a chorus boy. "During the production of *As Thousands Cheer*, there was great difficulty in finding an actor who resembled the prince of Wales for a sketch to be directed by Hart. Finally, a handsome young man named Thomas Hamilton was discovered. When Short enthused that he would personally spend as much time as necessary to coach him, 'Billy Ladd pointed out coolly that directing the actors was Moss's job.'"[108] Similarly, in *42nd Street*, Billy orders Julian to stay away from rivals. Flo informs Peggy: "I hope you're not going to tell me that [Billy] didn't get poor Ray Hall fired—and didn't mess things up for Bobby Lynton. Your new friend is death on blondes—male blondes, at any rate."[109]

In *42nd Street*, Ropes depicts the homosexual Marsh more sympathetically, through his use of roman à clef, than he later did George White as the caddish, skirt-chasing Ted. Nevertheless, when Marsh reappears in *Go Into Your Dance*, Ropes does not spare the producer, as an "autocrat [and] lordly power of Broadway," from the unsentimental depiction of being "feared by the mass of performers and revered by the sycophant who managed to worm his way into his confidence."[110] Suggesting his defiant attention to the mechanisms of power in show business, Ropes repeatedly created fictional portrayals of Broadway's most powerful directors and producers. Florenz Ziegfeld Jr. died in a state of bankruptcy in 1932. Yet, brothers Lee and J. J. Shubert, White, and Short were very much alive when Ropes incorporated their public profiles into his backstage trilogy. So was his erstwhile employer, Gus Edwards.

A "Titan of the Entertainment World": Ropes's Portrayal of Mark Thorne in *Stage Mother*

In *42nd Street* and *Go Into Your Dance*, Ropes critically commented upon the risks of the "over-elaboration" of 1920s Broadway revues. In the latter novel, Ropes's chorus girls found themselves at the mercy of a producer unwilling to prioritize their health and safety at the expense of a dazzling number. By contrast, in *Stage Mother*, Ropes commented upon the predatory behavior of Broadway's male power brokers through the character of Mark Thorne.

Ropes clearly based Thorne upon Edwards, with whom he had toured in *The Fountain of Youth of 1925*. Ropes introduces Thorne as a sanctimonious showman who exploits the myth of himself as a Jewish immigrant embodying the American Dream, even as he has left his roots far behind by the 1920s. In *Stage Mother*, Ropes describes the celebrated Thorne as "a Jew of Ghetto extraction and inordinately proud of the fact. He hymned the glories of those humble surroundings with a sentimental tear in his eyes and a plenitude of heart-felt gestures. The East Side, from which had risen titans of finance and lords of the entertainment world."[111]

As one of these new entertainment "lords," Thorne is portrayed by Ropes as a man who exploits his power in his relationships with the young women in his cast. Ropes may not have been directly accusing his former employer of sexually predatory behavior toward underage women, and the book starts with the standard disclaimer: "All characters and incidents in this novel are fictitious—B.R." Additionally, Ropes may have distanced himself successfully from litigation by including Edwards as a separate individual from Thorne in the novel. Kitty tells Shirley, "We'll let Thorne take a look at you": "It's either him or Gus Edwards . . . and I don't think there's room for you with the Edwards gang."[112]

Yet, Ropes spikes his backstage trilogy with blunt feminist critique of Broadway's "titans" posing a threat to the teenage girls joining the vaudeville stage and the ensembles of Broadway's chorus lines. Ropes places Thorne within a systemic Broadway culture of patriarchal harassment, objectification, and sexual abuse connected to its publicity mechanisms and the normalization of fetishizing teenage girls. As Westover observes, "A major trope in press releases about the [chorus] girls was an emphasis on their incomparable beauty as well as their 'freshness,' a term meant to indicate they were mainly young, certainly innocent, and inexperienced and not far removed from the nineteenth-century definition of 'chick' or 'squab' for a child."[113]

The portrayal of Thorne's sexual predation joins other incidents in Ropes's backstage trilogy. In these portrayals, Ropes evokes *Stage Mother*'s "Miss Pathé News," Jack Thomas, in balancing scandal-sheet luridness with a reformer's zeal to expose corruption. An accusation of statutory rape, for example, plays a substantial role in *42nd Street*. Ropes shows Andy Lee's wife, Amy, hanging the episode "over his head like the sword of Damocles."[114] Ropes enters Andy's thoughts, leaving the reader's conclusions ambiguous yet tilted toward Andy's guilt. Ropes writes: "Here he was, as classy a guy as you found on Broadway, tied down to a hell cat like Amy. And all because he got drunk and went on a wild party with some fifteen year-old. Then the next thing he remembered was the groggy aftermath when they found him in the girl's bed and she accused him of an assault."[115] In the same novel, stage mother Mrs. Blair dangles her daughter Polly, "a minor," in front of gangster Walt McDermott. Mrs. Blair urges Polly to "watch McDermott that he don't get too free an' easy with his hands" while allowing him to dance with her at a nightclub. Yet she also disregards her daughter's fears as Polly informs her mother, "He tried to kiss me tonight."[116]

Whatever the level of direct inspiration from Edwards, Ropes uses the figure of Thorne to indict the systemic exploitation of young female performers within the "Broadway Beauty Trust." Seeking to cast "lovely girls" in his new vaudeville youth revue, Thorne flanks himself "on either side by two of the more comely ladies of his act" as he first appears to dramatic effect before the stage mothers waiting to audition their children at his theater. Here, after Kitty describes Shirley's talents to another mother, the latter informs Kitty: "How lovely; I hear Mr. Thorne likes toe dancers." The woman "lowers her voice discreetly" before continuing, "The only thing is . . . they say he's a little bit too fond of young girls."[117]

Ropes draws directly upon his experiences with Edwards as Kitty arranges for Shirley to become one of Thorne's "subdebs" in a touring vaudeville show that closely resembles *The Fountain of Youth*. Thorne not only markets the youth of the girls in his cast but appears to inappropriately interact with them. In one of the novel's most shocking scenes, Kitty leverages Thorne's sexual relationship with an adolescent female cast member into blackmail, allowing the stage mother to bargain (without her daughter's knowledge) for Shirley's promotion within the company. After taking compromising Kodak photos of Thorne and the young woman outside his hotel room, Kitty confronts him: "I was in one of my devilish moods an' nothin' could stop me. So I sneaked along the fire escape 'till I came to Margie Evans' room."[118]

While depicting the title character of *Stage Mother* as a relentlessly Machiavellian, even gangster-like, operator, Ropes ironically depicts a shrewd woman using the weapons of patriarchy against its perpetrators. Thorne joins a chorus of male producers manipulated and outsmarted by Kitty, even as she submits to the same dehumanizing capitalist machinery to advance her daughter as a Broadway star. "We're pretty ruthless, aren't we, Mummie? We're tough babies!," Shirley exclaims sardonically.[119]

Unfortunately, Ropes's critique cannot be separated from the antisemitic imagery of the lecherous Jew with which he characterizes not only Thorne but also Lew Hearn. Ropes describes Hearn as "the smartest agent on the Main Stem" but also as a "procurer de luxe" characterized by his extreme lechery and "tremendous nose."[120] Ropes writes that Hearn "profited by the lust of the Broadway overlords—acting as a procurer, supplying them with a never diminishing stream of blondes and brunettes who were willing to surrender to any reasonable demand so long as they were allotted front row positions in the chorus of a musical comedy."[121]

Ropes's depictions of Jewish characters in his early 1930s backstage trilogy express some degree of range. The kind taxi driver Abe Feinstein in *Go Into Your Dance* and the virtuosic pianist Gertrude in *42nd Street* populate the novels along with men like Hearn and *42nd Street*'s Friedman and Green. By the time of 1951's *Mr. Tilley Takes a Walk*, Ropes expressed more sympathy to "immigrants in yarmalkas" (as well as to Irish Americans, contradicting his own teenage rant against "Sinn Feiners").

Ropes's warming attitude toward Jewish Americans may have stemmed from his twelve-year-long partnership with Val Burton. In 1938, for the MGM film *Lord Jeff*, Ropes teamed up with the British Jewish songwriter and screenwriter Burton, born Isadore Harry Burns. The collaboration encompassed five films and the unproduced play *Twenty Little Working Girls*, as well as *Mr. Tilley Takes a Walk*.[122] On the back cover of the first edition of *Mr. Tilley Takes a Walk*, Ropes and Burton pose in affectionate camaraderie, gazing at each other and touching knees. Born in London to a politically prominent Jewish family, the son of a Sephardic mother and an Ashkenazi father, Burton had been a decorated fighter pilot for the Royal Air Force and a songwriter for World War I-era concert parties and revues, including shows for Charles B. Cochran. Joining the American Society for Composers, Authors, and Publishers in 1921, he gained fame as the writer of several Tin Pan Alley standards cowritten with Will Jason, including, most famously, 1931's "Penthouse Serenade."[123] Burton's Hollywood screenwriting career ended shortly after his final film, 1951's *Bedtime for Bonzo*. On September 29, 1952, writer-producer Roy Huggins named him as a Communist before the House Un-American Activities Committee, leading to Burton's ban from the movie industry.[124]

Years before Ropes's partnership with Burton, antisemitic portraits of Jewish men as agents, managers, and producers abounded in the early 1930s backstage trilogy. Here, Ropes joined writers like J. P. McEvoy (with his satiric team of "Kibbitzer and Eppus" in *Show Girl*) in portraying Jewish producers as greedy, coarse, and lecherous. The widespread antipathy against the Shubert Brothers and the Theatrical Syndicate (five out of six of whom were Jewish) may have contributed to these demeaning representations. Holmes observes, "Attacks on them frequently foregrounded their Jewishness, using it both to locate them as a hostile presence in the high-cultural landscape and to imagine them with an imagined mass audience that was both immigrant and ethnic."[125] John H. Houchin also notes the popularity of the Baptist pastor Dr. John Roach Straton, who inveighed that "the theater today has fallen almost entirely into the hands of a small group of Jews. It is very unfortunate for any race to have control of the whole of the theatrical business."[126]

Additionally, as the seven-year-old president of the Children of the American Revolution of Wollaston, Ropes had grown up in an Anglo-Saxon climate

Photo of Bradford
Ropes and Val Burton
from back dust jacket
of *Mr. Tilley Takes a
Walk*.
Reproduced by per-
mission of Thomas
Crane Public Library,
Quincy, MA.

BRADFORD ROPES and VAL BURTON
Co-authors of "Mr. Tilley Takes a Walk"

systemically antipathetic to Jews. As Cleveland Amory observed (quoting
Dixon Wecter), the Anglophilic Boston Society of the Brahmins promised
"a great bulwark against Irish, German and Jewish invasion."[127] Yet Ropes's
antisemitic imagery in the early 1930s novels drew from a much broader set
of cultural contexts. With the rejuvenation of the Ku Klux Klan in the early
1920s and the nativist Immigration Act of 1924, the reality of life in the United
States in the early twentieth century, within and outside Boston, clashed
harshly with the inclusive myths of American democracy that Billy Bradford
encountered among the melting-pot stages of vaudeville. If Ropes expressed a

feeling of outsider status through the character of Peggy, his distance from the pervasive Jewish American immigrant culture of the Broadway musical likely contributed to it.

Rather than excusing Ropes's demeaning depictions of Jewish men, and particularly Broadway theater managers, these contexts add further dimensions to the Puritan character that remained with Ropes into the early 1930s, even as his antisemitic sentiments appear to have abated during his 1940s partnership with the British Jewish Burton. In 1951, the *Quincy Patriot Ledger* reported that Ropes and Burton had conceived a surprising follow-up to *Mr. Tilley Takes a Walk*: a political novel with anti-Fascist themes. Ropes reported setting the unpublished *The Judas Sheep* "in the locale of the UN, once the site of a slaughterhouse, and liken[ed] the human race unto the 'Judas Sheep' which leads the others to the slaughter, approximated in life by such personalities as Hitler, Mussolini, and others."[128] While *The Judas Sheep* was never published, *Mr. Tilley Takes a Walk* steered Ropes into new directions of backstage narrative. As enfolded into an expansive landscape of turn-of-the-century Boston, the book pointed critically to the city's historical blind spots as well as to ongoing persecutions against gay men and lesbians throughout the country.

Back to Boston: *Mr. Tilley Takes a Walk*

Ropes's backstage trilogy of the 1930s autobiographically charts his contradictory navigations as a "greasepaint Puritan" through the vaudeville and Broadway stages of the Jazz Age. Less reliant upon roman à clef strategies than his 1930s novels, *Mr. Tilley Takes a Walk* suggests an autumnal novel of artistic reconciliation that partially resolves tensions between Proper Boston and Broadway. Here, Ropes critically reckons with the social stratifications of a culture that often discouraged "the lure of the theatre." At the same time, Ropes pays fond tribute to his own "call of home"; to progenitors like the suffragette-doctor Mercy Ruggles Bisbee; and to the enduring connections to Boston that gave him such distinctive insight into American show business.

Ropes continued his work as a reliable and dexterous Hollywood screenwriter into the early 1950s. From his vaudevillian years with Alyn Mann to his backstage trilogy, Ropes had defied the strictures of his upbringing. Ropes may have related to Ted's confidence to his sister Ellen in *Go Into Your Dance*: "Ma says you an' me were born to be rebels. . . . She says she don't know how we come by it."[129] Yet, by the 1930s, after years of vaudeville's "tough grind,"

Ropes embraced the security offered by his Hollywood screenwriting career. "It is always best to have an ace in the hole," Ropes informed the *Patriot Ledger*.[130]

After the war, Ropes's screenplays largely avoided overt allusions to gay life. Yet, the 1947 comedy *Buck Privates Come Home* (based on a story by Ropes and Richard Macaulay) contains surprising and subtle elements of a gay adoption allegory. Here, Corporal Slicker Smith and Private Herbie Brown, returning veterans played by Bud Abbott and Lou Costello, attempt to adopt a French orphan. After a French Embassy consul informs the duo that marriage is a prerequisite, Costello misinterprets Abbott's reminder as a proposal: "Oh, Slicker—you wouldn't marry me, would you?" When Slicker asks Herbie, "Did you ever hear of anyone marrying a man?," the latter replies, "Yes, sir . . . my mother."[131] Ropes plays the scenes for gentle laughs rather than ridicule.

After World War II, Hollywood joined the rest of the country in a Cold War-era "Lavender Scare" that viciously persecuted gay men and lesbians. The decade saw the beginnings of a visible gay rights movement, with the Mattachine Society and the Daughters of Bilitis, founded, respectively, in 1950 and 1955. Yet, as Wendell C. Stone writes of the 1950s and '60s, "Cold war hysteria had raised concern that 'deviates' posed a security risk, so various federal agencies engaged in aggressive efforts to identify and weed out their influence. Gay men and women were routinely fired from their jobs, denied housing, and arrested for open displays of affection."[132]

Published amid the oppression of gay men and women during the Lavender Scare, *Mr. Tilley Takes a Walk* evokes Ropes's earlier novels not only in its backstage elements but also in Ropes's conflicted portrayal of Brahmin spinster Dolly Scripture. Reflecting his earlier portrayal of the "sinister" Emmy in *Go Into Your Dance*, Ropes draws upon stereotypical language and imagery in his portrayal of Dolly, who exercises a "tenacious, masculine domination" over her sister, Martha.[133] Yet Ropes sympathetically portrays Dolly as ostracized from a homophobic early twentieth-century suffragette movement in Boston, as expressed by the "Amazon" Emily Endicott. Emily informs her niece Cornelia that her feminism has its limits: "I never meant that the two sexes should change places; that we ladies must start wearing the trousers or conduct ourselves like that odious Dolly Scripture."[134] Ropes also shows Dolly heroically, during World War I, as an "intrepid soul" chauffeuring the running board of the Red Cross care staff.

The subtle inclusion of Dolly's suicide interrupts *Mr. Tilley*'s nostalgic picture of Proper Boston and reveals that Ropes continued to be concerned with expressing the experiences of gay men and women during an oppressive era. Ropes depicts Dolly's suicide as prompted by her viewing of the censored 1926 Broadway lesbian drama, *The Captive (La Prisonnière)*. Written by Édouard Bourdet and translated by Arthur Hornblow Jr., *The Captive* joined *Sex* and *The Virgin Man* as one of the three plays shuttered in 1927 by the Wales Padlock Law. George Jean Nathan had derided the play as "nothing more or less than a document in favor of sexual degeneracy."[135] In *The Captive*, which portrays lesbians as "shadow" figures, the young Frenchwoman Irène feigns love for her fiancé, Jacques, even as Mme. d'Aiguines leaves violets for Irène as a symbol of their irreconcilable passion.

Ropes implies that Dolly, having been disturbed by viewing *The Captive* at the Empire Theatre, has killed herself in the recognition of her suppressed lesbianism. Ropes writes of George Tilley's reaction to the tragedy:

> It was a profound shock to learn of Dolly Scripture's death. The details were shrouded in uncertainty but everything pointed to suicide. . . . As the shrinking, tearful-eyed Martha related it, that last evening had been devoid of any circumstances which could possibly have led to Dolly's act. . . . The play had seemed a trifle odd and ambiguous to Martha, some adaptation from the French called *The Captive*.

The details of Dolly's suicide echo that of Miss Rogers in *Go Into Your Dance*: "And, three hours later, Dolly Scripture plunged from the window of their suite on the thirtieth floor."[136]

In a climate of intense homophobia, Ropes sweeps the brief incident of Dolly's suicide into an epic narrative that also affirms Ropes's love of the stage. *Mr. Tilley* eschews the elements of incisive critique aimed at the Broadway theater industry that marked his earlier books. Written during the disillusioned days of the Depression, the backstage trilogy foregrounded Ropes's barbed critiques of show business's industrial machines and myths of "the show must go on." Yet, Ropes's unabashed "passion for the theatre" had irradiated the earlier backstage trilogy, as well, suggesting a deep connection between Ropes's idealism about the stage and his dedication to exposing its flaws.

In *Mr. Tilley*, Ropes reprises his critique of anti-theatrical prejudice through the character of Katie Sheridan (née Brannigan), an Irish American parlormaid-turned-"First Lady of the Theatre." Patriarch David Endicott forbids Katie from performing at a "questionable" Boston cabaret, circa 1900.[137]

Evoking the anti-Puritan history of Merrymount, Ropes places his identification with Katie even more so than with the Irish American George Tilley or the Brahmin Endicotts. Suggesting the young Ropes with *The Dream Child* and other pageants, Katie makes a "hit as Fairy Queen in Mrs. Butler's May Festival over at the Mechanics Building." She also specifically evokes Ropes's vaudevillian past when she tells George, "There's a chance I'll be doin' my act at Keith's next summer. Keith's on Tremont Street!"[138]

Despite the initial deterrence of David Endicott, Katie perseveres. The "epicene" Winthrop Frothingham, lured from Beacon Hill to "the fleshpots of Broadway," casts Katie in his first Main Stem venture.[139] Underscoring the hypocrisy underlying anti-theatrical prejudice in Proper Boston, Ropes shows that David himself has maneuvered the casting of Katie as a bribe to frame George Tilley as the father of a spuriously unborn child—and to remove the postman from a romantic attachment with daughter Cornelia. Sharing a full first name with Kitty Lorraine, Katie—as "the tony *Miss* Katherine Sheridan"—scores a triumph in Winthrop's play. Streaking a "fiery path which led from subordinate roles with the ill-fated Frothingham Productions to the champagne era, as Manhattan's reigning queen of musical comedy," Katie eventually becomes a star for David Belasco, "the white-maned sybarite who wore his collar like a priest."[140]

Katie Brannigan evokes the early life of Ropes from a different vantage point than Maine minister's daughter Peggy. By contrast with *42nd Street, Mr. Tilley* valorizes the American immigrant experience. Both Ropes and his cowriter Burton suggest some of their identification with Italian American Bill Gianelli, denigrated as an "ill-bred scribbler of cheap songs," who flees MIT to become a Tin Pan Alley songwriter in the 1920s. As teamed with the rebellious Sarah Elizabeth Endicott, Bill eventually transforms into a Broadway songwriter for intimate revues. Like both Ropes and Burton, Bill ends up in LA: "Why, those Hollywood boys are crazy to get their hands on the tunes Sarah Elizabeth and I wrote together."[141]

In this complex set of identifications with Katie, George, and Bill, Ropes fulfills more of the promise of becoming American than he might have been capable of in the early 1930s, when he related to Peggy's alienation as a "Puritan in show business" as much as to vaudevillian Danny Moran's persona as a "greasepaint vagabond."[142] Ropes critiques the "beleaguered" upper-class Bostonians who flee in "exodus" from Beacon Hill, when called upon to share their neighborhoods with (according to their perception) "the Philistines who were armed with brogues, yarmalkas or darker-tinted skins."[143] Here, looking back at the Jazz Age, Ropes suggests that the immigrant diversity on display at Keith's provides the lure and beacon for Americans to follow into a tumultuous modernity.

Yet, Ropes published 1951's *Mr. Tilley Takes a Walk* in a present still intolerant of gay and lesbian rights. After returning to Boston in the mid-1950s, Ropes died in 1966: three years before the Stonewall Uprising but only shortly after the momentous 1964 publication of Susan Sontag's "Notes on 'Camp'" in the *Partisan Review*. Had Ropes lived a few years longer, he might have been toasted at college screenings of *42nd Street* and *The Gold Diggers of 1933*. Sontag hailed the films' choreographer Busby Berkeley as an exemplar of "Genuine Camp" at the same time the youthful counterculture celebrated his hallucinogenic human patterns.

Ropes's own gay camp aesthetic lived on in the 1960s and '70s thorough multiple adaptive engagements with *42nd Street* in Caffe Cino's Off-Off-Broadway production of the musical pastiche *Dames at Sea* (1966) and Ken Russell's outlandish 1971 reimagining of Sandy Wilson's *The Boy Friend*. At the same time, the dazzling, smash hit 1980 stage musical adaptation of *42nd Street*, produced by David Merrick at the dawn of the Reagan era, excised the explicitly queer content that the Warner Brothers film had already minimized. If Ropes had critiqued "Banned in Boston"-style censorship in the early 1930s, the 1980s marked a revival of homophobic censorial impulses as much as the paradoxical immortalization of *42nd Street* as a classic Broadway stage musical.

CHAPTER 6

Bringing Back Bradford Ropes

Nine years before David Merrick's production of *42nd Street* recreated a pastiche fantasy of the 1930s, an actual 1920s musical became an unlikely smash hit on Broadway. This was the 1971 revival of *No, No, Nanette*, whose success was attributed to Busby Berkeley. Coaxed out of retirement and initially touted as the director of *No, No, Nanette*, Berkeley in fact supervised a show with musical staging and choreography by Donald Saddler. More importantly to the box office, Berkeley symbolized the late-show glamour of the Warner Brothers musicals to a younger, Vietnam War-weary generation, serving as the Art Deco figurehead of "a production that saw Ruby Keeler's triumphant return and placed the nostalgia movement squarely on Broadway."[1] Now, Berkeley accepted a new billing. "Who else would be singled out—when everybody thought he was all washed up—as a leading figure in the Golden Age of 'Camp' (whatever that was)? Nobody," asserted Don Dunn in *The Making of No, No, Nanette*.[2]

Five years before the *Nanette* revival, Bradford Ropes died in Jamaica Plain, Massachusetts, at the age of sixty-one. An obituary did not appear in the *New York Times*, and few publications other than his hometown newspaper memorialized him: "Bradford Ropes of Quincy; Novelist, Writer, Dancer," headlined the *Quincy Patriot Ledger*.[3] Ropes had layered his backstage trilogy with piercing critical ironies about gay men's success on Broadway in relationship to their assimilation to the straight world. Having juxtaposed Billy Lawler's smoke-screened ambition with Jack Winslow's defiant "queer art of failure" in *42nd Street*, Ropes might have anticipated the spectacle of erasure that followed the *No, No, Nanette* revival. Yet he might not have been fully pleased, had he lived past 1966, to watch not only *42nd Street* but the pervasive 1960s discourse on camp attributed to Berkeley, famous for his eroticized abstractions of feminine beauty. Cultural critics followed the lead of Sontag in proclaiming Berkeley an exemplar of the ubiquitous yet elusive sensibility. At the same time, these narratives wrote the gay man who envisioned *42nd Street* out of the history of one of the most iconic American works of camp style, as carried over from novel to film.

Ropes's activities in the 1950s suggest that he did not want his career in show business to be forgotten. In 1951, with the soon-to-be-blacklisted Val Burton, Ropes published to glowing reviews *Mr. Tilley Takes a Walk*, dedicating it: "For Mr. and Mrs. Arthur D. Ropes."[4] On one level, *Mr. Tilley* represented a gesture of nostalgia, as Ropes looked back at his Boston-to-Broadway trajectory. In other ways, he evoked his mother, Alice, who had presented her lantern-illustrated travel lectures three decades earlier. From 1952 to 1954, Ropes toured Boston-area clubs with a talk called "Adventures in Three Make-Believe Worlds." As the *Patriot Ledger* noted of the talk, whose title Ropes later amended to "Four Make-Believe Worlds" to encompass television: "The 'three worlds' Mr. Ropes pointed out are footlights, movies, and books."[5] Ropes presented "Three Make-Believe Worlds" at the Women's Union of the Atlantic Memorial Congregational Church in Quincy and at the Men's Club in Dalton, Massachusetts, among other venues.

The "Adventures in Three Make-Believe Worlds" lecture for the Quincy Women's Union suggests a vibrant evening of biographical stories and show business anecdotes, the bawdiness of which Ropes tempered in response to the Congregational setting. Indeed, Ropes traced the beginnings of his career to his work with Gus Edwards rather than to *A Whirl of Dance* with Alyn Mann. According to the *Patriot Ledger*, the "annual Guest day meeting" began with an introduction of Ropes by the program chairman, Mrs. Mason Eastman, and also included devotions by Mrs. Joseph D. Parkman. Before more than 150 members and guests of the Women's Union, Ropes regaled the audience with details about the performers he had worked with during his vaudeville days. He mentioned not only James Cagney and Fanny Brice (with whom he shared a bill at the Orpheum Theatre in LA) but also Imogene Coca, then a major television celebrity for her appearances on *Your Show of Shows*.[6] The *Patriot Ledger* recounted: "Returning to New York, Mr. Ropes, in looking for a new dance partner, turned down Imogene Coca, who had applied for the position, on the grounds that she was not the type he was looking for at the time."[7] Ropes presented the talk before not only citizens of Wollaston but also representatives from neighboring Congregational churches in Houghs Neck, Squantum, Braintree, Hancock, and Lexington.

Some obscurity shadows the reasons for Ropes's return to Boston in the mid-1950s, after a brief period of living in New York in the early part of the decade.[8] In 1951, the same year as *Mr. Tilley*, Ropes wrote the book for a musical that, suggesting *Applause*, told "of the violent end of burlesque." With a score by Dana Suesse, *Prize Package* would have been brought to the stage by *Finian's Rainbow* producer Lee Sabinson.[9] Yet, like Ropes's 1935 musical *Home Town Boy*, *Prize Package* did not materialize on Broadway.

Ropes, too, made only tentative inroads into writing for television, with episodes of the Ralph Bellamy-starring detective series *Man Against Crime* (1953 and '54); the spy drama *The Hunter* (1954); and the immigrant family drama *Mama* (1954, based on the stories that inspired *I Remember Mama*). If Ropes had successfully reinvented himself as a novelist and screenwriter during the decline of vaudeville, he now resisted the forces of change. During a 1953 talk at the Wollaston Woman's Club, the *Patriot Ledger's* reporter recounted Ropes describing "TV as the voracious monster, exhausting imagination and talent in its Frankenstein combine."[10] If Ropes found it difficult to adjust to industrial shifts in Hollywood, the institutionalized homophobia of the Lavender Scare may have also played a role in his flight from Hollywood, the site of his mid-1930s revels with Roswell Black, Bruz Fletcher, and Queenie Smith. In 1957, Ropes found work as an advertising copywriter for the industrial marketing agency S. Gunnar Myrbeck and Co., Inc., based in Quincy and Washington, DC; he became a freelance writer a year later.[11]

Ropes's worsening alcoholism may also have played a role in his return to his hometown. Having grown up as the son of a prominent temperance leader, Ropes had written extensively about the dynamics of alcohol addiction in both *42nd Street* and *Stage Mother*. Now, in the 1960s, and without the guidance of Alice (who passed away at the age of 90 in 1960), Ropes lived a life that became increasingly affected by the disease.

Yet, Ropes found a rejuvenating source of camaraderie and care in the aid provided by his first cousin Marjorie Gale, the daughter of Malcolm and Edith Nichols and a kindred spirit with whom Ropes had long been close. She was the "heartbeat of her community," recalled Gale's daughter.[12] In 1964, Gale and members of her family came to pick up Ropes at 15 Wollaston Avenue, where he was then living with elderly aunts. The family found Ropes in a state of deep inebriation. "We picked him up off the floor," recalled Gale's daughter, who also remembered the "Colonial minutemen" pattern of the "nico-tinted" wallpaper, "slanted down because the house had settled." It was Gale, a "vivacious and artistic" woman "with a flair for the dramatic," who "brought him back."[13] She both emotionally "rescued" Ropes and offered him a new sense of family belonging in the Boston borough of Jamaica Plain.

Under Gale's care, Ropes entered a new phase of life: one in which he continued to struggle with his alcoholism but was also surrounded by loving family and friends. "Marjorie was very animated with him," Gale's daughter recalls of Ropes, who "loved people" and particularly found a rapport with children. In multiple screenplays, including *Lord Jeff, Glamour Boy, Nothing But Trouble*, and *Buck Privates Come Home*, Ropes had featured a series of spirited and precocious kids. Now in Jamaica Plain, Ropes made a memorable impression on young people, including Gale's daughter, as a "very vivacious" man who captivated their imaginations with new "adventures in make-believe worlds." "Most kids want to get up and leave when an adult starts telling stories . . . not us," she recalls. Appearing on the porch with a "gathering of little people at his feet," Ropes alternated between "making up a lot of stories" for the neighborhood kids and recounting fairy tales like "Jack and the Beanstalk." According to Gale's daughter, Ropes would aid the children by narratively "throwing out some bones," such as "what the giant would eat"—but he would let "the excitement come from the kids."[14]

If Ropes endeared himself to young people, he also made ample time for adult friendships. At night, the Gale family and Ropes often received visits from Raphael Guiu (the godfather of Gale's children), as well as Guiu's brother: the virtuosic Cuban-born pianist José Melis. A prolific recording artist, the latter had risen to national celebrity as Jack Paar's bandleader for *The Morning Show* and then *The Tonight Show*, which Melis departed in 1962. A few times a month, Melis, Guiu, Ropes, and Gale led musical porch parties that attracted friends from around the neighborhood. As Gale's daughter recalls, the "adults late at night had a grand old time." Ropes, who had played some piano in his youth, sat on the piano bench with the brilliant Melis as "music, laughter, and cigarettes" filled the porch. Leaving behind a number of unpublished novels, including *Preview, The Prince of 42nd Street* (a biographical novel about Boston-raised *The Merry Widow* star Donald Brian), and the "detective story" *The Della Robbia Plaque*, Ropes died suddenly at the Jamaica Plain VA Hospital on November 21, 1966.[15] The cause of death was listed as an aspiration of blood secondary to ruptured esophageal varices, complicated by fatty nutritional cirrhosis.[16] Gale's daughter recalls of the loss, which was devastating to Marjorie, "He was there one day, and then he wasn't."[17]

If Ropes's later years in Jamaica Plain were dappled ones, his work fell into neglect, and the backstage trilogy languished without republication. Opting to publically conceal his homosexuality upon his return to Boston, Ropes may have chosen not to follow the example of Forman Brown, who authorized *Better*

Angel for a 1951 reprint by the pulp label Universal Publishing under the new title *Torment*. The cover salaciously queried: "Is it evil for one man to lavish affection on another? Torn between the boy who cherished him and the girl who struggled for his love, Kurt Gray could not be sure." A 1990 reprint of *Better Angel* by Alyson Press revealed Richard Meeker as the pseudonym of the eighty-nine-year-old Brown, who now received long overdue acclaim as a pioneering gay writer. By contrast, by the time of Ropes's death, the 1933 Hollywood adaptation of *42nd Street* had emphatically eclipsed his novel.

The "Notes on 'Camp'" discourse of the 1960s brought *42nd Street* back, while leaving behind the author of the source novel. Enshrining Busby Berkeley as a "pure example" of genuine "naïve camp," Sontag's essay galvanized a prodigious wave of critical discourse throughout the decade, while minimizing the generative influence of gay men. "Nevertheless, even though homosexuals have been its vanguard, Camp taste is much more than homosexual taste," argued Sontag.[18] As J. Hoberman has observed, the identification of Berkeley with camp originated in the underground gay cinema cults of Jack Smith, who included "'all Busby Berkeley flix' in the list of 'secret flix' he invokes in the manifesto, 'The Perfect Filmic Appositeness of Maria Montez,' published in the Winter 1962-3 issue of *Film Culture*."[19]

To Smith's underground fuse, Sontag lit the flame of a Berkeley cult that exploded from European film festivals to college campuses, where the choreographer toured his show *An Evening with Busby Berkeley and the Fabulous Era of Hollywood Musicals*. As Hoberman notes, "By 1965, the Huntington Hartford Gallery of Modern Art in New York was aware of Berkeley Film Festivals popping up on college campuses everywhere. . . . The San Francisco Film Festival that year featured the pictures, and other festivals throughout the United States and Europe began paying homage to the director."[20]

The reputation of Berkeley as the camp visionary behind *42nd Street* soared, although the choreographer initially greeted the term with a "puzzled stare." The organizer of a Gallery of Modern Art retrospective entitled "A Tribute to Busby Berkeley: Master Builder of the American Film" explained to Berkeley the definition of a term that many outside gay communities continued to find elusive. "They call me the King of Camp," Berkeley told *Newsweek*, elaborating: "I didn't know what camp was, but Raymond Rohauer, who organized the show, explained to me that camp is anyone who reaches the top and does something unusual and enjoyable."[21]

Although the six-times-married Berkeley became an idol of camp culture, he personally expressed ambivalence around flamboyant gay men. Dunn recounts the heavy "scent of embarrassment" exuded by Berkeley, his sixth wife, Etta, and onlookers when the choreographer declined to engage with a quartet of starstruck drag queens who snuck into a callback of *No, No, Nanette* in 1970. According to Dunn, the queens arrived at the auditorium of the 46th Street Theatre "dressed in faded, midi-length gowns that have obviously come from attic trunks and rummage sales," with one of them trailing "a feather boa fully nine feet long."

Though using the stigmatizing language of the "screaming queen," Dunn illustrates the ways in which the gay men and transgender women who fueled the 1960s camp revival still faced the marginalization of their sexuality in the years after Stonewall. Dunn recorded: "'We're just thrilled, so *thrillllled* to meet you, Mr. Berkeley,' one of the queens screeches, holding out a hand that the director ignores. . . . One is still blowing kisses at Berkeley as he is led— rushed—offstage."[22] The incident reflected comments by film critic Andrew Sarris, the 1960s American ambassador to French auteur theory, that the contributions of Berkeley, as the "Méliès of Musicals," "deserved better than being consigned to the sniggerings of Camp followers."[23]

The Nostalgia Craze of the 1960s and '70s propelled *No, No, Nanette* at the Broadway box office and ran in a "parallel line" with camp, in the words of John Simon. Before *Nanette*, the cultural movement started with the 1966 Off-Off-Broadway musical pastiche *Dames at Sea, or Golddiggers Afloat*. As Wendell C. Stone notes, the sleeper success of *Dames at Sea* inspired the openly gay producer Harry Rigby to pitch the idea of a *Nanette* revival to Berkeley. In "Notes on 'Camp,'" Sontag had explored the connections between camp and a backward-looking impulse, observing that "so many of the objects prized by Camp taste are old-fashioned, out-of-date, démodé."[24]

Clive Barnes elaborated on the influence of "Notes on 'Camp'" on *Dames at Sea* in his review of the musical's 1968 Off-Broadway production at the Bouwerie Lane Theater. Surprised to find himself charmed by this "little gem of a musical," Barnes prompted readers: "Someone—Susan Sontag perhaps— should do a sociological essay on the manner in which the movies have developed a new kind of instant nostalgia." Barnes elaborated, "For the real lovers of the 30's are the people who have absorbed them through that new time machine called the late-night movie on television."[25] Rocketing the young, kewpie doll-faced Bernadette Peters to stardom, *Dames at Sea* collectively played 575 performances at the Bouwerie Lane Theatre and the Theatre de Lys.

Although *Dames at Sea* originated as a scrappy, one-act pastiche at the coffeehouse Caffe Cino, the zeitgeist fueled the commercial transfer of the musical. The dual cultural appetites of nostalgia and camp enabled a robust, if niche, commercial market for the work of gay male theater makers and filmmakers in the 1960s and '70s (as well as heterosexual-identifying artists with a gay sensibility, such as Ken Russell). Exemplifying this new wave of work, both *Dames at Sea* and Russell's 1971 film musical *The Boy Friend* incorporated *42nd Street*'s chorus girl-to-star plot, which the works transposed, respectively, onto an American battleship and into a provincial English touring production. Gravitating to the Berkeley film musicals rather than Ropes's novel as the primary reference point, these artists kept *42nd Street* vibrantly alive in popular culture.

As originally directed by Robert Dahdah, *Dames at Sea* marked the biggest commercial hit to play the small coffeehouse stage of the Caffe Cino, credited as the birthplace of Off-Off-Broadway, as well as "the first venue to regularly feature work by and about gay men."[26] The show featured music by Jim Wise and book and lyrics cowritten by Robin Miller and George Haimsohn, the latter also a poet who created gay erotic photography and fiction under the pseudonyms of Plato and Alexander Goodman.[27] *Dames at Sea* illustrated a collaboration steeped in the men's love of the classic Hollywood musical, shared in winking code among themselves and a predominately gay and lesbian audience at the Cino. Haimsohn recounted the musical's origins: "We were going to do something on the '*Gold Diggers*' movies, and when Robin met Jim, Robin said he felt he needed an American to work with. That's how the three of us came together."[28] In the interview, Miller, Wise, and Haimsohn shared a joint love not only for Ruby Keeler (also held up as an exemplar of camp by Sontag) but also for the more outré numbers of 1930s movie musicals. Haimsohn enthused over "the giant chocolate milkshake that everybody comes out of" in the 1934 Eddie Cantor movie musical *Kid Millions*.[29]

Marking a more commercial, uptown direction for the Cino, *Dames at Sea* has not been considered among the Cino's most countercultural works. Stone observes of *Dames at Sea*: "Though it embodies many of the traits of other Cino productions, it shuns the more subversive style or content of the most significant work presented at the Caffe."[30] At the same time, *Dames* drew potently upon the underground camp ethos of the Caffe Cino, as exemplified by playwrights like H. M. Koutoukas and Tom Eyen. Their peer Robert Patrick recalled Koutoukas as "a true poet who enshrined such Cino cult-objects as mirror-balls, cheap glitter, dyed feathers ('cobra feathers'), rhinestones, toy pianos . . . and all other forms of 'tacky glamour.'"[31] Like the work of Koutoukas, *Dames* epitomized the founding aesthetic of its proprietor, of whom Stone recounts, "The highest compliment Joe Cino could pay a performer was to call him a Rockette."[32]

With its resourceful repurposing of Berkeley-esque spectacle, staged at the Cino with a six-actor cast, *Dames* can also be put into dialogue with the contemporaneous Play-House of the Ridiculous and the Ridiculous Theatrical Company. Both of these companies, respectively founded by John Vaccaro and Charles Ludlam in 1965 and 1967, shared the "trash from treasure" aesthetic fueling the cult films of Jack Smith, whom José Esteban Muñoz describes as the "progenitor of queer utopian aesthetics" in his hallucinatory summoning of B movie Technicolor other worlds.[33] Stephen J. Bottoms describes *Dames at Sea*'s aesthetics, which drew from Wilde as well as from Warners: "The women's costumes, for example . . . were from a stash of old *Salome* costumes that Dahdah had acquired some years previously . . . and six white umbrellas had silver sequins stitched onto them, in order to catch the light like raindrops while being twirled during the song 'Raining in My Heart'—thus echoing another Busby Berkeley sequence from the same film."[34]

Soaked with affectionate irony, *Dames at Sea* reflected the wide-ranging knowledge shared by Wise, Haimsohn, and Miller of not only the musicals and routines of Berkeley but a gamut of 1930s Hollywood musicals. The writers conceived "an affectionate spoof of all the old Berkeley films rolled into one."[35] They also worked in references to *The Broadway Melody*; the "let's put on a show" tropes of Mickey and Judy; the songs of Cole Porter; and naval tap dance extravaganzas like *Follow the Fleet* (Ropes himself had cowritten the story for such an MGM musical: 1942's *Ship Ahoy*, starring Eleanor Powell). Molly Haskell observed in the *Village Voice*: "The aim is not to ridicule but to recapture the cherished tinsel-and-trouper banalities and backstage bathos of the Busby Berkeley musical period."[36]

Yet, while *Dames at Sea* incorporated dozens of allusions and quotations, Wise, Miller, and Haimsohn based its plot structure most closely upon *42nd Street*. *Dames at Sea* followed the rise of the naive but ambitious Ruby, a chorus girl from Utah. "I'm still just a simple girl from Centerville," she informs her castmates.[37] Championed by songwriting sailor Dick and wisecracking chorine Joan, Ruby replaces temperamental Mona Kent in Harry Hennessey's musical, also titled *Dames at Sea*. The musical opens on Captain Courageous's naval ship after the shuttering of Hennessey's Broadway theater by the forces of the same "Wall Street" to which Mona tap dances a peppy paean in the show's opening number.

Dames at Sea demonstrated that *42nd Street*'s climactic scene, involving

Peggy's replacement of Dorothy Brock, had long since transformed into cliché. *Dames at Sea* repeats Dorothy's lines in the words of Mona: "Ruby, I want you to be so darn good, I'll hate you for the rest of my life."[38] At the same time, emphasizing the chorus girls' solidarity, the musical redistributes Marsh's famous pep talk to Joan, who assures her friend: "Listen, Ruby, you're going out on that poopdeck a chorus girl but you're coming back a star!"[39]

Evoking the strategies of Ropes, *Dames at Sea* fused a heterosexual love plot with gay innuendo steeped in the imagery of painter Paul Cadmus, who had scandalized Depression-era America in paintings like *Sailors and Floosies* and *The Fleet's In*. Bottoms observes that heterosexual audience members at the Cino might have missed "the gender ambiguities of the title song, with its sexually frustrated sailor boys":

DICK AND LUCKY: In the Atlantic, we get so frantic, For girls we left on the shore / In the Adriatic, when things get static, / We'd love to have a matey with a name like Sal or Sadie.

LUCKY: He's a nice guy, Dick, he's really a pal.

DICK: And Lucky's my best friend but he ain't no gal.

BOTH: We need some frilly skirts to boost our morale, / Some dames at sea!

As Bottoms notes, "Whether or not the teasing innuendo was fully picked up on, *Dames at Sea*'s enduring fusion of Hollywood glamor and makeshift materials succeeded in drawing a whole new audience of 'straight' musical fans to the Cino."[40]

Produced five years after *Dames at Sea*, Ken Russell's big-budget MGM meta-movie musical *The Boy Friend* also drew heavily upon *42nd Street* as an intertextual pastiche. Like *Dames at Sea*, Russell's adaptation of *The Boy Friend* expressed the sensibility of a publically heterosexual-identifying filmmaker who frequently gravitated to LGBTQ+ history and homoerotic themes, in films like 1971's *The Music Lovers*. That year, Norm Goldenstein profiled the British filmmaker, who infused his historical and biographical fantasias with punk shock: "He is probably the most talked about and talked to director today, the most flamboyant and controversial, perhaps the most eccentric and excessive."[41]

Russell "revamped" and "recamped" the 1953 stage musical *The Boy Friend*, with book, music, and lyrics by Sandy Wilson.[42] Wilson veiled his homosexuality with "respectable discretion" in the 1950s.[43] Yet, he gravitated to musicals informed by the camp aesthetic, as well as to adaptations of writers like Ronald Firbank. Wilson's work premiered in a midcentury West End theatrical milieu that embraced the work of gay men while criminalizing its creators. In her biography of Wilson, Deborah Philips points to the "irony of the fact that this pillorying of gay men and the censorship by the Lord Chamberlain's Office of any mention of homosexuality in British theatre occurred at a time when the theatre in London and the provinces were largely controlled by homosexual men."[44] As Philips notes, this influential group included songwriter Ivor Novello and playwright Terence Rattigan, as well as Wilson's idol Noël Coward.[45]

Set in the 1920s of the Bright Young Things, Wilson's *The Boy Friend* not only influenced but also shared similar origins with *Dames at Sea*. *The Boy Friend* debuted at the cabaret-theater Players' Club in London. Like the coffeehouse stage of the Caffe Cino, the Players' Club presented a sanctuary space for gay men, offering programs steeped in a "highly stylized Victorian music hall pastiche."[46] The Players' Club "deployed nostalgia together with the disorienting effects of pastiche and parody to project a coded 'gay' identity," as Robert Gordon describes.[47] Like the later chamber musical *Dames at Sea*, *The Boy Friend* moved from a fringe theater to the commercial stage, as the Broadway transfer of *The Boy Friend* catapulted to stardom Julie Andrews as ingenue Polly Browne.

Wilson's *The Boy Friend* had been marked by "delicate charm."[48] By contrast, Russell transformed Wilson's intimate musical into a film marked by his signature maximalism. Kurt Gänzl writes of Wilson's *The Boy Friend*: "When the laughs came they were to be laughs of recognition, of affection, of nostalgia as well . . . not laughs aroused by grotesquerie or campy parody."[49] Drawing the outrage of Wilson, who denounced Russell's film as "a walpurgisnacht of self-indulgence," the British filmmaker concocted a spectacle steeped in outlandish mannerisms.[50]

Though opening to a divided critical reception, Russell's *The Boy Friend* earned praise for its sophisticated demystification of genre, which included another riff on *42nd Street*. Using show-within-a-show devices, Russell frames the intrigues of a ragtag 1930s touring British production, performing Wilson's *The Boy Friend*, within a backstage plot lifted from *42nd Street*. Russell reimagines Peggy Sawyer as Polly Browne (played by Twiggy), a meek assistant stage manager called to go on in *The Boy Friend* for the Brock-like Rita Monroe, who has injured her high-heeled foot on a tram. As Goldenstein observed in his profile of Russell, *The Boy Friend* "is a film on three levels. It is the story of the member of a British provincial theater troupe and their back-stage lives; it is the play itself; and—here's the Russell rub—it is the fantasy of a Busby Berkeley musical of the 1930s, as dreamed by a director who sees the play performed at a near-empty stage matinee."[51]

Russell's *The Boy Friend* used many of the same structural inflection points and ironized quotation marks as *Dames at Sea*. As played with saccharine savagery by Glenda Jackson, Rita tells Polly: "Now get out there and be so great you'll make me hate you." Impresario Mr. Max also quotes Marsh: "Now Polly, listen to me. You're going out there a youngster—but you've got to come back a star."[52] Like *Dames at Sea* before it, Russell's *The Boy Friend* flattened *42nd Street*'s characters into Depression-era commedia archetypes. *Dames at Sea* had named its characters Ruby, Dick, and Joan in tribute to the 1930s Warner Brothers stock players. *The Boy Friend* goes further, collapsing the names of characters and actors. Polly and her love interest, the juvenile Tony, answer to "Polly and Tony" both within the touring *Boy Friend* company and within the show. Both *Dames at Sea* and *The Boy Friend* satirically queer the respective couplings of Ruby and Dick, and Polly and Tony. In both, pastiche, quotation, and artifice replace sincere heterosexual ardor. Russell follows the lead of *Dames at Sea*, in which Ruby and Dick—falling in love at first sight—duet on "It's You" without exchanging a word of dialogue, since Ruby has just woken up from a fainting spell.

The Boy Friend's extravagant pastiche led film critics to connect the film to the discourse that continued in the wake of Sontag's essay. Russell poured into his *Boy Friend* overripe touches including, in the words of Joseph Lanza, "exaggerated set designs, outlandish camera swoops, garish costumes and overblown acting, replete with fluttering eyelids and catty dialogue delivered through clenched teeth."[53] The film's designer, Tony Walton, commented: "I never dreamed I would have the opportunity to create such things as an Arabian Nights extravaganza, an airplane with dancers on the wings, a giant revolving gramophone turntable for another number, and even a complete Pixieland."[54] Russell also summons the gay roots of *42nd Street* in the effete-ness of the Marsh-like Mr. Max (Max Adrian), who, draped in a butterfly-patterned kimono, suggests Ropes's original vision of the character as a "syb-arite among producers."[55]

By contrast, the *Baxter's Beauties of 1933* segment of Stanley Donen's *Movie Movie* (1978), a third pastiche of *42nd Street*, removed the queer subtexts prominent in *Dames at Sea* and still detectable in Russell's reimagining of *The Boy Friend*. In her original review of the film, Pauline Kael opined that the "over-reverential" pastiche might have swerved further into Ludlam-esque Ridiculous camp; it "could use some of that golden hysteria of taking the situation in old movies to a logical extreme."[56] Framed as a double feature, *Baxter's Beauties of 1933* merged satire and melodrama, as George C. Scott's director Spats Baxter tearfully reunites with Kitty Simpson, the Peggy Sawyer-like chorine who turns out to be his long-lost daughter: "You're going out on that stage a Simpson, but you're coming back a Baxter."[57]

As pastiches and parodies of *42nd Street*, *Dames at Sea*, *The Boy Friend*, and *Movie Movie* collectively framed a paradox. They confirmed the Warner Brothers film as the paradigm of the backstage musical and sealed Berkeley's reputation as the "King of Camp." Yet, in identifying *42nd Street* so synonymously with Berkeley (who also worked with director Lloyd Bacon on the film), they displaced Ropes's novel from collective memory. These adaptations distanced the characters further and further away from the characters of Ropes's book. Most strikingly, Peggy moved further away from the wisecracking, self-aware, and even calculating career girl of Ropes's novel into "naïve, blank-faced Ruby."[58] As Peggy turned more and more guileless with every new pastiche, she also moved further away from the Maine minister's daughter that rooted Ropes's book in New England Puritan culture as much as Times Square.

These adaptations, which satirically emphasized the climatic portions of the screenplay, also moved cultural associations of *42nd Street* further away from Ropes's own contexts and thematic concerns. With James Seymour, the novelist and journalist Rian James, rather than Ropes, wrote most of the dialogue that the musicals and films repeatedly parodied from the 1960s onward, including what Ethan Mordden calls Marsh's "famous command . . . half shopgirl's dream and half egalitarian imperative."[59] Ropes had cynically portrayed "the show must go on" myths and Cinderella narratives of the 1920s. By contrast, the pastiches of the 1960s and '70s cemented *42nd Street* as a Depression-era celebration of collective solidarity fueled by the trouper ethos and individualist gumption. Although *Dames at Sea*, *The Boy Friend*, and *Movie Movie* enshrined this folklore in the popular imagination, these 1960s and '70s works eclipsed Ropes's framing of scarcity and opportunism as driving forces of the Broadway musical comedy "machine."

In 1977, the librettists Michael Stewart and Mark Bramble embarked on a Broadway musical adaptation of *42nd Street* after Stewart saw the "granddaddy" of backstage movies at a Manhattan revival house.[60] After Bramble, too, became excited about its prospects, the two started on an arduous search. Stewart reported that it took six months for him to get a copy of the novel and "another six months to trace [Ropes's] heirs for the rights."[61] They finally located Ropes's cousin Bess Bigue: the same woman who had inspired the character of Sarah Elizabeth Endicott in *Mr. Tilley Takes a Walk*. Descended from a brother of Arthur Dudley Ropes who had settled in Sacramento, the spirited Bigue, a former amateur model and fashion show organizer, had moved to Ajijic, Mexico, with her Ecuadorian American husband, Emile.[62] Stewart and Bramble launched a national search "to find the heirs of Bradford Ropes," which finally reached Bigue while she was shopping in Albuquerque. Bramble recounted in 2017:

> Our agent said, "Look, I'm going to start advertising in magazines across the country." . . . And for months, we had no response at all. . . . And suddenly, in Albuquerque, New Mexico, a lady and her pal were in a dress shop . . . and saw the notice. And [the pal] said, "Bess, isn't this your cousin, Bradford Ropes?" . . . And so we were able to make an arrangement with her and acquire the rights to the novel.[63]

In correspondence surrounding the February 1978 "Ropes Contract" signed by Bigue and her siblings, the librettists' lawyers noted, with some confusion, that Bigue had insisted on including, as part of the sale, *Mr. Tilley Takes a Walk*: a novel of personal resonance for the former Sarah Elizabeth Pottinger.[64] David Merrick then followed up by purchasing the rights to the *42nd Street* film from United Artists.[65]

By this time, *42nd Street*'s mythology had fixed itself in the popular psyche. Yet, the 1980 musical's origins differed substantially from those of the intimate spoof *Dames at Sea* and the source Wilson musical that inspired Russell's *The Boy Friend*. By contrast with these works, the foundational involvement of two Broadway legends, director-choreographer Gower Champion and producer Merrick, steered Bramble and Stewart's *42nd Street* to the commercial Broadway stage from its inception. Merrick informed Stewart and Bramble of his opulent vision for the production: "I want to do the biggest musical since the Second World War. . . . I want it to be the biggest show I've ever done."[66]

As directed and choreographed by Champion, with assistance from Larry Carpenter and Jerry Orbach on the staging of book scenes,[67] *42nd Street* premiered during a mythic opening night at the Winter Garden Theatre on August 25, 1980. With Orbach (as Marsh), Tammy Grimes (as Dorothy), and Wanda Richert (as Peggy) as its first stars, *42nd Street* eventually ran 3,486 performances. Considered a monumental legacy to the brilliance of Champion,

42nd Street skyrocketed at the box office, as fueled by the most infamous of Merrick's many publicity stunts. Since the late 1950s, Merrick—dubbed "the Abominable Showman"—had aspired to the bravado and "demonic flair for publicity" flaunted by Broadway's golden age impresarios. While boasting an artistically eclectic producing portfolio that ranged from *Gypsy* and *Hello, Dolly!* to *Becket* and *Marat/Sade*, Merrick "became a living symbol in the 1980s of the old-time strong leaders of the 1920s and 1930s, like Flo Ziegfeld and Lee and J.J. Shubert."[68]

Merrick's shocking curtain-speech announcement of the death of Champion on *42nd Street*'s opening night made international headlines. Merrick had known since the afternoon of August 25 that Champion had died of a rare blood disease—but he strategically hid the news from his *42nd Street* cast throughout the day. Merrick's opening night speech, played as much to reporters as to grief-stricken cast members, culminated a complex career marked as much by reports of "diabolical, manipulative, and mercurial" behavior as by flamboyantly entertaining box office pranks.[69] *42nd Street*'s opening night lived up to Merrick's expectation for a box office bonanza—but Merrick's actions also inflicted hurt and dismay among the company. As Otis Guernsey Jr. recounts, "Its opening night was not merely the presentation of a new hit, it turned out to be an unforgettable moment of theater history, when fact became more poignant than fiction, and the dream of a Broadway show turned into a nightmare that wouldn't go away after the curtain came down."[70]

Yet, Merrick's stunt had been anticipated by fiction: that of Ropes. In his backstage trilogy, Ropes had consistently placed at the center of his critique impresarios who place the demands of the box office above performers' safety and health. With the Lionel Crane episode in *42nd Street*, Ropes illustrated how, for Marsh, "each tragedy lost some of its force because the show was dominant."[71] Ropes's fictional account can be read less as a prophecy of Merrick's opening night speech than as a cautionary depiction of commercial calculation superseding human concerns. In Ropes's *42nd Street*, Marsh and his coproducers attempt to halt an inquest that will delay *Pretty Lady*'s Philadelphia opening. Resonating with this scene, on the day of *42nd Street*'s opening, Merrick reportedly shared with only a few insiders, including his former office boy Bramble, the top-secret news that Champion had died that afternoon and that he was determined to go on with the show.[72]

In both fictional and historical accounts, private rituals of grief transform into public performance. In Ropes's novel, Marsh rallies *Pretty Lady*'s performers toward the show he intends as a smash. In 1980, many observers of the infamous opening night considered that Merrick exploited the shock of Champion's death as a spectacle for the media, despite his own private grief. In a profile of the *42nd Street* opening night for *New York* magazine, Marie Brenner wrote, "There were big bucks involved this night. The director had died at noon. Merrick felt he had to keep that fact secret—God knows how he kept it from Wanda Richert for nine hours, but he did."[73] Writing of Richert, *42nd Street*'s star and Champion's girlfriend, Brenner observed how "her surprise, her horror, and her anguish became a matter of public record," as she was filmed by the camera crews orchestrated by Merrick and his PR team.[74] Although Tammy Grimes, among others, rebuked the act as "tasteless," Merrick also insisted that the opening night party must go on.[75] Brenner's account reflects Ropes's own fictional portrayal of the macabre rose garden scene of Crane's death, as Brenner mused: "All those black ties wandered around Park Avenue in search of the right thing to do on an evening when there was no right thing to do."[76]

The blatantly profit-driven ethos with which Merrick, as sole "angel" as well as single-billed producer, approached his production of *42nd Street* reflects the broader cultural and ideological contexts against which the show was produced. In 1933, Warner Brothers had aligned its *42nd Street* with FDR's New Deal. Hoberman observes: "Its production spans the 1932 Presidential election campaign and its release—together with that of *Gold Diggers of 1933*, which opened in Los Angeles and New York the very week that Congress passed the National Recovery Act—coincided almost exactly with the celebrated 'first hundred days' of the Roosevelt administration."[77] By contrast, Warren Hoffman observes that the "run of *42nd Street* coincides almost perfectly with Reagan's two-term presidency, coming to exemplify his administration's capitalist, money-hungry politics."[78] Hoffman notes that the 1980 *42nd Street* opened on a Broadway that "was becoming more artistically conservative" throughout the decade of Ronald Reagan and Margaret Thatcher.[79]

As both Hoffman and Laura MacDonald have discussed, Merrick's *42nd Street* reflected the Neoconservatism that increasingly defined the era. In his novel, Ropes had focused upon the scarcity and lack of power shared among the ensemble: a status mostly unalleviated by the breakthrough of one of their own. At the end of Ropes's *42nd Street*, Peggy expresses the self-preserving "Forty-Second Street code."[80] She rebukes stage manager Harry to "tell Phillips not to start the second verse so soon, will you? Who the hell does he think he *is*?"[81] By contrast, Merrick's *42nd Street* positions its wide-eyed Peggy as the fulfillment of the dreams of the chorus kids, not only her own. Anytime Annie rallies the other chorus girls: "She's gotta come through! Not for Jones or Barry or any of those stuffed-shirts out there, but for us! The kids in the line." Annie urges: "You're not just Peggy Sawyer tonight, you're every girl who ever kicked up a heel in the chorus. Get out there in front, kid, and show them what we can do."[82]

Merrick's *42nd Street* also reflected the decade's backlash to the feminist and civil rights progress of the 1970s, the decade of both the women's liberation and the Black Power movements. Bramble and Stewart added some modern updates to their adaptation of the 1933 *42nd Street* screenplay, transforming the male producer Jones into Maggie Jones, also *Pretty Lady*'s co-librettist. Yet, as MacDonald has argued, Merrick produced a 1980 *42nd Street* streaked with retrogressive strokes, including its focus on "pitting one generation of women against another" in the rivalry between diva Brock and ingenue Peggy.[83] For Merrick, Bramble and Stewart also added a Pygmalion romance between Marsh and the considerably younger Peggy, now from Allentown, Pennsylvania. After her triumph in the Philadelphia tryout of *Pretty Lady*, Peggy tells Marsh, "Oh, I said the lines and sang the songs and did the steps. But you were inside me pulling the strings."[84] MacDonald observes that, along with 1977's *Annie*, *42nd Street* showed Depression-era female protagonists who "relied on men to re-fashion their identities and fulfill their desires."[85] By contrast, Ropes's Peggy scoffed at the thought of living with "a bucolic husband and the prospect of red-cheeked babies" in Paris, Maine.[86]

"Told against the unspoken context of whiteness," Merrick's *42nd Street* reflected the Reagan administration's rejection of affirmative action policies and neglected to address racial politics, as Hoffman has argued.[87] He notes that the stage musical frames Peggy as an avatar of "the great American rags-to-riches success story, a combo of luck, hard work, and talent that has the hero come out on top." Hoffman observes that "while the show is predicated on the idea that hard work will pay off and that anyone can get the job as long as he or she has talent, what is unspoken is that this mythology only holds for whites."[88] By contrast, Ropes's novel had satirized pluck-and-luck myths and engaged with themes of cultural appropriation through the characters of Andy Lee and Gertrude. In all of his backstage novels, Ropes too marginalized Black characters in his focus upon white aspiration. Yet, with his frequent allusions to performers such as Bill "Bojangles" Robinson, the dancer who had been praised in Europe as an "incontestable master of the Black Bottom" did not ignore Black performers' presence or their struggles in a white show business world.

Even more than the 1933 film, in which subtextual and coded elements haunt the narrative, Merrick's *42nd Street* avoided the direct representation of gay male sexuality. The musical featured the contributions of numerous openly gay men in the cast and on the creative team. These included Lee Roy Reams, as well as Stewart and Bramble, whose once dialogue-dense script was demoted by Merrick from "book by" to "lead-ins and crossovers."[89] The sexuality of Billy Lawlor, played by Reams, was safely neutralized as that of a "tenor."[90] Yet, in 1982, a Broadway audience member wrote to the *Sandy Creek News* that they were "startled" by the revelation, while paging through a playbill, that the director and young dancer played by Orbach and Reams were lovers in Ropes's novel. Responding to the letter writer's inquiry about how they felt about this "bizarre disclosure," Orbach and Reams told columnist Robin Adams Sloan "with a twinkle in their eyes": "Please, we're just good friends."[91]

Stewart and Bramble themselves eschewed too close an identification of their *42nd Street* libretto with a camp aesthetic and also sought distance from the "hard" tone of the Ropes novel. In a May 1979 letter to Michael Bennett, whom the team approached to stage *42nd Street* during Champion's temporary withdrawal from the project, Stewart assured the *A Chorus Line* director: "No trace of 'camp' is intended."[92] Stewart elaborated upon the team's artistic aims in a 1985 interview with *The Blade*:

> "Ropes wanted to show the shoddiness of it all," Stewart said, and even the movie had a harsher edge than Stewart and Bramble preferred. . . . "We were intent on glorifying the world of theater, of looking at it with lovely eyes. . . . In that sense, it's a love song to musical comedy."[93]

Yet, the earliest drafts of *42nd Street* illustrate that the team considered other tonal avenues for their *42nd Street* adaptation. Bramble, in particular, appears to have originally sought a closer engagement with Ropes's novel than Stewart. The first draft, from August 1978 and credited as "done by Mark Bramble," blends the structure of James and Seymour's screenplay with extensive portions of dialogue directly quoting Ropes's novel, as mixed with famous lines from the movie. In particular, Bramble imported much of the chorus girls' cynical repartee from Ropes, including such barbed feminist insights as Peggy's "But can't a girl at least eat supper with a man without becoming immoral?" To this, Lorraine answers, "She probably can, but it isn't worth the trouble because no one will believe her."[94] Although the first draft preserves the heterosexual relationships of the 1933 film, Bramble reintroduces Jack Winslow, now referred to only as "Boy." Appearing only briefly at the cast party in Jones and Barry's Philadelphia hotel suite, "Boy" endures insults from Terry and dishes the dirt: "My dear, that gin would make Mrs. Fiske do rolling splits."[95]

By the time *42nd Street* opened on Broadway, almost none of Ropes's dialogue remained in the libretto. This final draft of the libretto, completed three years before the game-changing 1983 success of Jerry Herman and Harvey Fierstein's *La Cage aux Folles* on Broadway, may have reflected Stewart's stated intention to write a musical without "a trace of camp." At the same time, *42nd Street* opened against a context of systemic homophobia that would reach cataclysmic proportions with the Reagan administration's institutional neglect of the AIDS crisis starting in 1981. After the progress of the 1969 Stonewall Uprising and the protests of the Gay Liberation Front, the conservative activism of Phyllis Schlafly and Anita Bryant gained cultural traction at the end of the Carter administration.[96] "By late 1979, a decade after Stonewall, gayness was more visible in pop culture than ever before. But that very visibility was starting to inspire an equally tangible homophobic backlash," as Karina Longworth details the antigay ferment that followed Harvey Milk's assassination and the White Night riots in San Francisco.[97] Redevelopment in New York City also pushed city officials and the Broadway community to appeal to middle-of-the-road family values. The tourist-luring "I love New York" campaign swept onto Times Square in 1977, two years after the city declared bankruptcy.

Both this homophobic backlash and the onset of a "cleaner" Times Square affected the tone of Merrick's *42nd Street*, with its patina of "postmodern pastiche."[98] Though comparably lavish with Russell's MGM *The Boy Friend*, the stage *42nd Street* embraced a more reverent sense of nostalgia, resonating with the Neoliberal "gentrification of the mind" that, as Sarah Schulman argues, emerged in cultural counterpoint with the Reagan administration's economic policies.[99] Merrick and Champion mounted the show with consummate skill as a "suitably Ziegfeldian spectacular," featuring four hundred costumes and a dozen sets.[100] Yet, the production might be considered to have followed the crest of the "tidal wave of nostalgia" beginning with *Dames at Sea*.[101] According to Guernsey, "The show found its place, not in awe or mockery, but in a dreamland combination of nostalgic affection and spectacular musical comedy technique: Broadway as fable, embellished by masters."[102]

Critics commented on how Merrick and Champion's show steered away from the more satiric camp aesthetic that had defined *Dames at Sea* and *The Boy Friend*. In one of the production's few outright pans, *The New Yorker*'s Brendan Gill wrote: "What we observed on the stage of the Winter Garden is Jerry Orbach, Tammy Grimes, and Wanda Richert playing, with approximately straight faces, the roles created almost a half a century ago."[103] Both Frank Rich and John Simon echoed Gill, with the former observing: "When we watch their characters overcome quintessential showbiz adversities to bring their musical to Broadway, it's hard to know whether we are to laugh or to cheer or merely to float off on a cloud of nostalgia."[104]

At the same time, as critics hailed Champion's dazzling staging, the 1980 musical called upon the virtuosic dance in which Ropes, as Billy Bradford, had thrived in the 1920s. Simon marveled at how Champion's choreography "grabs you by the throat or entrails—sometimes; indeed, by the heart, and carries you beyond razzmatazz, beyond even pizzazz, into elation."[105] If Ropes anticipated Merrick's exploitation of Champion's death in the Lionel Crane scene of his novel, he would likely have greatly appreciated *42nd Street*'s sheer terpsichorean splendor. The musical continued to centralize hoofing in 2001 Broadway and 2017 West End revivals directed by Bramble, featuring new choreography by Champion's former *42nd Street* assistant Randy Skinner, who, with Karin Baker, had helped the legendary artist on the show's tap routines in 1980.[106]

Even by 1980, *42nd Street* no longer belonged to Ropes in the cultural imagination. The same year that the musical opened on Broadway, the University of Wisconsin Press published the screenplay with an introduction in which Rocco Fumento offered contradictory assessments of the novel. Comparing Ropes's acerbic vision to that of Rodgers and Hart in the 1940 musical *Pal Joey*, Fumento speculated, "If the movie version of *42nd Street* had been as frank and as gritty as the novel, it would have been a genuine first for American musicals."[107] Yet, Fumento qualified his praise: "Not that the Ropes novel is a great novel. It is, in fact, a bad one."[108] In measuring Ropes's *42nd Street* as a "deadly, sleep-inducing bore," Fumento equated literary excitement with "overt sex" and "bedroom scenes," while overlooking Ropes's own frequent allusions to gay male sexuality. Fumento wrote of Ropes's *42nd Street*, "Sex cannot improve a good novel, but it can prevent the reader of a bad one from falling asleep."[109] A small number of chronicles of gay male literary history took notice of Ropes's *42nd Street*, which otherwise persisted as a footnote and a prelude to the film and stage adaptations.

In the early 2020s, in the midst of an American culture more receptive to forgotten and hidden LGBTQ+ histories, signs of a Ropes revival started to appear. In his May 2020 essay on Ropes's "remarkable out-of-print book," Richard Brody quoted the *New York Times*'s Beatrice Sherman, on *Go Into Your Dance*: "He has the Broadway patter of hoofers, actors and producers down pat." Brody added, "And how!" The critic placed *42nd Street* in the context of the novel's 1927-28 Broadway setting, against which Ropes chronicled a theater world "of poverty, of widespread economic despair—in the milieu of actors—at a time of over-all prosperity." Brody praised the authenticity of Ropes's observation in *42nd Street*, as a novel about "the world of the theatre" and "the nuts and bolts of rehearsals and stagings." Among other elements, Brody also lauded Ropes's "delicious and gaudy theatrical slang" and his keen sensitivity to the lives of "young women like Peggy struggling to make their way in the theater."[110] As of this writing, both *42nd Street* and *Go Into Your Dance* have been independently republished with afterwords by Scott Miller.

In both his style and his themes, Ropes can be appreciated as a major popular artist and storyteller of the Modernist era. By comparison with fellow Thayer Academy alum John Cheever (who attended the school from 1926 to 1928), Ropes wrote within a commercial genre idiom rather than the sphere of literary fiction. Using the form of the popular backstage novel, Ropes drew upon his experiences in show business to critique the abuses of power that he witnessed, "governing his pen" in solidarity with a wide array of stage performers. Anticipating many contemporary conversations, against the contexts of the #MeToo movement and calls to reform the commercial theater industry on levels of racial, economic, and labor equity, Ropes's novels shine hard lights upon sexual harassment, exploitation, and unsafe workplace conditions in the theater. Additionally, Ropes's keen awareness of the Boston Brahmin caste hierarchy in which he had grown up influenced his subtle insights about the ways in which 1920s and '30s show business replicated larger societal disparities.

Stylistically, Ropes's novels might be aligned with a term coined by film critic Manohla Dargis. Writing about the directorial style of Ryan Murphy in her 2020 review of *The Prom*, Dargis observed, "Murphy likes to go big and lightly bonkers, and his aesthetic is best described as Showbiz Expressionism."[111] In their distinctive mixture of Broadway razzle-dazzle with the sordid, grotesque, and macabre, aspects of "Showbiz Expressionism" also flavor Ropes's backstage novels, which share the 1920s Expressionists' critique of the Machine Age.

Ropes's demystifying approach to backstage narrative aligns him with the innovators of the 1970s concept musical. Ropes died the same year that *Cabaret* ushered in a new era of razor-edged American show business stories, shaped by the disillusionments of the Vietnam War. Ropes's observation of musical comedy as "a bed of roses, thorny side up" in his *42nd Street* anticipated the through-a-glass-darkly visions of director-choreographer Bob Fosse and songwriters John Kander and Fred Ebb, as well as Sondheim (particularly with 1971's *Follies*). *A Chorus Line*, too, staged by Michael Bennett in 1975, shared with Ropes's *42nd Street* the image of Broadway as a machine both fueled by the romance of individual dreams and synchronized into the glittering, Tiller Girl-like kickline of "One."

Too racy to evade censorship even during Pre-Code Hollywood, Ropes's work also invites comparisons to the grittiness of New Hollywood cinema. Hoberman observes that even watered down from Ropes's vision, the 1933 *42nd Street* retained much of his candor: "Nevertheless, in its matter-of-fact acknowledgement of backstage prostitution, the movie *42nd Street* anticipates the less glamorous representation of '42nd Street' found in such post-Code films as John Schlesinger's 1968 *Midnight Cowboy* or Paul Morrissey's 1982 *Forty Deuce*."[112] Brody argues for a new *42nd Street* adaptation rooted in Ropes's work: "The novel would make an ideal basis for a closed-end TV series—it should include everything that's in the book and many things that aren't."[113]

The recent resurgence of the backstage novel and theater fiction, greeted avidly amid the absence of live theater during the COVID-19 pandemic, also affirms Ropes's lasting relevance. The 2021 novel *We Play Ourselves*, by the versatile playwright and television writer Jen Silverman, strikingly resonates with Ropes's tone, style, and themes. Silverman informed Alexis Soloski: "The book began as a love letter to the theater. . . . But it's a love letter where you know the dark side. It's not an idealized love."[114] Like Ropes before them, Silverman explores in *We Play Ourselves* the lure to the stage as a blood-deep calling: "It's the sort of feeling that becomes a constant longing. It's the sort of longing upon which you build an entire life."[115] At the same time, Silverman critiques its industrial conditions, writing in the acknowledgments of the novel: "Theatre is an art form with many contradictions folded into it: the deep intimacy of lifelong collaborations juxtaposed against an economic model that can be lonely and brutal."[116]

Beyond the novels' shared themes, the narratives of *42nd Street* and *We Play Ourselves* can be productively compared. Like Ropes, Silverman explores dynamics of romance, sexuality, gender, and power in the theater, as their bisexual protagonist Cass becomes infatuated with the brilliant, French-born director Hélène. Though romantically unreciprocated by Hélène, the relationship evokes aspects of the affair between Billy Lawler and Julian Marsh. In a passage that evokes Ropes's writing about the aesthete Marsh, Silverman describes Hélène: "She was in her element, an Old World god corralling chaos into beauty."[117] Like Ropes, Silverman examines themes of women's exploitation in the theater and in film. Yet in Silverman's novel, American capitalism pressures women to exploit themselves, as Cass's agent seems to rhapsodize of a bloody play by a "feminist" enfant terrible: "Wasn't this play the most amazing exploration of female trauma-slash-sexual awakening that you've ever seen?"[118]

Connecting the 2020s with the 1920s, Silverman shares with Ropes an intense focus upon not only women's roles but also the scarcities of resources in commercial theater. In the work of both authors, this fuels the stigma of failure within a gossip-prone theater world that remains "always alive and vibrating with lines of communication."[119] As Silverman told Soloski: "The arts economy in the U.S. is defined by scarcity, because we don't have government funding. . . . If you are a woman, queer, an artist of color, it's very clear that there is a slot and the people who are your community, your collaborators, your family, are also being positioned as your competitors."[120] With a more limited demographic focus, Ropes had critiqued these strictures in characters like Billy Lawler, who informs Peggy, "If you're not tough, they'll lick you after a few seasons. There's no such thing as sentiment in our business. It's dollars and sex!"[121] If Ropes frequently portrays a cynical world of actors who diminish their own humanity in pursuit of commercial success, he acknowledges a foundational culture of scarcity.

For all his modernity, Ropes must be placed into the context of his own times. He came of age in a Massachusetts Puritan culture in the proximity of the Boston Brahmins. Yet—also the hometown of Ruth Gordon and Billy De Wolfe—the Quincy of Ropes's youth cultivated his theatricality. Here, Ropes absorbed a deep love of Shakespeare; participated amply in school plays and pageants; and benefited from an educational structure that invested in the intellectual life of its students. Articles in the *Patriot Ledger* and the *Golden Rod* published between the mid-1920s and early 1950s illustrate that Quincyites regarded Ropes as a local hero, however compelled he was to conceal his sexuality. The dancer and writer once known as "Ropesy" remained a source of pride in Braintree in 1990, when the Thayer Academy staged *42nd Street* and noted Ropes as "T.A. Graduating Class of 1922" in the show's program.[122]

At the same time, Ropes's work also reflects his internalization of some exclusionary aspects of early twentieth-century Puritan and Brahmin codes. This includes the antisemitic imagery that mars the early 1930s backstage trilogy. Ropes grew up as the beneficiary of substantial racial, social, and economic privilege. At the same time, a robust rejection of the value systems that turned "Banned in Boston" into an infamous slogan buoys Ropes's work, as the writer used his camp wit to celebrate gay men's sexuality and women's independence and sexual agency. Ropes's dirt-dishing backstage novels consistently identify his rebellious spirit, his defiance of authority, cant, narrow-mindedness, and abuses of power.

Ropes also expressed a deep awareness of the contradictions of his story, having perceived that show business "did not want" Puritans. Descended from Pilgrims, Ropes likely appreciated the parallel life and lyrics of Cole Porter, a fellow rebel gay WASP who, hailing from the American Midwest, satirized the Boston Brahmin "Sabbot" family in his 1928 musical *Paris* before turning Plymouth Rock upside down in *Anything Goes*. Ropes, whom his Thayer Academy yearbook had called "Gilbert and Sullivan rolled into one," tried his hand at a number of unproduced Broadway musicals. Yet choosing the pages of the backstage novel as his main stage, Ropes no less than Porter explored the topsy-turvy modernity of America in the 1920s and '30s.

Ropes's blending of the Puritan ethos with theatrical glamour marks him as a distinctive figure in American show business history: one formed equally by Broadway and Boston. By contrast with the bustle of Times Square, Ropes affectionately mocked the tight "area-ways" between the houses of Beacon Hill in *Mr. Tilley Takes a Walk*. Yet, Ropes portrayed Boston and Broadway as comparably expansive regions of the country's cultural imagination, equally American in their scandals, follies, and "town talks." In the pages of Ropes's novels, Mayflower descendants, Masons, college boys, and stenographers at Boston's South Station jostle against the "society dowagers, hard-headed newspapermen, theatrical celebrities and racketeers" that fill the "night haunts of Manhattan."[123] Understanding that Puritan legacies define Americans as much as the desire to see names emblazoned in neon lights, Ropes powerfully collided these tensions in his work. The capacious imagination, flamboyant language, and defiant queer gaze of Bradford Ropes brought the characters of *42nd Street* memorably to life—and its creator should not be forgotten.

Notes

Introduction

1. J. Hoberman, *42nd Street*, BFI Film Classics (London: BFI Publishing, 1993), 9.

2. Otis Guernsey Jr., "*42nd Street*," in *The Best Plays of 1980–1981*, ed. Guernsey (New York: Bookthrift), 135–36.

3. Leonard Melfi, quoted in Guernsey, "*42nd Street*." Accounts of the number of curtain calls during *42nd Street*'s opening night vary, with others putting the number closer to ten (Patrick Hayward, "It Was a Rocky Road for *42nd Street* on Broadway," Overtures, June 16, 2017, https://overtures.org.uk/?p=13269).

4. David Boehm, Erwin S. Gelsey, Ben Markson, and James Seymour, *The Gold Diggers of 1933*, directed by Mervyn LeRoy (1933; Los Angeles: Warner Brothers Archive Collection, 2017), DVD.

5. J. Hoberman, "*42nd Street* and Looney Tunes Classics: Showstoppers Live and Animated," *New York Times*, May 29, 2015, https://www.nytimes.com/2015/05/31/movies/homevideo/42nd-street-and-looney-tunes-classics-showstoppers-live-and-animated.html

6. "Bradford Ropes, Local Writer, to Be Honored at Theater Here: Wollaston Man Wrote Novel *42nd Street* Now in Films," *Quincy Patriot Ledger*, March 13, 1933, 7.

7. "Bradford Ropes, Local Writer," 7.

8. Bradford Ropes, *Stage Mother*, dust jacket, 1st edition (New York: Alfred H. King, 1933).

9. Clinton Cuthbert, "The Book of the Day," *New York Sun*, May 8, 1933, 22.

10. Bradford Ropes, *Go Into Your Dance* (New York: Alfred H. King, 1934), 249.

11. Quoted in "About *Stage Mother*," dust jacket of Ropes, *Go Into Your Dance*, Worthpoint, accessed August 24, 2021, https://www.worthpoint.com/worthopedia/dance-bradford-ropes-hc-book-1934-1940547999

12. Richard Brody, "What to Read and Stream: The Remarkable Out-of-Print Book That Inspired *42nd Street*," the Front Row, *The New Yorker*, May 6, 2020, https://www.newyorker.com/culture/the-front-row/what-to-read-and-stream-the-remarkable-out-of-print-book-that-inspired-42nd-street

13. Wood Soanes, "42nd Street Outstanding Film Novelty," *Oakland Tribune*, April 1, 1933, 9.

14. Michael Nava, "Creating a Literary Culture: A Short, Selective, and Incomplete History of LGBT Publishing, Part I," *Los Angeles Review of Books*, June 5, 2021, https://lareviewofbooks.org/article/creating-a-literary-culture-a-short-selective-and-incomplete-history-of-lgbt-publishing-part-i/

15. Rick Altman, *The American Film Musical* (Bloomington: Indiana University Press, 1988), 208.

16. Hoberman, *42nd Street*, 72.

17. "'3 Make-Believe Worlds' Outlined by Actor-Author," *Quincy Patriot Ledger*, April 16, 1953, 22.

18. Bradford Ropes, *42nd Street* (New York: Alfred H. King, 1932), 89.

Interlude

1. Bradford Ropes, *42nd Street* (New York: Alfred H. King, 1932), 39.

2. Ropes, *Street*, 3.

3. Ropes, *Street*, 38.

4. Ropes, *Street*, 53.

5. Ropes, *Street*, 70.

6. Ropes, *Street*, 72.

7. Ropes, *Street*, 87.

8. Ropes, *Street*, 86.

9. Ropes, *Street*, 182.

10. Ropes, *Street*, 278.

11. Dorothy's sprained back and concussion were changed to a sprained ankle in the film and stage musicals.

12. Ropes, *42nd Street*, 329.

13. Ropes, *Street*, 335.

14. Ropes, *Street*, 337.

15. Ropes, *Street*, 345.

16. Bradford Ropes, *Stage Mother* (New York: Alfred H. King, 1933), 36.

17. Ropes, *Mother*, 59.

18. Ropes, *Mother*, 124.

19. Ropes, *Mother*, 152.

20. Ropes, *Mother*, 163.

21. Ropes, *Mother*, 312.

22. Ropes, *Mother*, 284.

23. Ropes, *Mother*, 297.

24. Ropes, *Mother*, 363.

25. Ropes, *Mother*, 366.

26. Bradford Ropes, *Go Into Your Dance* (New York: Alfred H. King, 1934), 155.

27. Ropes, *Dance*, 156.

28. Ropes, *Dance*, 235.

29. Ropes, *Dance*, 254.

30. Ropes, *Dance*, 302.

31. Ropes, *Dance*, 314.

32. Ropes, *Dance*, 316.

Chapter 1

1. Val Burton and Bradford Ropes, *Mr. Tilley Takes a Walk* (New York: Austin-Phelps, 1951), 7.

2. "Bradford Ropes' Novel of Boston *Mr. Tilly* [sic] *Takes a Walk* Out Feb. 19," *Quincy Patriot Ledger*, February 17, 1951, 6.

3. Burton and Ropes, *Mr. Tilley Takes a Walk*, 29.

4. Burton and Ropes, *Tilley*, 7.

5. Burton and Ropes, *Tilley*, 95.

6. Ropes, *42nd Street* (New York: Alfred H. King, 1932), 39.

7. Ropes, *Street*, 40.

8. Al Dubin and Harry Warren, "42nd Street," *42nd Street*, directed by Lloyd Bacon (1933; Los Angeles: Warner Brothers Archive Collection, 2006), DVD.

9. George Chauncey, *Gay New York: Gender, Urban Culture, and the Making of the Gay Male World, 1890-1940* (New York: Basic Books, 1994), 319.

10. Burton and Ropes, *Mr. Tilley Takes a Walk*, 46.

11. "Movie of Show Business," *Brooklyn Citizen*, August 29, 1932, 14.

12. "Quincy C.A.R. Has Fifty Charter Members," *Quincy Patriot Ledger*, April 8, 1921, 1.

13. Henry Whittemore, *The Founders and Builders of the Oranges* (Newark, NJ: L. J. Hardham, 1896), 274.

14. John Meehan and Bradford Ropes, *Stage Mother*, directed by Charles Brabin (1933; Los Angeles: Warner Brothers Archive Collection, 2017), DVD.

15. "Isaac Sprague," Geni, 2021, accessed January 18, 2021, https://www.geni.com/people/Issac-Sprague/6000000000284171112

16. Oliver Wendell Holmes Sr., *Elsie Venner: A Romance of Destiny* (Cambridge, MA: Houghton, Mifflin, 1861), 7.

17. Burton and Ropes, *Mr. Tilley Takes a Walk*, 168.

18. Thomas Harrison Eames, "The Wreck of the Steamer 'Portland,'" *New England Quarterly* 13, no. 2 (June 1940): 191.

19. Franklin de Ronde Furman, *Morton Memorial: A History of the Stevens Institute of Technology* (Hoboken, NJ: Stevens Institute of Technology, 1905), 544.

20. Whittemore, *Founders and Builders*, 275.

21. Whittemore, *Founders*, 275-76.

22. Charles P. Bowditch and Harrison Ellery, *The Pickering Genealogy: Being an Account of the First Three Generations of the Pickering Family of Salem, Mass., and of the Descendants of John and Sarah (Burrill) Pickering, of the Third Generation, Volume 2* (Princeton, NJ: J. Wilson and Son, 1897), 407.

23. Bowditch and Ellery, *Pickering Genealogy*, 669.

24. *Clark's Boston Blue Book: The Elite Private Address and Carriage Directory, Ladies' Visiting and Shopping Guide for Boston, Dorchester, Brookline, Cambridge, Jamaica Bay, and Charlestown District* (Boston: Edward E. Clark, 1885), 40; and Ednah C. Silver, *Sketches of the New Church in America on a Background of Civil and Social Life* (Boston: Massachusetts New Church Union, 1920), 87.

25. Cleveland Amory, *The Proper Bostonians* (New York: Dutton, 1947), 31.

26. Silver, *Sketches*, 87.

27. Amory, *The Proper Bostonians*, 39.

28. David Strauss, *Percival Lowell: The Culture and Science of a Boston Brahmin* (Cambridge, MA: Harvard University Press, 2001), 19.

29. Wendell Holmes, *Elsie Venner*, 3.

30. Strauss, *Percival Lowell*, 3, 10, 16.

31. Jack Beatty, *The Rascal King: The Life and Times of James Michael Curley (1874-1958)* (New York: Macmillan, 1992), 10.

32. Amory, *The Proper Bostonians*, 13.

33. Burton and Ropes, *Mr. Tilley Takes a Walk*, 110.

34. Beatty, *Rascal King*, 260.

35. Carl Leon Bankston, *Encyclopedia of American Immigration* (Hackensack, NJ: Salem Press, 2010), 120.

36. Amory, *The Proper Bostonians*, 345.

37. Burton and Ropes, *Mr. Tilley Takes a Walk*, 252.

38. J. Madison Watson, *Independent Fifth Reader* (New York: A. S. Barnes, 1876), 215.

39. Meehan and Ropes, *Stage Mother*.

40. Martyn Whittock, *Mayflower Lives: Pilgrims in a New World and the Early American Experience* (New York: Pegasus Books, 2019), 123.

41. Fullerton erroneously referred to Charles F. Williams II as Ropes's uncle rather than his maternal grandfather.

42. Mabelle Fullerton, "Wollaston Man Rings Bell with Novel about Postman," *Quincy Patriot Ledger*, January 24, 1951, 5.

43. Eames, "The Wreck of the Steamer 'Portland,'" 193.

44. Eames, "Steamer," 193.

45. Ropes, *42nd Street*, 31.

46. Ropes, *Street*, 166.

47. Ropes, *Street*, 24.

48. Ropes, *Street*, 267.

49. Amory, *The Proper Bostonians*, 14.

50. Ropes, *42nd Street*, 54.

51. Neil Kane et al., *Improper Bostonians: Lesbian and Gay History from the Puritans to Playland*, compiled by the History Project (Boston: Beacon Press, 1998), 15.

52. Henry Adams, *The Education of Henry Adams: An Autobiography* (Cambridge, MA: Houghton, Mifflin, 1918), 14.

53. Adams, *Education*, 9.

54. Amory, *The Proper Bostonians*, 144.

55. Adams, *Education of Henry Adams*, 10.

56. Kane et al., *Improper Bostonians*, 15.

57. Kane et al., *Improper*, 14.

58. Kane et al., *Improper*, 15.

59. Kane et al., *Improper*, 11.

60. Kane et al., *Improper*, 14-15.

61. Colin Marshall, "America's First Banned Book: Discover the 1637 Book That Mocked the Puritans," Open Culture, September 29, 2021, accessed Septem-

ber 30, 2021, https://www.openculture.com/2021/09/americas-first-banned-book
-discover-the-1637-book-that-mocked-the-puritans.html

62. Kane et al., *Improper Bostonians*, 15.

63. John H. Houchin, *Censorship of the American Theatre in the Twentieth Century* (Cambridge: Cambridge University Press, 2009), 6.

64. Houchin, *Censorship*, 23.

65. Ropes, *42nd Street*, 145.

66. Bowditch and Ellery, *Pickering Genealogy*, 672.

67. Burton and Ropes, *Mr. Tilley Takes a Walk*, 203.

68. "Arthur D. Ropes, Father of Screen Writer, Succumbs," *Quincy Patriot Ledger*, March 19, 1952, 18.

69. "From Swedenborg to the New Church—Interview with Jane Williams-Hogan," Religioscope, June 9, 2006, accessed June 2, 2021, https://english.religion
.info/2006/06/09/from-swedenborg-to-the-new-church-interview-with-jane
-williams-hogan/.

70. Quoted in "Swedenborgianism (New Church): An Evaluation from the Theological Perspective of the Lutheran Church—Missouri Synod," Lutheran Church Missouri Synod, September 2013, accessed June 10, 2021, https://files
.lcms.org/wl/?id=mjrjrwByyMlFYBoEWknSpbYkIWndcIHO

71. "From Swedenborg to the New Church."

72. "Arthur D. Ropes, Father of Screen Writer, Succumbs," 18.

73. M. G. Bullard, personal interview with author, Boston, June 17, 2021.

74. "Arthur D. Ropes, Father of Screen Writer, Succumbs," 18; and *Catalog of Copyright Entries: Part Three* (Washington, DC: Library of Congress, 1933), 14.

75. "*42nd Street* Author Sells Second Novel for Motion Picture," *Quincy Patriot Ledger*, April 25, 1933, 1.

76. "Mrs. Ropes in Beer Attack," *Quincy Patriot Ledger*, April 25, 1933, 1.

77. "Mrs. Arthur D. Ropes, Longtime Leader of WCTU, Dies at 94," *Quincy Patriot Ledger*, October 14, 1960, 21.

78. Ian Tyrrell, *Woman's World/Woman's Empire: The Woman's Christian Temperance Union in International Perspective, 1880–1930* (Chapel Hill: University of North Carolina Press, 1991), 2.

79. Allan J. Lichtman, *White Protestant Nation: The Rise of the American Conservative Movement* (New York: Grove Press, 2009), 21–22.

80. "Quincy Woman Blames Press for Moist Era," *Quincy Patriot Ledger*, May 3, 1927, 1.

81. "Mrs. Ropes in Beer Attack," 1.

82. Amory, *The Proper Bostonians*, 96.

83. Burton and Ropes, *Mr. Tilley Takes a Walk*, 228.

84. Amory, *The Proper Bostonians*, 103.

85. Amory, *Bostonians*, 102.

86. Amory, *Bostonians*, 102.

87. "Women's Clubs," *Newton Graphic*, March 26, 1920, 8.

88. "Ruskin Club," *Sixty-Fifth Annual Report of the Trustees of the Public Library of the City of Boston, 1916–1917* (Public Library of the City of Boston, 1917), 63.

89. Burton and Ropes, *Mr. Tilley Takes a Walk*, 214.

90. Burton and Ropes, *Tilley*, 178.

91. Burton and Ropes, *Tilley*, 12.

92. "California, U.S. Voter Registrations, 1866–1898" (1884), for Charles Franklin Ropes, 110, accessed August 29, 2021, Ancestry.com; and "Thirteenth Census of the United States: 1910-Population, San Francisco City," for Clarita Bigué, accessed August 29, 2021, Ancestry.com

93. "Miss Beth Pottinger Weds Emile E. Bigue," *San Francisco Examiner*, March 5, 1933, 14.

94. "Work of the Chapters," *Daughters of the American Revolution Magazine* 56, no. 11 (November 1922) (Philadelphia: J. P. Lippincott), 679.

95. "Work of the Chapters," 679.

96. "'3 Make-Believe Worlds' Outlined by Actor-Author," *Quincy Patriot Ledger*, April 16, 1953, 22.

97. "Thirteenth Census of the United States: 1910-Population, Quincy City," accessed June 30, 2020, Ancestry.com

98. "Playwright Visits Quincy High," *Quincy Patriot Ledger*, November 12, 1946, 16.

99. "Long-Lost Yule Poem of Wollaston Man Is Found," *Quincy Patriot Ledger*, December 24, 1945, 6.

100. Bradford Ropes, "The Influence of the Pilgrims upon the Twentieth Century, Bradford Ropes, 1921, Honorable Mention," *Quincy Patriot Ledger*, May 21, 1920, 5.

101. Ropes, "The Influence of the Pilgrims," 5.

102. "Author of *42nd Street* Started Career in Barn," *Buffalo Evening News*, December 20, 1933, 17.

103. "Bradford Ropes Author Speaks at Wollaston Woman's Club," *Quincy Patriot Ledger*, November 18, 1953, 14.

104. "Playwright Visits Quincy High," 16.

105. Samuel G. Freedman, "'The Actress' Returns, a Star Indeed, to Quincy," *New York Times*, November 11, 1984, 28.

106. Ruth Gordon, *Years Ago* (New York: Dramatists Play Service, 1947), 9.

107. Burton and Ropes, *Mr. Tilley Takes a Walk*, 105.

108. William Coates, "An Interview with Quincy's Own Novelist," *Golden Rod* 45, no. 3 (Spring 1933): 8.

109. John Clair Minot, "From a Wollaston Barn to Broadway," *Quincy Patriot Ledger*, May 18, 1933, 4.

110. Val Burton, F. Hugh Herbert, and Bradford Ropes. *Glamour Boy*, directed by Ralph Murphy (1941; Miami: Zeus DVDs, 2021), DVD.

111. "Playwright Visits Quincy High," 16.

112. "New Novel by Wollaston Man to Be Produced in Motion Pictures," *Quincy Patriot Ledger*, August 26, 1932, 1.

113. "Author of *42nd Street* Started Career in Barn," 17.

114. "Tribute Paid to Ropes by Mayor Ross: Quincy Author of Feature Film Is Lauded at Strand Theatre," *Quincy Patriot Ledger*, March 13, 1933, 2.

115. "Jean Donaldson, Movie Dancer, Spends Holiday at Home Here," *Quincy Patriot Ledger*, November 29, 1940, 11.

116. "Opening Night of *The Wishing Ring*," *Quincy Patriot Ledger*, April 28, 1917, 1; and "Wandering in Fairyland," *Quincy Patriot Ledger*, June 1, 1917, 1.

117. "Opening Night of *The Wishing Ring*," 1.

118. "School Boy Writes Play," *Quincy Patriot Ledger*, June 20, 1917, 1.

119. "School Boy," 1.

120. "School Boy," 1.

121. "Playwright Visits Quincy High," 16.

122. Ruth Kaulbeck, "A Private Correspondence Made Public," *Golden Rod* 31, no. 3 (June 1921): 18.

123. Kaulbeck, "Correspondence," 8.

124. "Peeks, but Not Piques," *Golden Rod* 31, no. 3 (June 1921): 15.

125. J. C. Schwartz, ed., *Who's Who in Law*, Vol. 1 (New York: 277 Broadway, 1937), 689.

126. "Nichols-Williams Wedding at Roxbury Church of New Jerusalem," *Boston Globe*, December 17, 1915, 15.

127. Amory, *The Proper Bostonians*, 86.

128. Amory, *Bostonians*, 45.

129. Amory, *Bostonians*, 81.

130. Bradford Ropes, "The Trembling Hour," *Golden Rod* 30, no. 1 (December 1919): 6.

131. Ropes, "Trembling," 7.

132. Ropes, "Trembling," 7.

133. Ropes, "Trembling," 8.

134. Ropes, "Trembling," 8.

135. Ropes, "Trembling," 8.

136. Ropes, "Trembling," 9.

137. Ropes, "Trembling," 9.

138. Bradford Ropes, "The Man Who Lost His Soul," *Golden Rod* 31, no. 3 (June 1921): 10.

139. Kane et al., *Improper Bostonians*, 58, 84.

140. Kane et al., *Improper*, 102.

141. Kane et al., *Improper*, 101.

142. Oscar Wilde, "The Truth of Masks: A Note on Illusion," in *Intentions* (Leipzig: Heinemann and Balestier, the English Library, 1891), 177.

143. Bradford Ropes, *Go Into Your Dance* (New York: Alfred H. King, 1934), 91.

144. Fullerton, "Wollaston Man," 5.

145. Mary Driscoll, "Alumni Notes." *Golden Rod* 32, no. 2 (February 1922): 21.

146. Larry Carlson, director of the Wentworth Archives, Thayer Academy, email correspondence, July 20, 2021.

147. Carlson, July 20, 2021.

148. Carlson, email correspondence, November 5, 2021.

149. "Bradford Ropes Author Speaks," 14.

150. "Bradford Ropes ('Brad,' 'Ropesy')," *The Black and Orange*, 1922, yearbook page provided to the author by Larry Carlson, April 27, 2021.

151. "Behind the Footlights," *Golden Rod* 43, no. 1 (November 1930): 38.

152. Sharon R. Ullman, "'The Twentieth-Century Way': Female Impersonation

and Sexual Practice in Turn-of-the-Century America," *Journal of the History of Sexuality* 5, no. 4 (April 1995): 591.

Chapter 2

1. Bradford Ropes, *Stage Mother* (New York: Alfred H. King, 1933), 175.

2. Ropes, *Mother*, 11.

3. Ropes, *Mother*, 175.

4. Robert W. Snyder, *The Voice of the City: Vaudeville and Popular Culture in New York* (1989), 2nd ed. (New York: Oxford University Press, 2000), 52.

5. Snyder, *Voice*, 43.

6. Snyder, *Voice*, xx.

7. Snyder, *Voice*, xix.

8. Ropes, *Mother*, 175.

9. "Palace," *Variety*, August 9, 1923, 29.

10. "Bradford Ropes, Local Writer, to Be Honored at Theater Here: Wollaston Man Wrote Novel *42nd Street* Now in Films," *Quincy Patriot Ledger*, March 13, 1933, 7.

11. Charles Stones, "Vogue et Black Bottom," *Terpsica*, November 24, 1926, 1.

12. "Dans les Music-Halls," December 7, 1926, *La Lanterne*, 3.

13. George Chauncey, *Gay New York: Gender, Urban Culture, and the Making of the Gay Male World, 1890-1940* (New York: Basic Books, 1994), 4.

14. "Book Notes," *New York Times*, May 5, 1933, 13.

15. "'3 Make-Believe Worlds' Outlined by Actor-Author," *Quincy Patriot Ledger*, April 16, 1953, 22. Yet Ropes, as Billy Bradford, never performed in *School Days*—he performed in Edwards's *The Fountain of Youth of 1925*.

16. "Behind the Footlights." *Golden Rod* 43, no. 1 (November 1930): 38.

17. Ropes, *Stage Mother*, 91.

18. Ropes, *Mother*, 95.

19. Stanley Walker, *The Night Club Era* (1933) (Baltimore: Johns Hopkins University Press, 1999), 94.

20. F. Scott Fitzgerald, "Echoes of the Jazz Age" (1931), quoted in *A Critical Companion to F. Scott Fitzgerald: A Literary Reference to His Life and Work*, ed. Mary Jo Tate (New York: Facts on File, 2007), 6.

21. Walker, *The Night Club Era*, 199.

22. "Keith's Bushwick," *Brooklyn Standard Union*, September 9, 1923, 16.

23. Anna Steese Richardson, "Lady Broadway: How the Woman Playwright Has Captured the Great White Way," *McClure's Magazine*, December 1917, 13.

24. Richardson, "Lady," 13.

25. Mark Henry, "This Week's Review of Vaudeville Theaters," *The Billboard*, August 11, 1923, 16.

26. C. J. Bulliet, *Venus Castina* (Olympia, WA: Olympia Press, 2009), 72.

27. "Fashion Creations of the Stage," *Evening Star*, September 2, 1923, 35.

28. Jack Lait, "Alyn Mann and Co.," *Variety*, March 8, 1923, 20.

29. Lait, "Mann," 20.

30. Lait, "Mann," 20.

31. "Amusements," *Indianapolis Times*, November 24, 1923, 5.

32. Lait, "Mann," 20.

33. "New Shows This Week," *Variety*, December 20, 1923, 31.

34. Bradford Ropes, *Go Into Your Dance* (New York: Alfred H. King, 1934), 63.

35. Lait, "Mann," 20.

36. Lait, "Mann," 20.

37. Henry, "This Week's Review," 16.

38. "New Shows This Week," 31.

39. "New Shows This Week," 31; and "At Boston Theaters," *Christian Science Monitor*, September 18, 1923, 4.

40. Len Libbey, "Boston," *Variety*, September 20, 1923, 47.

41. "Palace," 29.

42. "Lauder Never More Popular," *Vancouver Sun*, February 16, 1918, 5.

43. Sharon R. Ullman, "'The Twentieth-Century Way': Female Impersonation and Sexual Practice in Turn-of-the-Century America," *Journal of the History of Sexuality* 5, no. 4 (April 1995): 589.

44. "Orpheum Circuit Vaudeville," *Seattle Star*, March 22, 1923, 10.

45. Ropes, *Go Into Your Dance*, 144.

46. Ropes, *Dance*, 147.

47. Ropes, *Dance*, 216.

48. Walker, *The Night Club Era*, 213.

49. Bradford Ropes, *42nd Street* (New York: Alfred H. King, 1932), 71.

50. "Wollaston Woman Is Elected State President of W.C.T.U.," *Quincy Patriot Ledger*, October 20, 1922, 1.

51. Martin F. Glendon, "Bradford Ropes Reviews His Years in the Theatre," *Berkshire Evening Eagle*, February 10, 1954, 28.

52. "Bradford Ropes Author Speaks at Wollaston Woman's Club," *Quincy Patriot Ledger*, November 18, 1953, 14.

53. Debby Applegate, *Madam: The Biography of Polly Adler, Icon of the Jazz Age* (New York: Doubleday, 2021), 183-84.

54. Walker, *The Night Club Era*, 109.

55. Walker, *Night Club*, 122.

56. Applegate, *Madam*, 46.

57. "Van and Schenck at the Silver Slipper," *New York Telegram and Evening Mail*, February 29, 1924, 23.

58. "Three New Cabaret Shows," *The Billboard*, March 29, 1924, 12.

59. "Jan.-March," *New York Times Index* 12, no. 1 (New York: New York Times, 1924), 435.

60. Jimmy Durante and Jack Kofoed, *Night Clubs* (New York: Alfred A. Knopf, 1931), 67.

61. Ropes, *Go Into Your Dance*, 274.

62. Ropes, *Dance*, 274.

63. Ropes, *Dance*, 230.

64. "Bradford Ropes Author Speaks," 14.

65. "Author of *42nd Street* Started Career in Barn," *Buffalo Evening News*, December 20, 1933, 17.

66. Ropes, *Stage Mother*, 143.

67. "Bradford Ropes, Local Writer," 7.

68. Ropes, *Stage Mother*, 143.

69. Ropes, *Mother*, 253.

70. Ropes, *42nd Street*, 69, 14.

71. "More or Less in the Spotlight," *New York Times*, September 11, 1927, X2.

72. Ropes, *Stage Mother*, 122.

73. "Gus Edwards Tops Bushwick Bill," *Brooklyn Daily Eagle*, June 17, 1924, 9.

74. Snyder, *Voice of the City*, 110.

75. "*School Days* at Lyric Theatre," *Buffalo Courier*, October 31, 1909, 73.

76. Arthur Pollock Jr., "Vaudeville Theaters," *Brooklyn Daily Eagle*, June 21, 1925, 2E.

77. Palace Theatre program, June 29, 1925, Worthpoint, accessed December 10, 2021, https://www.worthpoint.com/worthopedia/palace-theatre-vaudeville-playbill-3666850315

78. "New Brighton Theatre," *Brooklyn Life and Activities of Long Island Society*, June 20, 1925, 17.

79. "Gus Edwards Heads Galaxy of Stars at the New Albee," *Brooklyn Standard Union*, March 3, 1925, M1.

80. Ropes, *Stage Mother*, 184.

81. Personal documents reveal the spelling of Hamilton's first name as "Marian." Yet spellings of her name in 1920s newspaper reviews vary widely between "Marian" and "Marion," with the latter the most common spelling.

82. Jacqui Malone, "Jazz Music in Motion: Dancers and Big Bands," in *The Jazz Cadence of American Culture*, ed. Robert G. O'Meally (New York: Columbia University Press, 1998), 280.

83. Ropes, *Go Into Your Dance*, 83.

84. Ropes, *Dance*, 125.

85. "Town and County," *Leavenworth Echo*, November 1, 1907, 3; and "Vodville Fans Delighted with Pantages' Bill," *Vancouver Sun*, July 4, 1922, 16.

86. "Amusements; Poli's: *Mr. Battling Buttler*," *Evening Star*, January 12, 1925, 12.

87. "S.S. Mauritania Names and Descriptions of Alien Passengers," New York to Southampton, Arrivals, November 30, 1925, accessed January 5, 2019, Ancestry.com

88. "'3 Make-Believe Worlds' Outlined by Actor-Author," 22.

89. *Daily Sketch* review quoted in "Billy Bradford: The Dancing Sensation of *The Blue Kitten* at the Gayety, London," *Variety*, February 24, 1926, 58.

90. "Billy Bradford," 58.

91. "Wollaston Woman Is Guest of Son Acting in London," *Quincy Patriot Ledger*, April 16, 1926, 1.

92. Patrick Newley, *Bawdy but British! The Life of Douglas Byng* (London: Third Age Press, 2009), 21.

93. Stanley Green, *Rodgers and Hammerstein Fact Book: A Record of Their Works Together and with Other Collaborators* (New York: Ganis and Harris, 1980), 689.

94. Steven Suskin, *Show Tunes: The Songs, Shows and Careers of Broadway's Major Composers* (New York: Oxford University Press, 2010), 84.

95. Green, *Rodgers and Hammerstein Fact Book*, 689.

96. Original program for *Cochran's Revue of 1926, The Magazine-Programme* (London, 1926), 1. Author's personal collection.

97. Ken Bloom and Richard Carlin, *Eubie Blake: Rags, Rhythm, and Race* (New York: Oxford University Press, 2020), 202.

98. Original program, *Cochran's*, 9.

99. Hermione Baddeley, *The Unsinkable Hermione Baddeley* (London: Collins, 1984), 52.

100. Quoted in Vivyan Ellacott, "London Revues: 1925-1929," "*Cochran's Revue of 1926*," Over the Footlights, accessed November 10, 2020, http://www.overthefootlights.co.uk/London%20Revues%201925-1929.pdf

101. "Cochran's New Revue, London, Entitled to Be Termed 'Smash,'" *Variety*, May 5, 1926, 3.

102. Frederick Nolan, *Lorenz Hart: A Poet on Broadway* (New York: Oxford University Press, 1995), 82; and "Bradford Ropes Author Speaks," 14.

103. Frank O'Connell, "Artists of All Nations Doing Well in London," *Vaudeville News and New York Star*, July 10, 1926, 14.

104. James Agate, "The Dramatic World: *Cochran's Revue* (1926)," *Sunday Times*, May 2, 1926, 6.

105. Newley, *Bawdy but British!*, 26.

106. Chauncey, *Gay New York*, 335.

107. Simon Callow, "Bawdy but British by Patrick Newley," *The Guardian*, August 28, 2009, accessed November 10, 2020, https://www.theguardian.com/books/2009/aug/29/bawdy-but-british-review.

108. Newley, *Bawdy but British!*, 25.

109. Newley, *Bawdy*, 22.

110. Henry M. Benshoff, *Monsters in the Closet: Homosexuality and the Horror Film* (Manchester, UK: Manchester University Press, 1997), 42.

111. Newley, *Bawdy but British!*, 21.

112. Original program, *Cochran's*, 13.

113. Karl K. Kitchen, "The Talk of New York," *Oakland Tribune*, September 26, 1932, 17.

114. "The Door: Barney," "The Greenwich Village Bookshop Door: A Portal to Bohemia, 1920-1925," edited by Molly Schwartzburg, Harry Ransom Center, accessed October 27, 2020, https://norman.hrc.utexas.edu/bookshopdoor/signature.cfm?item=126

115. Walker, *The Night Club Era*, 287.

116. Theodore Wolfram, "Paris," *The Billboard*, January 8, 1927, 35.

117. "In *A La Carte*," *The Billboard*, September 4, 1927, 2E.

118. Advertisement in *Paris Plaisirs*, December 1926, no. 54, 1.

119. Ulysse, "Le Music-Hall," *Paris Plaisirs*, no. 54, December 1926, 248.

120. René Nazelles, "'Spectacles': Casino de Paris," *Le Journal Amusante*, December 19, 1926, 16.

121. Nazelles, "Spectacles," 16.

122. Ulysse, "Le Music-Hall"; and Jacques Petin, "Les Premières," *Le Figaro*, December 6, 1926, 4.

123. Ulysse, "Le Music-Hall," 248.

124. Jane Catulle-Mendès, "Théâtre, Music-Hall, Cinema," *La Presse*, December 10, 1926, 2.

125. *Paris* program, 1926–27 season, Casino de Paris, 24. Author's personal collection.

126. Ulysse, "Le Music-Hall," 248.

127. *Paris* program, 48.

128. Catulle-Mendès, "Théâtre, Music-Hall, Cinema," 2.

129. Ulysse, "Le Music-Hall," 248.

130. Ropes, *Go Into Your Dance*, 270.

131. Ropes, *Dance*, 242.

132. Ropes, *Dance*, 253.

133. Louis Léon-Martin, "Les Spectacles," *Paris-Midi*, December 6, 1926, 4.

134. Ropes, *Go Into Your Dance*, 243.

135. "In A La Carte," 2E.

136. "In A La Carte," 2E.

137. Ropes, *Stage Mother*, 318.

138. "Spectacles et Concerts," *Le Figaro*, November 6, 1926, 4; and G.F.M., "Les Théâtres," *Le Gaulois*, November 5, 1926, 3.

139. "Music-Halls et Divers," *Excelsior*, November 26, 1926, 4.

140. Pierre Darius, "The *Black Bottom Follies* au Théâtre de l'Apollo," *Comoedia*, November 5, 1926, 5.

141. Legrand-Chabrier, "Pistes et Plateaux," *La Presse*, November 17, 1926, 2.

142. "Unique au Monde," *Le Matin*, December 1, 1926, 2.

143. Ropes, *Stage Mother*, 350.

144. Ropes, *Mother*, 350.

145. Ropes, *Mother*, 352.

146. Ropes, *Mother*, 353.

147. Ropes, *42nd Street*, 323.

148. Brenda Dixon Gottschild, *The Black Dancing Body: A Geography from Coon to Cool* (New York: Palgrave Macmillan, 2003), 167.

149. Walter Winchell, "Off Broadway," *Buffalo Evening News*, July 18, 1933, 15.

150. Jean Stearns and Marshall Winslow Stearns, *Jazz Dance: The Story of American Vernacular Dance* (New York: Da Capo Press, 1994), 146.

151. Will Marion Cook, "Spirituals and Jazz," *New York Times*, December 26, 1926, X8.

152. Langston Hughes, "When the Negro Was in Vogue," in *The Big Sea*, in *The Portable Harlem Renaissance Reader*, ed. David Levering Lewis (New York: Penguin Books, 1995), 80.

153. Snyder, *Voice of the City*, 44.

154. "Keith's Bushwick," 16.

155. "Thaddeus Drayton Collection 1926-1960: Overview," New York Public Library Archives and Manuscripts, accessed November 20, 2020, http://archives .nypl.org/scm/21003

156. "Anglo-American Press Dinner Is a Riot of Pleasure," *Chicago Tribune and the Daily News* (European ed.), December 8, 1926, 2.

157. Ropes, *Go Into Your Dance*, 249.

158. Ropes, *Stage Mother*, 69.

159. Ropes, *Mother*, 351.

160. Ropes, *Mother*, 146.

161. Ropes, *42nd Street*, 113.

162. Ropes, *Go Into Your Dance*, 75.

163. Although Ted and Eunice see Baker at the Casino de Paris in the late 1920s, Baker did not perform at this particular music hall until October 1930, singing "J'ai deux amours" in *Paris qui remue*.

164. Ropes, *Go Into Your Dance*, 244.

165. Ropes, *Dance*, 290.

166. David Savran, *Highbrow/Lowdown: Theater, Jazz, and the Making of the New Middle Class* (Ann Arbor: University of Michigan Press, 2009), 70.

167. Savran, *Highbrow/Lowdown*, 34.

168. Savran, *Highbrow/Lowdown*, 68.

169. Ropes, *42nd Street*, 148.

170. Ropes, *Street*, 155.

171. Ropes, *Street*, 155.

172. Savran, *Highbrow/Lowdown*, 175.

173. Ropes, *42nd Street*, 51.

174. Henry Whittemore, *The Founders and Builders of the Oranges* (Newark, NJ: L. J. Hardham, 1896), 275.

175. Ropes, *42nd Street*, 124.

176. Ropes, *Street*, 22.

177. Ropes, *Stage Mother*, 146.

178. Ropes, *Mother*, 275.

179. Ropes, *42nd Street*, 10.

180. "Dancer Elects Wifely Duties," *Brooklyn Standard Union*, October 25, 1928, 3.

181. "Plays and Players," *Brooklyn Life and Activities of Long Island Society*, August 13, 1927, 16.

182. Billy J. Harbin, "George Kelly, American Playwright: Characters in the Hands of an Angry God," in *Staging Desire: Queer Readings of American Theater History*, ed. Kim Marra and Robert A. Schanke (Ann Arbor: University of Michigan Press, 2002), 133.

183. Rowland Field, "The New Play," *Brooklyn Times Union*, August 18, 1927, 8.

184. "*A La Carte*," Internet Broadway Database, accessed December 5, 2020, https://www.ibdb.com/broadway-show/a-la-carte-1351

185. Ropes, *Go Into Your Dance*, 120.

186. "Jack Norworth at Flatbush," *Brooklyn Standard Union*, February 7, 1928, 10.

187. "Coast-to-Coast Vaudeville Reviews," *The Billboard*, January 14, 1928, 16.

188. Ropes, *Stage Mother*, 159.

189. Ropes, *Mother*, 74.

190. "Alumni," *Golden Rod* 40, no. 4 (June 1928): 55.

191. "School Boy Writes Play," *Quincy Patriot Ledger*, June 20, 1917, 1.

192. Arthur Pollock Jr., "The Theaters: *Billie*," *Brooklyn Daily Eagle*, October 2, 1928, 14A.

193. Ropes, *42nd Street*, 20.

194. "Cohan's Musical Play *Billie* Is Spirited," *New York Times*, October 2, 1928, 34.

195. Wilfred J. Riley, "*Billie*," *The Billboard*, October 12, 1928, 14.

196. Pollock, "The Theaters: *Billie*," 14A.

197. Pollock, "*Billie*," 14A.

198. "Dancer Elects Wifely Duties," 3.

199. "Cupid Wins on Broadway," *Brooklyn Standard Union*, October 31, 1928, 7.

200. "Marion Hamilton 1940 Census," accessed December 15, 2020, Ancestry.com

201. Ropes, *Stage Mother*, 266.

202. "List of United States Citizens, for the Inauguration Authorities," S.S. Republic, Cherbourg to New York, Arrivals, July 28, 1929, accessed January 5, 2019, Ancestry.com

203. "Wollaston Man Author of Book on Stage Life," *Quincy Patriot Ledger*, July 22, 1932, 6.

204. Ropes, *42nd Street*, 84.

205. "*The Silver Horde*, Rex Beach Western, on Silver Screen," *Rochester Times-Union*, November 1, 1930, 10.

206. "Stage Shows," *Exhibitors Herald-World*, December 20, 1930, 56.

207. Ropes, *42nd Street*, 84.

208. Snyder, *Voice of the City*, 158.

209. "Laughter Holds Lead in Orpheum Entertainment," *Seattle Daily Times*, January 10, 1931, 2.

210. "Stage Shows," 56.

211. Ropes, *42nd Street*, 35.

212. Ropes, *Street*, 91.

213. John H. Houchin, *Censorship of the American Theatre in the Twentieth Century* (Cambridge: Cambridge University Press, 2009), 111; and "Ministers Back Up Boston's Mayor," *North Adams Transcript*, September 24, 1929, 7.

214. Frank Rich, quoted in Neil Miller, *Banned in Boston: The Watch and Ward Society's Crusade Against Books, Burlesque, and the Social Evil* (Boston: Beacon Press, 2010), 120.

215. Miller, *Banned in Boston*, 208.

216. Miller, *Banned*, 120.

217. Houchin, *Censorship in the American Theatre*, 94.

218. Houchin, *Censorship*, 91.

219. H. L. Mencken, "The American: His New Puritanism," *Smart Set*, February 1914, the Grand Archive, accessed September 5, 2020, https://thegrandarchive.wordpress.com/2019/12/28/the-american-his-new-puritanism/

220. Cleveland Amory, *The Proper Bostonians* (New York: Dutton, 1947), 329.

221. Miller, *Banned in Boston*, 11.

222. "Boston's Censorship," *Chattanooga Daily Times*, October 6, 1929, 4.

223. "Biographical Note," Mayor Malcolm E. Nichols Collection, Boston Archives, accessed June 21, 2022, https://archives.cityofboston.gov/repositories /2/resources/43

224. "Today We Celebrate 'Sunday Sports Liberation Day,'" FenwayNation.com, January 31, 2017, http://www.fenwaynation.com/2017/01/today-we-celebrate -sunday-sports.html

225. Miller, *Banned in Boston*, 119.

226. Miller, *Banned*, 121.

227. "Ministers Back Up Boston's Mayor," 7.

228. "Ministers," 7.

229. Houchin, *Censorship in the American Theatre*, 113.

230. *Strange Interlude*'s run in Quincy launched the success of Howard Johnson's, as theatergoers sought dinner at the play's 9:00 p.m. intermission. According to Neil Miller, "The local restaurant, called Howard Johnson's, gained so much notoriety—and so many customers during the run of *Strange Interlude* that it soon emerged as a restaurant and hotel chain ubiquitous across the American landscape. Boston censorship had created yet another success story" (*Banned in Boston*, 123).

231. Miller, *Banned*, 122.

232. "Boston's Loss Is Other's Gain," *The Billboard*, October 12, 1929, 46.

233. Eugene O'Neill, *Strange Interlude*, in *Three Plays of Eugene O'Neill* (New York: Vintage Books, 1959), 62.

234. Houchin, *Censorship in the American Theatre*, 112.

235. O'Neill, *Strange Interlude*, 154.

236. O'Neill, *Strange*, 155.

237. O'Neill, *Strange*, 186.

238. Quoted in Savran, *Highbrow/Lowdown*, 21.

239. Ropes, *42nd Street*, 320.

240. Miller, *Banned in Boston*, 123.

241. Gilbert Swan, "Sidelights of New York: Kaleidoscope," *The Saratogian*, September 28, 1932, 4.

242. Mabelle Fullerton, "Wollaston Man Rings Bell with Novel about Postman," *Quincy Patriot Ledger*, January 24, 1951, 5.

243. Ropes, *Go Into Your Dance*, 77.

244. Snyder, *Voice of the City*, 84.

245. Snyder, *Voice*, 47.

246. Snyder, *Voice*, 47.

247. "Author of *42nd Street* Started Career in Barn," 17.

248. "Author of *42nd Street*," 17

249. William Coates, "An Interview with Quincy's Own Novelist," *Golden Rod* 45, no. 3 (Spring 1933): 8.

250. "Warnergram" from Jacob Wilk to M. Ebenstein, August 11, 1932, "From Book to Screen to Stage," *42nd Street*, directed by Lloyd Bacon (1933; Los Angeles: Warner Brothers Archive, 2015), Blu-ray.

251. "*Hobohemia* and *Shakuntala*," *Pearson's Magazine* 40, no. 7 (May 1919): 315.

252. "Movie of Show Business," *Brooklyn Citizen*, August 29, 1932, 14.

253. Swan, "Sidelights of New York: Kaleidoscope," 4.

254. "Harry Who?" *42nd Street Playbill* program, August 1981, 21.

255. Coates, "An Interview," 8.

256. Tim Carter, "'Hear the Beat of Dancing Feet': *42nd Street* (1933) and the 'New' Film Musical," in *The Oxford Handbook of the Hollywood Musical*, ed. Dominic Broomfield-McHugh (New York: Oxford University Press, 2022), 249. Carter's essay explores the 1933 adaptation in depth, charting changes from novel to shooting scripts to final film.

257. Dust jacket of Ropes, *42nd Street*.

258. John Selby, "Scanning New Books," *Evening Leader*, September 17, 1932, 4.

259. I.M.P., "Book Reviews and Literary Notes," *Oakland Tribune*, October 2, 1932, 8S.

260. J. Hoberman, *42nd Street*, BFI Film Classics (London: BFI Publishing, 1993), 67.

261. Mordaunt Hall, "The Screen: Putting on a Show," *New York Times*, March 10, 1933, 19.

262. "42nd Street Special Unique Train," *Waterbury Evening Democrat*, February 17, 1933, 9.

263. Leonard J. Leff, "'Come On Home with Me': *42nd Street* and the Gay Male World of the 1930s," *Cinema Journal* 39, no. 1 (1999): 8.

264. John Mosher, "The Current Cinema," *The New Yorker*, March 18, 1933, 62.

265. I.M.P., "Book Reviews and Literary Notes," 8S.

266. I.M.P., "Book Reviews," 8S.

267. Coates, "An Interview," 8.

268. "Tribute Paid to Ropes by Mayor Ross," 2.

269. "Bradford Ropes, Local Writer," 7.

270. Fullerton, "Wollaston Man," 5.

271. Louella O. Parsons, "Hollywood News Notes," *Albany Times*, May 9, 1934, 21.

272. "Bradford Ropes, Local Writer," 7.

273. Although Ropes has never been credited for possible work on *The Gold Diggers of 1933*, a review of *Stage Mother*'s film adaptation notes: "The author, incidentally, is Bradford Ropes, who was responsible for *42nd Street* and *The Gold Diggers*." ("S.R.," "Alice Brady Shares Loew's Met. Honors with Rudy Vallee," *Brooklyn Times Union*, September 30, 1933, 6A).

274. "Tribute Paid to Ropes by Mayor Ross," 2.

275. Ropes, *42nd Street*, 115.

276. The Hopwood character corresponding to Trixie Lorraine is not Trixie Andrews, however, but Mabel Munroe.

277. Ropes, *42nd Street*, 255.

278. "*42nd Street* Author Sells Second Novel for Motion Picture," *Quincy Patriot Ledger*, April 25, 1933, 1.

279. "Rialto Gossip," *New York Times*, February 4, 1934, X1.

280. Walter Winchell, "On Broadway," *Syracuse Journal*, September 15, 1934, 7.

281. Janet Adair, "Ropes's New Novel in Hands of Publisher," *Quincy Patriot Ledger*, September 26, 1940, 1B.

282. Kitchen, "The Talk of New York," 17.

Chapter 3

1. Clifton Cuthbert, "The Book of the Day," *New York Sun*, May 8, 1933, 22.

2. "Fiction in Lighter Vein: *Go Into Your Dance*," *New York Times*, February 4, 1934, 4.

3. "Broadway Show: *42nd Street*," *New York Times*, September 25, 1932, BR7.

4. "Broadway Show," BR7.

5. "Views and Reviews," *Evening News*, October 19, 1928, 20.

6. Ben Rosenberg, "Under the Reading Lamp," *Brooklyn Times Union*, August 12, 1928, 28.

7. Mario Puzo, "His Cardboard Lovers: *Tell Me How Long the Train's Been Gone*," *New York Times*, June 23, 1968, BR5.

8. Max Ewing, *Going Somewhere* (New York: Turtle Point Press, 2008), 51.

9. Quoted in Wallace K. Ewing, *Genius Denied: The Life and Death of Max Ewing* (Scotts Valley, CA: CreateSpace Independent Publishing, 2012), 53.

10. "The Smart Parade: *Going Somewhere*," *New York Times*, January 8, 1933, BR7.

11. George Chauncey, *Gay New York: Gender, Urban Culture, and the Making of the Gay Male World, 1890-1940* (New York: Basic Books, 1994), 324.

12. Roger Austen, *Playing the Game: The Homosexual Novel in America* (Indianapolis: Bobbs-Merrill, 1977), 65.

13. Austen, *Playing the Game*, 84.

14. Quoted in Austen, *Playing the Game*, xiv.

15. Sarah Schulman, *The Gentrification of the Mind: Witness to a Lost Imagination* (Berkeley: University of California Press, 2013), 31-32.

16. "Author of *42nd Street* Started Career in Barn," *Buffalo Evening News*, December 20, 1933, 17.

17. Graham Wolfe, *Theatre-Fiction in Britain from Henry James to Doris Lessing: Writing in the Wings* (Abingdon, UK: Routledge, 2019), 4.

18. Scott McMillin, *The Musical as Drama* (Princeton: Princeton University Press, 2014), 102.

19. Oscar Micheaux, "Harlem Double Feature: *Moon Over Harlem/Swing!*," directed by Micheaux (1938; West Conshohocken, PA: Alpha Video, 2007), DVD.

20. Andrea Most, *Theatrical Liberalism: Jews and Popular Entertainment in America* (New York: NYU Press, 2013), 58-61, 84-85.

21. Most, *Liberalism*, 46.

22. Martin Rubin, *Showstoppers: Busby Berkeley and the Tradition of Spectacle* (New York: Columbia University Press, 1993), 36.

23. Jessica Tanner, "Branding Naturalism: Dirt, Territory, and Zola's Aesthetics," *Dix-Neuf* 23, no. 2 (2019): 73.

24. Wolfe, *Theatre-Fiction in Britain*, 7.

25. Wolfe, *Theatre-Fiction*, 7.

26. Justin Gautreau, *The Last Word: The Hollywood Novel and the Studio System* (New York: Oxford University Press, 2021), 3.

27. Gautreau, *The Last Word*, 51.

28. Cuthbert, "The Book of the Day," 22.

29. Wolfe, *Theatre-Fiction in Britain*, 81.

30. Wolfe, *Theatre-Fiction*, 43.

31. Avery Hopwood, *The Great Bordello: A Story of the Theatre* (New York: Mondial, 2011), 579.

32. Cuthbert, "The Book of the Day," 22.

33. Wolfe, *Theatre-Fiction in Britain*, 5.

34. Anna Cora Mowatt, *Mimic Life, or Before and Behind the Curtain* (Boston: Ticknor and Fields, 1856), 19–20.

35. Wolfe, *Theatre-Fiction in Britain*, 138.

36. Wolfe, *Theatre-Fiction*, 18.

37. Paul Laurence Dunbar, *The Sport of the Gods* (Frankfurt am Main, Germany: Outlook Verlag, 2020), 42.

38. Dunbar, *The Sport of the Gods*, 53.

39. Dunbar, *Sport*, 72.

40. T. Austin Graham, *The Great American Songbooks: Musical Texts, Modernism, and the Value of Popular Culture* (New York: Oxford University Press, 2013), 192.

41. Graham, *The Great American Songbooks*, 203.

42. Ann Folino White, "In Behalf of the Feminine Side of the Commercial Stage: The Institute of the Woman's Theatre and Stagestruck Girls," *Theatre Survey* 60, no. 1 (January 2019): 39.

43. Graham, *The Great American Songbooks*, 173.

44. Gautreau, *The Last Word*, 40–41.

45. Gautreau, *Word*, 168.

46. Gautreau, *Word*, 185.

47. Wolfe, *Theatre-Fiction in Britain*, 137.

48. Fannie Hurst, *Star-Dust: A Story of an American Girl* (Amazon Public Domain Books, 2017), 109, Kindle.

49. Heywood Broun, "Brilliant Conversation in Fannie Hurst's First Novel," *New York Tribune*, May 5, 1921, 9.

50. Hopwood, *The Great Bordello*, 159–60.

51. Wolfe, *Theatre-Fiction in Britain*, 22–23.

52. Elizabeth L. Wollman, "How to Dismantle a (Theatric) Bomb: Broadway Flops, Broadway Money, and Musical Theater Historiography," *Arts* 9, no. 2 (May 2020), https://www.mdpi.com/2076-0752/9/2/66.

53. Jane Feuer, *The Hollywood Musical* (Bloomington: Indiana University Press, 1982), 80.

54. Feuer, *The Hollywood Musical*, 80.

55. Feuer, *Hollywood*, 80.

56. Rick Altman, *The American Film Musical* (Bloomington: Indiana University Press, 1988), 206.

57. Feuer, *The Hollywood Musical*, 44.

58. Altman, *The American Film Musical*, 208.

59. Beth Brown, *Applause* (New York: Horace Liveright, 1928), 196.

60. Christin Essin, *Working Backstage: A Cultural History and Ethnography of Technical Theatre Labor* (Ann Arbor: University of Michigan Press, 2021), 184.

61. Quoted in Hurst, *Star-Dust*, 86.

62. Martin Kasindorf, "Raven-Haired, Deeply Tanned and Radiant," *New York Times Magazine*, August 12, 1973, 11.

63. Kasindorf, "Raven-Haired," 11.

64. Stephen Rebello, *Dolls! Dolls! Dolls! Deep Inside "Valley of the Dolls," the Most Beloved Bad Book and Movie of All Time* (New York: Penguin, 2020), 32.

65. Kasindorf, "Raven-Haired," 11.

66. Tanner, "Branding Naturalism," 72.

67. Elmer Rice, *The Show Must Go On* (New York: Viking Press, 1949), 10.

68. Quoted in *"Show Girl*: The Outstanding Book Sensation of the Season," advertisement in the *Times Herald*, September 19, 1928, 7.

69. J. P. McEvoy, *Show Girl* (New York: Simon and Schuster, 1928), i.

70. Steven Moore, "The Avant-Pop Novels of J.P. McEvoy," *Numero Cinq* 8, no. 3 (March 2017), http://numerocinqmagazine.com/2017/03/02/the-avant-pop-novels-of-j-p-mcevoy-essay-steven-moore/

71. McEvoy, *Show Girl*, 212.

72. McEvoy, *Girl*, 64.

73. McEvoy, *Girl*, i.

74. "Views and Reviews," 20.

75. McEvoy, *Show Girl*, 42.

76. McEvoy, *Girl*, 98.

77. McEvoy, *Girl*, 113.

78. McEvoy, *Girl*, 50.

79. McEvoy, *Girl*, 14.

80. McEvoy, *Girl*, 20.

81. McEvoy, *Girl*, 193.

82. McEvoy, *Girl*, 167.

83. McEvoy, *Girl*, 94.

84. McEvoy, *Girl*, 195.

85. "'Ziggy' One of Trio Seeking Show Girl Like Dixie Dugan," *Brooklyn Times Union*, September 26, 1928, 45.

86. "Kitty Had That Something, and That Something Makes a Novel, *Applause*," *Brooklyn Citizen*, October 21, 1928, 7.

87. "All Story Tellers Go to Heaven," *Rockland County Journal News*, August 23, 1971, 7.

88. Brown, *Applause*, 131.

89. "Kitty Had That Something," 7.

90. Brown, *Applause*, 185–86.

91. "*Applause* by Beth Brown," *Variety*, April 10, 1929, 50.

92. Sydney Valentine, "The Baby Author: The Story of Beth Brown," *Screenland*, August 1929, 32.

93. Marion Clyde McCarroll, "Beth Brown, Five Feet Tall and an Author, Sighs Because She Doesn't Look Like One," *New York Evening Post*, July 24, 1930, 8.

94. Valentine, "The Baby Author," 32.

95. Regina Crewe, "Beth Brown Uses Pen to Pry Open Filmland's Purse," *Syracuse American*, October 20, 1929, 6S.

96. Gilbert Swan, "In New York," *Selma Times-American*, January 7, 1929, 4.

97. McCarroll, "Beth Brown," 8.

98. Beth Brown, "Man-Màde Movies for Women!," *Screenland*, June 1934, 80-82.

99. Brown, *Applause*, 184.

100. Brown, *Applause*, 125.

101. Brown, *Applause*, 128.

102. Brown, *Applause*, 10.

103. Brown, *Applause*, 108.

104. Brown, *Applause*, 200.

105. Brown, *Applause*, 203.

106. Brown, *Applause*, 288.

107. Brown, *Applause*, 289.

108. Wolfe, *Theatre-Fiction in Britain*, 7.

109. Brown, *Applause*, 291.

110. Brown, *Applause*, 293.

111. Brown, *Applause*, 292.

112. Chauncey, *Gay New York*, 324.

113. Chauncey, *Gay New York*, 324.

114. Austen, *Playing the Game*, 62.

115. Austen, *Game*, 58-59.

116. Bradford Ropes, *Go Into Your Dance* (New York: Alfred H. King, 1934), 270.

117. Gore Vidal, "Foreword," in *Miss Knight and Others*, by Robert McAlmon (Albuquerque: University of New Mexico Press, 1992), x.

118. Quoted in Kim Clarke, "Blue Angel," University of Michigan Heritage Project, accessed June 5, 2021, https://heritage.umich.edu/stories/blue-angel/.

119. Drewey Wayne Gunn, *Gay American Novels, 1870-1970: A Reader's Guide* (Jefferson, NC: McFarland, 2016), 14.

120. "The Book of the Day," *New York Sun*, January 3, 1933, 26.

121. Kate Hext, "Rethinking the Origins of Camp: The Queer Correspondence of Carl Van Vechten and Ronald Firbank," *Modernism/modernity* 27, no. 1 (January 2020): 169.

122. Henry McBride, "Max Ewing as a Camera Man," *New York Sun*, January 28, 1933, 9.

123. McBride, "Max Ewing," 9.

124. John Selby, "The Literary Guidepost." *Las Vegas Daily Optic*, January 9, 1933, 7.

125. Ewing, *Going Somewhere*, 6.

126. Ewing, *Going*, 246.

127. "The Book of the Day," 26.

128. José Esteban Muñoz, *Cruising Utopia: The Then and There of Queer Futurity* (New York: NYU Press, 2009), 1.

129. Ewing, *Going Somewhere*, 25-26.

130. "The Book of the Day," 26.

131. *"Show Girl* Opens Winter's Season on Eveready Hour," *Nashville Banner*, September 23, 1928, 30.

132. Austen, *Playing the Game*, 71.

133. Hopwood, *The Great Bordello*, 165.

134. Ropes, *Go Into Your Dance*, 254.

135. Austen, *Playing the Game*, 74.

136. "Bradford Ropes Gives Picture of Times Square," *Oakland Tribune*, October 2, 1932, 18.

137. "Broadway Show," BR7.

138. Leonard J. Leff, "'Come On Home with Me': *42nd Street* and the Gay Male World of the 1930s," *Cinema Journal* 39, no. 1 (1999): 8.

139. Rocco Fumento, "Introduction," *42nd Street*, Wisconsin/Warner Bros. Screenplay Series (Madison: University of Wisconsin Press, 1980), 14.

140. Leff, "Come On Home with Me," 8-12.

141. Leff, "Home," 10.

142. Leff, "Home," 13.

143. Leff, "Home," 18.

144. Cuthbert, "The Book of the Day," 22.

Chapter 4

1. Dust jacket of Bradford Ropes, *42nd Street* (New York: Alfred H. King, 1932).

2. Bradford Ropes, *Stage Mother* (New York: Alfred H. King, 1933), 29.

3. Ropes, *Mother*, 189.

4. John Worthen, *D. H. Lawrence: The Life of an Outsider* (New York: Counterpoint, 2005), 253. Invoking British slang for the male and female sex organs, *John Thomas and Lady Jane* was the 1927 title of D. H. Lawrence's second of his three versions of *Lady Chatterley's Lover* (1928). Before its 1959 unexpurgated edition in the United States and 1960 obscenity trial in the United Kingdom, *Lady Chatterley* made its first appearance as privately published in Florence by Lawrence in 1928.

5. Ropes, *Stage Mother*, 282.

6. Ropes, *Mother*, 297.

7. Ropes, *Mother*, 308.

8. Ropes, *42nd Street*, 250.

9. "Peeks, but Not Piques," *Golden Rod* 31, no. 3 (June 1921): 15.

10. Bradford Ropes, "The Man Who Lost His Soul," *Golden Rod* 31, no. 3 (June 1921): 10.

11. Bradford Ropes, *Go Into Your Dance* (New York: Alfred H. King, 1934), 91.

12. Esther Newton, *Mother Camp: Female Impersonators in America* (Chicago: University of Chicago Press, 1972), 103-4.

13. Ropes, *42nd Street*, 149.

14. Ropes, *Street*, 152.

15. Ropes, *Stage Mother*, 44.

16. Ropes, *42nd Street*, 26.

17. Ropes, *Street*, 33. The wisecrack references the famous *Ziegfeld Follies* slogan: "Glorifying the American Girl."

18. George Chauncey, *Gay New York: Gender, Urban Culture, and the Making of the Gay Male World, 1890-1940* (New York: Basic Books, 1994), 59.

19. Ropes, *42nd Street*, 257.

20. Ropes, *Street*, 250.

21. Chauncey, *Gay New York*, 5.

22. Chauncey, *Gay*, 141.

23. Chauncey, *Gay*, 148.

24. Chauncey, *Gay*, 9.

25. Chauncey, *Gay*, 172.

26. Chauncey, *Gay*, 61.

27. Mae West, *The Drag*, in *Three Plays by Mae West*, ed. Lillian Schlissel (New York: Routledge, 1997), 102.

28. Chauncey, *Gay New York*, 73.

29. Ropes, *42nd Street*, 341.

30. Ropes, *Street*, 250.

31. Robert J. Corber, "Recovering *A Scarlet Pansy*: An Introduction," in *A Scarlet Pansy*, by Robert Scully, edited by Corber (New York: Fordham University Press, 2016), 7-8.

32. Anthony Slide, *The Encyclopedia of Vaudeville* (Jackson: University Press of Mississippi, 2012), 457.

33. "Amusements," *Evening Star*, August 22, 1923, 34.

34. Chauncey, *Gay New York*, 149.

35. Chauncey, *Gay*, 176.

36. Ropes, *Go Into Your Dance*, 92.

37. Laurence Senelick, *The Changing Room: Sex, Drag and Theatre* (London: Routledge, 2000), 314.

38. Edmond Wilson, "Memoriam to Bert Savoy," *Syracuse Herald*, August 17, 1923, 3.

39. Senelick, *The Changing Room*, 317.

40. Senelick, *Room*, 316.

41. Senelick, *Room*, 312.

42. "Obituary: Bert Savoy," *Variety*, June 28, 1923, 7.

43. Robert McAlmon, "Miss Knight," in *Miss Knight and Others*, ed. Edward N. Lorusso (Albuquerque: University of New Mexico Press, 1992), 14.

44. Corber, "Recovering *A Scarlet Pansy*," 17.

45. Scully, *A Scarlet Pansy*, 174, 175.

46. Scully, *Scarlet*, 175.

47. Lillian Schlissel, "Introduction," in *Three Plays by Mae West* (New York: Routledge, 1997), 4.

48. Mae West, *The Pleasure Man*, in *Three Plays by Mae West*, ed. Lillian Schlissel (New York: Routledge, 1997), 184.

49. West, *The Pleasure Man*, 186-87.

50. Ropes, *42nd Street*, 82.

51. Ropes, *Street*, 85.

52. Ropes, *Street*, 250.

53. Ropes, *Street*, 332.

54. Ropes, *Street*, 251.

55. Ropes, *Street*, 251.

56. See José Esteban Muñoz, *Cruising Utopia: The Then and There of Queer Futurity* (New York: NYU Press, 2009), 153-54; and Halberstam, *The Queer Art of Failure* (Durham: Duke University Press, 2011), 88.

57. Ropes, *Street*, 296.

58. Jack Halberstam, *The Queer Art of Failure* (Durham: Duke University Press, 2011), 88.

59. Ropes, *42nd Street*, 250.

60. Muñoz, *Cruising Utopia*, 174.

61. Warren Hoffman, *The Great White Way: Race and the Broadway Musical* (New Brunswick, NJ: Rutgers University Press, 2014), 174.

62. Ropes, *42nd Street*, 329.

63. Chauncey, *Gay New York*, 48.

64. Chauncey, *Gay*, 16.

65. Forman Brown (as Richard Meeker), *Better Angel* (1933) (Los Angeles: Photo Friends Publications, 2020), quoted in Chauncey, *Gay*, 95.

66. Chauncey, *Gay*, 103.

67. Senelick, *The Changing Room*, 315.

68. Quoted in Schlissel, "Introduction," 24.

69. Ropes, *42nd Street*, 9.

70. Ropes, *Street*, 89.

71. Ropes, *Street*, 9.

72. Quoted in Jonas Westover, *The Shuberts and Their Passing Shows: The Untold Tale of Ziegfeld's Rivals* (New York: Oxford University Press, 2016), 113.

73. Chauncey, *Gay New York*, 301.

74. Ropes, *42nd Street*, 53.

75. Ropes, *Street*, 53.

76. Ropes, *Street*, 73.

77. Ropes, *Street*, 299.

78. Ropes, *Street*, 86.

79. Ropes, *Street*, 293.

80. Ropes, *Street*, 244.

81. Ropes, *Street*, 106.

82. Ropes, *Street*, 263, 336.

83. Ropes, *Street*, 327.

84. Chauncey, *Gay New York*, 106.

85. Leonard J. Leff, "'Come On Home with Me': *42nd Street* and the Gay Male World of the 1930s," *Cinema Journal* 39, no. 1 (1999): 8.

86. Ropes, *42nd Street*, 86.

87. Ropes, *Street*, 310.

88. Ropes, *Street*, 116.

89. Ropes, *Street*, 332.

90. Ropes, *Street*, 145, 296.

91. Ropes, *Street*, 107.

92. Ropes, *Street*, 216.

93. Ropes, *Street*, 217.

94. Ropes, *Street*, 107.

95. Ropes, *Street*, 253.

96. Ropes, *Street*, 281.

97. Ropes, *Street*, 298.

98. Ropes, *Street*, 295.

99. Ropes, *Street*, 298.

100. Ropes, *Street*, 330.

101. Chauncey, *Gay New York*, 104.

102. Ropes, *42nd Street*, 329.

103. Ropes, *Street*, 331.

104. Ropes, *Street*, 333.

105. Ropes, *Street*, 334.

106. Ropes, *Street*, 335.

107. Ropes, *Street*, 335.

108. Muñoz, *Cruising Utopia*, 153-54.

109. Muñoz, *Utopia*, 73.

110. Ropes, *42nd Street*, 327.

111. Halberstam, *The Queer Art of Failure*, 88.

112. Ropes, *42nd Street*, 335.

113. "Behind the Scenes: *Stage Mother* by Bradford Ropes," *New York Times*, May 14, 1933, BR13.

114. Quoted in "About *Stage Mother*," dust jacket of Ropes, *Go Into Your Dance*, Worthpoint, accessed August 24, 2021, https://www.worthpoint.com/worthopedia/dance-bradford-ropes-hc-book-1934-1940547999

115. "About *Stage Mother*."

116. Ropes, *Stage Mother*, 9.

117. Red Smith, quoted in Donald L. Miller, *Supreme City: How Jazz Age Manhattan Gave Birth to Modern America* (New York: Simon and Schuster, 2014), 3.

118. Quoted in Miller, *Supreme City*, 3.

119. Miller, *City*, 6.

120. Stanley Walker, *The Night Club Era* (1933) (Baltimore: Johns Hopkins University Press, 1999), 227.

121. Miller, *Supreme City*, 16.

122. Miller, *City*, 17.

123. Miller, *City*, 32.

124. Debby Applegate, *Madam: The Biography of Polly Adler, Icon of the Jazz Age* (New York: Doubleday, 2021), 298.

125. Walker, *The Night Club Era*, 231.

126. Rachel Shteir, "The Dead Woman Who Brought Down the Mayor," *The Smithsonian*, February 25, 2013, accessed May 20, 2020, https://www.smithsonianmag.com/history/the-dead-woman-who-brought-down-the-mayor-27003776/

127. Shteir, "The Dead Woman."

128. Ropes, *Stage Mother*, 283.

129. Ropes, *Mother*, 308.

130. Chauncey, *Gay New York*, 61.

131. Ropes, *Stage Mother*, 282.

132. Hugh Ryan, *When Brooklyn Was Queer: A History* (New York: St. Martin's Griffin, 2020), 156.

133. Ropes, *Stage Mother*, 292.

134. John H. Houchin, *Censorship of the American Theatre in the Twentieth Century* (Cambridge: Cambridge University Press, 2009), 109.

135. Ropes, *Stage Mother*, 271.

136. Ropes, *Mother*, 274.

137. Ropes, *Mother*, 270.

138. Jack Lait, "Preface," in *Behind the Curtains of Broadway's Beauty Trust*, by Will A. Page (New York: Monroe Press, 1926), i–ii.

139. Ropes, *Stage Mother*, 306.

140. Ropes, *Mother*, 264.

141. Ropes, *Mother*, 171.

142. Ropes, *Mother*, 264.

143. "Marion Hamilton to Wed: Dancer and David S. Ludlum Jr. Obtain a License," *New York Times*, October 26, 1928, 30.

144. Ropes, *Stage Mother*, 266.

145. Ropes, *Mother*, 274.

146. Ropes, *Mother*, 282.

147. Ropes, *Mother*, 283.

148. Ropes, *Mother*, 284.

149. Ropes, *Mother*, 288.

150. Ropes, *Mother*, 288.

151. Ropes, *Mother*, 291.

152. Ropes, *Mother*, 292.

153. Ropes, *Mother*, 294.

154. Ropes, *Mother*, 296.

155. Ropes, *Mother*, 296.

156. Ropes, *Mother*, 297.

157. Ropes, *Mother*, 322.

158. Ropes, *Mother*, 296.

159. Ropes, *Mother*, 288.

160. Ropes, *Mother*, 297.

161. Ropes, *Go Into Your Dance*, 15.

162. Jack Babuscio, "The Cinema of Camp (aka Camp and the Gay Sensibility)," in *Camp: Queer Aesthetics and the Performing Subject: A Reader*, ed. Fabio Cleto (Ann Arbor: University of Michigan Press, 2002), 127.

163. Chauncey, *Gay New York*, 333.

164. Chauncey, *Gay*, 335–37.

165. Rachel Shteir, *Striptease: The Untold History of the Girlie Show* (New York: Oxford University Press, 2004), 174.

166. Chauncey, *Gay New York*, 335-42.

167. Ropes, *Go Into Your Dance*, 33.

168. Ropes, *Dance*, 34.

169. Ropes, *Dance*, 81.

170. Ropes, *Dance*, 91.

171. Ropes, *Dance*, 96.

172. Ropes, *Dance*, 91.

173. Ropes, *Dance*, 92.

174. Ropes, *Dance*, 91.

175. Ropes, *Dance*, 91.

176. Ropes, *Dance*, 93.

177. Ropes, *Dance*, 95.

178. Ropes, *Dance*, 94.

179. Ropes, *Dance*, 95.

180. Ropes, *Dance*, 96.

181. Ropes, *Dance*, 97.

182. Ropes, *Dance*, 98.

183. Ropes, *Dance*, 100.

184. Ropes, *Dance*, 101.

185. Chauncey, *Gay New York*, 196.

186. Ropes, *Go Into Your Dance*, 107.

187. Ropes, *Dance*, 315.

188. Janet Adair, "Ropes's New Novel in Hands of Publisher," *Quincy Patriot Ledger*, September 26, 1940, 1B.

189. "Bradford Ropes Author Speaks at Wollaston Woman's Club," *Quincy Patriot Ledger*, November 18, 1953, 14.

190. Letter from Bradford Ropes to "Jimmy," April 30, 1947. Author's personal collection. "Jimmy" here may refer to Jimmy Fidler or Jimmy Starr, both columnists at the time.

191. Tyler Alpern, "Songs of Bruz Fletcher with Glossary and Commentary," accessed August 21, 2020, http://www.tyleralpern.com/bf3.html

192. Eddie Cherkose and Jule Styne, *Melody Ranch*, directed by Joseph Santley, screenplay by Betty Burbridge, F. Hugh Herbert, Jack Moffitt, and Bradford Ropes (1940; Los Angeles: Image Entertainment, 2003), DVD.

193. Ropes, *Go Into Your Dance*, 101.

194. Read Kendall, "Around and About in Hollywood," *Los Angeles Times*, July 1, 1938, 15; and Paul Chester, "Miss Gardner Gives Chinese Dinner," *Los Angeles Times*, May 1, 1938, D8.

195. "Alonzo Black," 1910 United States Federal Census, accessed March 15, 2020, Ancestry.com

196. "De Molay," *The Spartan Yearbook*, 1929, 38, accessed March 16, 2020, Ancestry.com

197. "Register of Marriage Statistics for Skagit County, State of Washington," 1930, accessed March 15, 2020, Ancestry.com

198. "New Novel by Wollaston Man to Be Produced in Motion Pictures," *Quincy Patriot Ledger*, August 26, 1932, 1.

199. "Chaperon Notebook," *Syracuse Journal*, November 24, 1933, 28.

200. "Bradford Ropes, on Visit Home, Takes Time from Novel," *Quincy Patriot Ledger*, November 28, 1933, 1.

201. "An Alumnus in Hollywood," *Golden Rod* 49, no. 2 (1937): 72.

202. Brett L. Abrams, *Hollywood Bohemians: Transgressive Sexuality and the Selling of the Movieland Dream* (Jefferson, NC: McFarland, 2014), 133.

203. Hal Eaton, "Going to Town," *Long Island Star-Journal*, June 5, 1953, 15.

204. Kendall, "Around and About in Hollywood." Ropes died in 1966 at the Veterans Administration Hospital in Jamaica Plain, Massachusetts. His death certificate issued by the Massachusetts Department of Public Health lists his marital status as "Divorced." However, I have found no additional evidence of Ropes as having married, beyond this prediction of "early marriage" to Smith.

205. Louella O. Parsons, "Studio Plans New Film for Sonja Henie's Return," *Schenectady Gazette*, July 29, 1939, 14.

206. "Roswell J. Black," "Index to Register of Voters," Los Angeles County, 1942, accessed March 16, 2020, Ancestry.com; and Bradford Ropes, "Index to Register of Voters," Los Angeles County, 1942, accessed February 19, 2021, Ancestry.com

207. Edwin Meserve, "Ball Attracts Smart Set Tomorrow," *Los Angeles Times*, August 25, 1938, A5.

208. "Man Ends Life after Arrest," *Santa Ana Register*, March 30, 1942, 3.

209. "Scenarist's Secretary Kills Self in Jail," *Los Angeles Times*, March 30, 1942, 7.

210. "Roswell Jolly Black," Memorials, accessed March 16, 2020, FindAGrave.com

211. "Bradford Ropes of Quincy; Novelist, Writer, Dancer," *Quincy Patriot Ledger*, November 22, 1966, 4.

212. Edwin Schallert, "Drama and Film," *Los Angeles Times*, March 23, 1943, 14.

213. Noël Coward, *Design for Living*, in *Noël Coward: Collected Plays: Three*, ed. Sheridan Morley (London: Methuen Drama, 1979), 95.

Chapter 5

1. Bradford Ropes, *Stage Mother* (New York: Alfred H. King, 1933), 57.

2. "From Swedenborg to the New Church—Interview with Jane Williams-Hogan," Religioscope, June 9, 2006, accessed June 2, 2021, https://english.religion.info/2006/06/09/from-swedenborg-to-the-new-church-interview-with-jane-williams-hogan/

3. Ropes, *Stage Mother*, 43.

4. Ropes, *Mother*, 47.

5. Ropes, *Mother* 189.

6. Bradford Ropes, *Go Into Your Dance* (New York: Alfred H. King, 1934), 42.

7. Ropes, *Dance*, 48.

8. Ropes, *Dance*, 17.

9. Andrea Most, *Theatrical Liberalism: Jews and Popular Entertainment in America* (New York: NYU Press, 2013), 77.

10. Ropes, *42nd Street*, 290.

11. Ropes, *Go Into Your Dance*, 82.

12. Alfred L. Bernheim, *The Business of the Theatre: An Economic History of the American Theatre, 1750-1932*, reprint of 1st ed. (1932) (New York: Benjamin Blom, 1964), 209.

13. Ropes, *42nd Street*, 37.

14. Ropes, *Street*, 116.

15. Ropes, *Street*, 112.

16. Ropes, *Street*, 324.

17. Ropes, *Street*, 39.

18. Ropes, *Street*, 308.

19. Ropes, *Street*, 258.

20. Ropes, *Street*, 151.

21. Ropes, *Street*, 253.

22. Ropes, *Street*, 254.

23. Ropes, *Street*, 258.

24. Ropes, *Street*, 259.

25. Ropes, *Street*, 258.

26. Ropes, *Street*, 259.

27. Bernheim, *The Business of the Theatre*, 161.

28. John Murray Anderson and Hugh Abercrombie Anderson, *Out Without My Rubbers: The Memoirs of John Murray Anderson, as Told to and Written by Hugh Abercrombie Anderson* (New York: Library Publishers, 1954), 51.

29. Ropes, *42nd Street*, 99.

30. Ropes, *Street*, 191.

31. Ropes, *Street*, 180, 181.

32. Ropes, *Street*, 181.

33. Bradford Ropes, "The Influence of the Pilgrims upon the Twentieth Century, Bradford Ropes, 1921, Honorable Mention," *Quincy Patriot Ledger*, May 21, 1920, 5.

34. Ropes, *Stage Mother*, 217.

35. Ropes, *Mother*, 24.

36. Ropes, *Mother*, 33.

37. Ropes, *Mother*, 92.

38. Ropes, *Mother*, 43.

39. Ropes, *Mother*, 39.

40. Ropes, *Mother*, 49.

41. Ropes, *Mother*, 35.

42. Ropes, *Mother*, 214-15.

43. Ropes, *Mother*, 225.

44. Ropes, *Mother*, 226.

45. Ropes, *Mother*, 334.

46. Ropes, *42nd Street*, 34.

47. Ropes, *Stage Mother*, 87.

48. Ropes, *Mother*, 83.

49. Ropes, *Mother*, 256.

50. Ropes, *Mother*, 87.

51. Ropes, *Mother*, 260.

52. Ropes, *Mother*, 200.

53. Ropes, *Mother*, 147.

54. Gypsy Rose Lee, *Gypsy: A Memoir* (Berkeley, CA: North Atlantic Books, 1999), 6

55. Ropes, *Stage Mother*, 169.

56. Lee, *Gypsy: A Memoir*, 46

57. Ropes, *Stage Mother*, 96.

58. Ropes, *Mother*, 106.

59. Lee, *Gypsy: A Memoir*, 29

60. Ropes, *Stage Mother*, 110.

61. Arthur Laurents, Stephen Sondheim, and Jule Styne, *Gypsy*, in *Ten Great American Musicals of the American Theatre*, ed. Stanley Richards (Boston: Chilton, 1973), 342–43.

62. Ropes, *Stage Mother*, 364.

63. Laurents, Sondheim, and Styne, *Gypsy*, 384.

64. Laurents, Sondheim, and Styne, *Gypsy*, 384.

65. Ropes, *Stage Mother*, 366.

66. Ropes, *Go Into Your Dance*, 230.

67. The Major was likely based on gangster Arnold Rothstein, also one of the silent investors in the Silver Slipper. According to Gary Flannery, White had raised $50,000 for the 1919 edition of *George White's Scandals*. White lost the money over a game of craps—and ended up borrowing it from Rothstein (Flannery with David Armstrong, "Episode 78: George White and His Scandals! (Part One)," *Broadway Nation* podcast, September 1, 2022, https://www.broadway-nation.com/episode-78-george-white-and-his-scandals/).

68. Ropes, *Stage Mother*, 14.

69. Ropes, *42nd Street*, 308.

70. Siegfried Kracauer, *The Mass Ornament: Weimar Essays*, ed. Thomas Y. Levin (Cambridge, MA: Harvard University Press, 1995), 75.

71. Sunny Stalter-Pace, *Imitation Artist: Gertrude Hoffmann's Life in Vaudeville and Dance* (Evanston, IL: Northwestern University Press, 2020), 152.

72. Ropes, *42nd Street*, 161.

73. Ropes, *Go Into Your Dance*, 243.

74. Bernheim, *The Business of the Theatre*, 207.

75. Bernheim, *Business*, 149.

76. Ropes, *42nd Street*, 244.

77. Ropes, *Street*, 47.

78. Ropes, *Street*, 21.

79. Ropes, *Street*, 92.

80. Mark Bramble and Michael Stewart, *42nd Street* (1980), directed for touring production by Bramble, originally directed by Gower Champion (Tokyo: NHK-TV Japan, 1986), accessed September 10, 2020, YouTube, https://www.youtube.com/watch?v=HprEpDF4Cy8

81. Ropes, *42nd Street*, 63.

82. Ropes, *Street*, 230.

83. Ropes, *Street*, 229.

84. Ropes, *Street*, 230.

85. Ropes, *Street*, 192.

86. Ropes, *Street*, 232.

87. Rocco Fumento, "Introduction," *42nd Street*, Wisconsin/Warner Bros. Screenplay Series (Madison: University of Wisconsin Press, 1980), 30.

88. Bernheim, *The Business of the Theatre*, 142.

89. Westover, *The Shuberts and Their Passing Shows: The Untold Tale of Zieg-feld's Rivals* (New York: Oxford University Press, 2016), 145.

90. Ropes, *Go Into Your Dance*, 281.

91. The stage manager named Friedman in *Go Into Your Dance* is not to be confused with Si Friedman from *42nd Street*, who also appears as Ted's "business manager" in the former book.

92. Ropes, *Go Into Your Dance*, 283.

93. Ropes, *Dance*, 282.

94. Ropes, *Dance*, 287.

95. Ropes, *Dance*, 288.

96. Ropes, *Dance*, 289.

97. Ropes, *Dance*, 291.

98. Ropes, *Dance*, 146.

99. Ropes, *42nd Street*, 147.

100. Ropes, *Go Into Your Dance*, 179.

101. Ropes, *Dance*, 174–75.

102. Sean P. Holmes, *Weavers of Dreams, Unite! Actors' Unionism in Early Twentieth-Century America* (Carbondale: Southern Illinois Press, 2013), 86.

103. David Armstrong, "Episode 5: Cole Porter and the Queers That Invented Broadway," *Broadway Nation* podcast, June 6, 2020, https://broadwaypodcastnetwork.com/broadway-nation/episode-5-cole-porter-the-queers-that-invented-broadway/

104. Ropes, *42nd Street*, 26.

105. Kevin Winkler, "Hassard Short," in *The Gay and Lesbian Theatrical Legacy*, ed. Billy J. Harbin, Kim Marra, and Robert A. Schanke (Ann Arbor: University of Michigan Press, 2007), 334.

106. Winkler, "Hassard Short," 337.

107. Winkler, "Short," 336–37.

108. Winkler, "Short," 337.

109. Ropes, *42nd Street*, 328.

110. Ropes, *Go Into Your Dance*, 88.

111. Ropes, *Stage Mother*, 143.

112. Ropes, *Mother*, 145.

113. Westover, *The Shuberts and Their Passing Shows*, 95.

114. Ropes, *42nd Street*, 47.

115. Ropes, *Street*, 47.

116. Ropes, *Street*, 96.

117. Ropes, *Stage Mother*, 147.

118. Ropes, *Mother*, 192.

119. Ropes, *Mother*, 259.

120. Ropes, *Mother*, 270, 195.

121. Ropes, *Mother*, 194.

122. "Lone Ranger to England," *Hollywood Citizen News*, November 29, 1938, 6.

123. "Life of Val Burton," Burton History, Google Sites, accessed June 1, 2021, https://www.sites.google.com/site/burtonhistory/home/life-of-val-burton

124. Robert Vaughn, *Only Victims: A Study of Show Business Blacklisting* (Newark, NJ: Limelight Editions), 295; and J. Hoberman, "The Star Who Fell to Earth," in *Vulgar Modernism: Writing on Movies and Other Media* (Philadelphia: Temple University Press, 1991), 61.

125. Holmes, *Weavers of Dreams*, 30.

126. Quoted in John H. Houchin, *Censorship of the American Theatre in the Twentieth Century* (Cambridge: Cambridge University Press, 2009), 80.

127. Cleveland Amory, *The Proper Bostonians* (New York: Dutton, 1947), 246.

128. "*Judas Sheep* to Be Next Ropes' Opus," *Quincy Patriot Ledger*, February 24, 1951, 6.

129. Ropes, *Go Into Your Dance*, 116.

130. "Playwright Visits Quincy High," *Quincy Patriot Ledger*, November 12, 1946, 16.

131. John Grant, Robert Lees, and Frederick I. Rinaldo, based on a story by Richard Macaulay and Bradford Ropes, *Buck Privates Come Home*, directed by Charles T. Barton (1947; Woodland Hills, CA: Image Entertainment, 1998), DVD.

132. Wendell C. Stone, *Caffe Cino: The Birthplace of Off-Off-Broadway* (Carbondale: Southern Illinois University Press, 2005), 35.

133. Val Burton and Bradford Ropes, *Mr. Tilley Takes a Walk* (New York: Austin-Phelps, 1951), 171.

134. Burton and Ropes, *Tilley*, 88.

135. Quoted in Houchin, *Censorship of the American Theatre*, 97.

136. Burton and Ropes, *Mr. Tilley Takes a Walk*, 232.

137. Burton and Ropes, *Tilley*, 105.

138. Burton and Ropes, *Tilley*, 70.

139. Burton and Ropes, *Tilley*, 128.

140. Burton and Ropes, *Tilley*, 141.

141. Burton and Ropes, *Tilley*, 235.

142. Ropes, *42nd Street*, 87.

143. Burton and Ropes, *Mr. Tilley Takes a Walk*, 158.

Chapter 6

1. Wendell C. Stone, *Caffe Cino: The Birthplace of Off-Off-Broadway* (Carbondale: Southern Illinois University Press, 2005), 181.

2. Don Dunn, *The Making of "No, No, Nanette"* (New York: Citadel Press, 1972), 101-2.

3. "Bradford Ropes of Quincy; Novelist, Writer, Dancer," *Quincy Patriot Ledger*, November 22, 1966, 4.

4. Val Burton and Bradford Ropes, *Mr. Tilley Takes a Walk* (New York: Austin-Phelps, 1951), 3.

5. "'3 Make-Believe Worlds' Outlined by Actor-Author," *Quincy Patriot Ledger*, April 16, 1953, 22.

6. Brice performed at Los Angeles's Orpheum Theatre in June 1923, August 1926, and November 1929.

7. "'3 Make-Believe Worlds,'" 22.

8. "Writer Honored at Holiday Party," *Quincy Patriot Ledger*, January 4, 1952, 6.

9. Mabelle Fullerton, "Wollaston Man Rings Bell with Novel about Postman," *Quincy Patriot Ledger*, January 24, 1951, 5.

10. "Bradford Ropes Author Speaks at Wollaston Woman's Club," *Quincy Patriot Ledger*, November 18, 1953, 14.

11. "Bradford Ropes of Quincy," 4.

12. M. G. Bullard, personal interview with author, Boston, June 17, 2021.

13. Bullard, interview.

14. Bullard, interview.

15. "Bradford Ropes Joins Staff of Gunnar Myrbeck," *Quincy Patriot Ledger*, February 8, 1957, 18; and "Bradford Ropes of Quincy," 4.

16. Bradford Ropes Death Certificate, Commonwealth of Massachusetts Department of Public Health Registry of Vital Records and Statistics, signed November 29, 1966, accessed via public record request May 20, 2021.

17. Bullard, interview.

18. Susan Sontag, "Notes on 'Camp'" (1964), in *Camp: Queer Aesthetics and the Performing Subject—A Reader*, ed. Fabio Cleto (Ann Arbor: University of Michigan Press, 2002), 64.

19. Hoberman, *42nd Street*, BFI Film Classics (London: BFI Publishing, 1993), 72.

20. Hoberman, *Street*, 46-47.

21. Quoted in Hoberman, *Street*, 72.

22. Dunn, *The Making of "No, No, Nanette,"* 128.

23. Hoberman, *42nd Street*, 73.

24. Sontag, "Notes on 'Camp,'" 60.

25. Clive Barnes, "Musical Pastiche of the 30's with Panache," *New York Times*, December 21, 1968, 46.

26. Stone, *Caffe Cino*, 43.

27. Wolfgang Saxon, "George Haimsohn, 77, Dies; a Writer of *Dames at Sea*," *New York Times*, January 25, 2003, A17.

28. "Talk of the Town: From Off Off to Off," *The New Yorker*, February 8, 1969, 28.

29. "Talk of the Town," 29.

30. Stone, *Caffe Cino*, 126.

31. Quoted in Stone, *Cino*, 103.

32. Stone, *Cino*, 175.

33. José Esteban Muñoz, *Cruising Utopia: The Then and There of Queer Futurity* (New York: NYU Press, 2009), 169.

34. Stephen J. Bottoms, *Playing Underground: A Critical History of the 1960s Off-Off-Broadway Movement* (Ann Arbor: University of Michigan Press, 2004), 281-82.

35. Dunn, *The Making of "No, No, Nanette,"* 48.

36. Molly Haskell (as "MH"), "Off-Broadway Theatre," *Village Voice,* January 30, 1969, 35.

37. George Haimsohn, Robin Miller, and Jim Wise, *Dames at Sea* libretto (New York: Samuel French, 1969), 51.

38. Haimsohn, Miller, and Wise, *Dames at Sea,* 48.

39. Haimsohn, Miller, and Wise, *Dames,* 47.

40. Bottoms, *Playing Underground,* 282.

41. Norm Goldenstein, "Ken Russell's New Film *Boy Friend* Stars Twiggy as Polly Brown," *Leader Herald,* November 3, 1971, 16.

42. Jerry Finkelstein, "The Movie Scene," *Utica Observer Dispatch,* March 13, 1972, 14C.

43. Deborah Philips, *And This Is My Friend Sandy: Sandy Wilson's "The Boy Friend," London Theatre and Gay Culture* (London: Methuen Drama, 2021), 37.

44. Philips, *And This Is My Friend Sandy,* 48.

45. Philips, *Sandy,* 39.

46. Philips, *Sandy,* 68, 64.

47. Quoted in Philips, *Sandy,* 65.

48. Philips, *Sandy,* 131.

49. Quoted in Philips, *Sandy,* 84.

50. Quoted in Philips, *Sandy,* 133.

51. Goldenstein, "Ken Russell's New Film," 16.

52. Quoted in Ken Russell, *The Boy Friend,* directed by Russell (1971; Los Angeles: Warner Brothers Archive Collection, 2011), DVD.

53. Joseph Lanza, *Phallic Frenzy: Ken Russell and His Films* (Chicago: Chicago Review Press, 2007), 131.

54. Quoted in Lanza, *Phallic Frenzy,* 130-31.

55. Ropes, *42nd Street,* 26.

56. Quoted in Hoberman, *42nd Street,* 75.

57. Quoted in Larry Gelbart and Sheldon Keller, *Movie Movie,* directed by Stanley Donen (1978; New York: Kino Lorber, 2014), DVD.

58. John S. Wilson, "Happily Afloat with *Dames,*" *New York Times,* July 6, 1969, D24.

59. Quoted in Hoberman, *42nd Street,* 51.

60. Rebecca Morehouse, "400 Tapping Toes," playbill for *42nd Street,* August 1980, 6, Michael Stewart Papers, 33.3, New York Public Library for the Performing Arts, Billy Rose Theatre Division.

61. Tom Gearhart, "Michael Stewart Says *42nd Street* Is One of a Kind," *The Blade,* November 19, 1985, Section E, Michael Stewart Papers, 33.1, New York Public Library for the Performing Arts, Billy Rose Theatre Division.

62. Rights agreement between Michael Stewart and Mark Bramble, and Bess Bigue, John S. Pottinger, Peggy Koll, and Dorothea Anderson, February 27, 1978, Michael Stewart Papers, 32.9, New York Public Library for the Performing Arts, Billy Rose Theatre Division.

63. Dominic Cavendish, "Mark Bramble on the Birth of Tap-Dancing Mega-Hit *42nd Street*," TheatreVoice, April 15, 2017, accessed July 27, 2021, http://www.theatrevoice.com/audio/mark-bramble-birth-42nd-street/

64. Letter from Alvin Deutsch to Helen Harvey, December 15, 1977, Michael Stewart Papers, 32.9, New York Public Library for the Performing Arts, Billy Rose Theatre Division.

65. Letter from Darcie A. Denkert to Alvin Deutsch, United Artists Corporation. August 21, 1978, Michael Stewart Papers, 32.6, New York Public Library for the Performing Arts, Billy Rose Theatre Division; and Jon Maas, telephone interview with author, February 3, 2022.

66. Cavendish, "Mark Bramble."

67. Maas, interview.

68. Front cover of Howard Kissel, *David Merrick: The Abominable Showman* (New York: Applause Books, 1993); and Ernest Harburg and Bernard Rosenburg, *The Broadway Musical: Collaboration in Art and Commerce* (New York: New York University Press, 1993), 46.

69. Michael Riedel, *Razzle Dazzle: The Battle for Broadway* (New York: Simon and Schuster, 2015), 195.

70. Otis Guernsey Jr., ed., *"42nd Street,"* in *The Best Plays of 1980-1981*, ed. Guernsey (New York: Bookthrift), 132.

71. Ropes, *42nd Street*, 63.

72. Kissel, *The Abominable Showman*, 16-20; and Maas, interview.

73. Marie Brenner, "Like No Business I Know," *New York* magazine, September 8, 1980, 12.

74. Brenner, "Like No Business," 12.

75. Kissel, *The Abominable Showman*, 23.

76. Brenner, "Like No Business," 12.

77. Hoberman, *42nd Street*, 68.

78. Warren Hoffman, *The Great White Way: Race and the Broadway Musical* (New Brunswick, NJ: Rutgers University Press, 2014), 183.

79. Hoffman, *The Great White Way*, 168.

80. Ropes, *42nd Street*, 333.

81. Ropes, *Street*, 345.

82. Bramble and Stewart, *42nd Street* (1980), directed for touring production by Bramble, originally directed by Gower Champion (Tokyo: NHKTV Japan, 1986), accessed September 10, 2020, YouTube, https://www.youtube.com/watch?v=HprEpDF4Cy8

83. Laura MacDonald (as Laura Pollard), "Consuming 'Little Girls': How Broadway and New York City Capitalized on Peggy Sawyer and Little Orphan Annie's Big Apple Dreams," *Journal of American Drama and Theatre* 21, no. 2 (Spring 2009): 71.

84. Bramble and Stewart, *42nd Street*.

85. MacDonald, "Consuming 'Little Girls,'" 85.

86. Ropes, *42nd Street*, 145.

87. Hoffman, *The Great White Way*, 183.

88. Hoffman, *Way*, 176.

89. Kissel, *The Abominable Showman*, 22.

90. Bramble and Stewart, *42nd Street*. Billy's last name is spelled as "Lawler" in the 1932 novel and 1933 film, but as "Lawlor" in the 1980 Broadway musical adaptation.

91. Robin Adams Sloan, "Town and Country News: Celebrity Circle," *Sandy Creek News*, September 1982, 7.

92. Letter from Michael Stewart to Michael Bennett, May 9, 1979, Michael Stewart Papers, 32.7, New York Public Library for the Performing Arts, Billy Rose Theatre Division.

93. Gearhart, "Michael Stewart Says *42nd Street* Is One of a Kind," Section E.

94. Mark Bramble and Michael Stewart, first draft of *42nd Street*, finished August 23, 1978, 1-6-34, Michael Stewart Papers, 26.1, New York Public Library of the Performing Arts, Billy Rose Theatre Division.

95. Bramble and Stewart, first draft, 1-12-66.

96. Allan J. Lichtman, *White Protestant Nation: The Rise of the American Conservative Movement* (New York: Grove Press, 2009), 320-21.

97. Karina Longworth, "1980s: Richard Gere and *American Gigolo*," *You Must Remember This* podcast, April 18, 2022, http://www.youmustrememberthispodcast.com/episodes/1980-richard-gere-erotic-80s-part-3

98. Hoffman, *The Great White Way*, 171-72.

99. Sarah Schulman, *The Gentrification of the Mind: Witness to a Lost Imagination* (Berkeley: University of California Press, 2013), 14.

100. Hoberman, *42nd Street*, 75.

101. Dunn, *The Making of "No, No, Nanette,"* 14.

102. Otis Guernsey Jr., ed., "*42nd Street*," 132.

103. Brendan Gill, "Hoofers," *The New Yorker*, September 8, 1980, 100.

104. Frank Rich, "Musical *42nd Street*: A Backstage Story," *New York Times*, August 26, 1980, C7.

105. John Simon, "And Still Champion," *New York Magazine*, September 8, 1980, 75.

106. Alison Durkee, "Interview: Choreographer Randy Skinner on 42nd Street," *Everything Theatre*, May 2, 2017, https://everything-theatre.co.uk/2017/05/randy-skinner-42nd-street-west-end-interview.html

107. Rocco Fumento, "Introduction," *42nd Street*, Wisconsin/Warner Bros. Screenplay Series (Madison: University of Wisconsin Press, 1980), 10-11.

108. Fumento, "Introduction," 11.

109. Fumento, "Introduction," 12.

110. Richard Brody, "What to Read and Stream: The Remarkable Out-of-Print Book That Inspired *42nd Street*," the Front Row, *The New Yorker*, May 6, 2020, https://www.newyorker.com/culture/the-front-row/what-to-read-and-stream-the-remarkable-out-of-print-book-that-inspired-42nd-street

111. Manohla Dargis, "'*The Prom*' Review: Showbiz Sanctimony, and All That Zazz," *New York Times*, December 10, 2020, https://www.nytimes.com/2020/12/10/movies/the-prom-review.html.

112. Hoberman, *42nd Street*, 39.

113. Brody, "What to Read and Stream."

114. Alexis Soloski, "Working in TV, Jen Silverman Wrote a Novel. About Theater," *New York Times*, February 10, 2021, https://www.nytimes.com/2021/02/10/theater/jen-silverman-we-play-ourselves.html

115. Jen Silverman, *We Play Ourselves* (New York: Random House, 2021), 11, Kindle.

116. Silverman, *We Play Ourselves*, 322.

117. Silverman, *Play*, 93.

118. Silverman, *Play*, 159.

119. Silverman, *Play*, 151.

120. Soloski, "Working in TV."

121. Ropes, *42nd Street*, 331.

122. "*42nd Street* program," Thayer Academy, 1990 production of *42nd Street*, directed by Donna Milani Luther. Courtesy of Larry Carlson.

123. Ropes, *Stage Mother*, 272.

Bibliography

Cited Interviews

Bullard, M. G. Personal interview, Boston, MA, June 17, 2021.
Carlson, Larry. Email correspondence, July 20, 2021, and November 5, 2021.
Maas, Jon. Telephone interview, February 3, 2022.

Works Cited

Abrams, Brett L. *Hollywood Bohemians: Transgressive Sexuality and the Selling of the Movieland Dream.* Jefferson, NC: McFarland, 2014.
Adair, Janet. "Ropes's New Novel in Hands of Publisher." *Quincy Patriot Ledger*, September 26, 1940, 1B.
Adams, Henry. *The Education of Henry Adams: An Autobiography.* Cambridge, MA: Houghton, Mifflin, 1918.
Agate, James. "The Dramatic World: Cochran's Revue (1926)." *Sunday Times*, May 2, 1926, 6.
"All Story Tellers Go to Heaven." *Rockland County Journal News*, August 23, 1971, 7.
Alpern, Tyler. "Songs of Bruz Fletcher with Glossary and Commentary." Accessed August 21, 2020. http://www.tyleralpern.com/bf3.html
Altman, Rick. *The American Film Musical.* Bloomington: Indiana University Press, 1988.
"Alumni." *Golden Rod* 40, no. 4 (June 1928): 55-57.
"An Alumnus in Hollywood." *Golden Rod* 49, no. 2 (1937): 72.
Amory, Cleveland. *The Proper Bostonians.* New York: Dutton, 1947.
"Amusements." *Evening Star*, August 22, 1923, 34.
"Amusements." *Indianapolis Times*, November 24, 1923, 5.
"Amusements; Poli's: *Mr. Battling Buttler*." *Evening Star*, January 12, 1925, 12.
Anderson, John Murray, and Hugh Abercrombie Anderson. *Out Without My Rubbers: The Memoirs of John Murray Anderson, as Told to and Written by Hugh Abercrombie Anderson.* New York: Library Publishers, 1954.
"Anglo-American Press Dinner Is a Riot of Pleasure." *Chicago Tribune and the Daily News* (European ed.), December 8, 1926, 2.

Applegate, Debby. *Madam: The Biography of Polly Adler, Icon of the Jazz Age*. New York: Doubleday, 2021.

Armstrong, David. "Episode 5: Cole Porter and the Queers That Invented Broadway." *Broadway Nation* podcast, June 6, 2020. https://broadwaypodcastnetwork.com/broadway-nation/episode-5-cole-porter-the-queers-that-invented-broadway/

Armstrong, David, with Gary Flannery. "Episode 78: George White and His Scandals! (Part One)." *Broadway Nation* podcast, September 1, 2022. https://www.broadway-nation.com/episode-78-george-white-and-his-scandals/

"Arthur D. Ropes, Father of Screen Writer, Succumbs." *Quincy Patriot Ledger*, March 19, 1952, 18.

"At Boston Theaters." *Christian Science Monitor*, September 18, 1923, 4.

Austen, Roger. *Playing the Game: The Homosexual Novel in America*. Indianapolis: Bobbs-Merrill, 1977.

"Author of *42nd Street* Started Career in Barn." *Buffalo Evening News*, December 20, 1933, 17.

Babuscio, Jack. "The Cinema of Camp (aka Camp and the Gay Sensibility)." In *Camp: Queer Aesthetics and the Performing Subject: A Reader*, edited by Fabio Cleto, 117-35. Ann Arbor: University of Michigan Press, 2002.

Baddeley, Hermione. *The Unsinkable Hermione Baddeley*. London: Collins, 1984.

Bankston, Carl Leon. *Encyclopedia of American Immigration*. Hackensack, NJ: Salem Press, 2010.

Barnes, Clive. "Musical Pastiche of the 30's with Panache." *New York Times*, December 21, 1968, 46.

Beatty, Jack. *The Rascal King: The Life and Times of James Michael Curley (1874-1958)*. New York: Macmillan, 1992.

"Behind the Footlights." *Golden Rod* 43, no. 1 (November 1930): 38-39.

"Behind the Scenes: *Stage Mother* by Bradford Ropes." *New York Times*, May 14, 1933, BR13.

Benshoff, Henry M. *Monsters in the Closet: Homosexuality and the Horror Film*. Manchester, UK: Manchester University Press, 1997.

Bernheim, Alfred L. *The Business of the Theatre: An Economic History of the American Theatre, 1750-1932*. Reprint of 1st ed. (1932). New York: Benjamin Blom, 1964.

"Billy Bradford: The Dancing Sensation of *The Blue Kitten* at the Gayety, London." *Variety*, February 24, 1926, 58.

"Biographical Note." Mayor Malcolm E. Nichols Collection, Boston Archives. https://archives.cityofboston.gov/repositories/2/resources/43

Bloom, Ken, and Richard Carlin. *Eubie Blake: Rags, Rhythm, and Race*. New York: Oxford University Press, 2020.

Boehm, David, Erwin S. Gelsey, Ben Markson, and James Seymour. *The Gold Diggers of 1933*. Directed by Mervyn LeRoy, 1933. Los Angeles: Warner Brothers Archive Collection, 2017. DVD.

"The Book of the Day." *New York Sun*, January 3, 1933, 26.

"Book Notes." *New York Times*, May 5, 1933, 13.

"Boston's Censorship." *Chattanooga Daily Times*, October 6, 1929, 4.

"Boston's Loss Is Other's Gain." *The Billboard*, October 12, 1929, 46.

Bottoms, Stephen J. *Playing Underground: A Critical History of the 1960s Off-Off-Broadway Movement*. Ann Arbor: University of Michigan Press, 2004.

Bowditch, Charles P., and Harrison Ellery. *The Pickering Genealogy: Being an Account of the First Three Generations of the Pickering Family of Salem, Mass., and of the Descendants of John and Sarah (Burrill) Pickering, of the Third Generation, Volume 2*. Princeton: J. Wilson and Son, 1897.

"Bradford Ropes Author Speaks at Wollaston Woman's Club." *Quincy Patriot Ledger*, November 18, 1953, 14.

"Bradford Ropes Gives Picture of Times Square." *Oakland Tribune*, October 2, 1932, 18.

"Bradford Ropes Joins Staff of Gunnar Myrbeck." *Quincy Patriot Ledger*, February 8, 1957, 18.

"Bradford Ropes, Local Writer, to Be Honored at Theater Here: Wollaston Man Wrote Novel *42nd Street* Now in Films." *Quincy Patriot Ledger*, March 13, 1933, 7.

"Bradford Ropes' Novel of Boston *Mr. Tilly [sic] Takes a Walk* Out Feb. 19." *Quincy Patriot Ledger*, February 17, 1951, 6.

"Bradford Ropes of Quincy; Novelist, Writer, Dancer." *Quincy Patriot Ledger*, November 22, 1966, 4.

"Bradford Ropes, on Visit Home, Takes Time from Novel." *Quincy Patriot Ledger*, November 28, 1933, 1.

Bramble, Mark, and Michael Stewart. *42nd Street* (1980), directed for touring production by Bramble, originally directed by Gower Champion. Tokyo: NHKTV Japan, 1986. YouTube. Accessed September 10, 2020. https://www.youtube.com /watch?v=HprEpDF4Cy8

Bramble, Mark, and Michael Stewart. First draft of *42nd Street*. Finished August 23, 1978. Michael Stewart Papers, 26.1. New York Public Library of the Arts, Billy Rose Theatre Division.

Brenner, Marie. "Like No Business I Know." *New York* magazine, September 8, 1980, 12.

"Broadway Show: *42nd Street*." *New York Times*, September 25, 1932, BR7.

Brody, Richard. "What to Read and Stream: The Remarkable Out-of-Print Book That Inspired *42nd Street*." The Front Row, *The New Yorker*, May 6, 2020. https://www.newyorker.com/culture/the-front-row/what-to-read-and-stream -the-remarkable-out-of-print-book-that-inspired-42nd-street

Broun, Heywood. "Brilliant Conversation in Fannie Hurst's First Novel." *New York Tribune*, May 5, 1921, 9.

Brown, Beth. *Applause*. New York: Horace Liveright, 1928.

Brown, Beth. "Man-Made Movies for Women!" *Screenland*, June 1934, 80–82.

Brown, Forman (as Richard Meeker). *Better Angel* (1933). Los Angeles: Photo Friends Publications, 2020.

Bulliet, C. J. *Venus Castina*. Olympia, WA: Olympia Press, 2009.

Burbridge, Betty, Eddie Cherkose, F. Hugh Herbert, Jack Moffitt, Bradford Ropes, and Jule Styne. *Melody Ranch*. Directed by Joseph Santley, 1940. Los Angeles: Image Entertainment, 2003. DVD.

Burton, Val, F. Hugh Herbert, and Bradford Ropes. *Glamour Boy*. Directed by Ralph Murphy, 1941. Miami: Zeus DVDs, 2021. DVD.

Burton, Val, and Bradford Ropes. *Mr. Tilley Takes a Walk*. New York: Austin-Phelps, 1951.

Callow, Simon. "Bawdy but British by Patrick Newley." *The Guardian*, August 28, 2009. https://www.theguardian.com/books/2009/aug/29/bawdy-but-british -review

Carter, Tim. "'Hear the Beat of Dancing Feet': *42nd Street* (1933) and the 'New' Film Musical." In *The Oxford Handbook of the Hollywood Musical*, edited by Dominic Broomfield-McHugh, 227-51. New York: Oxford University Press, 2022.

Catulle-Mendès, Jane. "Théâtre, Music-Hall, Cinema." *La Presse*, December 10, 1926, 2.

Cavendish, Dominic. "Mark Bramble on the Birth of Tap-Dancing Mega-Hit *42nd Street*." TheatreVoice, April 15, 2017. http://www.theatrevoice.com/audio/mark -bramble-birth-42nd-street/

"Chaperon Notebook." *Syracuse Journal*, November 24, 1933, 28.

Chauncey, George. *Gay New York: Gender, Urban Culture, and the Making of the Gay Male World, 1890-1940*. New York: Basic Books, 1994.

Chester, Paul. "Miss Gardner Gives Chinese Dinner." *Los Angeles Times*, May 1, 1938, D8.

Clair Minot, John. "From a Wollaston Barn to Broadway." *Quincy Patriot Ledger*, May 18, 1933, 4.

Clarke, Kim. "Blue Angel." University of Michigan Heritage Project. Accessed June 5, 2021. https://heritage.umich.edu/stories/blue-angel/

Clark's Boston Blue Book: The Elite Private Address and Carriage Directory, Ladies' Visiting and Shopping Guide for Boston, Dorchester, Brookline, Cambridge, Jamaica Bay, and Charlestown District. Boston: Edward E. Clark, 1885.

"Coast-to-Coast Vaudeville Reviews." *The Billboard*, January 14, 1928, 16.

Coates, William. "An Interview with Quincy's Own Novelist." *Golden Rod* 45, no. 3 (Spring 1933): 8.

"Cochran's New Revue, London, Entitled to Be Termed 'Smash.'" *Variety*, May 5, 1926, 3.

"Cohan's Musical Play *Billie* Is Spirited." *New York Times*, October 2, 1928, 34.

Cook, Will Marion. "Spirituals and Jazz." *New York Times*, December 26, 1926, X8.

Corber, Robert J. "Recovering *A Scarlet Pansy*: An Introduction." In *A Scarlet Pansy*, by Robert Scully, edited by Corber, 1-23. New York: Fordham University Press, 2016.

Coward, Noël. *Design for Living*. In *Noël Coward: Collected Plays: Three*, edited by Sheridan Morley. London: Methuen Drama, 1979.

Crewe, Regina. "Beth Brown Uses Pen to Pry Open Filmland's Purse." *Syracuse American*, October 20, 1929, 6S.

"Cupid Wins on Broadway." *Brooklyn Standard Union*, October 31, 1928, 7.

Cuthbert, Clifton. "The Book of the Day." *New York Sun*, May 8, 1933, 22.

"Dancer Elects Wifely Duties." *Brooklyn Standard Union*, October 25, 1928, 3.

"Dans les Music-Halls." *La Lanterne*, December 7, 1926, 3.

Dargis, Manohla. "'The Prom' Review: Showbiz Sanctimony, and All That Zazz." *New York Times*, December 10, 2020. https://www.nytimes.com/2020/12/10/mo vies/the-prom-review.html

Darius, Pierre. "The *Black Bottom Follies* au Théâtre de l'Apollo." *Comoedia*, November 5, 1926, 5.

De Ronde Furman, Franklin. *Morton Memorial: A History of the Stevens Institute of Technology*. Hoboken, NJ: Stevens Institute of Technology, 1905.

Dixon Gottschild, Brenda. *The Black Dancing Body: A Geography from Coon to Cool.* New York: Palgrave Macmillan, 2003.

"The Door: Barney." "The Greenwich Village Bookshop Door: A Portal to Bohemia, 1920-1925," edited by Molly Schwartzburg, Harry Ransom Center. Accessed October 27, 2020. https://norman.hrc.utexas.edu/bookshopdoor/signature.cfm?item=126

Driscoll, Mary. "Alumni Notes." *Golden Rod* 32, no. 2 (February 1922): 21.

Dubin, Al, and Harry Warren. "42nd Street." *42nd Street*. Directed by Lloyd Bacon, 1933. Los Angeles: Warner Brothers Archive Collection, 2006. DVD.

Dunbar, Paul Laurence. *The Sport of the Gods* (1902). Frankfurt am Main: Outlook Verlag, 2020.

Dunn, Don. *The Making of "No, No, Nanette."* New York: Citadel Press, 1972.

Durante, Jimmy, and Jack Kofoed. *Night Clubs*. New York: Alfred A. Knopf, 1931.

Durkee, Alison. "Interview: Choreographer Randy Skinner on 42nd Street." Everything Theatre, May 2, 2017. https://everything-theatre.co.uk/2017/05/randy-skinner-42nd-street-west-end-interview.html

Eames, Thomas Harrison. "The Wreck of the Steamer 'Portland.'" *New England Quarterly* 13, no. 2 (June 1940): 191-206.

Eaton, Hal. "Going to Town." *Long Island Star-Journal*, June 5, 1953, 15.

Ellacott, Vivyan. "London Revues: 1925-1929," "Cochran's Revue of 1926." Over the Footlights. Accessed November 10, 2020. http://www.overthefootlights.co.uk/London%20Revues%201925-1929.pdf

Essin, Christin. *Working Backstage: A Cultural History and Ethnography of Technical Theater Labor*. Ann Arbor: University of Michigan Press, 2021.

Ewing, Max. *Going Somewhere* (1933). New York: Turtle Point Press, 2008.

Ewing, Wallace K. *Genius Denied: The Life and Death of Max Ewing*. Scotts Valley, CA: CreateSpace Independent Publishing, 2012.

"Fashion Creations of the Stage." *Evening Star*, September 2, 1923, 35.

Feuer, Jane. *The Hollywood Musical*. Bloomington: Indiana University Press, 1982.

"Fiction in Lighter Vein: *Go Into Your Dance*." *New York Times*, February 4, 1934, 4.

Field, Rowland. "The New Play." *Brooklyn Times Union*, August 18, 1927, 8.

Finkelstein, Jerry. "The Movie Scene." *Utica Observer Dispatch*, March 13, 1972, 14C.

Fitzgerald, F. Scott. "Echoes of the Jazz Age" (1931). Quoted in *A Critical Companion to F. Scott Fitzgerald: A Literary Reference to His Life and Work*, edited by Mary Jo Tate, 6. New York: Facts on File, 2007.

Folino White, Ann. "In Behalf of the Feminine Side of the Commercial Stage: The Institute of the Woman's Theatre and Stagestruck Girls." *Theatre Survey*, 60, no. 1 (January 2019): 35-66.

"*42nd Street* Author Sells Second Novel for Motion Picture." *Quincy Patriot Ledger*, April 25, 1933, 1.

"42nd Street Special Unique Train." *Waterbury Evening Democrat*, February 17, 1933, 9.

Freedman, Samuel G. "'The Actress' Returns, a Star Indeed, to Quincy." *New York Times*, November 11, 1984, 28.

"From Swedenborg to the New Church—Interview with Jane Williams-Hogan." *Religioscope*, June 9, 2006. https://english.religion.info/2006/06/09/from-sw edenborg-to-the-new-church-interview-with-jane-williams-hogan/

Fullerton, Mabelle. "Wollaston Man Rings Bell with Novel about Postman." *Quincy Patriot Ledger*, January 24, 1951, 5.

Fumento, Rocco. "Introduction." *42nd Street*. Wisconsin/Warner Bros. Screenplay Series. Madison: University of Wisconsin Press, 1980.

Gautreau, Justin. *The Last Word: The Hollywood Novel and the Studio System*. New York: Oxford University Press, 2021.

Gearhart, Tom. "Michael Stewart Says *42nd Street* Is One of a Kind." *The Blade*, November 19, 1985, Section E. Michael Stewart Papers, 32.7. New York Public Library for the Performing Arts, Billy Rose Theatre Division.

Gelbart, Larry, and Sheldon Keller. *Movie Movie*. Directed by Stanley Donen, 1978. New York: Kino Lorber, 2014. DVD.

G.F.M. "Les Théâtres." *Le Gaulois*, November 5, 1926, 3.

Gill, Brendan. "Hoofers." *The New Yorker*, September 8, 1980, 100–101.

Glendon, Martin F. "Bradford Ropes Reviews His Years in the Theatre." *Berkshire Evening Eagle*, February 10, 1954, 28.

Goldenstein, Norm. "Ken Russell's New Film *Boy Friend* Stars Twiggy as Polly Brown." *Leader Herald*, November 3, 1971, 16.

Gordon, Ruth. *Years Ago*. New York: Dramatists Play Service, 1947.

Graham, T. Austin. *The Great American Songbooks: Musical Texts, Modernism, and the Value of Popular Culture*. New York: Oxford University Press, 2013.

Green, Stanley. *Richard Rodgers Fact Book: A Record of Their Works Together and with Other Collaborators*. New York: Ganis and Harris, 1980.

Guernsey, Otis, Jr. "*42nd Street*." In *The Best Plays of 1980–1981*, edited by Guernsey, 129–38. New York: Bookthrift.

Gunn, Drewey Wayne. *Gay American Novels, 1870–1970: A Reader's Guide*. Jefferson, NC: McFarland, 2016.

"Gus Edwards Heads Galaxy of Stars at the New Albee." *Brooklyn Standard Union*, March 3, 1925, M1.

"Gus Edwards Tops Bushwick Bill." *Brooklyn Daily Eagle*, June 17, 1924, 9.

Haimsohn, George, Robin Miller, and Jim Wise. *Dames at Sea* libretto. New York: Samuel French, 1969.

Halberstam, Jack. *The Queer Art of Failure*. Durham: Duke University Press, 2011.

Hall, Mordaunt. "The Screen: Putting on a Show." *New York Times*, March 10, 1933, 19.

Harbin, Billy J. "George Kelly, American Playwright: Characters in the Hands of an Angry God." In *Staging Desire: Queer Readings of American Theater History*, edited by Kim Marra and Robert A. Schanke, 126–54. Ann Arbor: University of Michigan Press, 2002.

Harburg, Ernest, and Bernard Rosenburg. *The Broadway Musical: Collaboration in Art and Commerce*. New York: New York University Press, 1993.

"Harry Who?" Playbill for *42nd Street*. August 1981, 21.

Haskell, Molly (as "MH"). "Off-Broadway Theatre." *Village Voice*, January 30, 1969, 35.

Hayward, Patrick. "It Was a Rocky Road for *42nd Street* on Broadway." Overtures, June 16, 2017. https://overtures.org.uk/?p=13269

Henry, Mark. "This Week's Review of Vaudeville Theaters." *The Billboard*, August 11, 1923, 16.

Hext, Kate. "Rethinking the Origins of Camp: The Queer Correspondence of Carl Van Vechten and Ronald Firbank." *Modernism/modernity* 27, no. 1 (January 2020): 165–83.

Hoberman, J. *42nd Street*. BFI Film Classics. London: BFI Publishing, 1993.

Hoberman, J. "*42nd Street* and Looney Tunes Classics: Showstoppers Live and Animated." *New York Times*, May 29, 2015. https://www.nytimes.com/2015/05/31/movies/homevideo/42nd-street-and-looney-tunes-classics-showstoppers-live-and-animated.html

Hoberman, J. "The Star Who Fell to Earth." In *Vulgar Modernism: Writing on Movies and Other Media*, 57–64. Philadelphia: Temple University Press, 1991.

"*Hobohemia* and *Shakuntala*." *Pearson's Magazine* 40, no. 7 (May 1919): 315.

Hoffman, Warren. *The Great White Way: Race and the Broadway Musical*. New Brunswick, NJ: Rutgers University Press, 2014.

Holmes, Sean P. *Weavers of Dreams, Unite! Actors' Unionism in Early Twentieth-Century America*. Carbondale: Southern Illinois Press, 2013.

Hopwood, Avery. *The Great Bordello: A Story of the Theatre*. 1928; reprint, New York: Mondial, 2011.

Houchin, John H. *Censorship of the American Theatre in the Twentieth Century*. Cambridge: Cambridge University Press, 2009.

Hughes, Langston. "When the Negro Was in Vogue." In *The Big Sea*, in *The Portable Harlem Renaissance Reader*, edited by David Levering Lewis, 77–91. New York: Penguin Books, 1995.

Hurst, Fannie. *Star-Dust: A Story of an American Girl* (1921). Amazon Public Domain Books, 2017. Kindle.

I.M.P. "Book Reviews and Literary Notes." *Oakland Tribune*, October 2, 1932, 8S.

"In *A La Carte*." *The Billboard*, September 4, 1927, 2E.

"Jack Norworth at Flatbush." *Brooklyn Standard Union*, February 7, 1928, 10.

"Jan.-March." *New York Times Index* 23, no. 1: 435. New York: New York Times, 1924.

"Jean Donaldson, Movie Dancer, Spends Holiday at Home Here." *Quincy Patriot Ledger*, November 29, 1940, 11.

"*Judas Sheep* to Be Next Ropes' Opus." *Quincy Patriot Ledger*, February 24, 1951, 6.

Kane, Neil, et al. *Improper Bostonians: Lesbian and Gay History from the Puritans to Playland*. Compiled by the History Project. Boston: Beacon Press, 1998.

Kasindorf, Martin. "Raven-Haired, Deeply Tanned and Radiant." *New York Times Magazine*, August 12, 1973, 11.

Kaulbeck, Ruth. "A Private Correspondence Made Public." *Golden Rod* 31, no. 3 (June 1921): 18.

"Keith's Bushwick." *Brooklyn Standard Union*, September 9, 1923, 16.

Kendall, Read. "Around and About in Hollywood." *Los Angeles Times*, July 1, 1938, 15.

Kissel, Howard. *David Merrick: The Abominable Showman.* New York: Applause Books, 1993.

Kitchen, Karl K. "The Talk of New York." *Oakland Tribune,* September 26, 1932, 17.

"Kitty Had That Something, and That Something Makes a Novel, *Applause." Brooklyn Citizen,* October 21, 1928, 7.

Kracauer, Siegfried. *The Mass Ornament: Weimar Essays.* Edited by Thomas Y. Levin. Cambridge, MA: Harvard University Press, 1995.

Lait, Jack. "Alyn Mann and Co." *Variety,* March 8, 1923, 20.

Lait, Jack. "Preface." In *Behind the Curtains of Broadway's Beauty Trust,* by Will A. Page. New York: Monroe Press, 1926.

Lanza, Joseph. *Phallic Frenzy: Ken Russell and His Films.* Chicago: Chicago Review Press, 2007.

"Latest Books Received." *New York Times,* September 3, 1933, BR17.

"Lauder Never More Popular." *Vancouver Sun,* February 16, 1918, 5.

"Laughter Holds Lead in Orpheum Entertainment." *Seattle Daily Times,* January 10, 1931, 2.

Laurents, Arthur, Stephen Sondheim, and Jule Styne. *Gypsy.* In *Ten Great American Musicals of the American Theatre,* edited by Stanley Richards, 331-90. Boston: Chilton, 1973.

Lee, Gypsy Rose. *Gypsy: A Memoir* (1957). Berkeley, CA: North Atlantic Books, 1999.

Leff, Leonard J. "'Come On Home with Me': *42nd Street* and the Gay Male World of the 1930s." *Cinema Journal* 39, no. 1 (1999): 3-22.

Legrand-Chabrier. "Pistes et Plateaux." *La Presse,* November 17, 1926, 2.

Léon-Martin, Louis. "Les Spectacles." *Paris-Midi,* December 6, 1926, 4.

Libbey, Len. "Boston." *Variety,* September 20, 1923, 47.

Lichtman, Allan J. *White Protestant Nation: The Rise of the American Conservative Movement.* New York: Grove Press, 2009.

"Life of Val Burton." Burton History, Google Sites. Accessed June 1, 2021. https://www.sites.google.com/site/burtonhistory/home/life-of-val-burton

"Long-Lost Yule Poem of Wollaston Man Is Found." *Quincy Patriot Ledger,* December 24, 1945, 6.

Longworth, Karina. "1980s: Richard Gere and *American Gigolo." You Must Remember This* podcast, April 18, 2022. http://www.youmustrememberthispodcast .com/episodes/1980-richard-gere-erotic-80s-part-3

Macaulay, Richard, and Bradford Ropes, (based on a story by) John Grant, Robert Lees, and Frederick I. Rinaldo. *Buck Privates Come Home.* Directed by Charles T. Barton, 1947. Woodland Hills, CA: Image Entertainment, 1998. DVD.

MacDonald, Laura (as Laura Pollard). "Consuming 'Little Girls': How Broadway and New York City Capitalized on Peggy Sawyer and Little Orphan Annie's Big Apple Dreams." *Journal of American Drama and Theatre* 21, no. 2 (Spring 2009): 67-90.

Malone, Jacqui. "Jazz Music in Motion: Dancers and Big Bands." In *The Jazz Cadence of American Culture,* edited by Robert G. O'Meally, 278-97. New York: Columbia University Press, 1998.

"Man Ends Life after Arrest." *Santa Ana Register,* March 30, 1942, 3.

"Marion Hamilton to Wed: Dancer and David S. Ludlum Jr. Obtain a License." *New York Times*, October 26, 1928, 30.

Marshall, Colin. "America's First Banned Book: Discover the 1637 Book That Mocked the Puritans." Open Culture, September 29, 2021. https://www.openc ulture.com/2021/09/americas-first-banned-book-discover-the-1637-book-th at-mocked-the-puritans.html

McAlmon, Robert. "Miss Knight." In *Miss Knight and Others*, edited by Edward N. Lorusso. Albuquerque: University of New Mexico Press, 1992.

McBride, Henry. "Max Ewing as a Camera Man." *New York Sun*, January 28, 1933.

McCarroll, Marion Clyde. "Beth Brown, Five Feet Tall and an Author, Sighs Because She Doesn't Look Like One." *New York Evening Post*, July 24, 1930, 8.

McEvoy, J. P. *Show Girl*. New York: Simon and Schuster, 1928.

McMillin, Scott. *The Musical as Drama*. Princeton: Princeton University Press, 2014.

Meehan, John, and Bradford Ropes. *Stage Mother*. Directed by Charles Brabin, 1933. Los Angeles: Warner Brothers Archive Collection, 2017. DVD.

Mencken, H. L. "The American: His New Puritanism." *Smart Set*, February 1914. The Grand Archive, December 28, 2019. https://thegrandarchive.wordpress .com/2019/12/28/the-american-his-new-puritanism/

Meserve, Edwin. "Ball Attracts Smart Set Tomorrow." *Los Angeles Times*, August 25, 1938, A5.

Micheaux, Oscar. "Harlem Double Feature: *Moon Over Harlem/Swing!*" Directed by Micheaux, 1938. West Conshohocken, PA: Alpha Video, 2007. DVD.

Miller, Donald L. *Supreme City: How Jazz Age Manhattan Gave Birth to Modern America*. New York: Simon and Schuster, 2014.

Miller, Neil. *Banned in Boston: The Watch and Ward Society's Crusade Against Books, Burlesque, and the Social Evil*. Boston: Beacon Press, 2010.

"Ministers Back Up Boston's Mayor." *North Adams Transcript*, September 24, 1929, 7.

"Miss Beth Pottinger Weds Emile E. Bigue." *San Francisco Examiner*, March 5, 1933, 14.

Moore, Steven. "The Avant-Pop Novels of J.P. McEvoy." *Numero Cinq* 8, no. 3 (March 2017). http://numerocinqmagazine.com/2017/03/02/the-avant-pop-novels-of -j-p-mcevoy-essay-steven-moore/

"More or Less in the Spotlight." *New York Times*, September 11, 1927, X2.

Morehouse, Rebecca. "400 Tapping Toes." Playbill for *42nd Street*, August 1980, 6. Michael Stewart Papers, 33.3. New York Public Library for the Performing Arts, Billy Rose Theatre Division.

Mosher, John. "The Current Cinema." *The New Yorker*, March 18, 1933, 62.

Most, Andrea. *Theatrical Liberalism: Jews and Popular Entertainment in America*. New York: NYU Press, 2013.

"Movie of Show Business." *Brooklyn Citizen*, August 29, 1932, 14.

Mowatt, Anna Cora. *Mimic Life, or Before and Behind the Curtain*. Boston: Ticknor and Fields, 1856.

"Mrs. Arthur D. Ropes, Longtime Leader of WCTU, Dies at 94." *Quincy Patriot Ledger*, October 14, 1960, 21.

"Mrs. Ropes in Beer Attack." *Quincy Patriot Ledger*, April 25, 1933, 1.

Muñoz, José Esteban. *Cruising Utopia: The Then and There of Queer Futurity*. New York: NYU Press, 2009.

"Music-Halls et Divers." *Excelsior*, November 26, 1926, 4.

Nava, Michael. "Creating a Literary Culture: A Short, Selective, and Incomplete History of LGBT Publishing, Part I." *Los Angeles Review of Books*, June 5, 2021. https://lareviewofbooks.org/article/creating-a-literary-culture-a-short-select ive-and-incomplete-history-of-lgbt-publishing-part-i/

Nazelles, René. "'Spectacles': Casino de Paris." *Le Journal Amusante*, December 19, 1926, 16.

"New Brighton Theatre." *Brooklyn Life and Activities of Long Island Society*, June 20, 1925, 17.

"New Novel by Wollaston Man to Be Produced in Motion Pictures." *Quincy Patriot Ledger*, August 26, 1932, 1.

"New Shows This Week." *Variety*, December 20, 1923, 31.

Newley, Patrick. *Bawdy but British! The Life of Douglas Byng*. London: Third Age Press, 2009.

Newton, Esther. *Mother Camp: Female Impersonators in America*. Chicago: University of Chicago Press, 1972.

"Nichols-Williams Wedding at Roxbury Church of New Jerusalem." *Boston Globe*, December 17, 1915, 15.

Nolan, Frederick. *Lorenz Hart: A Poet on Broadway*. New York: Oxford University Press, 1995.

"Obituary: Bert Savoy." *Variety*, June 28, 1923, 7.

O'Connell, Frank. "Artists of All Nations Doing Well in London." *Vaudeville News and New York Star*, July 10, 1926, 14.

O'Neill, Eugene. *Strange Interlude*. In *Three Plays of Eugene O'Neill*. New York: Vintage Books, 1959.

"Opening Night of *The Wishing Ring*." *Quincy Patriot Ledger*, April 28, 1917, 1.

"Orpheum Circuit Vaudeville." *Seattle Star*, March 22, 1923, 10.

"Palace." *Variety*, August 9, 1923, 29.

Parsons, Louella O. "Hollywood News Notes." *Albany Times*, May 9, 1934, 21.

Parsons, Louella O. "Studio Plans New Film for Sonja Henie's Return." *Schenectady Gazette*, July 29, 1939, 14.

"Peeks, but Not Piques." *Golden Rod* 31, no. 3 (June 1921): 15.

Petin, Jacques. "Les Premières." *Le Figaro*, December 6, 1926, 4.

Philips, Deborah. *And This Is My Friend Sandy: Sandy Wilson's "The Boy Friend," London Theatre and Gay Culture*. London: Methuen Drama, 2021.

"Plays and Players." *Brooklyn Life and Activities of Long Island Society*, August 13, 1927, 16.

"Playwright Visits Quincy High." *Quincy Patriot Ledger*, November 12, 1946, 16.

Pollock, Arthur, Jr. "The Theaters: *Billie*." *Brooklyn Daily Eagle*, October 2, 1928, 14A.

Pollock, Arthur, Jr. "Vaudeville Theaters." *Brooklyn Daily Eagle*, June 21, 1925, 2E.

Puzo, Mario. "His Cardboard Lovers: *Tell Me How Long the Train's Been Gone*." *New York Times*, June 23, 1968, BR5.

"Quincy C.A.R. Has Fifty Charter Members." *Quincy Patriot Ledger*, April 8, 1921, 1.

"Quincy Woman Blames Press for Moist Era." *Quincy Patriot Ledger*, May 3, 1927, 1.

Rebello, Stephen. *Dolls! Dolls! Dolls! Deep Inside "Valley of the Dolls," the Most Beloved Bad Book and Movie of All Time*. New York: Penguin, 2020.

"Rialto Gossip." *New York Times*, February 4, 1934, X1.

Rice, Elmer. *The Show Must Go On*. New York: Viking Press, 1949.

Rich, Frank. "Musical *42nd Street*: A Backstage Story." *New York Times*, August 26, 1980, C7.

Richardson, Anna Steese. "Lady Broadway: How the Woman Playwright Has Captured the Great White Way." *McClure's Magazine*, December 1917, 13, 67.

Riedel, Michael. *Razzle Dazzle: The Battle for Broadway*. New York: Simon and Schuster, 2015.

Riley, Wilfred J. "Billie." *The Billboard*, October 12, 1928, 14.

Ropes, Bradford. *42nd Street*. New York: Alfred H. King, 1932.

Ropes, Bradford. *Go Into Your Dance*. New York: Alfred H. King, 1934.

Ropes, Bradford. "The Influence of the Pilgrims upon the Twentieth Century." *Quincy Patriot Ledger*, May 21, 1920, 5.

Ropes, Bradford. "The Man Who Lost His Soul." *Golden Rod* 31, no. 3 (June 1921): 10.

Ropes, Bradford. *Stage Mother*. New York: Alfred H. King, 1933.

Ropes, Bradford. "The Trembling Hour." *Golden Rod* 30, no. 1 (December 1919): 6.

Rosenberg, Ben. "Under the Reading Lamp." *Brooklyn Times Union*, August 12, 1928, 28.

Rubin, Martin. *Showstoppers: Busby Berkeley and the Tradition of Spectacle*. New York: Columbia University Press, 1993.

"Ruskin Club." *Sixty-Fifth Annual Report of the Trustees of the Public Library of the City of Boston, 1916-1917*. Public Library of the City of Boston, 1917.

Russell, Ken. *The Boy Friend*. Directed by Russell, 1971. Los Angeles: Warner Brothers Archive Collection, 2011. DVD.

Ryan, Hugh. *When Brooklyn Was Queer: A History*. New York: St. Martin's Griffin, 2020.

Savran, David. *Highbrow/Lowdown: Theater, Jazz, and the Making of the New Middle Class*. Ann Arbor: University of Michigan Press, 2009.

Saxon, Wolfgang. "George Haimsohn, 77, Dies; a Writer of *Dames at Sea*." *New York Times*, January 25, 2003, A17.

"Scenarist's Secretary Kills Self in Jail." *Los Angeles Times*, March 30, 1942, 7.

Schallert, Edwin. "Drama and Film." *Los Angeles Times*, March 23, 1943, 14.

Schlissel, Lillian. "Introduction." In *Three Plays by Mae West*, edited by Schlissel, 1-29. New York: Routledge, 1997.

"School Boy Writes Play." *Quincy Patriot Ledger*, June 20, 1917, 1.

"*School Days* at Lyric Theatre." *Buffalo Courier*, October 31, 1909, 73.

Schulman, Sarah. *The Gentrification of the Mind: Witness to a Lost Imagination*. Berkeley: University of California Press, 2013.

Selby, John. "The Literary Guidepost." *Las Vegas Daily Optic*, January 9, 1933, 7.

Selby, John. "Scanning New Books." *Evening Leader*, September 17, 1932, 4.

Senelick, Laurence. *The Changing Room: Sex, Drag and Theatre*. London: Routledge, 2000.

"*Show Girl* Opens Winter's Season on Eveready Hour." *Nashville Banner*, September 23, 1928, 30.

"*Show Girl*: The Outstanding Book Sensation of the Season." Advertisement in the *Times Herald*, September 19, 1928, 7.

Shteir, Rachel. "The Dead Woman Who Brought Down the Mayor." *The Smithsonian*, February 25, 2013. https://www.smithsonianmag.com/history/the-dead-woman-who-brought-down-the-mayor-27003776/

Shteir, Rachel. *Striptease: The Untold History of the Girlie Show*. New York: Oxford University Press, 2004.

Silver, Ednah C. *Sketches of the New Church in America on a Background of Civil and Social Life*. Boston: Massachusetts New Church Union, 1920.

"*The Silver Horde*, Rex Beach Western, on Silver Screen." *Rochester Times-Union*, November 1, 1930, 10.

Silverman, Jen. *We Play Ourselves*. New York: Random House, 2021. Kindle.

Simon, John. "And Still Champion." *New York* magazine, September 8, 1980, 75.

Slide, Anthony. *The Encyclopedia of Vaudeville*. Jackson: University Press of Mississippi, 2012.

Sloan, Robin Adams. "Town and Country News: Celebrity Circle." *Sandy Creek News*, September 1982, 7.

"The Smart Parade: *Going Somewhere*." *New York Times*, January 8, 1933, BR7.

Snyder, Robert W. *The Voice of the City: Vaudeville and Popular Culture in New York* (1989). 2nd ed. New York: Oxford University Press, 2000.

Soanes, Wood. "*42nd Street* Outstanding Film Novelty." *Oakland Tribune*, April 1, 1933, 9.

Soloski, Alexis. "Working in TV, Jen Silverman Wrote a Novel. About Theater." *New York Times*, February 10, 2021. https://www.nytimes.com/2021/02/10/theater/jen-silverman-we-play-ourselves.html

Sontag, Susan. "Notes on 'Camp'" (1964). In *Camp: Queer Aesthetics and the Performing Subject: A Reader*, edited by Fabio Cleto, 53–65. Ann Arbor: University of Michigan Press, 2002.

"Spectacles et Concerts." *Le Figaro*, November 6, 1926, 4.

"S.R." "Alice Brady Shares Loew's Met. Honors with Rudy Vallee." *Brooklyn Times Union*, September 30, 1933, 6A.

"Stage Shows." *Exhibitors Herald-World*, December 20, 1930, 56.

Stalter-Pace, Sunny. *Imitation Artist: Gertrude Hoffmann's Life in Vaudeville and Dance*. Evanston, IL: Northwestern University Press, 2020.

Stearns, Jean, and Marshall Winslow Stearns. *Jazz Dance: The Story of American Vernacular Dance*. New York: Da Capo Press, 1994.

Stone, Wendell C. *Caffe Cino: The Birthplace of Off-Off-Broadway*. Carbondale: Southern Illinois University Press, 2005.

Stones, Charles. "Vogue et Black Bottom." *Terpsica*, November 24, 1926, 1.

Strauss, David. *Percival Lowell: The Culture and Science of a Boston Brahmin*. Cambridge, MA: Harvard University Press, 2001.

Suskin, Steven. *Show Tunes: The Songs, Shows and Careers of Broadway's Major Composers*. New York: Oxford University Press, 2010.

Swan, Gilbert. "In New York." *Selma Times-American*, January 7, 1929, 4.

Swan, Gilbert. "Sidelights of New York: Kaleidoscope." *The Saratogian*, September 28, 1932, 4.

"Swedenborgianism (New Church): An Evaluation from the Theological Perspective of the Lutheran Church—Missouri Synod." Lutheran Church Missouri Synod, September 2013. Accessed June 10, 2021. https://files.lcms.org/wl/?id=mjrjrwByyMlFYBoEWknSpbYkIWndcIHO

"Talk of the Town: From Off Off to Off." *The New Yorker*, February 8, 1969, 28.

Tanner, Jessica. "Branding Naturalism: Dirt, Territory, and Zola's Aesthetics." *Dix-Neuf* 23, no. 2 (2019): 71–89.

"Thaddeus Drayton Collection 1926–1960: Overview." New York Public Library Archives and Manuscripts. Accessed November 20, 2020. http://archives.nypl.org/scm/21003

"'3 Make-Believe Worlds' Outlined by Actor-Author." *Quincy Patriot Ledger*, April 16, 1953, 22.

"Three New Cabaret Shows." *The Billboard*, March 29, 1924, 12.

"Today We Celebrate 'Sunday Sports Liberation Day.'" FenwayNation.com, January 31, 2017. http://www.fenwaynation.com/2017/01/today-we-celebrate-sunday-sports.html

"Town and County." *Leavenworth Echo*, November 1, 1907, 3.

"Tribute Paid to Ropes by Mayor Ross: Quincy Author of Feature Film Is Lauded at Strand Theatre." *Quincy Patriot Ledger*, March 13, 1933, 2.

Tyrrell, Ian. *Woman's World/Woman's Empire: The Woman's Christian Temperance Union in International Perspective, 1880–1930*. Chapel Hill: University of North Carolina Press, 1991.

Ullman, Sharon R. "The Twentieth-Century Way': Female Impersonation and Sexual Practice in Turn-of-the-Century America." *Journal of the History of Sexuality* 5, no. 4 (April 1995): 573–600.

Ulysse. "Le Music-Hall." *Paris-Plaisirs*, no. 54, December 1926, 248.

"Unique au Monde." *Le Matin*, December 1, 1926, 2.

Valentine, Sydney. "The Baby Author: The Story of Beth Brown." *Screenland*, August 1929, 32.

"Van and Schenck at the Silver Slipper." *New York Telegram and Evening Mail*, February 29, 1924, 23.

Vaughn, Robert. *Only Victims: A Study of Show Business Blacklisting*. Newark, NJ: Limelight Editions, 1996.

Vidal, Gore. "Foreword." In *Miss Knight and Others*, by Robert McAlmon, ix–xiii. Albuquerque: University of New Mexico Press, 1992.

"Views and Reviews." *Evening News*, October 19, 1928, 20.

"Vodville Fans Delighted with Pantages' Bill." *Vancouver Sun*, July 4, 1922, 16.

Walker, Stanley. *The Night Club Era* (1933). Baltimore: Johns Hopkins University Press, 1999.

"Wandering in Fairyland." *Quincy Patriot Ledger*, June 1, 1917, 1.

"Warnergram" from Jacob Wilk to M. Ebenstein. August 11, 1932. "From Book to Screen to Stage." *42nd Street*, 1933. Los Angeles: Warner Brothers Archive, 2015. Blu-ray.

Watson, J. Madison. *Independent Fifth Reader*. New York: A. S. Barnes, 1876.

Wendell Holmes, Oliver, Sr. *Elsie Venner: A Romance of Destiny*. Cambridge, MA: Houghton, Mifflin, 1861.

West, Mae. *The Drag*. In *Three Plays by Mae West*, edited by Lillian Schlissel, 95–141. New York: Routledge, 1997.

West, Mae. *The Pleasure Man*. In *Three Plays by Mae West*, edited by Lillian Schlissel, 95–141. New York: Routledge, 1997.

Westover, Jonas. *The Shuberts and Their Passing Shows: The Untold Tale of Ziegfeld's Rivals*. New York: Oxford University Press, 2016.

Whittemore, Henry. *The Founders and Builders of the Oranges*. Newark, NJ: L. J. Hardham, 1896.

Whittock, Martyn. *Mayflower Lives: Pilgrims in a New World and the Early American Experience*. New York: Pegasus Books, 2019.

Wilde, Oscar. "The Truth of Masks: A Note on Illusion." In *Intentions*. Leipzig: Heinemann and Balestier, the English Library, 1891.

Wilson, Edmond. "Memoriam to Bert Savoy." *Syracuse Herald*, August 17, 1923, 3.

Wilson, John S. "Happily Afloat with *Dames*." *New York Times*, July 6, 1969, D24.

Winchell, Walter. "Off Broadway." *Buffalo Evening News*, July 18, 1933, 15.

Winchell, Walter. "On Broadway." *Syracuse Journal*, September 15, 1934, 7.

Winkler, Kevin. "Hassard Short." In *The Gay and Lesbian Theatrical Legacy*, edited by Billy J. Harbin, Kim Marra, and Robert A. Schanke, 334–40. Ann Arbor: University of Michigan Press, 2007.

Wolfe, Graham. *Theatre-Fiction in Britain from Henry James to Doris Lessing: Writing in the Wings*. Abingdon, UK: Routledge, 2019.

Wolfram, Theodore. "Paris." *The Billboard*, January 8, 1927, 35.

"Wollaston Man Author of Book on Stage Life." *Quincy Patriot Ledger*, July 22, 1932, 6.

"Wollaston Woman Is Elected State President of W.C.T.U." *Quincy Patriot Ledger*, October 20, 1922, 1.

"Wollaston Woman Is Guest of Son Acting in London." *Quincy Patriot Ledger*, April 16, 1926, 1.

Wollman, Elizabeth L. "How to Dismantle a (Theatric) Bomb: Broadway Flops, Broadway Money, and Musical Theater Historiography." *Arts* 9, no. 2 (May 2020). https://www.mdpi.com/2076-0752/9/2/66

"Women's Clubs." *Newton Graphic*, March 26, 1920, 8.

"Work of the Chapters." *Daughters of the American Revolution Magazine* 56, no. 11 (November 1922): 678–79. Philadelphia: J. P. Lippincott.

Worthen, John. *D. H. Lawrence: The Life of an Outsider*. New York: Counterpoint, 2005.

"Writer Honored at Holiday Party." *Quincy Patriot Ledger*, January 4, 1952, 6.

"'Ziggy' One of Trio Seeking Show Girl Like Dixie Dugan." *Brooklyn Times Union*, September 26, 1928, 45.

Index